Gleanings in Europe: England

The Writings of
James Fenimore Cooper

Gleanings in Europe

England

James Fenimore Cooper

Historical Introduction and
Explanatory Notes by Donald A. Ringe
and Kenneth W. Staggs
Text Established by James P. Elliott,
Kenneth W. Staggs and R. D. Madison

State University of New York Press   Albany

The preparation of this volume was made possible (in part) by a grant from the Program for Editions of the National Endowment for the Humanities, an independent Federal agency.

CENTER FOR
SCHOLARLY EDITIONS
AN APPROVED EDITION
MODERN LANGUAGE
ASSOCIATION OF AMERICA

The Center emblem means that one of a panel of textual experts serving the Center has reviewed the text and textual apparatus of the printer's copy by thorough and scrupulous sampling, and has approved them for sound and consistent editorial principles employed and maximum accuracy attained. The accuracy of the text has been guarded by careful and repeated proofreading according to standards set by the Center.

Published by
State University of New York Press, Albany

For information, address State University of New York Press, State University Plaza, Albany, N.Y., 12246

Library of Congress Cataloging in Publication Data
Cooper, James Fenimore, 1789-1851.
    Gleanings in Europe, England.

    (Cooper editions)
    Includes index.
    1. England—Social life and customs—19th century. 2. London—Description—1801-1900.
3. Cooper, James Fenimore, 1789-1851—Journeys—England. I. Title. II. Series: Cooper,
James Fenimore, 1789-1851. Selected works. 1979.
DA533.C77 1981   942   80-16993
ISBN 0-87395-367-3
ISBN 0-87395-459-9 (pbk.)

Contents

Acknowledgments   ix

Illustrations   xi

Historical Introduction   xvii

Cooper's Preface   1

Gleanings in Europe: England   5

Explanatory Notes   309

Appendix A   325

Textual Commentary   333

Textual Notes   347

Emendations   349

Word-Division   359

Index   363

Acknowledgments

The several editors who have shared in the preparation of this volume over an extended period have contracted so many obligations, recorded and unrecorded, that a full accounting would be impossible. Under these circumstances, the editors wish to express their warmest gratitude to all persons and institutions, mentioned or unmentioned, whose contributions have found place in the pages of this edition.

They wish especially to express their appreciation to the Fenimore Cooper family, particularly to the novelist's great-grandsons Dr. Henry S. Fenimore Cooper, the late Paul Fenimore Cooper, and to their sons, Mr. Henry S. Fenimore Cooper, Jr., and Dr. Paul Fenimore Cooper, Jr. They are grateful also to Clark University and the American Antiquarian Society, institutions which have encouraged and sponsored this volume as a part of the total edition of *The Writings of James Fenimore Cooper,* and to Trinity University in San Antonio and the University of Kentucky, which have assisted this volume additionally in many practical ways. Their thanks are doubly due to the National Endowment for the Humanities which, through the award of a Young Humanist Grant in the summer of 1971, enabled Mr. Staggs to examine editions and collect bibliographical information in the British Isles and on the continent. A subsequent grant from the National Endowment to Clark University on behalf of the Cooper Edition through the Division of Research Materials (for Research Materials Programs) insured the completion of this and other volumes.

Among the many librarians and curators whose assistance has been invaluable are Frederick E. Bauer, Jr., Mary E. Brown, Marion R. Snow, Carolyn A. Allen, and Dorothy M. Gleason of the American Antiquarian Society; Tilton M. Barron, Marion Henderson, and Irene Walch of the Goddard Library of Clark University; Donald C. Gallup of the American Literature Collection, Beinecke Library, Yale University; Kathleen Blow and June Moll of the University of Texas Library; John Dobson of the University of Tennessee Library; Stanley Gillam of the London Library; Harriet C. Jameson of the University of Michigan Library, Dean H. Keller of the Kent State University Library, D. MacArthur of the University Library, St. Andrews, Scotland; Frank Paluka of the University of Iowa Library; John L. Sharpe III of the Duke University Library; Glenn B. Skillin of the George Arents Research Library of Syracuse University; Lawrence Towner of the Newberry Library; Nicholas B. Wainwright of the Historical Society of Pennsylvania; and Henry Waltemade of the University of Colorado Library.

Among the institutions whose staffs have responded to questions or furnished books on inter-library loan are: the British Museum, the Westminster City Libraries, Sir John Soane's Museum, and the Greater London Council—all of London; the Bodleian Library, Oxford University, the New Jersey Historical Society, the Archibald Stevens Alexander Library, Rutgers University, the Boston Public Library; and the Public Library of Cincinnati and Hamilton County.

Permissions to use or quote from unpublished materials have been graciously provided by the Fenimore Cooper family, the trustees of the estate of Richard Bentley, and Mr. Henry Lea Hudson of Lea & Febiger, Publishers, successors to Carey & Lea in Philadelphia. For making available materials from the Yale Cooper Collection, the editors are grateful to Dr. Donald C. Gallup, Curator, Collection of American Literature, the Beinecke Rare Book and Manuscript Library, Yale University.

The prints which supply the illustrations are from the personal collection of Donald and Lucy Ringe or from the collections of the Widener Library of Harvard University. Photographs were prepared by the photographic staff of the Widener Library and by Herbert Walden of Worcester.

Mr. Ringe wishes to extend his particular thanks to John Clubbe of the University of Kentucky and Kay S. House of the San Francisco State University for suggestions used in the Historical Introduction. Mr. Staggs wishes to thank the many students who volunteered assistance; and the Editorial Board wishes to thank Wayne R. Kime for his extremely generous and valuable contribution to the volume.

Illustrations

Two of the engravings selected for this book, "Holland House" and "Lansdown House," were drawn in 1815 by John Preston Neale (1780-1847), for John Britton and Edward Wedlake Brayley, *The Beauties of England and Wales,* 18 vols. (London, 1801-1816). Though he sometimes worked in landscape, Neale is best known for his architectural drawings, especially those in his massive *Views of the Seats of Noblemen and Gentlemen, in England, Wales, Scotland, and Ireland,* First series, 6 vols. (London, 1818-1823); Second series, 5 vols. (London, 1824-1829). "Holland House" and "Lansdown House" are reproduced from engravings owned by Donald and Lucy Ringe.

The thirty other engravings were drawn by Thomas Hosmer Shepherd (fl. 1825-1840) and are reproduced from the illustrations in two books: *London and Its Environs in the Nineteenth Century, Illustrated by a Series of Views from Original Drawings, by Thomas H. Shepherd* (London, 1829); and James Elmes, *Metropolitan Improvements; or London in the Nineteenth Century: Displayed in a Series of Engravings... from Original Drawings... by Mr. Thos. H. Shepherd* (London, 1827). Since Shepherd is recognized for the great accuracy of his drawings, the illustrations give a faithful view of London around the time of Cooper's visit in the Spring of 1828. Shepherd also published views of Edinburgh and Bath.

Most of the illustrations show places that Cooper mentions in the text, though a few present views that he does not name, but which help the reader to visualize the London of his time. Plates I to IV depict St. Paul's Cathedral and views in Westminster; V to VIII, the royal palace and various houses that Cooper either saw or visited; IX to XII, views in the old City; and XIII to XVI, improvements in Regent Street recent in 1828, and some miscellaneous sights.

The house at 33 St. James's Place, where Cooper lived in 1828, is no longer standing, and no picture of it is available.

Following p. 68

PLATE I   London
                St. Paul's Cathedral

PLATE II   Westminster Abbey
                Westminster Hall

PLATE III   The Parliament House, from Old Palace Yard
                The King's Entrance to the House of Lords

PLATE IV   Banqueting House, Whitehall
                Westminster Bridge

Following p. 130

PLATE V   St. James's Palace
                York House, St. James's Park

PLATE VI   Holland House
                Spencer House, Green Park

PLATE VII   Lansdowne House
                Somerset House

PLATE VIII   Northumberland House, Charing Cross
                Statue of Charles I, Charing Cross

Following p. 187

PLATE IX   Tower of London, from Tower Hill
                Tower of London, from the Thames

PLATE X   Cheapside, looking down Poultry and Bucklersbury
                High Street, Aldgate

PLATE XI   Ludgate Hill, from Fleet Street
                The Guildhall

PLATE XII   Bank of England
                East India House

Following p. 249

PLATE XIII   Piccadilly, from Coventry Street
Regent Street, from Piccadilly Circus

PLATE XIV   Waterloo Place and Part of Regent Street
Regent Street, from the Quadrant

PLATE XV   Theatre Royal, Covent Garden
Christ Church, and Part of Christ's Hospital

PLATE XVI   Old London Bridge
London Docks

Pages 335, 336

PLATE XVII   Manuscript leaf of pp. 224-225 (*recto*)

PLATE XVIII Manuscript leaf of pp. 225-227 (*verso*)
(*Courtesy Paul Fenimore Cooper, Jr.*)

HISTORICAL INTRODUCTION

Gleanings in Europe: England, fourth of Cooper's European travel books in the sequence of publication, was the second volume in the chronology of travels recorded in the series. Its relative position, together with the variant titles under which it originally appeared, is indicated in the following chart:

Chronology	Title in Cooper Edition	Title in American First Edition	Title in British First Edition
14 July — 15 Oct. 1828	*Gleanings in Europe: Switzerland*	*Sketches of Switzerland* (1836)	*Excursions in Switzerland* (1836)
20 Aug. 1830 — 17 July 1832 passim 18 July — 11 Oct. 1832	*Gleanings in Europe: the Rhine*	*Sketches of Switzerland. Part Second* (1836)	*A Residence in France; with an Excursion up the Rhine, and a Second Visit to Switzerland* (1836)
1 June 1826 — 27 Feb. 1828	*Gleanings in Europe: France*	*Gleanings in Europe* (1837)	*Recollections of Europe* (1837)
28 Feb. — 29 May 1828	*Gleanings in Europe: England*	*Gleanings in Europe. England* (1837)	*England. With Sketches of Society in the Metropolis* (1837)
16 Oct. 1828 — 11 May 1830	*Gleanings in Europe: Italy*	*Gleanings in Europe. Italy* (1838)	*Excursions in Italy* (1838)

Historical Introduction

I

When James Fenimore Cooper landed at Dover on 28 February 1828, he began his fourth and most important visit to England. In 1806-07, as a young merchant seaman of the *Stirling*, he had visited London twice during a voyage to Spain; and, in the summer of 1826, at the beginning of his extended European residence, he had landed at Cowes, on the Isle of Wight, left his family with friends and relatives in Southampton, and spent ten days in London on publishing business and sightseeing before returning to take his family to Paris. Two visits in the summer of 1833 were still to come, but his three month stay in England from 28 February to 28 May 1828 provided his most intimate experience of London and most of the material for his *Gleanings in Europe: England*, though that book would be some nine years in gestation.

His purpose was business. Cooper brought with him the half finished manuscript of *Notions of the Americans*, intending to complete the book and see it through the press in no more than six weeks. That done, he planned to settle his family in Germany and accompany a friend, Gouverneur Wilkins, on a tour through Scandinavia and around the Gulf of Bothnia that would have taken them as far as St. Petersburg and Moscow. But though he worked very hard—even to the point of nervous exhaustion—*Notions* outgrew his original plans, and he did not complete it until about 17 May. By then, he had abandoned the northern trip for lack of time and projected instead a summer visit to Switzerland.

The extended delay in London had an unexpected result, however, in affording Cooper a splendid opportunity to study English society. Arriving in London on 29 February, the Coopers established themselves on 5 March at 33 St. James's Place, a blind, L-shaped street near the royal palace and both Green and St. James's Parks. It was a most desirable location. William Wilberforce lived next door, and just around the "L" at number 22 was the home of Samuel Rogers, who entertained persons of eminence, usually literary or artistic, at his celebrated breakfast table. Lord Spencer lived but a few steps away in an impressive house facing Green Park, and Sir James Mackintosh resided on Clarges Street, off Piccadilly, within easy walking distance. The London season was soon in full swing, and Cooper found himself in the midst of it. Though he had not expected to enter London society, William Spencer, a minor poet he had met in Paris, arranged calls and invitations from important Englishmen, and the American, much to his surprise, soon found himself with an impressive visiting list.

Cooper's social engagements cannot be fully calendared, nor can many of them be dated with certainty. Enough is known, however, to indicate their range and frequency. Cooper went alone to all of them, for on 6 March, Mrs. Cooper learned from a news-paper of her father's death and went into deep mourning. She accompanied her husband on a number of tourist trips—to West-minster Abbey on 10 March, the Tower of London on 27 March, Richmond Hill and Twickenham on 26 April, and Windsor Castle on 5 May—and she visited her sister Anne (Mrs. John L. McAdam) at her home at Hoddeston on 14 March, where Cooper joined her on 17 March, returning to London the following day.[1] But she attended none of the social functions to which she and her husband were invited.

She was pleased, however, with the attention he received and mentioned, in a letter to her daughters, who had remained in Paris, that the "Johnny Bulls" had been "very civil to him."[2] They were more than civil. By 11 March, Cooper had received calls from Thomas Campbell and Samuel Rogers and breakfasted with the latter,[3] and he met Lord John Russell at a Rogers breakfast on 19 March.[4] Three days later, on 22 March, he dined at Holland House,[5] and by 27 March, "the Duke of Devonshire, Lord Hol-land, Lord Spencer," and other distinguished Englishmen were "on his visiting list."[6] On 17 April, he attended a dinner at Rogers' house, where Sir Walter Scott, whom Cooper had met in Paris, was guest of honor; and he dined with William Sotheby on 22 April. On this occasion, Sir Walter Scott, Samuel Taylor Cole-ridge, and John Gibson Lockhart were among those present.[7] Escorted by Sotheby, Cooper visited Coleridge at Highgate and

Joanna Baillie at Hampstead between 27 and 30 April.[8] On the day before he left, 27 May, Cooper met Thomas Moore, the Irish poet, at a Rogers breakfast.[9]

These are only a few of Cooper's social engagements. The many breakfasts and other dinners with Rogers, the reception at Devonshire House, and the dinners at Lansdowne House, Spencer House, and the homes of Sir George Phillips and Lord Grey—to mention only the major ones—cannot now be dated, but they clearly indicate the welcome he received from many eminent members of the Whig aristocracy. On only one occasion did he truly have cause to complain about his reception. Invited to dinner at some unidentified house, he was all but ignored in the drawing room, left behind when the company went to dinner, and placed at the lowest position at table. Elsewhere, however, he was accorded the courteous treatment befitting a man who was, at the time, famous throughout Europe for his literary talent and accomplishments.

Though Cooper was warmly received by a prominent part of London society, he conducted himself always with the simplicity and independence of an American gentleman, and he observed with a critical eye. As he wrote to Charles Wilkes toward the close of his stay in England, he had "taken the opportunity of seeing London society, in which I have circulated quite as much as was desirable." He had "dined with all the Whigs," whom he considered "the most talented part of the aristocracy," but he had not been "enchanted with polite life" in London.[10] His self-consciously independent posture did not pass unnoticed. To some of his hosts, his behavior seemed truculent. Elizabeth, Lady Holland, thought him intelligent and handsome, but quickly detected his ambivalence toward England and, in personal letters, noted his restless, irritable appearance in society.[11] Cooper, on his part, "did not like Lady Holland,"[12] but his behavior was not inspired by any dislike for individual Britons. He was determined, rather, to maintain his dignity as an American in the face of the condescension he expected from them as a group.

Cooper was later attacked in the United States for Anglophobia. Critics would say that he gave himself airs in England, that he had not met the civilities extended to him as he ought to have done. Cooper vigorously denied this accusation. He had not, he insisted, neglected the social code of any country he visited and took special care in England not to do so.[13] He could not accept, however, the hypocrisies of English society, the ostensible concern for etiquette, yet the lack of any true civility. Nor could he forget that the lords he moved among, Whigs though they might be, were nonetheless "disciples of the doctrine of exclusion." Although "amiable and intelligent men," they owed their position not to superior abilities, but to adventitious causes. With few exceptions, there was "scarcely a man of superior mind among them all." Some were simply men "of the common stamp, merely polished by the friction of society."[14] The American democrat would not be impressed.

However much he may have relished their company, Cooper was fully aware that these educated and polished gentlemen formed a landed aristocracy whose control of British government was all but complete. The king's power was limited, and, in Parliament, Lords and Commons were drawn from the same landed class. Through the borough system, large numbers, rich and poor alike, were disenfranchised. The newly burgeoning industrial cities had no direct representation, and men whose wealth derived from commerce were largely excluded from power—unless they bought boroughs. Yet supporters of this oligarchical system decried the institutions of the United States, as if England and not America were the true champion of liberality and freedom. Cooper understood that the landed class was bound to defend the system which gave it power, but he could not like a country where social and political inequalities were so blatantly unmerited.

II

Cooper's ambivalence toward England had deeply personal roots. From childhood associations in his father's Otsego mansion and elsewhere, he early developed a profound reverence for England, somewhat qualified, perhaps, by the bigoted Anglophilia of his Oxford trained tutor in Albany, the Reverend Thomas Ellison, and by his own experience as a merchant seaman. As a youth of seventeen, he had seen his Yankee vessel, the *Stirling*, boarded by a British officer and a native American shipmate rudely impressed in the British navy. Shortly thereafter, another fell victim to the press gangs in London, and even the ship's master, Captain Johnston, escaped from them only with difficulty.[15] But if Cooper learned on this voyage a lesson in national weakness that he never forgot, his experience in London introduced him to the sharp difference in social and political circumstances between England and the United States. Permission to enter Green Park as a royal favor and not as a right, for instance, brought home to him—as he writes in Letter XVII of this book—"the broad distinction that exists between political *franchises* and political *liberty*."

Cooper's experience after his return home could only have stirred his feelings of nationalism. From 1808 to 1811, he served as midshipman in the United States navy, and he took great pride in American naval accomplishments during the War of 1812. His interest in naval affairs never slackened thereafter, and he argued throughout his life for a strong American naval force to protect national rights abroad. Yet with his marriage to Susan Augusta De Lancey, he united himself with a family that had remained loyal to the king during the Revolution and which had given high ranking officers to both the colonial government of New York and the British army. Indeed, his wife's oldest sister, Mrs. John L. McAdam, lived her whole life in England and was reared a Tory. Cooper apparently valued the De Lancey connection and became much interested in the family's genealogy, but alliance with them could only have increased the ambivalence of his feelings toward England.

Yet however strong those personal feelings may have been, Cooper's mature attitude toward England cannot be attributed solely to emotional causes nor can his behavior in London society only be seen in terms of psychological motives. Those motives were always present to some degree, but Cooper was also a keenly intelligent man who gave much thought to social and political questions, and who based his conclusions on sound principles and accurate knowledge of the countries he visited. By the spring of 1828, he was well equipped to compare the British and American systems. He had already lived in Europe for nearly two years and had closely observed the social and political institutions of both France and England. He had studied carefully American Constitutional principles, and he had begun *Notions of the Americans* to correct erroneous European impressions of America.

In a long footnote to the opening letter in that book—a note that is really a carefully argued appendix—Cooper wrote his first important analysis of British and American intellectual relations. Since the passage was probably written in England during the visit of 1828,[16] it has particular relevance to the attitudes expressed in *England*. Through his persona, John Cadwallader, a thinly disguised mask for the author, Cooper recalls at length the development of English and American relations since the Revolution, the source of English hostility in the growing power and commerce of the United States, the gross European ignorance of things American, and the servile American dependence on British opinion. This last was a major point of contention. That English and American institutions should differ was only to be expected, but that Americans should defer to an assumed British superiority in social and political matters was not to be condoned.

Cooper was aware of the enormous opportunities the British had to exert an intellectual dominance. Because the two countries shared language and history, the influence of British thought was bound to be great. After the political bonds were severed, it was natural that such an influence should continue, so long as Americans cherished English literature and read British books without a literature of their own. Cooper was disturbed by the unnatural perpetuation of that influence. The absence of an international copyright law encouraged the pirating of English books. As a result, the development of a native literature was seriously retarded, and American readers were exposed to a large number of works affirming a social system inimical to their institutions. The extremely popular romances of Sir Walter Scott, saturated as they were with the values of an aristocratic society, could not fail to insinuate in uncritical American minds a strong bias in favor of social principles that America had rejected. Continued over a long period of time and supported by a myriad of other English books, such a bias would necessarily be detrimental to the creation of a distinctively American society.

Cooper was convinced, moreover, that some Englishmen took advantage of this situation and deliberately sought things to criticize in American society. The reports of some British travelers in America intensified, if they did not inspire, this conviction, for many of these visitors were openly hostile and did not conceal their hope that the American experiment would fail. At best, they saw the United States through British eyes and condemned it for not resembling England. In *Travels in North America,* for example, a book which appeared in England after Cooper's visit of 1828, Captain Basil Hall stoutly affirms his acceptance of British institutions: the monarchy, the established church, the aristocracy, and even the unreformed Parliament.[17] His insistence on judging the United States in terms of these institutions could only lead him to unfavorable conclusions about American society and culture.

Americans recounting their visits to England faced a difficult problem: how to respond to these British misunderstandings. Washington Irving was conciliatory. Though well aware of the growing literary animosity between England and the United States, he alluded to it gently in *The Sketch Book,*[18] and both there and in *Bracebridge Hall,* evoked an image of English life that bore little relation to nineteenth-century realities. On the other hand, Nathaniel H. Carter, a friend of Cooper, describes in detail many aspects of contemporary England—including the new industrial cities and their mills. He occasionally reveals a strong American bias in his passing comments upon the artificiality of British society and the juxtaposition of wealth and poverty, power and servility that he observed on his tour.[19] And Richard Rush, whose work Cooper knew, recounts his experience while serving as minister of the United States to Great Britain and includes in his books diplomatically correct descriptions of the many social functions he attended.[20]

Cooper felt no desire to conciliate and, as a private citizen, none of the restraint that influenced Rush. Nor did he wish to write the tourist guide that Carter's book, with its circumstantial description of places, sometimes resembles. His primary interest was political and social analysis. Americans, he believed, had to understand conditions in England to estimate their own advantages justly. Preoccupied with externals, they did not know the truth about British society, and they lacked the sophistication to concede the inferiority of some American things, while maintaining the superiority of their own institutions. Until they could achieve that detachment, Americans could not hope to win intellectual independence from England. Though Cooper had no expectation that *England* would bring about that grand result, he hoped that his book might contribute in some degree to the education of his countrymen.

III

Nine years elapsed between Cooper's visit to London in 1828 and his account of it in *England* in 1837. During that time, he had published five novels, including three set in Europe; a satire, *The Monikins,* directed against British, French, and American society; and a large quantity of non-fiction, including *A Letter to His Countrymen,* the "A. B. C." letters for the New York *Evening Post,* and three of his five books of European travels. He had also become involved in controversy. Because of the role he assumed in Europe of defending American institutions, Cooper had been attacked by the antirepublican press in France, and some of the hostile reviews had been reprinted at home. He soon found himself in the anomalous position of being attacked in the United States by American editors who allowed their attitude toward him to be influenced by politically inspired foreign opinion. Stung by his fellow Americans' apparent repudiation of him, Cooper returned to the United States in 1833 determined to end his career as a novelist.

Cooper did not stop writing. The issue of American intellectual independence was too important for him to remain silent, and despite his dissatisfaction with social and political conditions in the United States, he devoted much time and effort to the instruction of his fellow citizens in American principles. Although *A Letter to His Countrymen* provoked a storm of criticism and personal ridicule from the Whig press and *The Monikins* turned out to be a complete failure, Cooper persevered in his purpose. As early as January 1828, he had begun to project a series of travel books to reaffirm his position as an American democrat and to justify his conduct during his residence abroad. At first Cooper envisioned a single work in several volumes,[21] but the series eventually grew to five full-sized books. *Gleanings in Europe: England,* the second in point of time of the events described, was the fourth to be written.

Cooper began *England* sometime during the fall of 1836, for on 19 November, he forwarded the printed sheets of *Gleanings in*

Europe: [*France*] to Richard Bentley, his English publisher, and announced that *England* would be next in the series.[22] By 25 January 1837, the writing must have been well advanced. Visiting Philadelphia on business with his American publisher, Carey, Lea, and Blanchard, Cooper wrote his wife that he would "not remain to finish the book, but long enough to get through with a good deal, and to make my arrangements,"[23] implying thereby that the work was almost finished. On 6 March, Cooper informed Bentley, whose reply to Cooper's November letter had not yet arrived, that the book was "nearly printed" and that he was sending him the sheets of volume I.[24] Cooper was again reading proof in Philadelphia on 5 April, and on 14 April he forwarded to Bentley, whose letter he had at last received, the sheets of volume II. By that time, however, the writing of *England* had long been completed, for Cooper also informed his English publisher that "work on Italy," the fifth and last book in the series, was "nearly done."[25]

Though *England* must have been written very rapidly, the book shows few, if any, signs of undue haste. It seems rather to have been well thought out and carefully constructed. Cooper originally suggested to Bentley that he might organize the material around "[f]our visits to London, with views at different times," but he soon decided to limit the scope to "a visit or a winter in London."[26] He structured the book, therefore, on the sojourn of 1828 and presented his material through the device of letters ostensibly written at that time. Though they are addressed to actual people, no manuscripts of them have ever been found, and they seem to have been written expressly for this book. The epistolary device afforded him a number of advantages. By directing the letters to identifiable people, he could fit the content to the supposed recipients. Descriptions of social events, for example, are addressed to Mrs. Jay or Mrs. H. H. Comstock, while accounts of visits to Parliament and discussions of the British press are addressed to William Jay, who would presumably be more interested in public affairs. By this means, Cooper was able to construct what are in effect a number of essays on particular subjects yet give them the variety and human interest of a series of letters written for different people.

The device caused him some problems, however. To maintain the illusion that these had been actual letters of 1828, Cooper had to include material that he knew was out of date in 1837. The Reform Bill of 1832 had been passed, and a greater knowledge of and better feeling toward Americans, it was said, now existed in Great Britain. Yet to maintain the integrity of the book—and of the series of which it formed but one part— Cooper had to limit himself to those conditions which had existed during his visit. He includes in the text, therefore, such statements as his prediction that reform or revolution lay in store for Great Britain, when he knew full well, at the time of publication, that some reform had already occurred. A footnote declares—probably correctly—that this statement was actually made in 1828, but whether it was or not, it does indeed contribute to the desired effect.

Although the events of 1828 determined the basic character of *England*, Cooper felt free to reorganize his material for thematic purposes. The basic structure of the book accords with the facts of his visit: his arrival at Dover in February, his journey through Canterbury to London, and his departure in May by steamboat for Amsterdam; but in describing his experience in London, he did not follow strictly the actual order of events. The trips to Richmond Hill (26 April) and Windsor (5 May), for example, appear in Letter XV, before the description, in Letter XX, of the visit to the Tower of London (27 March), and all three events had occurred after the visit to Hoddeston (17 March), described in Letter XXII. Thus, although Cooper maintains the illusion that the events have taken place in the order described in the letters, he rearranges the material to fit the larger purpose he had in writing his book: to present his important theme in an entertaining manner.

Cooper arranged the letters with considerable skill. The opening ones are largely descriptive, detailing the arrival in London and describing the sights and sounds that would first attract the attention of the tourist—or the reader of travel books. In succeeding letters, however, Cooper includes increasing amounts of social and political commentary, until, toward the end, we find a number of letters that are largely analytical. Yet even in these later pages, the social and political analysis is freely interspersed with accounts of tourist attractions and descriptions of famous persons and social events, as if Cooper consciously sought to make his themes palatable to his audience. He seems to have been aware of the need to entertain his readers as well as to instruct them, and to lead them gradually toward an understanding and acceptance of the social analysis that was his primary purpose in writing.

To accomplish his aims, Cooper was willing to include material unavailable in 1828 and to transfer to that year experiences from other times and places. He compares Westminster Hall with the great halls of the Stadhuis in Amsterdam and of the Palazzo Gran Duca in Florence, and he describes the size and general effect of St. Paul's Cathedral in terms of St. Peter's basilica in Rome, though he did not visit either Holland or Italy until after his residence in London. These and a number of other incidental comparisons—of Roman women with those of England and America, of Neapolitan and English weather, and of music and art in Italy with their counterparts in London—add greatly to the reader's interest in the book, and Cooper may have included them for just that reason.

Other incidents and events, transposed to 1828, serve a thematic function. The incident at Major André's monument in Westminster Abbey, used in Letter IV to exemplify British feelings toward Americans, apparently took place on 21 June 1833, for Cooper reported in his journal of that date the mutilation of the figure of Washington and the cicerone's comment that some Americans must have done it.[27] Another incident is transposed from an earlier date. In Letter XVII, Cooper contrasts the white, ringless hands of an English duke with those of a prince on the continent whose dirty fingers were covered with jewels. This observation had appeared in a letter of 26 March 1827 to Mrs. Peter Augustus Jay, in which Cooper had contrasted his own clean, unadorned fingers with the bejewelled, grimy ones of an Italian prince.[28] Thus, an occurrence in Paris was changed to illustrate a social difference between England and the continent.

Other, more obvious anachronisms also appear in the book. Michael T. Sadler's maiden speech in the House of Commons, mentioned in Letter X, was not delivered until 17 March 1829,[29] so that Cooper could not have discussed it with a Whig peer during his visit. Captain Basil Hall's *Travels in North America*, alluded to in several of these letters, did not appear until 1829; and Sir James Mackintosh's *History of the Revolution in England in 1688*, quoted in Letter XIII, was not published until 1834.[30] Cooper used them, no doubt, as he used other incidents and comparisons that he could not have known or made during his residence in London. That they were anachronistic was apparently less important to him than that they admirably suited his thematic purpose: to illustrate a point about British society or to illuminate a British attitude.

England would seem to be, therefore, a carefully prepared, if rapidly written book, and Cooper hoped that it would reach a wide audience. He thought it a better book than his other travel volumes, and he had asked more money for it from Richard Bentley because of the interest he believed it would excite in Great Britain. Bentley, on his part, urged Cooper to return to fiction with a tale of the sea or woods. He had made no profit, he wrote, on his last books of travels, and he was clearly reluctant to undertake more of them. He did agree, however, that *England* would be more interesting to the British public, and he settled on £300, £50 less than Cooper had asked.[31] Entitled *England, with Sketches of Society in the Metropolis,* the book was published in London on 29 May 1837 in an edition of 1250 copies,[32] and another English language edition, derived from it, appeared in Paris on 12 August 1837 under the separate imprints of Baudry's European Library and A. and W. Galignani.[33]

Cooper had even more trouble with his American publishers. Carey, Lea, and Blanchard claimed, on 13 September 1837, that they had not yet made a cent on Cooper's last eight books to repay them for the "capital & time employed in them,"[34] and though they had, in January, 1837, readily accepted *England* when it was offered them,[35] they paid him only $750 for an edition of 2000 copies, the same terms that they had allowed him for *France.* This was $250 less than he had received for the volumes on Switzerland and the Rhine, and less than one-third of what he had been paid for *The Monikins* ($2500).[36] Cooper had fallen on hard times. They would not soon improve.

The spring and summer of 1837 were extremely difficult ones for both Cooper and the country. On the personal level, the tensions that had been developing between the Cooper family and many of the residents of Cooperstown since their return from Europe came to a head in the Three Mile Point controversy, which was soon to subject Cooper to vilification in the Whig press and involve him in a series of lawsuits; while on the national scene, the country plunged into the depression of 1837. Book

publishers were, of course, hit as hard as other businessmen, and
Carey, Lea, and Blanchard put no books to press throughout the
summer. *England* had been printed in April,[37] and was announced
in at least two journals as soon to be published in June.[38] But
Carey wrote to Cooper on 26 June that he was withholding publication because of the gloomy business prospects.[39] He delayed so
long, indeed, that Cooper bluntly wrote on 8 September: "What
the deuce have you done with England?—Burnt it?" By that
time, the American edition had in fact appeared, but a great deal
of damage to the book was already being done, for, his publisher
wrote, it—"or rather its author"—had come under regular attack
in the newspapers.[40]

IV

Cooper did not yet know how the English edition, already published for over three months, was faring, but he soon learned from
a returning traveler, Colonel Joseph M. White, that the book
had "made a stir in London, where," Cooper wrote, he was both
"abused and read à la Trollope."[41] This was only part of the truth.
Though *England* and its author had indeed been sharply attacked,
both were better received in some quarters than anyone might
have expected. At first, even the censure was mild. An early notice
in the *Literary Gazette* (20 May 1837) merely excerpts a few passages to illustrate the spirit of the book and to support its one
main criticism: that Cooper dwells too often "on the ridiculous
features" of society.[42] A review in the *Athenæum* in June was a bit
more critical. The reviewer had expected a better book from
Cooper and contends that the three volumes should have been
condensed into one. He attributes the failure in part to Cooper's
dislike for England, yet he concedes that English writers had
committed the similar fault of basing their social analysis on too
meager an experience in America, and he selects a few excerpts
from the "best passages," mainly descriptions of London and some
amusing anecdotes.[43]

Other reviewers found much to praise in *England*. On 27 May,
the *Spectator* called the book "unquestionably the most searching
and thoughtful, not to say philosophical, of any which have been
published by an American on England"; on 4 June, the *Examiner*

wrote that it contained "many valuable *home-truths*"; and in July, the *Monthly Review* found in the "graver passages a great deal that is impressive, and calculated to expose error, as well as to chastise folly."[44] There is high praise, too, for the author. The *Spectator* praises his judgment and taste, and though it regrets his Anglophobia and occasional personal pique, it believes he does "justice to the manners and character of England." The *Examiner* thinks him "an acute observer," who "often displays superior sagacity," and though it detects in his writing a certain irritable humor and a tendency to view things "altogether too much as they immediately affect himself," it notes his "strong regard for the truth" and his "candid and just mind." The *Monthly Review* also deplores his irritable mood and thinks him far too sensitive and prejudiced in his view of English and American relations, but it too considers him "a close, a searching observer," who is "critical, and corrective in no ordinary degree."

What these reviewers found attractive in the book was the liberal social view that Cooper expressed. They took no offense at his analysis of English society. They thought him right. Thus, the *Spectator* thinks "[h]is comments on the strength of the aristocracy" worthy of consideration, and the *Examiner* calls his "remark [sic] on the House of Lords . . . on the whole just and forcible" and reprints a passage from Letter XII in which Cooper depicts the peers of England as usurpers who, under the guise of supporting liberty, had perverted the institutions of England to their own advantage. Though it does not agree with him wholly, it is only because he gives them too much credit for "[t]he affair of 1688," which, in the reviewer's opinion, was "something like a swindling transaction when compared with the single year of government that followed the meeting of the parliament of 1640." In a similar fashion, both the *Spectator* and the *Monthly Review* close their notices with an excerpt from the beginning of Letter XXV, wherein Cooper contends that the artificiality of British society has choked up the channels of human sympathy and describes the particularly hard lot of the English female domestics. This passage, the *Monthly Review* concludes, "should be daily read in many an English family."

Reviews in Tory journals completely ignored such passages. They resorted instead to indirection in sometimes savage efforts to demolish the author and his book. Political implications are apparent in these reviews—as in *Blackwood's* sneer at *The Heiden-mauer* and *The Bravo,* books known for their liberal themes, or in the brief statement in *Fraser's* dismissing the politics of *England* as "merely trash"—but by and large, the reader's attention is directed to other matters. George Croly, who noticed the book in both the August and September issues of *Blackwood's,* quoted directly only a brief passage comparing English and American women, and both he and William Maginn, who probably wrote the review in the August issue of *Fraser's,* devote considerable space to the famous dinner in which Cooper was given the lowest place at table (Letter XX). Maginn also includes a number of similar anecdotes to depict the author as a man of vast conceit who continually sought admission to high society while pretending to care nothing about it, and both he and Croly attempt to pin on him the charge of vulgarity, a trait which Croly accounts for by his having been "bred to the sea."[45] Because these attacks are so personal, one suspects the reviewers of attempting to deflect attention from the meaning of Cooper's book.

A long review by John Wilson Croker[46] in the October *Quarterly* epitomizes the strategy. It simply ignores the issues that Cooper raises and turns instead to a vicious attack on the author. Beginning with the assumption that "[t]he subject of the book is not England, but Mr. J. Fenimore Cooper," Croker creates and sustains through some thirty-five pages an image of Cooper as ignorant, narrow-minded, egotistical, even malicious. He had spent, Croker maintains, "the most important years of his life" as a "common seaman," and had probably risen only lately into polite society. Hence, he exhibits the "vulgar vanity" that "natural, professional, personal, and national" circumstances had produced in him. A book by such a man, Croker implies, is not to be taken seriously, for it is only the "*autobiography of excoriated vanity.*" Croker meets Cooper's arguments with personal attack designed to destroy his credibility. He even attempts to damage him with his American audience by printing a long sequence of brief passages from *England* in which Cooper criticizes America and Americans.[47] The review resembles those in *Blackwood's* and *Fraser's,* but surpasses them both in its gross unfairness.

The English were not alone in treating Cooper so scornfully. A brief review in *Magazin für die Literatur des Auslands,* published 12 June 1837, is as withering in its criticism as were the Tory journals in Great Britain. Five years before, in its first year of publication, the *Magazin* had taken an antirepublican stand, and though the reviewer of Cooper's book has praise for such republicans as Franklin and Irving, it accuses the plebeian Cooper of crudity and pettiness in his treatment of England. He had, the reviewer admits, once seemed a colossal figure, but now that he has exchanged his tales of the prairies and maritime adventures for travel books on Europe, he appears small. Since their publication "ist sein literarischer Ruhm so krank geworden, dass ihm die kritischen Aerzte in der alten wie in der neuen Welt kein langes Leben mehr versprechen." The refined reading public will now bid him farewell.[48] As William Maginn was later to do in *Fraser's Magazine,* the German reviewer predicts the early demise of Cooper as a writer.

The reception of *England* in the United States was strongly influenced by British opinion and complicated by the war with the Whig press that Cooper was beginning to wage. Depending upon their political bent, the first reviews often cited either favorable or unfavorable British opinion. William Cullen Bryant printed a friendly notice in his *Evening Post* (5 September 1837), taking exception to Cooper's stand against free trade, but praising the book's liveliness and quoting a statement attributed to the *Examiner* that *England* is "the most searching and thoughtful work that has been written concerning England by an American."[49] The *Journal of Belles Lettres,* on the other hand, reported, on 12 September, that the British journals had treated the book "with severity on account of its snarling and want of liberal feeling," and reprinted Croly's notice from the August *Blackwood's.* The American editor goes on to say that he is tired of Cooper's nonfiction, that the author "has a *kink,*" and that he exhibits, through his sensitiveness, too much "deference towards the opinions and modes of action in vogue in England."[50]

Most newspapers were hostile. On 8 September, the *Morning Courier and New-York Enquirer* attacked the style of the book as "careless and clumsy," but devoted most of its attention to the long footnote at the end of Letter XXVI. Cooper's belief that American character abroad suffered more under Jackson's than Adams' administration supplies occasion for a political jibe at the Democrats. On 16 September, the *New-York American,* which had earlier reprinted the notice from the London *Literary Gazette,* read into Cooper's report on British society "an ardent longing for aristocratic distinctions" and accused him of the very "tuft-hunting" that he had condemned in others. And on 4 October, the *Chenango Telegraph* deliberately interjected the book into the Three Mile Point controversy by reprinting the notice from the August *Blackwood's* on the same page as its announcement of the beginning of Cooper's suit against the editor. Indeed, it explicitly calls Cooper's attention to the review to "edify his feelings."[51]

Similar attacks appeared in the October issues of two monthly journals. Both the *Gentleman's Magazine* and the *American Monthly Magazine* direct their critical fire against the author. In the words of the former journal, "Mr. Cooper has turned his European tour to a profitable account: and has shown his proficiency in the vice of book making, by manufacturing his trip into several volumes of questionable merit." He "has become an errant grumbler." In search of things to criticize, he acts like the ass in the eastern fable who defiles a beautiful garden "in an eager search after his favorite thistle. But Mr. Cooper outdoes the Oriental asinine, for when he has obtained his weedy prize, he grumbles in the height of his delight, and laments the bitterness of the thing he has taken such pains to discover." The *American Monthly Magazine* projects an image of Cooper as a man laughed to scorn by his countrymen for his recent ridiculous books and considers him too egotistical and insensitive to feel the just rebukes that both English and American journals have administered. It cites with approval the August review in *Fraser's Magazine* and claims that the American journal would have ignored the book completely if the English magazines had not "deemed it worthy of considerable remark and animadversion."[52]

Other American journals were fairer in their estimates. Although the *Oasis,* a magazine published in Oswego, New York, was by no means favorable in its October review, it was somewhat more balanced. It disliked the tone of the book, objected to the way that Cooper "allowed himself to grumble at and contemn every thing he met with in England," and was quite out of patience with him for outraging the feelings of his hosts. It admitted, nonetheless, that the book was well written in an independent spirit and contained "some admirable descriptions of men and things —

some pointed and judicious reflections upon society, which may be read with profit." The October *Knickerbocker*, too, found "much to condemn" in the book, particularly the assumption of British hatred of Americans, the sensitivity of the author, and his supposed admiration for titles. Yet it also found much to admire. It agreed with "Cooper, entirely, in very many of his views in relation to the society and manners of England and America," and was pleased "to see, by the squirming of the *malevoli* among the English critics, who are nibbling away at the excrescences of the work," that Cooper's criticism had struck home.[53]

Here the matter might have ended had American journals not given wide publicity—and support—to Croker's attack in the *Quarterly Review. Brown's Literary Omnibus* announced the arrival of the October issue on 5 January 1838 and used it immediately against Cooper. Though it reprinted only the journal's table of contents. it replaced the actual British title of the book with Croker's satiric one: "J. Fennimore Cooper, Esquire, in England, with sketches of his behaviour in the metropolis." On 16 January, the *Journal of Belles Lettres* called the review "a biting and severe attack, justly earned by [Cooper's] vanity and weakness," and on 19 January, the *National Gazette and Literary Register* printed a few paragraphs from it. Two complete reprints of Croker's article followed in February: in the *Museum of Foreign Literature* and in two issues (6 and 13 February) of the *Journal of Belles Lettres.* The latter journal appended a few editorial comments to each issue calling the reader's attention to the list of quotations, critical of America and Americans, that Croker had culled from *England,* and expressing its mortification "that one of our citizens should give occasion for so biting and unwarrantable a satire upon our manners and habits."[54]

Croker's article became at once the focus of discussion on Cooper's *England.* In February, the *Gentleman's Magazine* cited with approval the "potent causticity" with which the reviewer "developes the gangrene of the author's mind in its most foul and diseased state," and went on to say that "[t]he annals of criticism do not exhibit a parallel instance of such talented and well applied severity." The February issue of the *Knickerbocker,* in a sharp reversal of its earlier position, summarized Croker's article, repeating much of the original abuse, and pronounced the review in many respects a "justly pungent and deserved" criticism.[55] And as late as July 1838, the *American Monthly Magazine,* in a review of Cooper's *Gleanings in Europe: Italy,* was still citing with delight "[t]he delicious article" in the *Quarterly Review,* and trusted "most fervently" that "the same hand and the same thongs are ready for a new and lustier infliction" of "the magnificent flogging."[56] Croker's article had thus become a rallying point for those who wished to attack the book—or, more properly, its author.

Other American journals rose to his defense. The *New-York Mirror,* in January, sharply attacked the review in the London *Quarterly* as a "clever and ingenious piece of special pleading" and, recognizing its Tory bias, hoped that some liberal British journal, like the *Westminster Review,* would reply. Sensible readers, it observes, will not form their opinion of *England* from "the garbled extracts" in the *Quarterly Review,* which, by cutting and splicing quotations, made the author appear "a gross libeller" of both England and America. The notice ends with strong support for Cooper himself: though Americans may deplore the caustic tone of *England,* Cooper's "essential manliness of character, his haughty independence and high-toned principal [sic] as a republican, an American and a gentleman, not less than his unquestioned superiority of talent, and his commanding station as one of the pioneers of our infant literature, intrench him too deeply in their esteem, their pride and patriotism for a hundred reviewers, though all as clever as he of the Quarterly, to shake or impair. When such ephemeral comments shall have passed away, the world will judge the writings of Cooper by their intrinsick merits, and not by the opinions which individuals or parties may have expressed concerning them."[57]

Two southern magazines were equally strong in his support. The bitterness of the attack in the *Quarterly Review,* the *Southern Literary Journal* shrewdly observed in February, clearly shows that Cooper was not so insignificant, nor his accusations so groundless as the British journal suggests. The English do assume an air of superiority over everything American, and Americans are indeed too often sycophantic in their attitude toward the British. Yet because Cooper states "his opinions without fear or favor," he "stands very little chance of receiving justice at home or abroad." The *Baltimore Monument,* a journal that had already published a plea for American intellectual independence, made an even stronger point in May. It was not "surprised that foreign reviewer's [sic] should do their utmost to injure an author, who has written as fearlessly and acted as independnetly [sic] as" Cooper, but it was "somewhat mortified [to] find that envious rivals at home, have so far forgotten the respect due to American talent as to become the echoes for foreign abuse, and retailers of malignant vituperation, which is becoming a very marketable article among us."[58] Cooper's plea for American intellectual independence had not fallen on deaf ears. These writers understood him perfectly.

Other references to Cooper and his work between October 1837 and July 1838, while not reviews of *England,* might possibly have been provoked by the controversy marking its appearance. The review of *Gleanings in Europe: [France]* in the January 1838 *North American Review* seems to have had *England,* too, as part of its target,[59] and brief biographies of Cooper in the *Rural Repository* (November 1837) and the *Southern Literary Messenger* (June 1838) are related to the controversy in that they support his ideas or actions.[60] So too does a brief passage in the April 1838 issue of Orestes Brownson's *Boston Quarterly Review.* In an article on Francis J. Grund's *The Americans in their Moral, Social, and Political Relations,* the reviewer accounts for the attacks on Cooper in this way: "Cooper was a favorite, so long as he wrote only to amuse, and took good care to show no sympathy with the democracy; but since he has felt himself an American, and sought to infuse into his works some portion of American thought and feeling, he has fallen from grace, and must now be looked upon as under the ban of all the Quarterlies in the world,—except our own."[61]

Scattered attacks on Cooper's *England* continued both here and abroad for some time after the book had ceased to be a matter of current interest. In England, a brief derogatory reference appeared in Colburn's *New Monthly Magazine* a year after its British publication,[62] and as late as the end of 1839, a reviewer of Cooper's *History of the Navy* was still referring to *England* and assuring his readers that the book had been utterly demolished by the *Quarterly Review.*[63] In America, the book was depicted in the *Albany Evening Journal* (22 November 1841) as the work of a "snarler and scold" who seemed to have written both *England* and *Italy* with "no other object but to draw comparisons injurious to his own Country."[64] Such statements were, however, only incidental to their authors' larger purposes and simply indicate the long-lasting disparagement that the book was subjected to.

Cooper himself thought well of his book and took some delight in the stir it had caused in London. It ought, he believed, to do the English good.[65] Its reception in America, however, was a different matter. He had some private as well as public support, like that of Senator Bedford Brown of North Carolina, who wrote him, on 21 March 1838, concerning the book. But Cooper knew it was "not very well received in general," and he regretted that other writers would not sustain him. They feared for their popularity, and "half of them" had, he thought, "a most profound and provincial awe of the old island." He had little patience with those who considered *Italy* the better book, and he took the reception of *England* by one group of American editors as a sign of the strong and increasing hold of English opinion on the American mind. "[T]he English know it," Cooper replied to Senator Brown on 24 March, and "they are disposed to turn their power to account, in the way of promoting their own interests."[66] The message of his book had been lost on a large segment of the American public, which, in its attitude, showed unmistakably how correct he had been in his analysis of Anglo-American intellectual relations. For the sturdy American democrat, there was no consolation in that.

Notes

1. Mrs. Cooper to her daughters, London, 11 March, 19 March, 27 March, 26 April, 6 May [1828]; MSS: Yale Collection of American Literature, Beinecke Rare Book and Manuscript Library, Yale University (hereafter referred to as YCAL).
2. *The Letters and Journals of James Fenimore Cooper,* ed. James Franklin Beard (Cambridge, Mass., 1960-1968), I, 254, (hereafter referred to as *Letters and Journals*).
3. Mrs. Cooper to her daughters, London, 11 March [1828]; MS: YCAL.
4. Mrs. Cooper to her daughters, London, 19 March [1828]; MS: YCAL.
5. *Elizabeth, Lady Holland to Her Son, 1821-1845,* ed. The Earl of Ilchester (London, 1946), p. 79.
6. Mrs. Cooper to her daughters, London, 27 March [1828]; MS: YCAL.

7. *The Journal of Sir Walter Scott,* ed. W. E. K. Anderson (Oxford, 1972), pp. 460, 462. The dates seem certain, yet the first, 17 April, presents a problem in that Cooper claims in Letter XIV that Scott visited him the morning following this dinner to discuss some business concerning his consulship at Lyons. Scott mentions such a conversation in a journal entry dated 4 May (p. 468). Cooper would seem to be in error in linking the two events.

8. *Letters and Journals,* I, 261.

9. *Memoirs, Journal, and Correspondence of Thomas Moore,* ed. Lord John Russell (London, 1853-1856), V, 288-289.

10. *Letters and Journals,* I, 263.

11. Quoted from unpublished manuscripts by Robert E. Spiller in his introduction to *Gleanings in Europe: England* (New York, 1930) pp. xiii-xiv. These quotations are printed only in part in *Elizabeth, Lady Holland to Her Son,* p. 80. For Lord Holland's opinion of Cooper, see The Earl of Ilchester, *Chronicles of Holland House, 1820-1900* (London, 1937), p. 95. Yet another contemporary view of Cooper in society appears in John Gibson Lockhart's letter to John Wilson Croker, quoted in Myron F. Brightfield, *John Wilson Croker* (Berkeley, Cal., 1940), p. 390.

12. *Letters and Journals,* I, 357.

13. *Letters and Journals,* I, 354-355.

14. *Letters and Journals,* II, 95.

15. [James Fenimore Cooper], "America," *New Monthly Magazine,* XXXII (Oct. 1831), 309-310; *Ned Myers; or, A Life Before the Mast* (Philadelphia, 1843), pp. 24-25, 34-35.

16. Cooper's persona states: "I write under the observation of four visits to England," Cooper's own situation during the visit of 1828. *Notions of the Americans: Picked up by a Travelling Bachelor* (Philadelphia, 1828), I, 320.

17. *Travels in North America, in the Years 1827 and 1828* (Edinburgh, 1829), III, 393-436.

18. "English Writers on America," *The Sketch Book of Geoffrey Crayon, Gent.,* ed. Haskell Springer (Boston, 1978), pp. 43-49.

19. *Letters from Europe, Comprising the Journal of a Tour through Ireland, England, Scotland, France, Italy, and Switzerland in the Years 1825, '26, and '27,* second ed. (New York, 1829), I, 75, 80, 96-97.

20. Rush's two books are: *Memoranda of a Residence at the Court of London* (Philadelphia, 1833); *Memoranda of a Residence at the Court of London, Comprising Incidents Official and Personal, from 1819 to 1825* (Philadelphia, 1845). The second volume is a continuation of the first.

21. *Letters and Journals,* I, 241-242; see also I, 258; II, 175-176; III, 149.

22. *Letters and Journals,* III, 249.

23. *Letters and Journals,* III, 253.

24. *Letters and Journals,* III, 257.

25. *Letters and Journals,* III, 259, 261.

26. *Letters and Journals,* III, 152, 156.

27. *Letters and Journals,* II, 390.

28. *Letters and Journals,* I, 210. Elsewhere in the book (see p. 225), Cooper attributes an experience to "G_____." The single surviving manuscript leaf of *England* indicates that not "G_____" but Cooper himself suffered the snub described.
29. *Parliamentary Debates,* 20 n.s. (London, 1829), 1149-1171.
30. *Dictionary of National Biography,* XII, 621.
31. *Letters and Journals,* III, 249, 258.
32. Bentley Papers, BM Add MSS 46, 637, 40v-41r. Bentley appended to this edition a much abridged version of Cooper's *A Letter to His Countrymen* (1834).
33. *Bibliographie de la France* (Paris, 1837), XXVI, 4179-4180.
34. *Letters and Journals,* III, 290.
35. Carey and Lea to Cooper, Philadelphia, 4 January 1837; MS: YCAL. Although they do not mention the book by name, the work referred to is presumably *England.*
36. *The Cost Book of Carey & Lea, 1825-1838,* ed. David Kaser (Philadelphia, 1963), p. 221; David Kaser, *Messrs. Carey & Lea of Philadelphia: A Study in the History of the Booktrade* (Philadelphia, 1957), p. 81.
37. *The Cost Book of Carey & Lea,* p. 221.
38. *Waldie's Literary Omnibus,* 1 (16 June 1837), [8]; *The New-York Mirror,* 14 (24 June 1837), 414.
39. Carey and Lea to Cooper, Philadelphia, 26 June 1837; MS: YCAL.
40. *Letters and Journals,* III, 289-290. Carey and Lea informed him on 13 September that the book had "been out for three weeks past." It was announced as "published this day" in *The National Gazette and Literary Register,* 2 September 1837.
41. *Letters and Journals,* III, 291, 296.
42. *The Literary Gazette,* No. 1061 (20 May 1837), 347.
43. *The Athenæun,* No. 502 (10 June 1837), 412-413.
44. *The Spectator,* No. 465 (27 May 1837), 493-494; *The Examiner,* No. 1531 (4 June 1837), 355-357; *The Monthly Review,* 2 n.s. (July 1837), 346-357. All quotations in this and the following paragraph are from these three issues.
45. *Blackwood's Edinburgh Magazine,* 42 (Aug. 1837), 199; 42 (Sept. 1837), 328; *Fraser's Magazine,* 16 (Aug. 1837), 233-241. For the attribution of these articles to Croly and Maginn, see *The Wellesley Index to Victorian Periodicals, 1824-1900,* ed. Walter E. Houghton (Toronto, 1966-1979), I, 55; II, 357.
46. For the attribution of this article to Croker, see *The Wellesley Index to Victorian Periodicals,* I, 719. At the time the review appeared, it was thought by many, but not by Cooper, to be the work of John Gibson Lockhart, Sir Walter Scott's son-in-law. For Cooper's opinion, see *Letters and Journals,* III, 320-322. This letter was published in *The Knickerbocker,* 11 (April 1838), 380-386, and reprinted, in part, in *The Baltimore Monument,* 2 (5 May 1838), 245.
47. *The Quarterly Review,* 59 (Oct. 1837), 327-361.
48. *Magazin für die Literatur des Auslands,* 11 (12 June 1837), 280.
49. *The Evening Post,* 5 Sept. 1837. The quotation is not in the *Examiner.* It seems rather to be misquoted from the opening sentence of the review in the *Spectator,* a passage that had been reprinted, somewhat inaccurately, in the *National Gazette and Literary Register,* 2 Sept. 1837.

50. *The Journal of Belles Lettres*, 10, No. 11 (12 Sept. 1837), [2-3].

51. *Morning Courier and New-York Enquirer*, 8 Sept. 1837; *New-York American*, 29 July 1837, 16 Sept. 1837; *The Chenango Telegraph*, 4 Oct. 1837.

52. *The Gentleman's Magazine*, 1 (Oct. 1837), 290-291; *The American Monthly Magazine*, 4 n.s. (Oct. 1837), 391-393, reprinted in *The New-Yorker*, 4 (7 Oct. 1837), 462-463.

53. *The Oasis*, 1 (21 Oct. 1837), 46-47; *The Knickerbocker*, 10 (Oct. 1837), 350-352, reprinted in *The New-Yorker*, 4 (14 Oct. 1837), 476-477.

54. *Brown's Literary Omnibus*, 2 (5 Jan. 1838), [8]; *The Journal of Belles Lettres*, 11, No. 3 (16 Jan. 1838), [3]; *The National Gazette and Literary Register*, 19 Jan. 1838; *The Museum of Foreign Literature, Science, and Art*, 4 n.s. (Feb. 1838), 180-195; *The Journal of Belles Lettres*, 11, No. 6 (6 Feb. 1838), [1-4], and 11, No. 7 (13 Feb. 1838), [1-4]. For Cooper's reply to the *National Gazette*, see *Letters and Journals*, III, 309-311.

55. *The Gentleman's Magazine*, 2 (Feb. 1838), 131; *The Knickerbocker*, 11 (Feb. 1838), 184-185.

56. *The American Monthly Magazine*, 6 n.s. (July 1838), 75-76. Additional reviews of *Italy* which relate it to other volumes in the series, and sometimes to *England*, may be found in the *Morning Courier and New-York Enquirer*, 30 May 1838; *New-York American*, 2 June 1838; *The New-Yorker*, 5 (2 June 1838), 173. The *Quarterly Review* attack was still being mentioned by the last named journal four months later. See *The New-Yorker*, 6 (13 Oct. 1838), 61.

57. *New-York Mirror*, 15 (20 Jan. 1838), 239. *The Westminster Review* did not notice *England.*

58. *The Southern Literary Journal*, 3 n.s. (Feb. 1838), 159-160; *The Baltimore Monument*, 2 (9 Dec. 1837), 76; 2 (5 May 1838), 245. Additional defenses of Cooper may be found in *The Evening Post*, 31 Jan. 1838, where Croker's review is called "a tissue of petulant railing," and in *The Evening Post for the Country*, 1 Feb. 1838 (under 30 Jan. 1838 for this semi-weekly), where a short ironic letter in support of Cooper appears.

59. *The North American Review*, 46 (Jan. 1838), 16. The passage in which the reviewer advises Cooper not to "conceive that his country is wilfully insulted, because his own position at table does not accord with his wishes" may be a reference to the dinner at which Cooper sat near the foot of the table (Letter XX).

60. *The Rural Repository*, 14 (25 Nov. 1837), 93-94; *Southern Literary Messenger*, 4 (June 1838), 373-378.

61. *The Boston Quarterly Review*, 1 (April 1838), 165. An interesting defense of Cooper may also be found in *The Vision of Rubeta, An Epic Story of the Island of Manhattan*, [by Laughton Osborn] (Boston, 1838), pp. 347-351.

62. Michael J. Quin, "Ancient Days," *New Monthly Magazine*, 53 (May 1838), 89.

63. Cited in Thomas R. Lounsbury, *James Fenimore Cooper* (Boston, 1882), pp. 204-205.

64. Quoted in Ethel R. Outland, *The "Effingham" Libels on Cooper* (Madison, Wis., 1929), p. 113.

65. *Letters and Journals*, III, 296.

66. *Letters and Journals*, III, 300, 334, 316.

Gleanings in Europe: England

Preface

The American who should write a close, philosophical, just, popular, and yet comprehensive view of the fundamental differences that exist between the political and social relations of England and those of his own country, would confer on the latter one of the greatest benefits it has received since the memorable events of July 4, 1776. That was a declaration of political independence, only, while this might be considered the foundation of the mental emancipation which alone can render the nation great, by raising its opinion to the level of its facts.

This work lays no claim to a merit so distinguished. It is intended solely as a part of the testimony, of which an incalculable mass is yet required, that, under the slow operation of time, and in the absence of such an effort of genius as has just been named, it is to be hoped, will, sooner or later, produce something like the same result.

Some pains have been taken to persuade the reading world, that the writer of this book is peculiarly prejudiced against Great Britain, and it may be expedient to clear the way for the evidence he is about to give, by a few explanations. He might be content to refer to the work itself, perhaps, for proofs to the contrary; but there are many who would still insist on seeing antipathies in truths, and rancour in principle.

There is no very apparent motive, why the writer of this book should be particularly prejudiced against Great Britain. Personally, he was kindly treated, by many of her most distinguished men; he is as strongly convinced as his worst enemy can be, that, as an author, he has been extolled beyond his merits; nor has he failed to receive quite as much substantial remuneration, as he can properly lay claim to. In no country has he ever been as *well* treated, as in England; not even in his own; although, since some of his opinions have appeared, he has not escaped the usual abuse that seems to flow so easily from the Anglo-Saxon tongue.

The writer will now give his own account of what he conceives to be the origin of this erroneous notion. A part of the American travellers have earned for themselves, a well-deserved reputation of being the most flagrant tuft-hunters, who enter the British empire. Of this amiable peculiarity, the writer has not yet been accused, and they who have the consciousness of not having always preserved their own self-respect in the English circles, are a little too much disposed, perhaps, to quarrel with those who have.

Anecdotes have been circulated concerning the writer's "sayings and doings" while in England; some in print, and more verbally, and all to his prejudice. Many of these tales have reached his ears, but he has, hitherto, been content to let them circulate without contradiction. This may be a proper time to say that not one of them is true. He has given an account of a little occurrence, of this nature, expressly with the view to show the reader, the manner in which mole-hills become exaggerated into mountains, through the medium of three thousand miles, and with the hope that the better portion of his countrymen may see the danger of yielding credit to tales that have their origin in antipathies to their own nation.

The English do not like the Americans. There is a strong disposition in them to exaggerate and circulate any thing that has a tendency to throw ridicule and contumely on the national character—and this bias, coupled with the irritation that is a consequence of seeing others indifferent to things for which their own deference is proverbial, has given rise to many silly reports, that affect others besides the writer. On the other hand, so profound is the deference of the American to England, and so sensitive his feelings to her opinion, that he is disposed to overlook that essential law of justice which exacts proof before condemnation.

It is just to say that a traveller should go through a country observant, but silent as regards its faults; that, on the subject of the superior merits of his own system, modesty and deference to the feelings of others are his cue. But when we come to apply these rules they are liable to qualifications. If those he visits *will* provoke comparisons, they should not complain that they are made intelligently and with independence, so long as they are made temperately. Had the disposition in the English to comment freely and ignorantly on America, before natives of the country been early met with manliness and a desire, in particular, *to sustain the institutions,* the idle tales alluded to would never have had an existence. It is as natural, as it is easy, for those who have fallen short of the mark in this respect, to say that others have gone beyond it. Men who have been disposed to accept attentions on any terms, are not always the best judges of propriety.

England has experienced essential changes since the period of these letters. It is said more knowledge of, and a better feeling towards, America, now exist in the country. But, in carrying out the design of his whole work, the writer has been obliged to respect the order of time, and to portray things as he saw them when he was in the island. A future work may repair some of the faults that have arisen from this circumstance.

It is quite probable that this book contains many false notions. They are, however, the mistakes of a conscientious observer, and must be attributed solely to the head. Its opinions will run counter to the prejudices of much the largest portion of what are called the intelligent classes of America, and quite as a matter of course, will be condemned. An attempt to derange any of the established opinions of this part of American Society, more especially on subjects connected with the aristocratical features of the English government, meets with the success that usually accompanies all efforts to convince men against their wishes. There is no very profound natural mystery in the desire to be better off than one's fellows. The philosopher who constructs a grand theory of government, on the personal envy, the strife, and the heart-burnings of a neighbourhood, is fitted by nature to carve a Deity from a block of wood.

Letter I.

To Capt. W. Branford Shubrick, U. S. N.

It was a fine February day, when we left the *Hôtel Dessin* to embark for Dover. The quay was crowded with clamorous porters, while the *gendarmes* had an eye to the police regulations, lest a stray rogue, more or less, might pass undetected between the two great capitals of Europe. As I had placed myself in the hands of a regular *commissionnaire* belonging to the hotel, we had no other trouble than that of getting down a ladder of some fifteen steps, into the boat. The rise and fall of the water is so great, in these high narrow seas, that vessels are sometimes on a level with the quays, and at others three of four fathoms below them.

We had chosen the English steam-packet, a government boat, in preference to the French, from a latent distrust of Gallic seamanship. The voyage was not long, certainly, but, short as it was, we reaped the advantage of a good choice, in beating our competitor by more than an hour.

It is possible to see across the Straits of Dover, in clear weather, but, on this occasion, we had nothing visible before us, but an horizon of water, as we paddled through the long entrance of the little haven, into the North Sea. The day was calm, and, an unusual circumstance in swift tides and narrow passages, the channel was as smooth as a pond. Even the ground swell was too gentle to disturb the *omelettes* of M. Dessin's successor.

The difference of character in the two great nations that lie so near each other, as almost to hear each other's cocks crow, is even visible on the strait that separates them. On the coast of France, we saw a few fishing boats, with tanned sails, catering for the *restaurants* of Paris, while the lofty canvass of countless ships rose in succession from the bosom of the sea, as we shot over towards the English shore. I think we had made more than fifty square-rigged vessels, by the time we got close in with the land. Several were fine India-men, and not a few were colliers, bound to that focus of coal-smoke, London.

I passed the Straits of Dover, as a sailor, four times, during the years 1806 and 1807. At that period England was still jealous of the views of Napoleon. In the autumn of the former year, in particular, I remember that we were off Dungeness, just as the day dawned, and a more eloquent picture of watchfulness cannot be imagined, than the channel presented on that occasion. Near a hundred sail were in sight, and, including a fleet just anchoring in the Downs, much the greater portion of them were cruisers. The nearness of the two coasts enabled the French occasionally to pick up a prize in the narrow waters, and all this care had become necessary to protect the trade of London. No better proof of the inferiority of the French, as a maritime people need be given, than the simple fact that they have ports, which no skill can blockade, within thirty leagues of the mouth of the Thames, and that England maintained the commerce of her capital throughout the whole of a long and vindictive war. I think a maritime people would have driven half the trade to Liverpool, or Bristol, within the first five years. If the Yankees had a hole to run into, so near the river, it would be unsafe punting above the bridges.

The packet was admirably managed, though we had nothing but smooth water to contend with, it is true; still, the quiet and order that prevailed were good proofs that the people could have been used to a proper purpose at need. I was struck, however, with the diminutive appearance of the crew, which was composed of short little waddling fellows, who would have been bothered to do their work on the lower yard of a heavy ship. I have remarked this peculiarity, on several occasions, and I feel very certain that the specimens of English seamen that you and I formerly knew, at home, were much above the level of the class. High wages usually command a high quality of service, and to this circumstance, I presume, we must look for the explanation. Certainly, I never saw any of these little fry, under our flag, and our old friend, Jack Freeman, would have made three or four of them.

After a run of two hours, the cliffs of Dover became distinctly visible, the haze having concealed them until we got pretty close in with the English coast. Although these celebrated hills will bear no comparison with the glorious shores of the Mediterranean, so well known to you, they are noble eminences, and merit the distinction of being mentioned by Shakspeare.

The town of Dover lies partly in a ravine between two of the cliffs, and partly on the strand at their bases. It appears as if nature had expressly left a passage to the sea between the hills, at this point, for, while the latter cannot be much less than three or four hundred feet high, there is scarcely a perceptible rise in the road which runs into the interior. The place is both naturally and poetically fine, for, when one reflects that this accidental formation is precisely at the spot where the island is nearest to the continent, it has the character of a magnificent gate-way to a great nation. The cliffs extend several miles on each side of the town, melting away in swelling arable land, in the direction of Hastings and Dungeness. The latter is the point where the Conqueror landed, and I should think it the spot most favourable for a descent, anywhere on the English coast. The shore is still dotted with the remains of works erected during the period of the threatened invasion, and I well remember the time when they groaned under their bristling guns.

The view of Dover and of its cliffs, as we approached the shore, was pleasing, and, in some respects, fine. There was nothing of the classically picturesque in the artificial parts of the picture, it is true, but the place was crowded with so many recollections from English history, that even the old chimney-pots, with which the cliffs had pretty well garnished the place, had a venerable and attractive look. The castle, too, which stands on the eastern or rather northern hill, is a reasonably suitable edifice, and may be conveniently peopled by the imagination. I believe some part of it is ascribed to that extensive builder Cæsar.

The port is small, but very convenient, lying fairly embosomed in the town. The entrance is altogether artificial, but I saw no gates. I believe that vessels of some size may enter, though the trade is chiefly confined to the communication with France. The pier is a fine promenade of itself, and the whole of the public works connected with it, are solid and respectable. We glided quietly into this little haven about one o'clock, and landed on the soil of old England once more.

If we were struck with the contrast between England and France, on first reaching the latter country, I think we were still more so on returning to the former. Four hours before we were in the region of politeness, vociferation, snatching, fun and fraud, on the quay of Calais; and now we were in that of quiet, sulkiness, extortion, thank'ees and half crowns, on that of Dover. It would be hard to say which was the worst, although, on the whole, one gets along best, I think, with the latter; for, provided he will pay, he gets his work done with the fewest words. The western people sometimes call a "rowdy" a "screamer," but they have nothing that deserves the name, in comparison with a true French *prolétaire*, who has his dinner still to earn. In England, a fellow will at least starve to death in silence.

We proceeded to Wright's tavern, certainly one of the best in Dover, and it proved to be as unlike a French, or what an American inn would have been, in similar circumstances, as possible. The house was small, by no means as large as most of the village taverns at home, and altogether unworthy to be mentioned, as respects size, with the hotel we had just left, on the other side of the channel; but it was quiet and clean. I do not know that it was any cleaner than *Dessin's*, or a good American house, but the silent manner in which the servants did their several duties, was, of itself, an indescribable luxury. At a thoroughfare like this, we should cause a huge pile to be reared, with cells for bed-rooms, a vast hall for a dining-room, and a kitchen fit for barracks, and with this *respublica* of a structure, the travellers, without remorse, would indiscriminately be elevated, or depressed, to the same level of habits; it being almost an offence against good morals, in America, for a man to refuse to be hungry when the majority is ravenous, or to have an appetite when the mass has dined. In the midst of noise and confusion, one would be expected to allow, that in such a caravansery, he was living in, what in American parlance, is called "splendid style." "Splendid misery" would be a better term, were not the use of the first term, as applied to a tasteless shell, absurd.

I have long thought that the regularity, silence, order, cleanliness, and *decencies* of an English inn, added to the beds, elegance, table, and liquors of a French inn, would form the *ne plus ultra* of inn-ism; and the house at Calais, which has, in some measure, become Anglicised by its position, goes to prove that the notion is not much out of the way. It quite puts its English competitor at Dover into the shade. We missed the mirrors, the service for the table, and the *manner*, but we got in their places a good deal of solid unpretending comfort.

While W[illiam] went to the custom house, Mrs. [Cooper] and myself took a guide, and walked out to look at the cliffs. On one side the chalk rises like a wall, the houses clinging to its base, and, at this point, a shaft has been cut in it, containing a circular flight of steps, by which we ascended to the heights. This passage was made to facilitate the communications between the different military works. On quitting the stairs, we found ourselves on an irregular acclivity that forms the summit of the cliffs, and which was in grass. Of the perpendicular elevation, I should think about two-thirds of it was in the chalky precipices, looking towards the channel and the town, and the other third in the verdant cap on which we stood.

Here we found works of the modern school, consisting of the usual parapets, ditches, and glacis. The guide, who was anxious to show off his wares, led us up to a fort, into which we entered by a passage, from which he affirmed it was possible to abstract the air, a new device in warfare, and one that I should think rather supererogatory here, since the enemy that got as far as this gate at the *pas de charge*, would already be pretty short-winded. As we climbed, I more than once inquired, with old Gloster, "When shall we come to the top of that same hill?" The honour of the invention was ascribed to the Duke of Wellington, by our companion, who was an old campaigner. But the military features were the least of the attractions of the spot. We were on the very cliffs of the "samphire gatherers:"—

          _____"Half way down
Hangs one that gathers samphire; dreadful trade!
Methinks he seems no bigger than his head:
The fishermen, that walk upon the beach,
Appear like mice; and yon tall anchoring bark
Diminished to her cock; her cock a buoy
Almost too small for sight. The murmuring surge,
That on the unnumbered idle pebbles chafes,
Cannot be heard so high."

It is quite evident Edgar did not deal fairly with the old man, little of this fine description being more than poetically exact. After ascending to the summit of the height, which, without the stairs, could only be done from the rear, one would have to descend a long distance, across the verdant cap mentioned, in order to reach the verge of the cliffs.

Still the view was both imposing and beautiful. We overlooked the channel of course, and, for a few moments, we had a glimpse of the cliffs of France. Tall ships were stealing along the water, though neither their "cocks" nor "buoys" were visible. Dr. Johnson has complimented Shakspeare for his knowledge of nautical phrases, but this is a mistake into which neither you nor I will be so likely to fall. In the quotation I have just given you, the great bard makes the gradation in diminutiveness pass from the ship to her boat, and from the boat to the buoy! This is poetry, and as such it is above comment; but one of the craft would have been more exact.

About a dozen years ago, I made an essay in nautical description, a species of writing that was then absolutely new. Anxious to know what the effect would be on the public, I read a chapter to our old shipmate [Midshipman], now Captain [Cooper], which contained an account of a ship's working off-shore, in a gale. It had been my aim to avoid technicalities, in order to be poetic, although the subject imperiously required a minuteness of detail to render it intelligible. My listener betrayed interest, as we proceeded, until he could no longer keep his seat. He paced the room furiously until I got through, and just as I laid down the paper he exclaimed, "It is all very well, but you have let your jib stand too long, my fine fellow!" I blew it out of the bolt-rope, in pure spite.

The part of the view from the heights of Dover, which struck us as altogether the most unusual, was the inland. France, from Paris to Calais, was brown, and altogether without vegetation, while we now found England covered with a dark verdure that I had never before seen in February. In short, this country was much greener than when we left it, in July, 1826. It is true, the fields were not covered with the lively green of young grasses, but it had a dark, rich look, that conveyed the idea of a strong soil and of good husbandry. Something of this might have been owing to local causes, for I think the peculiarity was less observable nearer London, than on the coast.

The absence of wood would have left a sense of nakedness and sterility, but for the depth of the verdure. As it was, however, the whole district, visible from the heights, had a sort of Sunday air, like that of a comfortable mechanic, who was just shaved and attired for the day of rest. Few buildings appeared in the fields, and most of those we saw, the castle and public works excepted, singularly reminded us of the small, solid, unpretending but comfortable brick abodes, that one sees in New Jersey, Maryland, and Delaware, rather than in any other part of America. This is just the section of the United States which most resembles the common English life, I think, and it is also the region in which the purest English is spoken. I believe it to be, on the whole, the nearest approach we have to England, in architecture, domestic habits and language, and I ascribe the fact to the circumstance, that this part of the Union was principally settled with emigrants from the midland counties of the mother country. I now refer, however, solely to the every-day rustic habits and usages.

We looked at this view of England with very conflicting sensations. It was the land of our fathers, and it contained, with a thousand things to induce us to love it, a thousand to chill the affections. Standing, as it might be, in the very portal of the country, I imagined what was to occur in the next three months, with longing and distrust. Twenty-two years before, an ardent boy, I had leaped ashore, on the island, with a feeling of deep reverence and admiration, the fruits of the traditions of my people, and with a love almost as devoted as that I bore the land of my birth. I had been born, and I had hitherto lived, among those who looked up to England as to the idol of their political, moral, and literary adoration. These notions I had imbibed, as all imbibed them in America down even as late as the commencement of the last war. I had been accustomed to see every door thrown open to an Englishman, and to hear and think that his claim to our hospitality was that of a brother, divided from us merely by the accidents of position. Alas! how soon were these young and generous feelings blighted. I have been thrown much among Englishmen throughout the whole of my life, and for many I entertain a strong regard—one I even ranked among my closest friends—and I have personally received, in this kingdom itself, more than cold attentions; and yet among them all I cannot recall a single man, who, I have had the smallest reason to think, has ever given me his hand the more cordially and frankly because I was an American! With them, the tie of a common origin has seemed to be utterly broken, and when I have made friends, I have every reason to believe it has been in despite, and in no manner in consequence, of my extraction. Other Americans tell me the same, and I presume no one enters the country from our side of the water, who has not first to overcome the prejudice connected with his birth, before he can meet the people on an equality with other strangers. We may have occasion to look into this matter before the next three months shall be passed.

On returning to the inn, we found that our effects were passed, at some little cost, and that we were expected to present ourselves, in person, at the alien office. This ceremony, far more exacting than any thing we had hitherto encountered in Europe, was not of a nature to make us feel at home. We went, however, even to the child, and were duly enregistered. I shall not take it on myself to say the form is unnecessary, for the police of two such towns as London and Paris must require great vigilance; but it had an ungracious appearance to compel a lady to submit to such a rule. We were treated with perfect civility, in all other respects, and, as the law was then new, it is possible its agent had interpreted its provisions too literally.

Mrs. [Cooper] had also to pay a heavy duty on one or two of her dresses, although they formed part of her ordinary wardrobe. This regulation, however, might very well be necessary also, in the situation of the two countries, and it was not an easy matter to make an available distinction, in this respect, between the natives of the country and mere travellers. I have had every reason to speak favourably of the English custom-houses, which, on all occasions, have manifested a spirit of liberality, and, in one or two instances, in which I have been a party, a generous and gentlemanlike feeling, that showed how well their officers understood the spirit of their duties. In my case, the revenue has never lost a farthing by this temper, and both parties have been spared much useless trouble.

After dining, which was done without napkins, a change we instantly observed on coming from France, I made my arrangements to proceed. The French *calèche* had of course been left at Calais, but Mr. Wright gave me a regular post-coach, that held us very comfortably, together with the whole of the luggage. This vehicle differed but little from a stage coach, resembling what the *amateur* Jehus of London call a "drag."

As this equipage drove up to the door, we had, at once, a proof of the superiority of English over French travelling. The size and weight of the vehicle compelled me to order four horses, which appeared in the shape of so many blooded animals, a little galled in the withers, it is true, but in good heart, and which were under the management of two smart postillions, in top-boots, white hats, and scarlet jackets.

I inquired as to the condition of the roads. "Very bad, sir," exclaimed Mr. Wright, who had a well-fed, contented air, without a particle of sulkiness about him—"quite rotten, sir." I was curious to see a rotten road. The word was given, and we moved off at a pace that did credit to the stables of Dover. The day was raw and windy, and the "boys," one of whom was fifty years old, got off at a turnpike, and concealed their finery under great coats. I took the opportunity to inquire when we should reach the "rotten roads," and was told that we were then on them. Occasionally the water lay on the surface, and cavities were worn an inch or two deep, and this was termed a rotten road! W[illiam] laughed, and wondered what these fine fellows would think of a road in which "the bottom had fallen out," and of which we have so many in America.

The rate at which we moved did not appear very rapid, the whole team quite evidently travelling perfectly at their ease, and yet we did the distance between Dover and Canterbury, some sixteen miles, in about an hour and a-half. French cattle to do this, would have been on a cowish jump the whole time.

The road was quite narrow, following the natural windings of the ground, and, in all respects, its excellence excepted, resembled one of our own country roads. Indeed it is not usual to find so little space between the fences, as there was between the hedges of this great thoroughfare, most of the way. We passsed a common or two, and a race-course over an uneven track. The scenery was *petite*, if you can make out the meaning of such an expression, by which I would portray, narrow vales, low swells, and limited views. This, I think, is the prevailing character of English scenery, which owes its beauty to its finish, and a certain air of rural snugness and comfort, more than to any thing else. We missed the wood of France, for, at this season, the hedges are but an indifferent substitute.

We found Canterbury on a plain, and drove to another Mr. Wright's, for, to make a bad travelling pun, it was literally "all Wright," on this road. We had four of the name, including Dover and London. We ordered tea, and it was served redolent of home and former days. The hissing urn, the delicious toast, the fragrant beverage, the warm sea-coal fire, and the perfect snugness of everything, were indeed grateful, after so many failures to obtain the same things in France. Commend me to a French breakfast, and to an English or an American "tea!"

Letter II.
To Capt. W. B. Shubrick, U. S. Navy

Early the following morning, on looking out of my window, I saw a gentleman in a scarlet coat, and a hunting-cap, mounting in the yard of the inn. He had been hunting the previous day, and had evidently made a night of it. Soon after we went to look at the metropolitan church of England. Canterbury itself is a place of no great magnitude, but it is neat. Coming from France the houses struck us as being diminutively low, though they are very much the same sort of buildings one sees in the country towns of the older parts of the middle states. Burlington, Trenton, Wilmington, Bristol, Chester, &c. &c., will give you a very accurate idea of one of these small provincial towns, as will Baltimore, its night-caps apart, of one of the larger. It is usual to say that Boston is more like an English town, than any other place in America, but I should say that the resemblance is stronger in Baltimore, as a whole, and in Philadelphia, in parts. There are entire quarters of the latter town, which, were it not for their extreme regularity, might be taken for parts of London, though there are others which are quite peculiar to Philadelphia itself. As for New-York, it is a perfect rag-fair, in which the tawdry finery of ladies of easy virtue, is exposed, in the same stall, and in close proximity to the greasy vestments of the pauper.

As we walked through the streets of Canterbury, I directed the attention of my companions to the diminutive stature of the people. I feel certain that the average height of the men we have met since landing, is fully an inch below that of one of our own towns. And yet we were in the heart of Kent, a county that the English say contains the finest race of the island. Though short, and not particularly sturdy, the people had a decent air, that is wanting in the French of the same classes, with all their *manner*. Mrs. [Cooper] was delighted with this peculiarity in her own sex, which strongly reminded her of home. Even the humblest wore some sort of a hat in the streets, and a large proportion wore those scarlet cloaks that used to be so common among the farmers' wives in America.

In this particular, the common people had the appearance of having adhered to fashions that our own population dropped some forty years since.

The cathedral of Canterbury is a fine church, without being one of the best of its class. It is neither as large nor as rich as some others in England, even, and in both respects, it is much inferior to many on the continent. Still it is large and noble, its length exceeding five hundred feet. Like all the great English churches, this cathedral is free from the miserable adjuncts that clerical cupidity has stuck against the walls of similar edifices, in France. It stands isolated from all other buildings, with grass growing prettily up to its very walls. This, of itself, was a great charm, compared to the filthy pavements, and the garbage that is apt to defile the temple, on the other side of the channel.

We found the officials at morning prayers, in the choir. It sounded odd to us, to hear our own beautiful service, in our own tongue, in such a place, after the Latin chants of the deep-mouthed canons, and we stood listening with reverence, although without the skreen. These English cathedrals maintain so much of the Romish establishments as still to possess their chapters, but instead of the ancient cloisters, the protestants having wives, there is a sort of square of snug houses around the edifice, for the residences of the prebendaries and other officials. I believe this is called a *close*, a word that we do not use, but which has the same signification as place, or *cul de sac*, not being a thoroughfare. Perhaps the term *close fellow* came from these churchmen; no bad etymology, since it has a direct reference to the pocket. It has always been matter of astonishment to me, that a man of liberal attainments should possess one of these clerical sinecures, grow sleek and greasy on its products, eat, drink, and be merry, and fancy, all the while, that he was serving God! Men become accustomed to any absurdity. Were Christ to reappear on earth, and preach again his doctrine of self-denial and humility, he who should attempt to practice on his tenets, according to modern notions would be regarded as not only a fool himself, but as believing others weak as himself; but time has hallowed the abuses that were begotten by cupidity on ignorance.

The cathedral of Canterbury was the scene of Becket's murder. His shrine was here, and for centuries, it was the resort of pilgrims. It merited canonization to be slain at the horns of the altar. The building still contains many curious relicks of this nature, but mere descriptions of such things, are usually very unsatisfactory.

After passing most of the morning exploring, and taking a tea breakfast, *à l'Anglaise*, we proceeded. The road took us through Rochester, Sittingbourne, Chatham, Gravesend, and the edge of Woolwich. The distance was fifty-five miles, and we passed at least five towns, which contained, on an average, ten thousand souls. Although the day was windy and raw, I stuck to the box the whole time, preferring to encounter the marrow-chilling weather of an English February, to missing the objects that came within our view. In the course of the morning we saw a party of horsemen, with a pack of hounds, dashing through a turnip field, but what they were after could not be seen.

You probably know that a principal naval station is at Sheerness, on the Medway. We did not pass immediately through this town, though Chatham forms almost a part of it. The river was full of ships, as was the Thames in a reach above Gravesend. Most of the vessels in the latter place, were frigates. They lay in tiers, and appeared to be well cared for. These ships were chiefly of the class of the old thirty-eights, or vessels that we call thirty-sixes, mounting eight-and-twenty eighteens below, and two-and-twenty lighter guns above.

It may be known to you, that after our last war, the English admiralty altered its mode of rating. The old thirty-eights are now called forty-sixes, though why, it is not easy to see. The pretext that we under-rated our ships, because we did not number the guns, is absurd, since we derived the usage directly from the English themselves; nor do their changes meet the difficulty, as no large vessel is now probably rated exactly according to her armament. The number of the guns, moreover, is no criterion of the force of a vessel, since the metal and powers of endurance make all the difference in the world. An old-fashioned English thirty-two, mounted twenty-six twelves below, with as many light guns as she could conveniently carry on her quarter-deck and forecastle, differing from the thirty-six merely in the weight of metal, which in the latter was that of eighteens. I have seen a thirty-two that carried as many guns as a thirty-six, and yet the latter was at least a fourth heavier, if not a third. Fetches of this nature, are every way unworthy of two such navies as those of England and America, nor can they mislead any but the extremely ignorant. In my estimation the Duke of Wellington deserves more credit for the frank simplicity of his account of the battles he has fought, than for the victories he has gained; other men having been successful as well as himself, though few, indeed, are they who have been content with the truth.

It is a point of honour with the post-boys, on an English road, to pass all the stage coaches. For this purpose they use cattle of a different mould; animals that possess foot rather than force. The loads are lighter, usually, and in this manner they are able to carry their point. I was pleased with the steady, quiet, earnest manner in which this essential object was always attained, every thing like the appearance of strife and racing being studiously avoided.

The terrible Shooter's Hill offered no longer any terrors, and as for Blackheath, it had more the air of a village green than of a waste. The goodness of the roads, the fleetness of the cattle, and, more than all, the system of credits, have rendered highwaymen and footpads almost unknown in England. Robberies of this nature are now much more frequent in France than in this island, for several flagrant instances have lately occurred in the former country. A single footpad is said to have rifled a *diligence*, sustained by a platoon of *paddies*, armed with sticks, and arrayed by moonlight! The story is so absurd, that one wishes it may be true.

In travelling along these beautiful roads, at the rate of ten or eleven miles the hour, in perfect security, we are irresistibly led to recall the pictures of Fielding, with his carriers, his motley cargoes, and his footpads!

London met us, in its straggling suburbs, several miles down the river. I cannot give you any just idea of our *carte de route*, but it led us through a succession of streets lined by houses of dingy yellow bricks, until we suddenly burst out upon Waterloo Bridge. Crossing this huge pile, we whirled into the Strand, and were set down at the hotel of Mrs. Wright, Adam street, Adelphi. Forty years since we should have been in the very focus of the fashionable world, so far as hotels were concerned, whereas we were now at its *Ultima Thule*. The Strand, as its name signifies, runs parallel to the river, and at no great distance from its banks, leaving room, however, for a great number of short streets between it and the water. Nearly all these streets, most of which are in fact "places," having no outlets at one end, are filled with furnished lodging-houses, and, in some of the best of them, I believe it is still permitted to a gentleman to reside. When, however, I mentioned to a friend that we were staying in Adam street, he exclaimed that we ought, on no account, to have gone east of Charing Cross. These were distinctions that gave us very little concern, and we were soon refreshing ourselves with some of worthy Mrs. Wright's excellent tea.

One of the merits of England is the perfect order in which every thing is kept, and the perfect method with which every thing is done. One sees no cracked cups, no tea-pots with broken noses, no knives thin as wafers, no forks with one prong longer than the other, no coach wanting a glass, no substitute for a buckle, no crooked poker or tongs loose in the joint, no knife that wont cut, no sugar cracked in lumps too big to be used, no hat unbrushed, no floor with a hole in it, no noisy servants, no bell that wont ring, no window that wont open, no door that wont shut, no broken pane, nor any thing out of repair that might have been mended. I now speak of the eyes of him who can pay. In France, half of these incongruities are to be met with amid silken curtains and broad mirrors, though France is rapidly improving in this respect; but, at home, we build on a huge scale, equip with cost, and take refuge in expedients as things go to decay. We are not as bad as the Irish are said to be, in this respect, but he who insists on having things precisely as they ought to be, is usually esteemed a most unreasonable rogue, more especially in the interior. We satisfy ourselves by acknowledging a standard of merit in comforts, but little dream of acting up to it. We want servants, and mechanical labour is too costly. The low price at which comforts are retailed here, has greatly surprised me. I feel persuaded that most of the common articles of English manufacture come to the consumer in America, at about thrice their original cost.

The second night we were in London, a party of street musicians came under the window and began to play. They had tried several tunes without success, for I was stretched on a sofa reading, but the rogues contrived, after all, to abstract half a crown

from my pocket, by suddenly striking up *Yankee Doodle!* It is
something, at all events, to have taught John Bull that we take
pride in that tune. You can scarcely imagine the effect it produced
on my nerves to hear it in the streets of London, though you and
I have heard it "rolling off for grog" so often with perfect indifference. I have since been told by a music-master, that the
air is German. He touched it for me, though with a time and
cadence that completely changed its character. The English took
the tune of an old song beginning with "Miss Nancy Locket lost
her pocket," and adapted their words of derision to it; but there is
strictly no such thing as an English school of music. Most of their
songs, I believe, have the *motives* of German airs. The prevalent
motive of all English music, however, is gold.

I cannot tell you how many furnished apartments and lodging-
houses London contains, but the number is incredible. They can
be had at all prices, and with nearly every degree of comfort and
elegance. The rush of people to town is so great, during the season, that there are periods when it is not easy to have a choice,
notwithstanding, though we were sufficiently early to make a
selection. In one thing I was disappointed. The English unquestionably are a neat people, in all that relates to their houses, and
yet the furnished lodgings of London are not generally as tidy as
those of Paris. The general use of coal may be a reason, but after
passing a whole day in examining rooms, we scarcely met with
any that appeared sufficiently neat. The next morning I tried a
new quarter, where we did a little better, though the effects of the
coal-dust met us everywhere.

We finally took a small house in St. James's Place, a narrow *inlet*
that communicates with the street of the same name, and which is
quite near the palace and the parks. We had a tiny drawing-room,
quite plainly furnished, a dining-room, and three bed-rooms, with
the use of the offices, &c., for a guinea a-day. The people of the
house cooked for us, went to market, and attended to the rooms,
while our own man and maid did the personal service. I paid a
shilling extra for each fire, and as we kept three, it came to another
guinea weekly. This, you will remember, was during the season,
as it is called; at another time the same house might have been
had, quite possibly, for half the money.

Many people take these furnished houses by the year, and more
still, by the quarter. I was surprised to find those in our neigh-

bourhood gradually filling with people of condition, many of the coaches that daily stood before their doors having coronets. Perhaps more than half of the peers of the three kingdoms lodge in this way when in town, and I believe a smaller proportion still actually own the houses in which they reside. Even in those cases in which the head of a great family has a town-house of his own, the heir and younger children, if married, seldom reside in it, the English customs, in this respect, being just the reverse of those of France.

There is a great convenience in having it in one's power to occupy a house that is in all respects private, ready furnished, and to come and go at will. Were the usage introduced into our own towns, hundreds of families would be induced to pass their winters in them, that now remain in the country from aversion to the medley and confusion of a hotel, or a boarding-house, as well as their expense. We have a double advantage for the establishment of such houses, in New York at least, in the fact that we have two seasons, yearly, the winter and the summer. Our own people would occupy them during the former portion of the year, and the southern travellers in the warm weather. The introduction of such houses would, I think, have a beneficial influence on our deportment, which is so fast tending towards mediocrity, under the present gregarious habits of the people. When there is universal suffrage at a dinner-table, or in the drawing-room, numbers will prevail, as well as in the ballot-boxes, and the majority in no country is particularly polite and well bred. The great taverns that are springing up all over America, are not only evils in the way of comfort and decency, but they are actually helping to injure the tone of manners. They are social Leviathans.

Letter III.

To Richard Cooper, Esq. Cooperstown, N. Y.

A London season lasts during the regular session of parliament, unless politics contrive to weary dissipation. Of course this rule is not absolute, as the two houses are sometimes unexpectedly convened; but the ordinary business of the country usually begins after the Christmas holidays, and, allowing for a recess at Easter, continues until June, or July. This division of time seems unnatural to us, but all national usages of the sort, can commonly be traced to sufficient causes. The shooting and hunting seasons occupy the autumn and early winter months; the Christmas festivities follow; then the country in England, apart from its sports, is less dreary in winter than in most other parts of the world, the verdure being perhaps finer than in the warm months, and London, which is to the last degree unpleasant as a residence from November to March, is most agreeable from April to June. The government is exclusively in the hands of the higher classes, or, so nearly so as to render their convenience and pleasure the essential point, and these inhabit a quarter of the town, in which one misses the beauties of the country far less than in most capitals. The west end is so interspersed with parks and gardens and the enclosures of squares, that, aided by high culture and sheltered positions, vegetation not only comes forward earlier in Westminster than in the adjacent fields, but it is more grateful to the eye and feelings. The men are much on horseback of a morning, and the women take their drives in the parks, quite as agreeably as if they were at their own country residences.

The season has gradually been growing later, I believe, though Bath of old, and Brighton and Cheltenham, and other watering places of late, attracted, or still attract the idler, in the commencement of the winter. Since the peace, the English have much frequented the continent, after June; Paris, the German watering places, and Switzerland being almost as easy of access as their own houses. It is made matter of reproach against the upper classes of England, that they spend so much of their time abroad, but, without adverting to the dearness of living at home, and the factitious state of society, both of which are strong inducements to multitudes to quit the island, I fancy we should do the same thing were we cooped up, in a country so small, and with roads so excellent that it could be traversed from one end to the other in eight and forty hours, having the exchanges always in our own favour, and with an easy access to novel and amusing scenes. Travelling never truly injured any one, and it has sensibly meliorated the English character.

A day or two after our arrival in London, an English friend asked me if I were not struck with the crowds in the streets; particularly with the confusion of the carriages. Coming from Paris I certainly was not, for, during the whole of March, the movement, if any thing, was in favour of the French capital.

As usual, I came to London without a letter. It may be an error, but on this point I have never been able to overcome a repugnance to making these direct appeals for personal attentions. In the course of my life, I do not think, much as I have travelled, that I have delivered half a dozen. I am fully aware of their necessity if one would be noticed, but, right or wrong, I have preferred to be unnoticed to laying an imposition on others that they may possibly think onerous. The unreflecting and indelicate manner in which the practice of giving and asking for letters is abused, in America, may have contributed to my disgust at the usage. Just before I left home, a little incident occurred, connected with the subject, that, in no degree, served to diminish this reluctance to asking favours and civilities of strangers. I happened to be present when an improper application was made to the son of one of our ministers in Europe, for letters to the father. Surprised that such a request should be granted, I was explicitly told that a private sign had been agreed upon, between the parties, whereby all applicants should be gratified, though none were really to have the benefit of the introduction but those who bore the stipulated mark! This odious duplicity, had its rise in the habits of a country, in which men are so apt to mistake their privileges. The practice of deferring leads to frauds in politics, and to hypocrisy in morals. Some will tell you this case was the fruits of democracy, but I shall say it savoured more of an artifice of aristocracy, and such, in fact, was the political bias of both father and son. Democracy merits no other reproach in the affair, than the weakness of allowing itself to be deceived by agents so hollow.

I had made the acquaintance of Mr. William Spencer, in Paris, a gentleman well known in England as the author of "A Year of Sorrow," and several very clever pieces of fugitive poetry. Hearing that I was about to visit London, he volunteered to give me letters to a large circle of acquaintances, literary and fashionable. Pleading my retired habits, I endeavoured to persuade him not to give himself the trouble of writing, but, mistaking the motive, he insisted on showing this act of kindness. Trusting to his known indolence, I thought little of the matter, until the very morning of the day we left Paris, when this gentleman appeared, and, instead of the letters, he gave me a list of the names of some of those he wished me to know, desiring me to leave cards for them, on reaching London, in the full assurance that the letters would be sent after me! I put the list in my pocket, and, as you will readily imagine, thought the arrangement sufficiently queer. The list contained, however, the names of several whom I would gladly have known, could it be done with propriety, including, among others, those of Rogers, Campbell, Sotheby, Lord Dudley, &c. &c.

Under these circumstances, I took quiet possession of the house in St. James's Place, with no expectation of seeing any part of what is called society, content to look at as much of the English capital as could be viewed on the outside, and to pursue my own occupations. This arrangement was rendered the less to be regretted by the circumstance that we had been met in London, by the unpleasant intelligence of the death of Mr. de [Lancey]. Of course it was the wish of your aunt to be retired. While things were in this state, I went one morning to a bookseller's, where the Americans are in the habit of resorting, and learned, to my surprise, that several of the gentlemen named on Mr. Spencer's list, had been there to inquire for me. This looked as if he had actually written, and to this kindness on his part, and to an awkward mistake, by which I was supposed to be the son of an Englishman of the same name and official appellation as those of your grand-father, I am indebted to nearly all of the acquaintances I made in England, some of whom I should have been extremely sorry to have missed.

The first visit I had, out of our own narrow circle of Americans, occurred about a fortnight after we were established in St. James's

Place. I was writing at the time, and did not attend particularly when the name was announced, but supposing it was some tradesman, I ordered the person to be admitted. A quiet little old man appeared in the room, and we stood staring near a minute at each other, he, as I afterwards understood, to ascertain if he could discover any likeness between me and my supposed father, and I wondering who the diminutive little personage might be. I question if the stature of my visitor much exceeded five feet, though his frame was solid and heavy. He was partly bald, and the hair that remained was perfectly white. He had a fine head, a benevolent countenance, and a fresh colour. After regarding me a moment, and perceiving my doubt, he said simply —"I am Mr. Godwin. I knew your father, when he lived in England, and hearing that you were in London, I have come, without ceremony, to see you." After expressing my gratification at having made his acquaintance on any terms, I gave him to understand there was some mistake, as my father had never been out of America. This led to an explanation, when he took his seat and we began to chat. He was curious to hear something of American literature, which I have soon discovered is very little known in England. He wished to learn, in particular, if we had any poets—"I have seen something of Dwight's and Humphrey's, and Barlow's," he said, "but I cannot say that either pleased me much." I laughed and told him we could do better than that, now. He begged me to recite something—a single verse, if possible. He could not have applied to a worse person, for my memory barely suffices to remember facts, of which I trust it is sufficiently tenacious, but I never could make any thing of a quotation. As he betrayed a childish eagerness to hear even half a dozen lines, I attempted something of Bryant's, and a little of Alnwick Castle, which pretty much exhausted my whole stock. I was amused at the simplicity with which he betrayed the little reverence he felt for our national intellect, for it was quite apparent he thought "nothing good could come out of Nazareth."

Mr. Godwin sat with me an hour, and the whole time the conversation was about America, her prospects, her literature, and her politics. It was not possible to believe that he entertained a favorable opinion of the country, notwithstanding the liberal tendency of his writings, for prejudice, blended with a few shrewd and judicious remarks, peeped out of all his notions. He had

almost a rustic simplicity of manner, that, I think, must be as
much attributed to the humble sphere of life in which he had
lived, as to character, for the portion of his deportment which was
not awkward seemed to be the result of mind, while the remainder
might easily enough be traced to want of familiarity with life. At
least, so both struck me, and I can only give you my impressions.
As Mr. Godwin has long enjoyed a great reputation, and the
English of rank are in the habit of courting men of letters, (though
certainly in a way peculiar to themselves) I can only suppose that
the tendency of his writings, which is not favorable to aristocracy,
has prevented him from enjoying the usual advantages of men of
celebrity.

It would savour of empiricism to pretend to dive into the depths
of character, in an interview of an hour, but there was something
about the manner of Mr. Godwin that strongly impressed me with
the sincerity of his philosophy, and of his real desire to benefit his
race. I felt several times, during his visit, as if I wished to pat the
old man's bald head, and tell him "he was a good fellow." Indeed,
I cannot recall any one, who, on so short an acquaintance, so
strongly impressed me with a sense of his philanthropy; and this
too, purely from externals, for his professions and language were
totally free from cant. This opinion forced itself on me, almost in
spite of my wishes, for Mr. Godwin so clearly viewed us with any
thing but favourable eyes, that I could not consider him a friend.
He regarded us as a *speculating* rather than as a *speculative* people,
and such is not the character that a philosopher most esteems.

I returned the visit of Mr. Godwin, in a few days, although I
was indebted to his presence to a mistake, and found him, living
in great simplicity, in the midst of his books. On this occasion he
manifested the peculiarities already named, with the same disposition to distrust the greatness of the "twelve millions." I fancy my
father has not sent him very good accounts of us.

A few days later I got an invitation to be present at an evening
party, given by a literary man, with whom I had already a slight
acquaintance. On this occasion, I was told a lady known a little in
the world of letters, was desirous of making my acquaintance,
and, of course, I had only to go forward and be presented. "I had
the pleasure of knowing your father," she observed, as soon as my
bow was made.—Forgetting Mr. Godwin and his visit, I observed

that she had then been in America. Not at all; she had known my father in England. I then explained to her that I was confounded with another person, my father being an American, and never out of his own country. This news produced an extraordinary change on the countenance and manner of my new acquaintance, who, from that moment, did not deign to speak to me, or hardly to look at me! As her first reception had been quite frank and warm, and she herself had sought the introduction, I thought this deportment a little decided. I cannot explain the matter, in any other way, than by supposing that her inherent dislike of America suddenly got the better of her good manners, for the woman could hardly expect that I was to play impostor for her particular amusement. This may seem to you extraordinary, but I have seen many similar and equally strong instances of national antipathy betrayed by these people, since my residence in Europe. I note these things, as matter of curious observation.

In the course of the same week I was indebted to the attention of Mr. Spencer for another visit, which led to more agreeable consequences. The author of the Pleasures of Memory was my near neighbour in St. James's Place, and, induced by Mr. Spencer, he very kindly sought me out. His visit was the first I actually received from the "list," and it has been the means of my seeing most of what I have seen, of the interior of London. It was followed by an invitation to breakfast for the following morning.

I certainly have no intention to repay Mr. Rogers for his many acts of kindness, by making him and his friends the subject of my comments, but, to a certain degree he must pay the penalty of celebrity, and neither he nor any one else has a right to live in so exquisite a house, and expect every body to hold their tongues about it.

It was but a step from my door to that of Mr. Rogers, and you may be certain I was punctual to the appointed hour. I found with him Mr. Cary, the translator of Dante, and his son. The conversation during breakfast was general. The subject of America being incidentally introduced, our host told many literary anecdotes, in a quiet and peculiar manner that gave them point. I was asked if the languge of America differed essentially from that of England. I thought not so much in words and pronunciation, as in intonation and in the signification of certain terms. Still I thought I could always tell an Englishman from an American, in the course of five minutes' conversation. The two oldest gentlemen professed not to be able to discover any thing in my manner of speaking to betray me for a foreigner, but the young gentleman fancied otherwise. "He thought there was something peculiar—provincial— he did not know what exactly." I could have helped him to the word—"something that was not cockney." The young man however was right in the main, for I could myself have pronounced that all three of my companions were not Americans, and I do not see why they might not have said that I was no Englishman. The difference between the enunciation of Mr. Rogers and Mr. Cary and one of our educated men of the middle states, it is true, was scarcely perceptible, and required a nice ear and some familiarity with both countries to detect, but the young man could not utter a sentence, without showing his origin.

Mr. Rogers had the good nature to let me see his house, after breakfast. It stands near the head of the place, there being a right-angle between his dwelling and mine, and its windows, in the rear, open on the Green Park. In every country in which men begin to live for enjoyment and taste, it is a desideratum to get an abode that is not exposed to the noise and bustle of a thoroughfare. One who has intellectual resources, and elegant accomplishments, in which to take refuge, scarcely desires to be a street gazer, and I take it to be almost a test of the character of a population, when its higher classes seek to withdraw from publicity, in this manner. One can conceive of a trader who has grown rich wishing to get a "good stand," even for a house, but I am now speaking of men of cultivated minds and habits.

On this side of the Green Park there is no street between the houses and the field. The buildings stand in a line, even with the place on one side, and having small gardens between them and the park. Of course, all the good rooms overlook the latter. The Green Park, and St. James's Park, are, in fact, one open space, the separation between them being merely a fence. The first is nothing but a large field, cropped down like velvet, irregularly dotted with trees, and without any carriage way. Paths wind naturally across it, cows graze before the eye, and nursery maids and children sprinkle its uneven surface, whenever the day is fine. There is a house and garden belonging to the ranger, on one of its sides, and the shrubbery of the latter, as well as that of the small private gardens just mentioned, help to relieve the nakedness. I should think there must be sixty or eighty acres in the Green Park, while St. James's is much larger. On one side the Green Park is open to Piccadilly; on another it is bounded by a carriage way in St. James's; a third joins St. James's, and the fourth is the end on which stands the house of Mr. Rogers.

It strikes me the dwellings which open on these two parks, (for more than half of St. James's Park is bounded by houses in the same manner) are the most desirable in London. They are central as regards the public edifices, near the court, the clubs, and the theatres, and yet they are more retired than common. The carriage way to them is almost always by places, or silent streets, while their best windows overlook a beautiful rural scene interspersed with the finer parts of a capital. As a matter of course, these dwellings are in great request. On the side of the Green Park is the residence of Sir Francis Burdett, Spencer-house, Bridgewater-house, so celebrated for its pictures, and many others of a similar quality, while a noble new palace stands at the point where the two parks meet, that was constructed for the late Duke of York, then heir presumptive of the crown.

The house of Mr. Rogers is a *chef-d'œuvre* for the establishment of a bachelor. I understood him to say that it occupied a part of the site of a dwelling of a former Duke of St. Albans, and so well is it proportioned that I could hardly believe it to be as small as feet and inches demonstrate. Its width cannot be more than eighteen feet, while its depth may a little exceed fifty. The house in which we lodge is even smaller. But the majority of the town-houses, here, are by no means distinguished for their size. Perhaps the average of the genteel lodging houses, of which I have spoken, is less than that of Mr. Rogers's dwelling.

This gentleman has his drawing-room and dining-room lined with pictures, chiefly by the old masters. Several of them are the studies of larger works. His library is filled with valuable books; curiosities, connected principally with literature, history, and the arts, are strewed about the house, and even some rare relics of Egyptian sculpture find a place in this tasteful abode. Among other things of the sort, he has the original agreement for the sale of Paradise Lost! The price, I believe, was twenty-five pounds. It is usual to rail at this meanness, but I question if there is a book-seller, now in London, who would pay as much for it.

I was much interested with a little circumstance connected with these rarities. In the drawing-room stands a precious antique vase, on a handsome pedestal of carved wood. Chantrey was dining with the poet, as a group collected around the spot, to look at the vase. "Do you know who did this carving?" asked the sculptor, laying his hand on the pedestal. Mr. Rogers mentioned the carver he employed. "Yes, yes, he had the job, but *I* did the *work*,"— being then an apprentice, or a journeyman, I forget which.

Letter IV.

To Thomas James De Lancey, Esquire.

I shall not entertain you with many cockney descriptions of "sights." By this time England, in these particulars, is better understood with us, than in points much more essential. Whenever I do diverge from the track prescribed to myself, with such an object, it will be to point out something peculiar, or to give you what I conceive will be juster notions than those you may have previously imbibed. Still, one can hardly visit London without saying something of its *matériel*, and I shall take this occasion to open the subject.

As your [aunt] had never before been in London, and might never be again, it became a sort of duty to examine the principal objects, one of the first of which was Westminster Abbey. I have already spoken of the exterior of this building, and shall now add a word of its interior.

The common entrance is by a small door, at the Poet's Corner; and it was a strange sensation to find one's self in the midst of tablets bearing the epitaphs of most of those whose names are hallowed in English literature, and English art. I can only liken it to the emotion one might feel in unexpectedly finding himself in a room with most of his distinguished contemporaries. It was startling to see such names as Shakspeare, and Milton, and Ben Jonson, even on a tomb-stone; and, albeit little given to ultra romanticism, I felt a thrilling of the nerves as I read them. The abbey is well filled with gorgeous monuments of the noble and politically great, but they are collected in different chapels, on the opposite side of the church, or beneath its nave, while the intellectual spirits are crowded together, in a sort of vestibule; as if entering, one by one, and finding good companions already assembled, they had stopped in succession to enjoy each other's society. Notwithstanding the gorgeous pomp of the monuments of the noble, one feels that this homely corner contains the best company. Westminster Abbey, in my judgment, is a finer church internally than on its exterior. Still it has great faults, wanting unity, and an unobstructed view. It has a very neat and convenient choir, in which the regular service is performed, and which bears some such proportion to the whole interior, as the chancel of an ordinary American church bears to its whole inside. It stands, as usual, in a range with the transept. This choir, however, breaks the line of sight, and impairs the grandeur of the aisles.

The celebrated chapel of Henry VIIth, like the body of the church itself, is finer even internally than externally, although its exterior is truly a rare specimen of the gothic. The stalls of the Knights of the Bath are in this chapel, and its beautiful vaulted roof is darkened by a cloud of banners, time worn and dingy. This is a noble order of chivalry, for its rolls contain but few names that are not known to history. Unlike the Legion of Honour, which is now bestowed on all who want it, and the Garter, an institution that owes all its distinction to the convention of hereditary rank, the Knights of the Bath commonly earn their spurs by fair and honourable service, in prominent and responsible stations, before they are permitted to wear them. There always will be some favouritism in the use of political patronage, but, I am inclined to think there never was an order of chivalry instituted, or indeed any other mode of distinction devised, in which merit and not favour has more uniformly controlled the selections, than in bestowing the red ribbands. The greatest evil of such rewards arises from the fact that men will not be satisfied with simply making a distinction of merit, but they invariably rear on a foundation so plausible, other and more mystified systems, in which there is an attempt to make a merit of distinctions.

Among the laboured monuments of the Abbey is one in honour of Admiral Sir Peter Warren, who died Rear Admiral of England, some seventy years ago, erected by his wife. Lady Warren was a native of New York, and a member of your own family; having been the sister of your father's grand-father. Her husband was a long time commander in chief on our coast, and was known in our history as one of the conquerors of Louisbourg. He was a good officer, and is said to have done most of the fighting on the occasion of Anson's victory, commanding the van-squadron. On his return, the worthy citizens of London were so much captivated with his bravery, that they offered to make him an alderman! Sir Peter Warren was also the uncle of Sir William Johnson, and this celebrated person first appeared in the interior of our country, as the agent of his relative, who then owned an estate on the Mohawk, at a place that is still called Warrensbush.

As a whole, there is little to be said in favour of the much-talked-of monuments of Westminster Abbey. Most of them want simplicity and distinctness, telling their stories badly, and some of the most pretending among them are vile conceits. There are some good details, however, and a few of the statues of more recent erection, are works of merit. A statue of Mr. Horner by Chantrey is singularly noble, although in the modern attire. The works of this artist strike me as having all the merit that can exist independently of the ideal. The monuments are very numerous; for any person, of reasonable pretensions, who chooses to pay for the privilege, can have one erected for a friend, though I fancy, the poet's corner is held to be a little more sacred. It is much the fashion of late, to place the monuments of distinguished men in St. Paul's.

You have heard that the heads of Washington and the other American officers, which are on a *bas-relief* of André's monument, have been knocked off. This fact of itself furnishes proof of the state of feeling here, as respects us, but an answer of our cicerone, when showing us the church, gives still stronger evidence of it. "Why have they done this?" I demanded, curious to hear the history of the injury. "Oh! sir, there are plenty of evil-disposed people get in here. *Some American* has done it, no doubt." So you perceive we are not only accused of hanging our enemies, but of beheading our friends!

In a room, up a flight of steps, is a small collection of figures in wax, bedizened with tinsel, and every way worthy of occupying a booth at Bartholomew Fair. It is impossible for me to tell you what has induced the dean and chapter, to permit this prostitution of their venerable edifice, but it is reasonable to suppose that it is the very motive which induced Ananias to lie, and Sapphira to swear to it. These crude and coarse tastes are constantly encountering one in England, and, at first, I felt disposed to attribute it to the circumstance of a low national standard, but, perhaps it were truer to say that the lower orders of this country, by being more at their ease, and by *paying* for their gratifications of this nature, produce an influence on all public exhibitions that is unfelt on the Continent, where the spectacle being intended solely for the intellectual is better adapted to their habits. As connected with religious superstition, moreover, the finest cathedrals of all Catholic countries enjoy monstrosities almost as bad as these of the Abbey.

There are many old monuments in Westminster, which, without possessing a particle of merit in the way of the arts, are very curious by their conceits, and as proofs of the tastes of our forefathers. Truly, there is little to be said in favour of the latter, it being quite evident that, as a nation, England was never so near the golden age, in every thing connected with intellect, as at this moment. Hitherto, nearly all her artists of note, have been foreigners, but now she is getting a school of her own, and one that, sustained by her wealth and improved by travelling, bids fair shortly to stand at the head of them all.

Westminster Abbey, exclusively of Henry VIIth's Chapel, which scarcely appears to belong to the edifice, although attached to it, is by no means either a very rich, or a very large, edifice of its kind. Still it is a noble structure, and its principal fault, to my eye, is that pinched and mean appearance of its towers, to which I have elsewhere alluded, externally; and internally the manner in which it is broken into parts. The chapels have a cupboard character, that well befits English snugness. The greatest charms of the Abbey are its recollections and its precious memorials of the mighty dead. As respects the latter, I should think it quite without a rival, but you must look elsewhere for descriptions of them. In travelling through Europe, one is occasionally startled by meeting the name of Erasmus, or Galileo, or Dante, or of some other immortalised by his genius; but these monuments are scattered not only in different countries and cities, but often in the different churches of the same place. There is moreover a homely air and a rustic simplicity, here, in the quiet, unpretending stones, that line the walls and flagging of the Poet's Corner, and which almost induce one to believe that he is actually treading the familiar haunts of the illustrious dead. The name of Shakspeare struck me as familiarly as if I had met it beneath a yew, in a country church-yard.

On leaving the Abbey we went to look at the Parliament-Houses, and Westminster Hall. These buildings are grouped together. on the other side of the street, lying on the banks of the river. They form a quaint and confused pile, though, coupled with their eventful history, their present uses, and some portions of architectural beauty and singularity, one of great interest. Now that my eye has become accustomed to Gothic cathedrals, I find myself looking at the Hall, with more feeling, than even at the old church.

Westminster Hall is the oldest and finest part of the pile. It dates from the time of William II., though it has been much improved and altered since, especially about the year 1400. Its style may be properly referred to the latter period, though the rude magnificence of the thought, perhaps, better comports with the former. You know it was intended as the banqueting hall of a palace. When we remember that this room is two hundred and seventy feet long, ninety high, and seventy-four wide, we are apt to conceive sublime things of the state of an ancient monarch. But, it is all explained by the usages of the times. The hall, or knight's hall, in the smaller baronial residences, was more than half the dwelling. In some instances, it was literally the whole of one floor of the tower, the recesses of the windows being used as bed chambers at night. Although we have no records of the time when the English nobles lived in this primitive manner, it is reasonable to suppose that they did no better, for that civilization which is now so perfect, is far from being the oldest of Europe.

These halls were formerly appropriated to the purposes of the whole establishment, the noble and his dependents using the same room and the same table, making the distinction of "the salt." Then a court, at which the courtier invariably appeared with a train of armed followers, had need of space, not only to entertain those who came to protect their lords, but those who were present to see they did no violence.

If one gets a magnificent idea of the appliances of royalty from this hall, he gets no very exalted one of the comforts of the period. The side walls are of naked stone, there is no floor, or pavement, and bating its quaint gothic wildness, the roof has a strong affinity to that of a barn. On great occasions it requires a good deal of dressing, to make the place, in the least, like a room. A part of it, just then, was filled with common board *shantys*, which, we were told, were full of records, and a line of doors on one side, communicates with the courts of law.

It is said that Westminster Hall is the largest room in Europe, that is unsupported by pillars, the roof being upheld by the ordinary gothic knees, or brackets. This may be true, though the great hall of the Stadt House, at Amsterdam, and that of the Palazzo Gran Duca at Florence, both struck me as finer rooms. There is also a hall at Padua which I prefer, and which I think is larger, and there are many in the Low Countries, that, on the whole, would well compare with this. The great gallery of Versailles, the hall of Louis XIV., is certainly not near as large, but in regal splendour and cost, this will no more compare with that, than a cottage will compare with a hotel. The uses, however, were very different.

I shall not attempt to give you any accurate notion of the arrangement of the rest of this pile. There is a garden on the river, and a house which is occupied by the speaker. We went into St. Stephen's chapel, the House of Lords, the painted chamber, robing room, star chamber, &c., &c., but, after all, I brought away with me but a very confused idea of their relative positions.

St. Stephen's is literally a small chapel, or church, having been constructed solely for religious purposes. The commons have assembled in it, originally, exactly as our associations occasionally use the churches. It has the regular old fashioned side and end galleries, the speaker's chair occupying the usual situation of the pulpit. The end gallery is given up to the public, but the side galleries, though not often used, are reserved for the members. The *bar* is in a line with the front of the end gallery, and of course immediately beneath, while the *floor* of the house occupies the rest of the lower part of the building. I should think the whole chapel internally might be about fifty-five feet long, by about forty-one or two wide. The floor I paced, and made it nearly forty feet square. It is not precisely of these dimensions, but more like thirty-nine feet by forty-one or two. A good deal of even these straitened limits is lost, by a bad arrangement of seats behind the speaker's chair, which is about a fourth of the way down the chapel; these seats rising above each other, like the transoms of a ship. The clerks are seated at one end of a long table in the centre of the room, and the benches run longitudinally, being separated into four *blocks*. They have backs, but nothing to write on. The distance between the table and the seats next it, may be three feet. It is sufficiently near to allow members on the first bench to put their feet against it, or on it, an attitude that is often assumed. The treasury bench is the one nearest the table, on the left, looking from the gallery, and the leaders of opposition sit on the right. The chair of the speaker has a canopy, and is a sort of throne. The wood is all of oak, unpainted; the place is lighted by candles, in very common brass chandeliers, and the whole has a gloomy and inconvenient air. Still it is not possible to view St. Stephen's with any other feelings than those of profound respect, its councils having influenced the civilized world, now for more than a century. I name this period, as that is about the date of the real supremacy of the parliament in this government. The chapel, however, has been used as its place of meeting, since the reign of Edward VI., or near three centuries. It is said that one hundred and thirty strangers can be seated in the end gallery. Small iron columns, with gilded Corinthian capitals, support the galleries.

The House of Lords is a very different place. The room may be about the size of St. Stephen's, though I think it a little smaller, and there is no gallery.* The throne, by no means a handsome one, is a little on one side, and the peers sit on benches covered with red cloth, in the centre, and within a railing. These benches occupy three sides of an area in the centre, while the throne stands on the fourth. In front of the latter are the wool sacks, which are a species of divan that do not touch a wall. Every thing is red, or rather crimson, from the throne down. There is a table, and places for the clerks, in the area. The chancellor is by no means as much cared for as the speaker. The seat of the latter is quite luxurious, but the former would have rather a hard time of it, were it not for a sort of false back that has been contrived for him, and against which he may lean at need. It resembles a fire-skreen, but answers its purpose.

The celebrated tapestry is a rude fabric. It must have been woven when the art was in its infancy, and it is no wonder that such ships met with no success. It is much faded, which, quite likely, is an advantage rather than otherwise. "The tapestry which *adorns* these walls" was a flight of eloquence that must have required all the moral courage of Chatham to get along with. Like so much of all around it, however, one looks at it with interest, and not the less for its very faults.

*This was in 1828; at the return of the writer to England, in 1833, there was a gallery in the House of Lords, and it is hardly necessary to say, that, since that time, both houses have been burnt.

I can tell you little of the adjuncts of the two houses of parliament. The rooms were all sufficiently common, and are chiefly curious on account of their uses, and their several histories. The eating and drinking part of the establishment struck me as being altogether the most commodious, for there is a regular coffee-house, or rather tavern, connected with them, where one can, at a moment's notice, get a cup of tea, a chop or a steak, or even something better still. In this particular, parliament quite throws congress and the *chambers* into the back ground. A dinner is too serious a thing with a Frenchman to be taken so informally, and then both he and the American are content with legislating in the day time. The late hours frequently drive the members of parliament to snatch a meal where they can. Tea is a blessed invention for such people, and Bellamy's is a blessed invention for tea.

After visiting Westminster, we gave part of a day to St. Paul's. This is truly a noble edifice. Well do I remember the impression it made on me, when, an uninstructed boy, fresh from America, I first stood beneath its arching dome. I actually experienced a sensation of dizziness, like that one feels in looking over a precipice. When I returned home, and told my friends, among other traveller's marvels, that the steeple of Trinity could stand beneath this dome, and that its vane should not nearly reach its top, I was set down as one already spoilt by having seen more than my neighbours! It is surprisingly easy to get that character in America, especially if one does not scruple to tell the truth. I was much within the mark as to feet and inches, but I erred in the mode of illustrating. Had I said that the dome of St. Paul's was a thousand feet high, I should have found a plenty of believers, but the moment I attempted to put one of our martin's boxes into it, self-love took the alarm, and I was laughed at for my pains. This was two and twenty years ago: have we improved much since that time?

Although I no longer looked on St. Paul's with the fresh and unpractised eyes of 1806, it appeared to me now, what in truth it is, a grand and imposing edifice. In many respects it is better than St. Peter's, though, taken as a whole, it falls far short of it. When the richness of the materials, the respective dimensions, the details, and the colonnade of St. Peter's are considered, it must be admitted that St. Paul's is not even a first class church, St. Peter's standing alone; but I am not sure that the cathedral of London is not also entitled to form a class by itself, although one that is inferior.

The architecture of St. Paul's is severe and noble. There is very little of the meretricious in it, the ornaments, in general, partaking of this character, both in their nature and distribution. A pitiful statue of Queen Anne, in front of the building, is the most worthless thing about it, being sadly out of place, without mentioning the monstrosity of the statue of a woman in a regular set of petticoats, holding a globe in her hand, and having a crown on her head. I am not quite sure she is not in a hoop. Had she been surrounded by a party of "the nobility and gentry," dressed for Almacks', the idea would have been properly carried out. Ladies who are not disposed to go all lengths, had better not be ambitious of figuring in marble.

The interior of St. Paul's was too naked, perhaps, until they began to ornament it with monuments. I remember it nearly in that state, not more than half a dozen statues having been placed, at my first visit to London. There are now many, and as they are all quite of the new school, they are chaste and simple. This church promises to throw Westminster Abbey, eventually, in the shade.

Of course we ascended to the whispering gallery. The effect is much the same as it is in all these places. I do not think Sir James Thornhill, who painted the dome with passages from the life of St. Paul, a Michael Angelo, or even a Baron Gros, though, like the latter, he painted in oil. The colours are already much gone, which, perhaps, is no great loss.

I ought to have said that we came up, what our cicerone called a "geometry stair-case," of which the whole secret appeared to be, that the steps are made of stones of which one end are built into a circular wall. This "geometry stair-case" greatly puzzled my friend, the traveller, Mr. Carter, who agreed with the cicerone that it was altogether inexplicable. It is a wonder to be classed with that of the automaton chess-player. The effect, however, is pleasing.

Not satisfied with the whispering gallery, we ascended to another on the exterior of the dome, where we found one of the most extraordinary bird's eye views of a town, I remember ever to have seen. The day was clear, cool, and calm, and, of course, the vapour of the atmosphere floated at some distance above the houses. The whole panorama presented a field of dingy bricks, out of which were issuing thousands of streams of smoke, ascending in right lines to the canopy of murky vapour above. The effect was to give this vast dusty-looking cloud, the appearance of standing on an infinity of slender vapoury columns, which had London itself for their bases. In a small district around the cathedral, there also arose a perfect *chevaux de frise* of spires and towers, the append-ages of the ordinary parish churches, of which London proper contains an incredible number. Some one said that three hundred might be counted from the gallery, and really it did not strike me that there could be many less.

Seen in this manner, London offers little to be mentioned in comparison with Paris. It has no back ground, wants the grey angular walls, the transparent atmosphere, the domes and mon-uments, for we were on the only one of the former, and the gen-eral distinctness, necessary to satisfy the eye. It was not always easy to see at all, in the distance, and the objects were principally tame and confused. I like mists, feathery, floating, shadowy mists, but have no taste for coal smoke.

We were much amused with a remark of a good woman, who opened some of the doors above. There were sundry directions to visitors to pay certain stipulated prices, only, for seeing the dif-ferent parts of the edifice. All the English cicerones have a for-mal, sing-song manner of going through their descriptions, that is often the greatest source of amusement one finds, but which nothing but downright mimicry can make intelligible to those who have not heard it. The woman in question, without altering the key, or her ordinary mode of speaking, concluded her history, with saying, "by the rules of the church, I am entitled to only two pence for showing you this, and we are strictly prohibited from asking any more, but gentlefolks commonly give me a shill-ing." They have a custom here of saying that such and such an act is *un-English*, but I fancy they will make an exception in favour of this.

If you are as much puzzled, as I was myself once, to understand in what manner such huge churches can be used, you will be glad to have the matter explained. In all Catholic cathedrals, you already know, there are divers chapels, that are more or less separated from the body of the building, in which different offices are frequently saying at the same time. Near the centre, or a little within the head of the cross (for this is the form they all have) is the choir. It is usually a little raised above the pavement, and is separated from the rest of the nave by a screen, by which it is more or less enclosed on the other sides. In this choir are performed all the cathedral services, the preaching taking place in a different part of the church; usually from movable pulpits. Frequently, however, these pulpits are fixtures against a pier, the size of the edifice rendering their appearance there of no moment.

In St. Paul's there is the screen and the choir, as at Canterbury. But instead of the canons' or prebends' stalls, only, there are also pews for a congregation. There are, moreover, a pulpit and a reading-desk, and, the organ forming part of the screen, an organ-loft for the choir. In this chapel, or "heart" of the church, then, is the usual service performed. In Catholic cathedrals, you will understand that laymen, except in extraordinary cases, are not admitted within the choir, and the organ is almost always at the end of the nave, over the great door, and beneath an oriel window. The cathedrals at Canterbury and Westminster, were both built for the Catholic worship, and they had their private chapels; but St. Paul's, having arisen under the Protestant régime, is a little different. I believe there are private chapels in this building, but they are detached and few. After excepting the church or the choir, and the parts appropriated more properly to business, the remainder of this huge edifice can only be used on the occasions of great ceremonies. There are, however, a utility and fitness in possessing a structure for such objects, in the capital of a great empire, that will readily suggest themselves. There is something glorious and appropriate in beholding the temple of God rearing its walls above all similar things, which puts the shallow and pettifogging sophistry of closet-edifices and whittling sectarianism to manifest shame.

The absence of the side chapels gives a nobleness to the centre of St. Paul's, that is rather peculiar to itself. It is true that the choir, with the screen, which partially cuts off the side aisles, in some measure intercepts the view, and the eye nowhere embraces the whole extent, as in St. Peter's; a fact, that, coupled with its vast dimensions, must always render the *coup d'œil* of the interior of the latter, a wonder of the world. But few churches show, relatively, as grand a transept and dome, as this. Apart from the dimensions, which, exclusively of the colonnades, the vatican, and the sacristy, are in all things, about one-sixth in favour of St. Peter's, the difference between the *coups d'œil* of the two churches, exists in the following facts. On entering St. Peter's, the eye takes in, at a glance, the whole of the nave, from the great door at one end, to the marble throne of the pope, at the other. In St. Paul's, this view is intercepted by the screen, and the appliances of protestant worship just mentioned. In St. Peter's, there is everywhere an ornate and elaborate finish, of the richest materials, while the claims of St. Paul's to magnificence, depend chiefly on the forms and the grandeur of the dimensions. In St. Peter's, all the statuary, monuments, and other accessories, are on a scale suited to the colossal grandeur of the temple, the marble cherubs being in truth giants. Whereas, in St. Paul's, individuals being permitted to erect memorials in honour of their friends, the proportions have been less respected.

To conclude, St. Paul's, in the severity and even in the purity of its style is, in some few particulars, superior to the great Roman Basilica; but, these admissions made, it will not do to urge the comparison further, since the latter in size, material, details, and in the perfection of its subordinate art, has probably never been approached, as a whole, since the foundations of the earth were laid. St. Paul's, like all Protestant churches, is wanting in the peculiar and grateful atmosphere of the temple. Still, like all large edifices, it is temperate, being cooler in summer and warmer in winter, than those that are smaller. At least, so it has always appeared to me.

Our visit happened to be made during the season of festivals, and more than a usual number of the officials were loitering about the church. Who they were, I cannot say, but several of them had the sleek, pampered air of well-fed coach horses; animals that did nothing but draw the family to church on Sundays, and enjoy their stalls. There was one fellow, especially, who had an unpleasantly greasy look. He was in orders, but sadly out of his place, nature having intended him for a cook.

Letter V.
To Richard Cooper, Esq. Cooperstown.

The ice once broken, visitors began to appear at my door, and since my last, I have been gradually looking nearer and nearer, at the part of the world which it is usual to call society. A friend who knew England well, remarked to me, just before we left Paris—"you are going from a town where there is little company and much society, to one where there is no society and much company." Like most ambitious and smart sayings, that aim at sententiousness, there is some truth, blended with a good deal of exaggeration, in this. It is easy enough to see that association of all degrees, is more laboured, less graceful, and less regulated by reasonable and common sense motives in London, than in Paris. It is usual to say, that as between us and England, the latter having prescribed and definite degrees of rank, its upper classes have less jealousy of place, and of intrusion on their rights, than the same classes in America, and that society is consequently under less restraint. There is some truth in this opinion, as relates to us; but when England comes to be considered in connection with other European nations, I think the consequences of such a comparison are exactly the other way.

On the continent of Europe, nobility has long formed a strictly social *caste*. Its privileges were positive, its landmarks distinct, and its rules arbitrary. It is true, all this is gradually giving way before the spirit of the age, and the fruits of industry, but its effects are every where still to be traced. There is no more need of jealousy of the intrusion of the inferior in most European capitals, than in America there is distrust of the blacks forcing their way into the society of the whites. France is an exception to this rule, perhaps, but the *pêle-mêle* produced by the revolution has been so complete, that just now one says and thinks little of origin and birth, from sheer necessity. It is too soon for things to fall into the ordinary channels, but when they do we shall probably see the effects of a reaction. Nothing can keep society unsettled, in this respect, but constant and rapid changes of fortunes, and, apart from revolutions, France is a country in which there is not likely to be much of these.

In England, it is very true there exists legal distinctions, as between the rights and powers of men. But it will be remembered that the real peers of England are a very small class. As a body they have neither the wealth, the blood, nor numbers, of their side. I met, not long since, on the continent, a gentleman of the name of G_____, who was the head of a very ancient and affluent family, in his own county. In the same place there happened to be a Lord G_____, the descendant of three or four generations of peers. It was rather matter of merriment to the lookers on, that Lord G_____ was very anxious to be considered as belonging to the family of Mr. G_____, while the latter was a little disposed to repudiate him. Now, it needs no demonstration to prove that the peer enjoyed but a very equivocal social superiority over his namesake, the commoner. Admitting them to be of the same root, the latter was the head of the family, he had the oldest and the largest estate, and, in all but his political rank, he was the better man. It is quite obvious, under such circumstances, that the legal distinction counts for but little, in a merely social point of view.

The fact is that the gentry of England, as a class, are noble, agreeably to the standard of the rest of Europe. It is true they want the written evidences of their rank, because few such have ever been granted in England except to the titled;* but they have every requisite that is independent of positive law. Of all the Howards descended from the "Jockey of Norfolk," and they are numerous, both in England and America, only four or five are esteemed noble, because no more possess peerages; and, yet, when we come to consider them as heirs of blood, it would be folly not to deem one as gentle as the rest.

Thus you see England is filled with those who have all the usual claims to birth, and in many cases that of primogeniture too, without enjoying any legal privileges, beyond the mere possession of their fortunes. The Earl of Surrey, the heir of the first peer of England, is just as much a commoner, in the eye of the law, as his butler. It is not the legal distinctions alone, therefore, that divide men into social castes in England, as on the continent

---

*Esquires were formerly created by patent.

of Europe, but opinion, and habit, and facts, as all are connected with origin, antiquity, estates, and manners. It is true that a peer enjoys a certain positive political consideration from the mere circumstance of his being a peer; and just as far as this class extends, the assertion that their privileges put them above jealousies, is, I believe, true. I ascribe the circumstance that an American will be more likely to meet with a proper degree of civility among the nobles of England than among the classes beneath them, to this very fact. But the number of the rigidly noble is too small, to give its character to a society as broad and as peculiar as that of England. They exist in it, themselves, as exceptions rather than as the rule.

If we remove the titled from English society, the principles of its formation and government are precisely the same as our own, however much the latter may be modified by circumstances. It is true, the fact that there is a small body at the summit of the social scale, protected in their position by positive ordinances, has an effect to render the whole system more factitious and constrained than it would otherwise be, but, nevertheless, with these distinctions, it is identical with our own. Though these privileged are not enough to give society its tone, they form its goal. The ambition of being in contact with them, the necessity of living in their circle, and their real superiority are the causes of the *shoving propensities* of the English, propensities that are so obvious and unpleasant as to render their association distinct from that of almost every other people. The arbitrary separation of the community between the gentle and the simple prevents these efforts in the other parts of Europe, nor is it any where else so obvious as among ourselves.* I take it that it exists with us (though in an infinitely lessened degree) because we are subject to so many of the same causes.

The moment you create a motive for this irritating social ambition, and supply the means of its gratification, a serious injury is given to the ease, nature and grace of society. In England the motive exists in the wish to mingle with the privileged classes,

---

*A little of this feeling is getting up in Paris, under the new order of things, which favour the pretensions of money, but France is in the transition state, and it is too soon to predict the result.

and the means in the peculiar character of the gentry, in the great prosperity of the commerce and manufactures of the country, and in the insensible manner in which all the classes glide into each other and intermingle.

There is much to admire in the fruits of such a social organization, while there is, also, a great deal to condemn. A principal benefit is the superior elevation and training that are imparted to those, who, under other systems, would be kept always in a condition of dependant degradation; and one of its principal disadvantages is the constant moral fermentation, that so sensibly impairs the charm and nature of the English circles. A looker-on here, has described the social condition of England to be that of a crowd ascending a ladder, in which every one is tugging at the skirts of the person above, while he puts his foot on the neck of him beneath. After the usual allowances, there is truth in this figure, and you will, at once, perceive that its consequences are to cause a constant social scuffle. When men (and more especially *women*) meet under the influence of such a strife, too much time is wasted in the indulgence of the minor and lower feelings, to admit of that free and generous communion that can alone render intercourse easy and agreeable. There must be equality of feeling to permit equality of deportment, and this can never exist in such a *mêlée*.

Nor is the English noble always as absolutely natural and simple as it is the fashion to say he is, or as he might possibly be demonstrated to be by an ingenious theory. Simple he is certainly in mere deportment, for this is absolute as a rule of good breeding; and he may be simple in dress, for the same law now obtains generally, in this particular; and, if it did not, in his peculiar position, it would be the old story of the *redingote grise* of Napoleon revived; but he is not quite so simple in all his habits and pretensions. I will give you a few laughable proofs of the contrary.

A dozen noblemen may have laid their own patrician hands on my knocker, within a fortnight. As I use the dining-room to write in, I am within fifteen feet of the street door, and no favour of this sort escapes my ears. Ridiculous as it may seem, there is a species of etiquette established, by which a peer shall knock louder than a commoner! I do not mean to tell you that parliament has passed a law to that effect, but I do mean to say that so accurate has my ear become, that I know a Lord by his knock, as one would know

Velluti by his touch. Now a loud knock may be sometimes useful as a hint to a loitering servant, but it was a queer thought to make it a test of station.

I had occasion to go into the country, a day or two since, with two ladies. On our return, the latter asked permission to leave cards, at one or two doors in the way. The footman was particularly cautioned about his rap, one of the ladies explaining to me, that the fellow had got a loud knock by living with Lord_____. Quite lately too, I saw an article in the Courier complaining of the knocks of the doctors, who were said to disturb their patients by their *tintamarres* and, moreover, were accused, in terms, of rapping as loud as noblemen!

While on the subject, I may as well add, that no one, but the inmates of the house, uses the bell in London, although there is always one. The postman, the beggar, the footman, the visitor, all have their respective raps, and all are noticed according to their several degrees of clamour. I walked into Berkeley Square, yesterday, to leave cards for Lord and Lady G_____. Determined to try an experiment, I knocked as modestly as possible, without descending quite as low as the beggar. At that hour, there were always two footmen in the hall of the house, and I saw the arm of one at the window, quite near the door. He did not budge. I waited fully two minutes, and raised the note, a little, but with no better success. I then rapped *à la peer of the realm,* and my hand was still on the knocker, as the lazy rogue opened the door. I think I could already point out divers other petty usages of this nature, but shall defer the account of them, until my opinions are confirmed by longer observation. In the meanwhile, these trifling examples have led me away from the main subject.

A chief effect of the social struggles of England is a factitious and laboured manner. As respects mere deportment, the higher ranks, and they who most live in their intimacy, as a matter of course, are the least influenced by mere forms. But, as one descends in the social scale, I think the English get to be much the most artificial people I know. Instead of recognising certain great and governing rules for deportment, that are obviously founded in reason and propriety, and trusting to nature for the rest, having heard that simplicity is a test of breeding, they are even elaborate and studied in its display. The mass of the people conduct in society like children who have had their hair combed and faces washed, to be exhibited in the drawing-room, or with a staid simplicity that reminds you always how little they are at their ease, and of the lectures of the nurse.

I have seen eight or ten men sitting at a dinner table for two hours, with their hands in their laps, their bodies dressed like grenadiers, and their words mumbled between their teeth, evidently for no reason in the world but the fact they had been told that quiet and subdued voices were the tone of the higher classes. This boarding-school finish goes much further than you would be apt to think in London society, though it is almost unnecessary to say, it is less seen in the upper classes than elsewhere, for no man accustomed to live with his equals, and to consider none as his betters, let him come from what country he may, will ever be the slave of arbitrary rules, beyond the point of reason, or no further than they contribute to his ease, and comfort, and tastes.

Something of this factitious spirit, however, extends itself all through English society, since a portion of even the higher classes have a desire to distinguish themselves by their habits. Thus it is that we find great stress laid on naked points of deportment, as tests of breeding and associations, that would be laughed at elsewhere, and which, while they are esteemed imperious during their reign, come in and go out periodically, like fashions in dress. Of course, some little of this folly is to be found in all countries, but so much more, I think, is to be found here, than any where else, as to render the trait national and distinctive.

While there is all this rigid and inexorable tyranny of custom in small things, there is also apparent, in English manners, an effort to carry out the dogmas of the new school, by ultra ease and nature. The union of the two frequently forms as odd a jumble of deportment as one might wish to see. I think it is the cause of the capriciousness, for which these people have a reputation. I have had a visit from a young man of some note here, and one who lives fully one half his time, by these conventional rules, and yet, in the spirit of ease, which is thought to pervade modern manners, he seated himself a-straddle of his chair, with his face turned inwards, in a first visit, and in the presence of ladies! Still this person is well connected, and a member of parliament. He reminded me of the man who advertised a horse to be seen, with its tail where the head ought to be. The rogue had merely haltered the animal, wrong end foremost, to the manger. Sitting on the floor, with the foot in a hand, or suspiciously like a tailor, is by no means unusual.

When one gets at all above the commoner classes in England, it strikes me there is much less of obtrusive vulgarity than with us, while there is much more of the easy impertinence of which I have just given a specimen. This is contrary to our own experience of the English, but we see few above a class that is quite below all comment, in describing a nation. In two or three instances, in houses where I have made first visits, I have observed the young men lolling at their length on the ottomans and sofas, and scarcely giving themselves the trouble to rise, in a way that would hardly be practised at Paris. Such things are disrespectful to strangers, and in exceedingly bad taste, and I think them quite English; still, you are not to suppose that they are absolutely common here, though they are more frequent than could be wished. I have seen them in noblemen's houses. But the go-by-rule simplicity, you will understand, is so common, in the imitative classes, as to be distinctive.

As for the remark of there being no society in London, it may be true as a rule, but there are glorious exceptions. An American, after all, is so much like an Englishman, and one has so much more pleasure in the interchange of thought, when the conversation is carried on in his own language, that I ought, perhaps, to distrust my tastes a little; but taking them as a criterion, I should say that the means of social and intellectual pleasures are quite as amply enjoyed in London, as in the capital of France. The dinners are not as easy, especially while the women are at table, but either I have fallen into a peculiar vein of breakfasts, or the breakfasts have fallen into my vein, for I have found some twenty of them, at which I have already been present, among so many of the pleasantest entertainments I have ever met with. It will scarcely do for us to affect disdain for the society of London, whatever may be the rights of a Frenchman in this respect.

Mr. Rogers, who is my near neighbour, you already know, asked me a second and a third time, in the course of a few days, and on each occasion I had the pleasure of seeing a few of the prominent men of the country. The first day I met Lord John Russell, and the second Sir James Mackintosh. One seldom hears of a distinguished man, without forming some notion, erroneous or not, of his exterior. I knew little of the former of these gentlemen, beyond the fact that he was rather prominent in opposition, and that he had enrolled himself on the page of letters; but I had been told he was conspicuous for a "bull-dog tenacity" in clinging to his object and in carrying his point. The term "bull-dog," and some vague notion of the Russells of old, led me to expect a man of thews and sinews, and one adapted, by his *physique*, to carry out the lofty designs of a vigorous intellect. Nothing could be farther from the truth. Lord John Russell is a small, quiet man, with an air of ill-health, reminding me a little, in his mouth and manner of speaking, of Captain Ridgely of the navy, though the latter has altogether the best physique. He complained of his health, and talked but little. I remember one of his remarks, however, for he said that parliament was "getting too thin-skinned" for a healthful state of things. Did he mean to compare the present times with those in which his illustrious ancestor lost his head?

Sir James Mackintosh I had figured a robust, brawny, negligent Scot, with a broad accent, and strong national peculiarities. Instead of realizing this picture, he appeared a man of good stature, and, considering his years, of an easy and graceful person, with somewhat of an air of the world, and with as little of Scottish provincialism as was necessary. His voice was gentle and pleasant, and it was quite difficult, though not impossible, to trace any of the marks of his origin in his speech. Of these he had much less even than Sir Walter Scott. He proved to be the best talker I have ever heard. I am acquainted with a Neapolitan, who is more eloquent in conversation, and Colonel C_____, of Georgia, is perhaps neater and closer in his modes of expressing himself, but neither discovers the same range of thought and information, through a medium as lucid, comprehensive, and simple. Sir James Mackintosh is a free, but by no means an oppressive, talker in company. He is full of material, and, evidently, is willing to give it vent, but he also is content to listen. I greatly prefer his oral to his written style. I believe the former would be thought the best, could it be written down as he utters his words. The bias of his mind is to philosophy, in which he is both comprehensive and ingenious, and it appears to me that he makes himself more clearly intelligible in conversation than on paper. It is very true that abstrusities occur in reasoning that require the closet to be comprehended, and which best suit the pen, while it would be a defect to exact the same attention in society; but what I mean is, that (in my estimation) Sir James Mackintosh would be more likely to express the same thought felicitously while conversing, than in deliberately committing it to paper.

That he entertains some such notion of himself I have reason to think by a remark he made, on quitting the table yesterday. We had been speaking of the powers of the different distinguished orators of England and America, and some comparisons had been made between Pitt, and Fox, and Burke, and Sheridan. "After all," observed Sir James, as we went out together, "conversation is the test of a man's powers. If it is in him, he can bring it out, and all are witnesses of the manner in which it is done." Too much importance ought not to be attached to a casual remark like this, but the opinion struck me as singularly in opposition to Addison's celebrated answer about his inability to pay a shilling on the spot, while he could draw for a thousand pounds. In this manner are we all influenced by our own personal qualities; Addison could write better than Mackintosh, and Mackintosh could talk better than Addison. A man may certainly have it in him, and not always be able to bring it out, as is proved by thousands besides Addison.

I found Sir James Mackintosh better informed on the subject of America than any European I have yet seen. His ideas of our condition are more accurate and more precise. He spoke of several of our jurists with commendation; not in the extravagant and exaggerated manner that is so much in fashion at home, but with moderate respect, and frankly. All this time, however, it was quite evident that he thought us a people who might yet do prodigies, rather than as a people who had performed them.

Mr. Rogers introduced the subject of American poetry. By general consent, it was silently agreed to treat all who had gone before the last ten years, as if they had not written. I named to them Messrs. Halleck and Bryant, of neither of whom did they appear to know any thing. In consequence of something that had previously fallen from our host, I had obtained an imperfect copy of light American poetry, from Mr. Miller, the bookseller. It contained Alnwick Castle, as well as several things by Mr. Bryant. I left it with them, and both gentlemen subsequently expressed themselves much pleased with what they found in it. Alnwick Castle, in particular, had great success, but I do not think the book itself did justice to Mr. Bryant.

While speaking of Mr. Rogers, I cannot avoid adverting to the manner in which a portion of the London press is in the practice of using his name. One of them especially, constantly speaks of him as a confirmed jester. I have been told there is a private pique and a malicious envy, in all this, and that he is represented as a jester because he has a peculiar aversion to jests. The motive is self-evident, and of itself places the offending party below a serious refutation. But, lest you may have imbibed some erroneous notions, in this respect, concerning a man whose name is familiar to all America, there may be no harm in giving you a traveller's views of the matter. Mr. Rogers is neither a jester, nor one who has any particular aversion to a clever saying. No man's tone of manner is better, and few men have a more pleasant way of saying pleasant things. He lives in the very best circles of London, where he appears to me to be properly appreciated and esteemed. Although as far as possible from being the incessant joker his enemies would represent him to be, I know no one who occasionally gives a keener or a finer edge to a remark, or one in better taste. I should say his house is positively a nucleus of the very best literary society of London, and, although a decided liberal in politics, he seems to me to be personally on equally good terms with all parties, with the exception of those, who, by their very tone towards himself, betray that they are unfit associates for any gentleman.

The *petits déjeuners* of Mr. Rogers have deservedly a reputation in London. Taking all in conjunction, the house, the host, the curiosities, the situation, the company and the tone, it is not easy to conceive of any thing better in their way. Women frequent them as well as men, and, by a tact in the master in making his selections and assorting his company, or by the atmosphere of the abode, or by some cause I shall not attempt to explain, it is unusual to see or hear any thing out of place, or out of season. Not satisfied with the mental treats he dispenses, the nicest care is had to the table, and but for these admirable breakfasts I should be apt to pronounce the meal one, of whose rare qualities and advantages, the English in general have no proper notion. There is no attempt at the French entertainment in all this, every thing being strictly simple, and one might say national; but, while I see England and America in the entire arrangement, both countries are made to appear so much better than common, that I have been driven to a downright examination of the details to make certain of the fact. Commend me, in every respect, to the delicious breakfasts of St. James's Place!

Letter VI.
To Mrs. J[ay], New York.

If one, in the least in the world, were to judge from the invitations that lie on his table, during the season, he would be very apt to pronounce London an eating and drinking town; but inferences are not to be rashly drawn, and, before we come to our conclusions, it will be well to remember the numbers there are to eat and drink. Westminster is a large town, entirely filled with the affluent of the greatest empire of modern times, and their dependants. Although comparatively few strangers circulate in the drawing-rooms of London, the gay and idle of the whole kingdom assemble in them periodically. Under the incessant fire of invitations that is let off on these occasions, it is not to be wondered at, if a few random shots should hit even a rambling American, like myself; for while we are not absolutely loved in the "British Isles," they do not churlishly withhold from us the necessaries of life.

I am very sensible that my experience is too limited to give you a proper and full idea of the gay world of England, but I may tell a portion of what I have seen, and, by adding it to the contributions of others, you may be able to get some more accurate notions than are to be derived from the novels of the day. As a traveller is a witness it is no more than fair that some idea should be given of the circumstances under which he obtained his facts, in order that one may know how to appreciate his testimony. I may have now been in fifty houses, since my arrival in London, including in this list that of the duke down to that of the merchant. Perhaps a third have been the residences of people of quality; a large portion have been in the intermediate class between nobility and trade, and the remainder have certainly savoured of the shop. To this list, however, may be added a dozen which embrace the indescribable *omnium gatherum* of men who have achieved notoriety as *littérateurs* without personal rank, players, artists, and managers. I say *littérateurs* without personal rank, for, in this age of book-making, half the men of fashion about town have meditated, or have actually perpetrated the crime of publishing. The mania of scribbling is not quite as strong here as at Paris, where it afflicts young and old, high and low, from the king on his throne to the driver of the *cabriolet* in his seat; but as Sir Walter Scott, who is now here, whispered me the other day, when I pointed out to him a young nobleman as a "brother chip" (and mere *chips* of *his log* are we in good sooth), "The peers are all going mad!"

One of my first essays of life, in a great house, beyond a morning call, was at a dinner at Lord [Holland]'s. [Holland] house is in the skirts of London, and was constructed as a country residence, though the growth of this mammoth town is gradually bringing it within the smoke and din of the capital. The lamps extend miles beyond it. Taking a hackney coach I drove to the gate, the lawn being separated from the high-way, or rather street, by a high blind wall. Here I alighted and walked to the house. The building is of bricks, and I should think of the time of Elizabeth, though less quaint than most of the architecture of that period. At any rate Lady [Holland] told me that in the room in which we dined, Sully had been entertained, and his embassy occurred in 1603. This building was once in a family different from the present, and is also celebrated as having been the abode of Addison, after his marriage with Lady Warwick. There were formerly Earls of [Holland] too, of another race. But I cannot tell you any thing of their history. The present possessors of [Holland] house are of a family too well known to need any explanation; Lord [Holland] being the grandson of the man who so long battled it with the first [Pitt], as his son did with the second.

The proximity of London and the value of land forbids the idea of a park, but the lawn was ample, and prettily enough arranged. It is scarcely necessary to say that it was neat, in a country where order and system and the fitness of things, seem to form a part of its morals, if not indeed of its religious faith. The lawn is about the size of your own at Rye, and I should think the house might contain twice as much room as that of the Patroon. The rooms were old fashioned, and, in some respects quaint, and, to me, they all seemed out of proportion narrow for their length. That in which we dined had a ceiling in the style of Elizabeth's reign, being much carved and gilded. It was not as large as the hall of the manor-house, at Albany, nor in any other respect, much more peculiar, although the ceiling was essentially higher.

[Holland] house as a country residence, in England, is but of a secondary class, though, for a town abode, it would rank among the first. Whoever may own it, fifty years hence, will probably enjoy a preferment so easily and quietly obtained, for the new improvements at Pimlico bid fair to push fashion into this quarter. We should pull the building down, however, if we had it in New York; firstly, because it does not stand on a thoroughfare, where one can swallow dust free of cost; secondly, because it wants the two rooms and folding doors, and thirdly, because it has no iron *chevaux de frise* in front.

The invitations to dinner, here, vary from seven to half-past seven. It is not common to receive one for an earlier hour, nor do regular people often dine at a later. As this was semi-rural, I had been asked to come early, and Sir James Mackintosh had been kind enough to leave word with the porter, that he was to be sent for when I arrived. Accordingly, I had the pleasure of passing half an hour with him, before the rest of the party assembled. He took me into the grounds in the rear of the house, which are still quite extensive for the situation, though I presume Kensington, which is beginning to enclose the spot on that side, has already curtailed them in a degree. I was told that a proposition had lately been made to the proprietor, to dispose of a part on lease, but that he preferred air and room to an addition of some thousands a year to his rental. There is an historical avenue of trees, behind the house, and a garden near by; but the latter struck me as insignificant.

We went into the library, which is a fine room, on the second floor, including the whole depth of the house. There were recesses for reading, and writing, and also for lumber, on one of its sides. My companion showed me tables at different ends of the room, and stated there was a tradition that Addison, when composing, was in the habit of walking between the two, and of aiding his inspirations, by using the bottles placed on them for that purpose. I beg you will not mention this, however, lest it excite a sensation among the "ripe scholars" of New York.

Our party at dinner was not large. There were present, besides the family, and a lady or two, Mr. Rogers, Sir James Mackintosh, Mr. Tierney, and an old nobleman, a Lord B_____ and his son. The table was square, and we sat round it without any attention to precedency, the master of the house occupying a corner, while the mistress had a seat in the centre. As this was done quietly, and without the parade of an *impromptu fait à loisir*, the effect was particularly good. So was the dinner. I do not think the tables of London, however, of a very high order. The viands are generally better than those of Paris, but the cookery is far less knowing, and the arrangement, while it is more pretending, is, I think, generally less elegant and graceful. It appears to be as much a matter of etiquette for a peer to dine off of silver here, as it is to keep a carriage. Wealthy commoners sometimes use plate also, but opinion has so much influence over things of this nature, in England, that it is not always sufficient to be able to buy a luxury, to be permitted to enjoy it in peace. In England certain indulgences are accorded to station, and it is deemed *contra bonos mores* to assume them without the necessary qualifications. Something of this feeling must exist every where when there are distinctions in rank, but, in this country, rank being so positive, while the competition is open to all, that the outs watch their fellows closely, as stealing a privilege is thought to be stealing from them. "Do you see that silly fellow," asked _____, as we were walking together, and pointing to a man who had just passed—"his father was in trade and left him a large fortune, and, now he is dashing upon the town, like a nabob. He actually had the impudence lately to give his footmen cockades." There was a fellow!

Nothing is in worse taste than to talk much of dishes and wines at table, I allow, but one may show his gratitude for good things of this sort, afterwards, I hope, without offending the *bienséances*. I believe the table of [Holland] house is a little peculiar in London; at least, such is its character according to my limited experience. As to the mere eating and drinking, New York is a better town than London. We set handsomer tables too, on the whole, with the exception of the size (our own being invariably too narrow), the plate, and the attendants. In porcelain, glass, cutlery, table linen, and the dishes, I am clearly of opinion, that the average of the respectable New York dinners, is above the average of those of London. There may be, now and then, a man of high rank here, who, on great occasions, throws us far into the shade, but these cases are exceptions, and I am now speaking of the rule. On the point of plate, I believe there is more of it, in the way of ounces, in the single city of London, than in the whole twenty-four states of the American Union, put together.

During dinner, as the stranger, I had the honour of a seat next to Lady [Holland]. She offered me a plate of herrings, between the courses. Being in conversation at the moment, I declined it, as I should not have done, according to strict etiquette, especially as it was offered by the mistress of the house. But my rule is the modern one of pleasing one's self on such occasions; besides I never suspected the magnitude of the interest involved in the affair. "You do not know what you say," she good humouredly added — "They are *Dutch*." I believe I stared at this, coming as it did from the mistress of a table so simply elegant and so *recherchée*. "*Dutch!*" I involuntarily repeated, though I believe I looked at the same time, as if it was a herring after all. "Certainly; we can only get them *through an ambassador*." What a luxury would a potato become, if we could contrive to make it contraband! I shall hold a Dutch herring in greater respect, as long as I live.

Unluckily there is nothing prohibited in America, and it is a capital oversight in graduating our comforts, it is such a pleasure to sin! I believe I got out of the difficulty by saying there were too many good things of native production, to require a voyage to Holland, on my account. Still I frankly avow I ought to have eaten one, even to the fins and tail. From some such feeling as this, has probably come the old saying of "fish, flesh, and red herring."

There are a thousand things in life, which will not stand the test of philosophical inquiry, but on which no small part of our daily enjoyments depend. I have mentioned this little anecdote, not because it is particularly pertinent to the house in which I was dining, which would be particularly impertinent in me, but, because I think it illustrative of a principle that pervades the whole structure of English society. Things appear to me, to be more than usually estimated here, by the difficulty there may be in attaining them, and less than usual by their intrinsic value. In citing such examples one is always obliged to keep a salvo for poor human nature (and why Esop made the animal in the manger a *dog* I never could discover) but, apart from this, England is singularly a begrudging country. Every thing is appreciated by its price. They have an expression always in their mouths that is pregnant of meaning, and which I fancy was never heard any where else. They say a thing is *"ridiculously cheap."* Now when one becomes ridiculous from buying a thing at a low price, common sense is in a bad way. This is one of the weaknesses of man from which we are more than usually exempt, and I believe that with us, free trade may boast of having done more on this point than on any other.

I was asked by the mistress of this house where I had learned to speak so good English? This surprising me quite as much as the herring!

The old nobleman I have mentioned, had the civility to offer to take me to town in his chariot; and I was safely deposited in St. James's Place, about ten.

As Lord [Holland] is a man of mark, it may be well if I add that he had an air of great benevolence, and that there were much nature and *bonhomie* in his manner. I thought his feeling towards America kind, and his disposition to speak of it stronger than usual. His wife is possessed of some property in New York, and he complained a little of the squatters; the land, he told me, lying on the Genessee, in Connecticut. You may judge from this single circumstance how much attention we attract, when a man made this mistake about his own property. The day may not be distant, when lands in either Connecticut, or New York, will more avail his heir than the lawn before [Holland] house. Reform must move fast in England, or it will be overtaken by revolution.* Sir James Mackintosh pithily observed, that he supposed "there was about the same danger of finding a squatter in Connecticut, as there would be of finding one in the county of Kent." He is the only man I have yet met in England who appears to have any clear and defined notions of us. They will not acquire this knowledge, simply because they do not wish to acquire it, until we bear hard on some of their interests, political or pecuniary, and then light will pour in upon them in a flood, as the sun succeeds the dawn. That day is not distant.

After the herring, and before the dessert, a page, attired in a very suspicious manner, entered with a regular censer, such as is

---

*In consequence of the delay in publishing these "gleanings," the writer is often doubtful whether he ought to indulge such prophecies. These words, however, were actually written in 1828.

used before the altar, smoking with frankincense, and, swinging it about, he perfumed the room. I thought this savoured a little of *"protestant emancipation."*

One of my next dinners was at [Spencer] house. This is a residence in the heart of London, and the invitation ran for a quarter past seven, *very precisely.* The English have a reputation, in America, for coming late, and I can understand it, as one accustomed to their hours must feel a reluctance to dine as early as five or six; but here, the sittings of parliament excepted, I think it rare to be behind the time.

I breakfasted a few mornings since with Mr. Rogers, who had invited five or six others. I was the first there, and I was punctual to the hour. Not another soul had come. On my laughing at their laziness, "you shall have the laugh all of your own side," said the poet, who forthwith ordered breakfast. We sat down alone. Presently Stuart Newton showed himself; then Kenney, the dramatist; then Mr. Luttrell, and the remainder in succession. We, who were first on the ground, treated the matter coolly, and the others were left to enjoy it as they might. A man who wilfully misses any portion of these delightful breakfasts, is quite beneath sympathy.

I sent my man to set my watch by the palace clock, and as the distance was short, a few minutes before the hour named, for the dinner just mentioned, I drew on my gloves and walked leisurely to the door, which was but a step from my own lodgings. It was exactly a quarter past seven when I knocked. On entering the drawing-room, I found it full of people. "Very precisely" means, then, a little before the hour. Among the guests were Sir [Henry Halford], one of the most fashionable physicians of London, and Dr. [Copleston], lately consecrated Bishop of [Llandaff]. The latter was the first dignified clergyman I had met, and, irreverent though it seem, his appearance diverted me out of measure. He wore a wig, in the first place, that set at naught both nature and art, and not satisfied with this, he had on a little silk petticoat, that I believe is called a stole. One may get accustomed to this clerical masquerade, as well as to any thing else, and there is little argument for or against it, in abstract philosophy; but I shall contend that neither the little wig, nor the *jupon*, is any more of a natural taste than olives, though I dare say one who has been envying others their possession half his life, may think them very becoming.

Both the bishop and the physician had a precise and potent manner with them, that showed how broad is the separation between *castes* and the professions, in this country.

"Mon tailleur m'a dit que les gens de qualité étoient comme cela le matin."

We were about to take our seats, when the bishop, who was on my left hand, bent over the table and uttered a sound that was singularly like that made by a hound gaping. He then commenced an apology to Lady [Spencer], who, in her turn, apologized to him, saying, "you were quite right, my lord." To my surprise, I learned the divine had been saying grace!

This dinner offered nothing worth repeating, except a short conversation I had with my neighbour, the bishop. He asked me if I knew Dr. *Hubbart*. I was obliged to answer, "No." "From what part of America do you come?" "From New York." "I thought Dr. *Hubbart* well known in that state. Is he not its bishop?" "You must mean Dr. *Hobart*, who was lately in England, I think." "Hubbart, or Hobart; we have a noble family in this country of the name of Hobart, which we pronounce *Hubbart*, and we called your bishop, *Hubbart* too, thinking it might flatter him." Here was a finesse, for a successor of St. Peter and St. Paul!

The bishop then began to speak of the well known sermon preached by Dr. Hobart, after his return from Europe, a sermon which was not very favourable to an established church, you will remember. I said a little in his defence, observing that he had probably written from his convictions, and that, however erroneous, a conscientious discharge of duty was not to be condemned. To this my neighbour had no objection; but he complained that Dr. Hobart held language so different when abroad, that he had disappointed and grieved his friends in England. This, you will perceive, was little short of accusing our good bishop of a vice as mean as a toad-eating hypocrisy. Something like this he is charged with in some of the church publications, here.

All who knew Dr. Hobart will exonerate him from the imputation of calculating disingenuousness. His fault, if fault it be, lay just the other way. Still I think a desire to avoid unpleasant topics, as well as the wish to say pleasant things, may have induced him to be silent, on some occasions, when it might have been better to speak, and not always to have measured the extent of his concessions. It moreover requires some time, and not a little practice, for an Englishman and an American fully to understand each other, though speaking the same language. I had a proof of this fact this very evening, and I will relate the circumstance, by way of illustrating my meaning.

The night previously I was in company with Lord N[ugent] and Mr. B_____, both of whom are members of the House of Commons, and whigs. The former was very particular in inquiring how we prevented frauds under the vote by ballot. I explained to these two gentlemen the process, which, as you have never attended an election, it may be well to explain to you. It is simply this. The ballot is put in the hands of a public officer, who is himself chosen by the people, and who is obliged to hold it in such a way that every one can see it is not changed. In this manner it is put into the box. Thus the elector is prevented from slipping in two tickets along side of each other; the officer cannot change the ticket; and when they come to count the votes, if two are rolled together, both are rejected.

To me this explanation seemed perfectly clear; but I saw, at the time, my auditors did not appear to be of the same way of thinking. After dinner, at [Spencer] house, when we had returned to the drawing-room, Lord A[lthorp], the son of the master of the house, and Lord John Russell, both prominent men in the opposition, came to me, and the former, who has stronger notions in favour of the ballot than is usual in England, observed that he had heard me quoted at Brooks's as giving an opinion against the vote by ballot. I answered that my opinion was strongly in favour of the ballot, and that I did not remember even to have spoken at all on the subject, except on the previous night to Lord N[ugent] and Mr. B_____, when the question was not of the *utility* of the ballot, but of the *manner in which we prevented frauds under the system.* I was desired to repeat our mode of proceeding, but neither of these gentlemen appeared to me to be perfectly satisfied. Of course, this ill-luck in explaining set me to reflecting, and by dint of thought, observation, and inquiries, I believe I have arrived at the truth. By *frauds* these gentlemen meant to ask me, "In what manner do you prevent the elector who has pledged himself to vote for you, from voting for another man at the polls?" As these pledges, in England, are four times in five given by the dependant to his patron, the tradesman to the employer, and the tenant to the landlord, the inquiry was to know, if we had discovered any means by which the very object for which the vote by ballot had been instituted, might be defeated under the ballot! It strikes me this is a peculiarly English mode of doing things.

Here, then, you see how easy it is for us to misunderstand each other; for Lord A[lthorp] admitted that it was Lord N[ugent] who quoted me in the manner he had mentioned; and how much care and experience are necessary for an Englishman to give a correct account of even the declared opinions of an American, and, of course, *vice versa.*

As respects Dr. Hobart, it is understood, that, like almost every clergyman of our church, who goes to England to pass any time, he saw reason to alter many of his previously cherished opinions. In the sermon to which there has been allusion, he said that, of the two, he should prefer for his church, the persecution of the state to a legal establishment, and this, an opinion that would be very likely to rankle in the breast of a new-made bishop, is also an opinion that he himself, probably, did not entertain, or at least in so strong a light, when he sailed from home. Now, some time and observation are necessary to produce these changes, and Dr. Hobart, or any other man, may very conscientiously think, and thinking, express himself differently, on quitting a country, from what he had done on entering it.

But I would strenuously urge on every American who really loves the institutions of his country, never to make any concessions to mere politeness, on these topics, when actually required to say any thing in England. Indeed, politeness has few claims when principles are concerned, and it is rare to meet an Englishman, in America or any where else, who thinks himself bound to sacrifice even a prejudice to such a claim.

There is another point of view in which this charge against Dr. Hobart ought to be considered. There is, quite evidently, here, a secret distrust of the justice of the present system, both political and religious, and a latent apprehension of its not enduring forever. Every thing wears out, even to the rock, and time is the parent of changes. Even they who maintain that our sytem is but a single step removed from despotism, know that our system must, in principle at least, be the next great change of England, and they search eagerly for testimony against its merits, from those who, having lived under it, are supposed to be acquainted with its action. Thus an American, who betrays the smallest leaning to their side of the argument, is eagerly quoted, and used as authority in their favour. Such may have been the case with Dr. Hobart, who, in the warmth of his feeling towards a church from which his own is derived, and which its worst enemies must admit has so much that is excellent, has probably uttered expressions to which too much meaning has been attached, or which, indeed, he may have seen good reason himself to change on a closer examination, after admitting the more comprehensive views that are always opened by travelling.

From [Spencer] house Mr. [Rogers] and myself proceeded to Berkeley Square, to make a call. As we were in the hall, Lord [Essex], one of the guests, understanding our intention, offered to take us in his chariot. As I had no acquaintance with this gentleman, I put myself at the disposition of my companion, who decided to accept the offer. Another carriage was standing before the door, and casting my eye at it, I was half inclined to think that the bishop, by some droll freak, had got up on its box. The coachman was in deep black, wore a cocked hat, and a wig so very like that I had been admiring in the house, that, to my uninstructed eye, they appeared to be one and the same. Some such conceit must have passed through the mind of Lord [Essex], for we were no sooner seated, than he began to discuss the subject of coachmen's wigs. It would seem that a fashion of decorating the heads of the Jehus of the "nobility and gentry" with this ornament, has lately come in, and most of the conceits of this nature being already monopolized by the bench, the bar, or parliament, they who invented the mode have been compelled to trespass a little on the sacred rights of the church. After some cogitation, pro and con, Lord [Essex] decided against the wigs.

On reaching the house to which we were going, we alighted, in the order in which we sat, which brought Lord [Essex] in advance. In this manner, as a matter of course, we ascended the stairs. When about half way up, my companion stopped, and appeared to be examining a vase filled with rose leaves, one of the customs that the extreme luxury of the age has introduced in London. It was some little time, however, before I discovered the real cause of the delay, which was merely to allow Lord [Essex], who was a fat old man, and walked slow, to get up stairs before us. This he did, was announced, and entered the drawing-room first, we following and entering as if we had not come in his party! It was very good natured in this gentleman to offer a stranger the use of his carriage, but now I understand the conditions, I shall not accept it the next time, even though he should change his mind and give his coachman a wig.

I exonerate the English for a portion of their want of manners, as respects us. It is, to a certain extent, our own fault. We have the reputation of being notorious tuft-hunters in England, and, I am afraid, not always without cause. Nothing is more natural than that one educated in American society, should feel a curiosity to see the higher classes of a country like England. Such a feeling would, under ordinary circumstances, be stronger perhaps, in the American accustomed to the really good company of his own country, than in another, for it would, in a degree, be necessary to his habits. Names, and titles, and local distinctions make little difference between men who have access to civilized society, and who are equally accustomed to consider themselves at its head. The usages of polite life, sentiment and training are accessible to all, and nothing is effected by dividing the community into *castes*, but depressing all beneath the highest. When you give a man education, manners, principles, tastes and money (and all are the certain fruits of civilization) you do not change his positive position by adding titles, though you do change it relatively, and these relations can only be obtained at the expense of the inferior. You compel the latter to stop in the middle of the stairs, without walking like a man to the top, but you do not elevate the other an inch. My companion and myself got into the drawing-room later, for this *coup de politesse*, but Lord [Essex] got there no sooner.

But, if it be natural for one accustomed to no superior in his own country to wish to see more of a similar class in other nations, it is unnatural for him to submit to the association under the penalty of losing his own self-respect. Very few of our people, certainly, are seen at all in English drawing-rooms, and fewer still, in those of the great; but I think if these few had uniformly maintained the tone they ought, that fifty years would have brought about in our behalf, a juster state of feeling than actually exists.

All our colonial traditions go to prove the little estimation that was enjoyed by our forefathers in the mother country. The descendants of the same ancestors looked upon their American cousins even more coldly than "country cousins" are usually regarded. Perhaps this was the natural consequence of the political relations between the two countries. The violent separation has superadded positive dislike and distrust, and we have to contend with all these feelings in associating with the English. One must eat a peck of dirt, they say, and look you, madam, I charge at least a quart of mine to this delay on the stairs.

I very well know there are would-be-philanthropists, and mawkish sentimentalists who will deny both my facts and my conclusions. As to the facts I specifically state to have befallen myself, you, at least, will believe them, and I ask with confidence if the anecdote I have just related is not eloquence itself, on the subject of the estimation in which we are held? Philanthropy is a very pretty thing to talk about, and so is sentiment, but they usually are not much gifted with either of a very pure quality, who deal with them most in phrases. That is the healthiest philanthropy which soonest and the most effectually cures an evil, and this can be best done by exacting for ourselves, all that we are willing to yield to others.

It is not easy for an American to imagine the extent of the prejudice which exists against his country in England, without close and long observation. One of its effects is frequently to cause those who were born on our side of the water, or who have connections there, to wish to conceal the fact. Two anecdotes connected with this feeling have come to my knowledge, and I will relate them.

A gentleman of one of our well known families was put young in the British army. Circumstances favoured his advancement, until he rose early to a situation of high honour, and of considerable emolument. Speaking of his prospects and fortune, not long since, to a near relative, who mentioned the anecdote to me, he felicitated himself on his good luck, adding, "that he should have been the happiest fellow in the world, had he not been born in America."

An Englishman married an American wife, and their first child was born in the country of the mother. Alluding to the subject, one day, an American observed—"but you are one of us; you were born in the United States." Observing his friend to change colour, he asked him if he really had any feeling on the subject, when the other frankly admitted "there was so strong a prejudice against America, in England, that he felt a reluctance to own that he was born there."

All the Americans resident here give the same account of the matter, whatever may be their own feelings towards England. Captain Hall, I see, virtually admits the same, and although occasionally one meets with an Englishman who is disposed to deny it, I think there are few who do not allow the existence of the dislike, when they are on terms of sufficient intimacy to speak frankly. I lay stress on this matter, because any mistake on our part would be peculiarly awkward, and because a knowledge of the truth, in this particular, may clear the way to our inquiries on other subjects.

Letter VII.

To Thomas Floyd-Jones, Esq. Fort Neck.

When we first arrived here from Paris, I was disposed to deny that the streets of London were as crowded as it is usual to pretend. My opinion was formed too soon. What was then true, is so no longer. London, or rather Westminster, in the height of the season, and Westminster out of the season, so far as the movement in the streets is concerned, are not the same town. When I was here in 1826, I saw no essential difference between Regent street and Broadway, as regards the crowd, but now, that we have passed the Easter holidays, every one appears to be at his post, and so far from having ever seen, any where else, the crowds of people, the display of rich equipages, the incessant and grand movement that adorn and bewilder the streets of London, I had never even pictured such a sight in my imagination. They who have not been here at this season of the year, know nothing of the place. There is a part of the day, between one and six, when it is actually a matter of risk for a pedestrian to cross the streets. I live near Piccadilly, which is not wider than Broadway, if quite as wide, and I have occasion to cross it frequently. You know I am no laggard, and am not deficient in activity, and yet I find it convenient to make my first run towards a stand of coaches in the middle of the street, protected by which I take a fresh departure for the other side. Regent street is still worse, and there is a place at Charing Cross, that would be nearly impracticable, but for a statue of Charles I., which makes a capital lee for one on foot. As for Broadway, and its pretended throng, I have been in the current of coaches in what is called the city, here, for an hour at a time, when the whole distance was made through a jam, as close as any you have ever seen in that street for the space of a hundred yards. Broadway will compare with the more crowded streets of London, much as Chestnut street will compare with Broadway.

I frequently stop and look about me in wonder, distrusting my eyes, at the exhibition of wealth and luxury that is concentrated

Plate I

London

St. Paul's Cathedral

Plate II

Westminster Abbey

Westminster Hall

Plate III

The Parliament House, from Old Palace Yard

The King's Entrance to the House of Lords

Plate IV

Banqueting House, Whitehall

Westminster Bridge

in such narrow limits. Our horses have none of the grand movement that the cattle are trained to in Europe generally, and these
of London seem, as they dash furiously along, as if they were
trampling the earth under their feet. They are taught a high
carriage, and as they are usually animals of great size as well as
fleetness, their approach is sometimes terrific. By fleetness, however, I do not mean that you, as a Queen's county man, and one
who comes of a sporting stock, would consider them as doing a
thing "in time," but merely the fleetness of a coach horse. As to
foot, I have little doubt that we can match England any day. I
think we could show as good a stock of roadsters, both for draught
and the saddle, but we appear to want the breed of the English
carriage horse; or, if we possess it at all, it is crossed, dwindled,and
inferior.

The English coachmen do not rein in the heads of their cattle
towards each other, as is practised with us, but each animal carries
himself perfectly straight, and in a line parallel to the pole. I
found this unpleasant to the eye, at first, but it is certainly more
rational than the other mode, and by the aid of reason and use I
am fast losing my dislike. The horses travel easier and wider in
this way than in any other, and when one gets accustomed to it, I
am far from certain the action does not appear nobler. The superiority of the English carriages is equal to that of their horses.
Perhaps they are a little too heavy; especially the chariots; but
every thing of this sort is larger here than with us. The best French
chariot is of a more just size, though scarcely so handsome. You
see a few of these carriages in New York, but, with us, they are
thought clumsy and awkward. One of our ordinary carriages, in
Regent street, I feel persuaded would have a mob after it, in
derision. There is something steam-boatish in the motion of a
fine English carriage—I mean one that is in all respects well
appointed—but their second class vehicles do no better than our
own, though always much heavier.

The men, here, are a great deal in the saddle. This they call
"riding;" going in a vehicle of any sort is *"driving."* The distinction is
arbitrary, though an innovation on the language. Were one to say he
had been *"riding"* in the park, the inference would be inevitable,
that he had been in the saddle, as I know from a ludicrous mistake
of a friend of my own. An American lady, who is no longer young,

nor a feather-weight, told an acquaintance of hers, that she had been *riding* in the Bois de Boulogne, at Paris. "Good Heavens!" said the person who had received this piece of news, to me, "does Mrs. _____ actually exhibit her person on horseback, at her time of life, and in so public a place as the Bois de Boulogne?" "I should think not, certainly; pray why do you ask?" "She told me herself that she had been *'riding'* there all the morning." I defended our country-woman, for our own use of the word is undeniably right. "Why if you *ride* in a coach, what do you do when you go on a horse?" demanded the lady. "And if you *drive in* a carriage, what does the coachman do, *out* of it?"

The English frequently make the *abuse* of words the test of *caste*. Dining with Mr. William Spencer, shortly before we left Paris, the subject of the difference in the language of the two countries was introduced. We agreed there was a difference, though we were not quite so much of a mind, as to which party was right, and which was wrong. The conversation continued good humouredly, through a *tête-à-tête* dinner, until we came to the dessert. "Will you have a bit of this *tart?*" said Mr. Spencer. "Do you call that a *tart,*—in America we should call it a *pie.*" "Now, I'm sure I have you—here, John," turning to the footman behind his chair, "what is the name of this thing?" The man hesitated and finally stammered out that he "believed it was a pie." "You never heard it called a *pie*, sir, in good society in England, in your life." I thought it time to come to the rescue, for my friend was getting to be as hot as his *tart*, so I interfered by saying—"Hang your good society—I would rather have the opinion of your cook or your footman, in a question of pastry, than that of your cousin the Duke of Marlborough."

To put him in good humour, I then told him an anecdote of a near relative of my own, whom you may have known, a man of singular readiness and of great wit. We have a puerile and a half-bred school of orthoepists in America who, failing in a practical knowledge of the world, affect to pronounce words as they are spelt, and who are ever on the rack to give some sentimental or fanciful evasion to any thing shocking. These are the gentry that call Hell Gate, Hurl Gate, and who are at the head of the *rooster school* A person of this class appealed to my kinsman to settle a disputed point, desiring to know whether he pronounced "quality," "*qual*-i-ty," or "*quol*-i-ty." "When I am conversing with a person of quality," he answered gravely, "I say *quol*-i-ty, and when with a person of *qual*-i-ty, I say *qual*-i-ty." As the wit depended in a great degree, on the voice, you will understand that he pronounced the first syllable of *qual*-i-ty, as *Sal* is pronounced in Sally. You will be very apt to call this digression *bolting*, a *qual*-i-ty that a true Long Islandman cordially detests. *Revenons à nos moutons.*

I have told you that the men are a great deal in the saddle in London. The parks afford facilities for this manly and healthful exercise. It is possible to gallop miles without crossing one's track, and much of the way through pleasant fields. But galloping is not the English pace. The horses appear to be hunters, with a good stride, and yet it is quite rare that they break their trot. The common paces are either a fast trot or a walk. During the first, the rider invariably rises and falls, a most ungraceful and, in my poor judgment, ungracious movement, for I cannot persuade myself a horse likes to have a Mississippi sawyer on his back. Nothing is more common than to see a man, here, scattering the gravel through one of the parks, leaning over the neck of his beast, while the groom follows at the proper distance, imitating his master's movements, like a shadow. I have frequently breakfasted with young friends, and found three or four saddle-horses at the door, with as many grooms in waiting for the guests, who were on the way to one or the other of the Houses. Nothing is more common than to see fifteen or twenty horses, in Old Palace Yard, whose owners are attending to their duties within.

We appear to possess a species of saddle horse that is nearer to the Arabian, than the one principally used here. The colours most frequent are a dull bay and chesnuts, very few of the true *sorrels* being seen. It was said the other day, that this word was American, but Lord H_____n replied that it was a provincial term, and still in use, in the north, being strictly technical. Johnson has "Sorel; the buck is called the first year a fawn; the third a *sorel*." He cites Shakspeare as authority. Can the term, as applied to a horse, come from the resemblance in the colour? I leave you to propound the matter to the Jockey Club.

England is a country of proprieties. Were I required to select a single word that should come nearest to the national peculiarities, it would be this. It pervades society, from its summit to its base, essentially affecting *appearances* when it affects nothing else. It enters into the religion, morals, politics, the dwelling, the dress, the equipages, the habits, and one may say all the opinions of the nation. At this moment, I shall confine the application of this fact to the subject before us.

It would not be easy to imagine more appropriate rules than those which pervade the whole system of the stable in England. It is so perfect, that I deem it worthy of this especial notice. One might possibly object to some of the carriages as being too heavy, but the excellence of the cattle and of the roads must be considered, and the size of the vehicles give them an air of magnificence. What would be called a *showy* carriage is rarely seen here, the taste inclining to an elegant simplicity, though, on state occasions at court, carriages do appear that are less under laws so severe.

The king is seldom seen, but when he does appear it is in a style as unlike that of his brother of France, as may be. I have witnessed his departure from St. James's for Windsor, lately. He was in a post-chariot, with one of his sisters, another carriage following. Four horses were in the harness, held by two postillions, while two more rode together, on horses with blinkers and collars, but quite free from the carriage, a few paces in advance. Four mounted footmen came in the rear, while a party of lancers, cleared the way, and another closed the *cortège*. There was no *piqueur*. He went off at a slapping pace. On state occasions, of course, his style is more regal.

Five and twenty years since, families of rank often went into the country with coaches and six, followed by mounted footmen. I have seen nothing of this sort, now. Post chariots and four are common, but most people travel with only two horses. The change is owing to the improvements in the roads. It is only at the races, I believe, that the great "turn outs" are now made.

Most of the fashionable marriages take place in one of two churches, in London; St. James's, Piccadilly, or St. George's, Hanover Square. We are at no great distance from the first, and I have several times witnessed the Hegiras of the happy pairs. They take their departure from the church door, and the approved style seems to be post-chariots and four, with the blinds closed, and postillions in liveries, wearing large white cockades, or bridal favours. The sight is so common as to attract little attention in the streets, though I dare say the slightest departure from the established seemliness might excite newspaper paragraphs. You have not the smallest conception of what a livery is. A coat of some striking colour, white, perhaps, covered with lace, red plush vest and breeches, white stockings, shoes and buckles, a laced round hat with a high cockade, a powdered head and a gold-headed cane constitute the glories of the footman. A shovel-nosed hat and a wig, with a coat of many capes spread on the hammercloths, in addition, set up the Jehu. Two footmen behind a carriage seem indispensable to style, though more appear on state ceremonies. Chasseurs belong rather to the continent, and are not common here. But all these things are brought in rigid subjection to the code of propriety. The commoner, unless of note, may not affect too much state. If the head of an old county family, however, he may trespass hard on nobility. If a *parvenu*, let him beware of cockades and canes! There is no other law but use, in these matters, but while an Englishman may do a hundred things that would set an American county in a ferment of police excitement, he cannot encroach on the established proprieties, with impunity. The reckless wretch would be cut as an Ishmaelite. Vanity sometimes urges an unfortunate across the line, and he is lampooned, laughed at, and caricatured, until it is thought to be immoral to appear in his society.

The arms are respected with religious sanctity; not that men do not obtain them clandestinely as with us, but the rules are strictly adhered to. None but the head of the family bears the supporters, unless by an especial concession; the maiden appears in the staid and pretty diamond; the peer in the coronet; not only every man, woman and child seems to have his or her place, in England, but every coach, every cane, and every wig!

Now, there is a great deal that is deadening and false, in all this, mixed up with something that is beautiful, and much that is convenient. The great mistake is the substitution of the seemly, for the right, and a peculiar advantage is an exemption from confusion and incongruities, which has a more beneficial effect, however, on things than on men. But, I forget; we are dealing with horses.

England is the country of the wealthy. So far as the mass can derive benefits from the compulsory regulations of their superiors (and positive benefits, beyond question, are as much obtained in this manner, as fleets and armies and prisons are made more comfortable to their *personnels* by discipline) it may expect them, but when the interests of the two clash, the weak are obliged to succumb.

The celebrated division of labour, that has so much contributed to the aggrandizement of England, extends to the domestic establishments. Men are assorted for service, as in armies; size and appearance being quite as much, and in many cases more, consulted, than character. Five feet ten and upwards, barring extraordinary exceptions, make a footman's fortune. These are engaged in the great houses; those that are smaller squeeze in where they can, or get into less pretending mansions. All the little fellows sink into pot-boys, grooms, stable-men, and attendants at the inns. The English footman I have engaged, is a steady little old man, with a red face and powdered poll, who appears in black breeches and coat, but who says himself that his size has marred his fortune. He can just see over my shoulder, as I sit at table. If my watch were as regular, as this fellow, I should have less cause to complain of it. He is never out of the way, speaks just loud enough to be heard, and calls me master. The rogue has had passages in his life, too, for he once lived with Peter Pindar, and accompanied Opie in his first journey to London. He is cockney born, is about fifty, and has run his career between Temple Bar and Covent Garden. I found him at the hotel, and this is his first appearance among the quality, whose splendour acts forcibly on his imagination. W[illiam] caught him in a perfect ecstacy the other day, reading the card of an Earl, which had just been given him at the door. He is much contemned, I find, in the houses where I visit, on account of his dwarfish stature, for he is obliged to accompany me, occasionally.

It is a curious study to enter into the house, as well as the human, details of this capital. As caprice has often as much to do with the decisions of the luxurious as judgment, a pretty face is quite as likely to be a recommendation to a maid, as is stature to a footman. The consequence is, that Westminster, in the season, presents as fine a collection of men and women, as the earth ever held within the same space. The upper classes of the English are, as a whole, a fine race of people, and, as they lay so much stress on the appearance of their dependents, it is not usual to see one of diminutive stature, or ungainly exterior, near their dwellings. The guards, the regiments principally kept about London, are picked men, so that there is a concentration of fine forms of both sexes to be met with in the streets. The dwarfs congregate about the stables, or mews as they are called here, and, now and then, one is seen skulking along with a pot of beer in his hand. But in the streets, about the equipages, or at the doors of the houses, surprisingly few but the well looking of both sexes are seen.

As strangers commonly reside in this part of the town, they are frequently misled by these facts, in making up their opinions of the relative stature of the English and other nations. I feel persuaded that the men of England, as a whole, are essentially below the stature of the men of America. They are of fuller habit, a consequence of climate, in a certain degree, but chiefly, I believe, from knowing how and what to eat; but the average of their frames, could the fact be come at, I feel persuaded would fall below our own. Not so with the women. England appears to have two very distinct races of both men and women; the tall and the short. The short are short indeed, and they are much more numerous than a casual observer would be apt to imagine. Nothing of the sort exists with us. I do not mean that we have no small men, but they are not seen in troops as they are seen here. I have frequently met with clusters of these little fellows in London, not one of whom was more than five feet, or five feet one or two inches high. In the drawing-room, and in public places frequented by the upper classes, I find myself a medium-sized man, whereas, on the continent, I was much above that mark.

In America it is unusual to meet with a woman of any class, who approaches the ordinary stature of the men. Nothing is more common in England, especially in the upper circles. I have frequently seen men, and reasonably tall men too, walking with their wives, between whose statures there was no perceptible difference. Now such a thing is very rare with us, but very common here; so common, I think, as to remove the suspicion that the eye may be seeking exceptions, in the greater throngs of a condensed population, a circumstance against which it is very necessary to guard, in making comparisons as between England and America.

It is a received notion that fewer old people, in proportion to whole numbers, are seen in America, than are seen here. The fact must be so, since it could not well be otherwise. This is a case in point, by which to demonstrate the little value of the common-place observations of travellers. Even more pretending statisticians frequently fall into grave blunders of this sort, for the tastes necessary to laboured and critical examinations of facts, are seldom found united with the readiness of thought, and fertility of invention, that are needed in a successful examination of new principles, or of old principles environed by novel circumstances. No one but an original thinker can ever write well, or very usefully of America, since the world has never before furnished an example of a people who have been placed under circumstances so peculiarly their own, both political and social. Let us apply our reasoning.

To be eighty years old one must have been born eighty years ago. Now eighty years ago, the entire population of America may have been about three millions, while that of England was more than seven. A simple proposition in arithmetic would prove to us, that with such premises, one ought to see more than twice as many people eighty years old in England, than in America; for as three are to seven, so are seven to sixteen and one-third. Setting aside the qualifying circumstances, of which there are some, here is arithmetical demonstration, that for every seven people who are eighty years old in America, one ought to meet in England with sixteen and one third, in order to equalize the chances of life in the two countries. The qualifying circumstances are the influence of immigration, which, until quite lately, has not amounted to much, and which perhaps would equal the allowance I have already made in my premises, as England had actually nearer eight than seven millions of souls, eighty years since: and the effect of surface. I say the effect of surface, for a mere observer, who should travel over a portion of America equal in extent to all England, would pass through a country that, eighty years ago, had not probably a population of half a million, and this allowing him, too, to travel through its most peopled part.

The comparative statistical views of Europe and America, that have been published in this hemisphere, are almost all obnoxious to objections of this character, the writers being unable to appreciate the influence of facts of which they have no knowledge, and which are too novel to suggest themselves to men trained in other habits of thinking.

I see no reason to believe that human life is not as long in our part of America, as it is here, and, on the whole, I am inclined to believe that the average of years is in our favour. I do not intend to say that the mean years of running lives is as high with us, as it is here, for we know that they are not. The number of children, and the facts I have just stated, forbid it. But I believe the child born in the state of New York, *cæteris paribus*, has as good a chance of attaining the age of nincty, so far as climate is concerned, as the child born in Kent, or Essex, or Oxford, and so far as other circumstances are concerned, perhaps a better. The freshness of the English complexion is apt to deceive inconsiderate observers. This, I take it, is merely the effect of fog and sea air, and, except in very low latitudes, where the heat of the sun deadens the skin, as it might be to protect the system against its own rays, is to be seen every where, under the same circumstances. There is something in the exhalations of a country newly cleared, beyond a question, unfavourable to health, and this the more so, in latitudes as low as our own; but now I speak of the older parts of the country, where time has already removed this objection. I can remember when it was not usual to see a woman with a good colour, in the mountains around C[ooperstow]n, while it is now unusual to find girls with a finer bloom than those of the present generation. At my residence at Angevine in West-Chester, a few years since, I could count ten people more than ninety years old, within ten miles of my own door. One of them had actually lived as a servant in the family of Col. Heathcote, of whom you know something, and who figured in the colony, at the close of the seventeenth century; and another was Mr. Augustus Van Cortlandt, a gentleman who drove his own blooded horses, at the ripe years of four score and ten. The old servant actually laboured for my oldest child, making five generations of the same family, in whose service she had toiled.

The notion of the comparative insalubrity of our climate, however, is not quite general, for, making a call, the other day, on Lady Affleck, a New York woman well advanced in life, she expressed her conviction that people lived to a greater age in America, than in England! She had been making inquiries after the members of the old colonial gentry, such as Mrs. White,* John

*This lady is just dead, in her ninety-ninth year.

Jay, Mr. John de Lancey, Mrs. Izard, Mr. Van Cortlandt, Mr. John Watts, Lady Mary Watts, and divers others, most of whom were octogenarians, and several of whom were drawing near to a century. It appeared to me that the good old lady wished herself back among them, to get a mouthful of native air.

Though Westminster, in the season, has the peculiarities I have mentioned, I do not think that the population of London, as a whole, is remarkable for either size or freshness. I have elsewhere said that, in my opinion, Paris has the advantage of London in these particulars, though certainly not in good looks. The English female face is essentially the same as the American, though national peculiarities are to be observed in both. It is a delicate office to decide on the comparative personal charms of the sex in different communities, but as you and I are both beyond the hopes and fears of the young, on this point, a passing word is no more than a tribute due to the incontestible claims of both. Were it not for the females of Rome, I should say that the women of England and America might bear away the palm from all other competitors, on the score of personal charms, so far as we are familiarly acquainted with the rest of the world. There is a softness, an innocence, a feminine sweetness, an expression of the womanly virtues, in the Anglo-Saxon female countenance, that is met with only as an exception, in the rest of Christendom. As between the English and American divisions of this common race, I think one may trace a few general points of difference. The English female has the advantage in the bust, shoulders, and throat. She has usually more colour, and, on the whole, a more *delicacy* of complexion. The American is superior in general delicacy of outline, as well as in complexion; she has a better person, bust and shoulders excepted, and smaller hands and feet. Those who pretend to know much on this subject, and to make critical comparisons, say, that it is usual to see most truly *beautiful* women in England, and most *pretty* women in America. Real beauty is an exception every where, and it must be remembered how much easier it is to find exceptions in a crowded population, than in one scattered over a surface as large as a third of Europe. Of one thing I am certain; *disagreeable* features are less frequently met, among the native females of America, than among any other people I have visited. I must hesitate as to the points of *beauty* and *prettiness,* for, judging merely by what one would see in London and New York, I think there is truth in the distinction. The English women appear better in high dress, the Americans in demi-toilettes. One other distinction, and I shall quit the subject. I have remarked that faces here, which appear well in the distance, often fail in some necessary *finesse* or delicacy, when closer, and I should say, as a rule, that the American female, certainly the American girl, will bear the test of examination better than her European rival. I do not mean, by this, however, under a fierce sun, that direful enemy of soft eyes, for there is scarcely such a thing as a bright sun, or what we should call one, known in England.

It would pollute this page, were I to return to the horses. I may, however, say, for the subject is, to a degree, connected with the ladies, that sedan chairs appear to have finally disappeared from St. James's street. Even in 1826, I saw a stand of them, that has since vanished. The chairs may still be used, on particular occasions, but were Cecilia now in existence, she would find it difficult to be set down in Mrs. Belfield's entry, from a machine so lumbering. Thank God! men have ceased to be horses;—when will the metamorphosis be completed by their relinquishing the affinity to the other quadruped?

Letter VIII.

To Edward Floyd De Lancey, Esq.

London justly boasts of her squares and parks. The former are both more numerous and more beautiful than are to be found in any other town; and, while Vienna has its Prater, Paris its Bois de Boulogne, and Berlin, Munich, Dresden, Brussels, and, indeed, nearly every capital of Europe, its particular garden, or place of resort, none of them offer the variety, range, and verdure, of the parks of this great town. As compared with their size, the smaller capitals of Germany perhaps possess this advantage in an equal degree with London; but the inhabitants of Leipsig, Dresden, or Munich, cannot enjoy the circuit and broad expanse of fields that are met with here. There are said to be eighty squares alone in this huge town, to say nothing of its parks.

You are too young to know much, even by report, of the London of the last century; but the squares, rendered nearly classical by the better novels of that period, are, I believe, with one solitary exception, already without the pale of fashion. I can remember Soho when it was still the residence of people of condition; but that and Leicester Square, with Lincoln's Inn Fields, the largest area of the sort in London, are now all abandoned to business. St. James's still maintains its character, owing, probably, to its position near the palace. Norfolk-house, the town-dwelling of the first peer of the realm, is in this square, as is also that of the Duke of St. Albans. In a country as aristocratical as this, in which there are but some twenty nobles of this high rank, the presence of a single duke will suffice to leaven the gentility of a neighbourhood. In this manner does Northumberland-house, standing on the confines of trade, serve as an outpost to protect the eastern flank of the *beau quartier*, extending its atmosphere a little beyond itself, in a sort of diluted fashion.

Norfolk-house,* on the street, (I have never entered it), shows a front of nine windows, I believe, differing but little in externals from one of our own dwellings, with the difference in length. There is one feature, however, in our architecture, that distinguishes it almost invariably from that of Europe. Here the details are on the same dimensions as the building. Thus a house of nine windows would not be exactly three times as long as one of three, but probably something longer. Houses of three or four windows in front, which are common enough in London, if intended for good abodes, are usually on a larger scale than our own: the fact that even a small building can get a noble aspect by fine details, being better understood here than with us. We multiply, but seldom enlarge rooms, though the size and proportions are indispensably necessary to effect.

Norfolk-house has neither court nor gate, and, of course, it can be entered only by crossing the side-walk, as with us; a circumstance that, of itself, does away with most of its air of grandeur. A private palace that is well known to me at Florence, has thirty-three windows in front, besides being built around a court!

I have been in but one house in St. James's Square, which belongs to Lord Clanricarde, though now occupied by Lord Wellesley. It is a house of the size, style, and appearance of one of our own better sort of town residences, with the difference I have named; that of having rather nobler details. The practice of living on the first floor, enables the English to take into the better rooms the whole width of the building. This practice prevailed with us thirty years since, when our architecture, like our society, was less ambitious, but in better taste than it is to-day. There may be in London, possibly, a hundred dwellings that, in Paris, might be called hotels, and which are deemed, here, worthy to bear names. They belong principally to the higher nobility, for I fancy it would be deemed social treason for a commoner to erect such an abode. Among them are Northumberland, Devonshire, Norfolk, Apsley, Lansdowne, Marlborough, Westminster, Bridgewater, Spencer, and Burlington-houses, &c. &c. &c. Neither of these dwellings would be considered first-rate on the continent of Europe; especially in Italy; nor do I think either is as large as the

*George III. was born in this house. See Wraxall.

President's house; though the residence of the Duke of Northumberland may be an exception. The unfinished building intended for the Duke of York, and which, since his death, has been purchased by the Marquis of Stafford, promises to be one of the noblest dwellings of London, and is truly a palace.*

It strikes me there is a sort of arbitrary line run between the quarters of London, following the direction of Regent's street. There are many squares on the eastern side of this thoroughfare, and some good streets, but rank and fashion appear to avoid them. When I was here in 1826, Mr. Canning facetiously asked, in parliament, if any one knew where Russell Square might be, and the question was thought to be derogatory to its standing. Still Russell, Bedford, Bloomsbury, and one or two more squares in that vicinity, are among the finest in London. They are chiefly occupied, I fancy, by people in the professions, or in trade. Cavendish, Hanover, St. James's, Grosvenor, Portman, Berkeley, and Manchester, are the squares most affected by people of condition. I presume a *parvenu*, who should wish to get into one of these squares, would have to make his advances with caution; not that houses may not be bought, or built, but because opinion draws arbitrary distinctions, on all these matters, in England. This feeling is inherent in man, and we are far from being free from it. If a person of one of our own recognized but impoverished families were to become rich suddenly, no one would think it extraordinary that he set up his carriage and extended his mode of living; for, by a sort of general but silent consent, it would be admitted there was a fitness in it; while the entirely new man would be commented on and sneered at. Institutions are of no avail in such matters, opinion being stronger than law. Mankind insensibly defer to the things and persons to whom they are accustomed. There is some just and useful sentiment, mingled with a good deal of narrow prejudice, in this feeling, and it should be the aim of those who influence opinion, to distinguish between the two; neither running into a bigotted exclusion, nor indulging in those loose and impracticable theories, that only tend to impair the influence of those who are capable of refining and advancing the

---

*Now Sutherland-house; the Marquis of Stafford having been raised to the rank of Duke of Sutherland.

tone and tastes, and frequently the principles, of society, without finding a substitute.

The English squares do not differ essentially from our own, though the houses around them are generally larger and more imposing, and the enclosures are usually laid out with a stricter adherence to taste in landscape gardening. I know of nothing on the continent of Europe of precisely the same nature, the squares there being usually, if not invariably, without trees, enclosures, or verdure.

The parks of London are four; St. James's, the Green, Hyde, and Regent's. The two first lie side by side, and their corners are separated from that of Hyde Park by Piccadilly only, so that in passing from one to the other, one is always in the fields; and Kensington Gardens, again, which differs from the parks only in the nature of the plantations, lie adjacent to the further extremity of Hyde Park. The latter alone contains nearly four hundred acres of land, and I should think a space of near, or quite, seven hundred acres lies, here, in contiguous fields and gardens, covered with what may almost be termed eternal verdure.

Regent's Park is at some distance from the others, though in a quarter inhabited by the upper classes, for, while London has so many areas for the enjoyments of the affluent, it is worse off than common, in this respect, in the quarters of the humble. An improvement of quite recent date, has entirely changed a portion of the capital. Carlton House, the former residence of the Prince of Wales, has been pulled down, and an opening made into St. James's Park, in a style resembling the French. Here is a *place*, or square, without verdure, which is surrounded by magnificent club-houses, and is called Waterloo Place. At this point Regent's street commences, running a distance of near two miles, though not exactly in a straight line. The deviations in the direction are made by means of architectural devices, that rather aid than impair the effect. The *coup d'œil* of this street is noble, and almost unequalled, though it is faulty in details, and mean in materials. The latter objection may be made to most of the modern improvements of the town, stuccoed bricks being used very generally, and sometimes in the public edifices. When the stucco stands, as it does pretty well in London, the appearance is better than that of the naked bricks however, and by far the greater portion of the towns of Europe are stuccoed, though usually on stone. It is only in Italy that one sees much true magnificence, and even there stucco is quite common. The best hotels of Paris, however, are of hewn stone.

The whole of Regent street is lined by buildings, erected in *blocks,* so as to resemble hotels, or palaces. The architecture is Grecian, varying between the several streets, no two *blocks* being exactly alike, perhaps; and many of them having columns, though none that project, or descend to the pavement. The buildings are chiefly used for shops, eating-houses, taverns, and other places of business. They are, in general, insignificant in depth, being principally outside. Still, the general effect is noble, and it is much aided by the breadth, beauty, and solidity of the flagging. The carriage-way is McAdamized.

Regent street, by a pleasing curvature, has been made to *débouche* in Portland Place, a short, but noble street, filled with plain, good dwellings. Portland Place, again, terminates at Regent's Crescent, where a series of beautiful enclosures commence. Here the houses are in circular colonnades, and passing them, you enter Regent's Park. This park better deserves the name of garden, as it is planted and decorated in that style, rather than in that of a park. It bids fair to be very beautiful, but is still too recent to develope all its rural charms. Certain favourites have been permitted to build in the park, and so long as this privilege shall be kept within proper limits, the effect will aid rather than impair the view. The Zoological Garden is also within the enclosure.

As the first peculiar object seen is apt to make the strongest impression, I ought perhaps to distrust my decision, but I think this collection, as yet, much inferior in taste, arrangement, and animals, to the *Jardin des Plantes.* It will, however, most probably improve fast, for no nation enjoys facilities equal to England to advance such an end. The whole of Regent's Park, a distance of about a mile and a-half, is encircled by a broad, smooth road, or drive, and this again is, in part, enclosed by rows of dwellings in terraces. These terraces stand a little back from the road, have carriage-sweeps and shrubbery in front, and are constructed on identified plans, so as to make a dozen dwellings resemble a single edifice. The material and designs are much like those of Regent street, though the scale is grander. Occasionally an isolated building breaks the uniformity of the arrangement, and prevents monotony.

The climate of London, a few of the summer months excepted, in the way of nerves and sensations, is any thing but pleasant. But the mists, when they do not degenerate to downright smoke and fogs, have the merit of singularly softening and aiding the landscape character of its scenes. I have driven into the Regent's Park, when the fields, casting upward their hues, the rows of houses seen dimly through the haze, the obscure glimpses of the hills beyond, the carriages rolling up, as it were out of vacuum, and the dim magnificence with its air of vastness, have conspired to render it one of the most extraordinary things, in its way, I have ever beheld.

There is a point near White-Hall, too, where I have stood often, to gaze at the dome of St. Paul's throwing up its grand outlines in the atmosphere of vapour, looking mystical and churchly. Such are the days in which I most like to gaze at London, for they carry out the idea of its vastness, and help to give it the appearance of an illimitable wilderness of human abodes, human interests, and human passions.

Many of the views from the bridges are rather striking, though in this particular, I think Paris has the advantage. Having an occasion to make a call on a member of the Admiralty, I found him in Somerset-house, in rooms that overlook the river. The day was clearer than usual, and my acquaintance pointed out to me views, which embraced the windings of the Thames, the noble bridges, the fields of roofs and chimneys, with a background of verdant hills, in Surrey, that might be deemed fine, for any town. Still it is the eternal movement, the wealth, the endless lines of streets, the squares and parks, and not its scenery, that characterize London. There is another peculiarity that, for most of the year, one cannot help feeling here. I mean the chilling dreariness of the weather, without, as it is contrasted to the comfort of an English home, within. There is not more of the latter than with us, perhaps, but there is so much more of the former, as to bring the warmth, coal-fires, carpets, and internal arrangements of the dwellings, into what may be truly termed a *high relief*. As we ordinarily find the best agriculture in inhospitable climates, and the richest inventions of man under circumstances that have called loudest for their exercise, so do I suspect that the far-famed comfort of England, within doors, owes its existence to the discomfort without.

Of the climate, I have not a word to say that is favourable. In America we have very cold and very hot weather; perhaps four months of the year are decidedly uncomfortable, from one or the other of these causes; though the cold being usually a dry, honest cold, may be guarded against, and be borne; and the cold certainly with us, is commonly weather that is exhilarating and otherwise healthful. The remaining eight months are such as are not surpassed, and hardly equalled, in any part of Europe, that I have visited. I should divide our New York weather in some such manner as this. Between November and March, there may be found, in all, a month of uncomfortable cold; between March and May, another month of disagreeable weather; between May and October, five or six weeks of lassitude, or of heat, that one could wish were not so, and then, I think, our positively bad weather is fully disposed of. The remainder of the year, under the necessary variations of the seasons, may be termed good.

I question if England can boast of half as much tolerable weather. I am aware that it requires long residences, and habits of comparison, to speak understandingly of climates; and, perhaps, there is no point on which travellers are more apt to be influenced by their own feelings, than on this; but, judging as much by the accounts of those who ought to know, as by my own experience, I believe four months in the year would fully include all the weather, of this island, that a stranger would not find uncomfortably bad. I have been disappointed in the English spring. I do not say it is not better than ours of the northern states, for nothing, in its way, can be less genial than our spring; but, this at London, strikes me as much less pleasant than that we have passed at Paris, though even that was afflicted with what the French call "*la lune rousse.*"

There is much verdure, many beautiful flowers, and a fine foliage in the parks, it is true, but the days in which all these can be thoroughly enjoyed, are few indeed. This English weather strikes me as possessing the humidity of the sea-air, without its blandness. It is too often raw, penetrating to the heart and marrow, and leaving a consciousness of misery. The Neapolitan scirocco is scarcely more withering.* In Paris the season advances more steadily and gracefully, and there are three months of progressive, calm, and stealthily increasing delight, until one has enjoyed all the gradations of vegetation between the bud, the blossom, and the leaf. With us the transitions are too rapid; in England they are accompanied by weather that constantly causes one to dread a return to winter.

June is *the* month of all this part of Europe. The Parisians extol their autumn, but it will not compare with our own. As for this island, between the first of October and January, it ought not to be inhabited. Nature has blessed me with a constitutional gaiety and a bouyancy of spirits, that are not to be mastered by trifles, but I have walked in the streets of this town, in certain conditions of the weather, when it appeared that every one I met was ready to point his finger at me, in mockery. At this season, in which we are now here, the verdure, and the trees in the parks, constantly invite one to walk, and yet there is rarely a day in which it is not pleasanter to be on the sunny side of the street. Still I prefer the English spring to our own, until we reach May, when, I think, we get the advantage. Mr. McAdam, who resided seventeen years in America, says, that in New York he was often very cold, whereas in England, he is almost always chilled. The distinction is significant, as between the bad seasons of the two countries.

As the town stretches along the parks, and contains so many squares, it is possible to ride, or *drive*, two or three miles, from a residence to Westminster-hall, without touching the stones, and almost without losing sight of verdure. Any one can enter Hyde Park on horseback, or in a carriage; hackney-coaches, stage-coaches, and the common vehicles excepted. This is the place usual for taking an airing. It is hardly necessary to say that, at certain times, the world does not afford similar exhibitions of taste, beauty, and a studied, but regulated magnificence, of the sort. Still carriages and four strike me as being less frequent, now, than they were in my youth. I think the taste for displays of this

---

*Mr. Washington Allston was once asked, "what is a scirocco?" The celebrated painter pithily described it, as a "Boston east-wind BOILED." It is a great advantage to be able to take the spring weather of London *raw;* and raw enough it is, of a verity.

nature is lessening in England; though, within the limits set by usage, I perceive no falling off in the equipages, but rather an improvement in form and lightness.

The *road* around Regent's Park appears open to every thing; but into St. James's, none but the privileged can enter except on foot. The Green Park is exclusively for pedestrians, being little more than a pretty and extensive play-ground for children. Kensington Gardens can be entered by all properly dressed pedestrians.

These parks are in the custody of the crown, and the privilege of entering St. James's, on horseback, or in a carriage, is much coveted. Like every thing else that is exclusive, men pine to possess it. I was told, the other day, that Lord _____, a nobleman, who in addition to his high rank, has filled many important offices in the ministry, cannot ride through this park, in going to or from the house, because he has had too much self-respect to solicit the favour; and they who regulate the matter, are too selfish and too narrow-minded to accord it, unasked. But this is the history of favours all over the world, the mean and truckling always obtaining them, while they who depend solely on their services are overlooked, unless, indeed, their names and presence become necessary to those in power.

They have a story, here, that some man of mark, wishing to get this privilege was denied; the friend, through whom he had preferred the request, telling him "it was impossible to get permission for him to go through the park, but he could have him made an Irish peer, if he wished it."*

Taking an airing, lately, with a friend, who is good authority in these matters, as indeed he is in others of a much higher character, he told me the following anecdote, pointing out, as we passed him, the hero of the story. A party was riding in Hyde Park, of

---

*Sir Nathaniel Wraxall, in his Posthumous Memoirs of his Own Time, has probably given the true version of this tale. A person of the name of Philipps was denied a request to have a carriage-road from the park to his door, and to soften the refusal, Mr. Pitt offered him an Irish peerage, which he accepted. One hears of many grounds for an *illustration,* but this is the queerest on record; that of ennobling a man "because a carriage-sweep may not be made between St. James's Park at his door! — — *'Comme vous voilà bâti!'* "

whom all but one had the privilege of passing through St. James's. The excluded offered to take twenty guineas that he got through the horse-guards (the place where the unprivileged are stopped), while none of the others should. With this understanding, he boldly entered the tabooed grounds, and rode with the rest, until he got within a certain distance of the gate of the horse-guards. Here he trotted ahead, and whispered the sentinel that neither of the gentlemen coming had a right to pass, but that they intended to attempt it, under false names, and he advised him to be on the alert. The soldier was mystified by this communication, and suffered the rogue to go through, while the others were stopped of course.

It is not easy to appreciate the effects that exclusion, in these trifling matters, produces on graver things. National character gets to be affected by such practices, which create a sort of a dog-in-the-manger propensity. Foreigners say, and I think not without reason, that the tone of English manners is injured by the system, for it renders the natives insensible to the claims of humanity, and especially to the obligations of hospitality. I have heard it said, that Mrs. _____, the wife of an American minister, was once excluded from a seat that was thought desirable, in a private assembly, by women of condition, who maintained that if she were privileged at court, she was not privileged there. The effect of all exclusiveness in deportment, that is not founded on taste, or sentiment, is to render people low-bred and vulgar; as the effect of all exclusiveness in institutions, which is purely factitious, is to depress the mass without elevating the superiors. I, myself, have seen English women of quality spread their petti-coats on a seat, when _____ and _____ were approaching it, in order to prevent their obtaining places, and manifest an alarm that was quite superfluous, as both of those whom they wished to exclude were too much accustomed to good company, to think of bringing themselves unnecessarily in contact with people who betrayed so gross an ignorance of its primary laws.

"Were you at the drawing-room," asked Sir _____ _____, of me, a fortnight since. I had not been. "You were wise, for, really, these things occur so rarely, now, that the press is nearly insup-portable. Many were compelled to wait hours for their carriages, and some were obliged to trudge it afoot, both going and coming." I mentioned that I had been told this difficulty would have been obviated by my going through rooms less thronged. "You mean by the private entrance.—Oh! But that is a privilege excessively difficult to be obtained, I do assure you; Lady ———, who went that way, had to exert all her influence; and it is a thing not to be had without a *ridiculous degree of favour.*"—"I was told by our *chargé*, that if I went, he would take me by some private entrance that is devoted to the diplomatic corps. You will remember that I should have to be presented."—"Ah! true; in that way it might *possibly* have been done." And he looked *ridiculously* envious of a foreigner who enjoyed this small privilege.

There is a diplomatic tradition that one of our ministers complained to our own government, of the treatment his wife received at court even, and a pithy anecdote is current concerning the mode in which Mr. Jefferson avenged her. It is not easy to see in what manner a minister can resent the slights of ordinary society; perhaps the best method would be to send his family to Paris, where it would be certain to meet with good-breeding, at least, and ask permission to visit it, from time to time, in a way that would leave no doubt of the cause. But a slight that proceeded from the court, ought to be met promptly. If a spirited remonstrance did not procure redress, the minister should ask his recall, and assign his reason. Were such a thing to occur once, in a case that was clear, and our government were to decline filling the mission, because it could ask no citizen to take a family into a country where its feelings were not properly regarded, the principle would be settled forever. If there ever was a nation that can afford to take high ground, in a matter like this, it is our own; for we are above fear, have no need of favour, and cannot accept of rewards. No people was ever more independent in its facts; would to heaven it were equally so in its opinions! If a case of this nature should occur, the trading part of the community would raise an outcry, lest it should derange commerce, the administration would probably be frightened by their clamour and the dignity of the republic would be abandoned, although the bone and sinew of the nation, when properly called on, would be ready and willing to maintain it. Still the dignity and the policy of a country are inseparable.

Letter IX.

To James Stevenson, Esq.

S ome favourable accidents have thrown me lately, more than I had a right to expect, in the circumstances under which I have visited England, into the society of the leading whigs. At dinner at Lord Grey's, I have met Lord Holland, Lord Lauderdale, Lord John Russell, Lord Duncannon, Lord Althorp, Lord Durham, and many men of less note, though all of the same way of thinking. Were it permitted to relate what passes when one is admitted within the doors of a private house, I could amuse you, beyond a question, by repeating the conversation and remarks of men of whom it is matter of interest to learn any thing authentic, but neither of us has been educated in a gossiping school. Still, without violating propriety, I may give you some notions of my distinguished host.

Lord Grey, notwithstanding his years, for he is no longer young, retains much of the lightness and grace of a young man, in his form. He is tall, well-proportioned, and I should think had once been sufficiently athletic, and there is an expression of suavity and kindness in his face, that report had not prepared me to see. He struck me as being as little of an actor in society, as any public man I have ever seen. Simple and well-bred, such a man could hardly escape being, but in Lord Grey's simplicity, there is a nature one does not always meet. He is not exactly as playful as Lord Holland, who seems to be all *bonhomie*, but he sits and smiles at the sallies of those around him, as if he thoroughly enjoyed them. I thought him the man of the most character in his set, though he betrayed it quietly, naturally, and, as it were, as if he could not help it. The tone of his mind and of his deportment was masculine. I find that the English look upon this statesman with a little social awe, but I have now met him several times, and have dined twice with him at his own table, and so far from seeing, or rather *feeling*, any grounds for such a notion, I have been in the company of no distinguished man in Europe, so much my senior, with whom I have felt myself more at ease, or who has appeared to me better to understand the rights of all in a drawing-room. I can safely say that his house is one of the very few in England, in which something has not occurred to make me feel that I was not only a foreigner, but *an American*. Lord Grey expressed no surprise that I spoke English, he spared me explanations of a hundred things that are quite as well understood with us as they are here, manifested liberality of sentiment without parade, and, on all occasions, acted and expressed himself precisely as if he never thought at all of national differences. His company was uniformly good, and as it was generally composed of men of rank, perhaps I fared all the better for the circumstance. *Castes* have a tendency to depress all but the privileged, and the losers are a little apt to betray the "beggar-on-horseback" disposition, when they catch one whom they can patronise or play upon. There was not the least of this about the manner of Lord Grey.

You may be curious to know in what the difference consists between the manner of living in a house like this, of which I am speaking, and in one of our own that corresponds to it, in social position. We have essentially larger and better houses than many of the town residences of the English nobility. Our rooms are, however, too apt to want height and dimension, for where we increase the number of the apartments these people increase the size. Almost every dwelling of any pretensions in London has a stone stair-case, and, although they are not to be compared to those of Paris, (the few great houses here, excepted) they give the arrangements a certain air of solidity and richness. In the other marbles, I think, on the whole, we have the advantage; though regular architects controlling that, which, with us, is too often left to a mere mechanic, I should think violations of taste and propriety do not as often occur in the domestic ornaments of the English, as in our own.

Our old practice of having the reception rooms on the first-floor, and the dining-room below, is very general in London, the only exceptions being in the comparatively few houses whose size admits of rooms *en suite*. Of course the stairs are more in use here than with us. This sadly impairs the effect, for nothing can be worse than to be obliged to climb and descend a long narrow flight of steps, in going to or from the table: I am wrong; it is worse to eat in a room that is afterwards used to receive in.

The English furnish their houses essentially as ours are furnished. French bronzes, clocks, &c., and, indeed, all continental and Chinese ornaments are perhaps less common, but they use much more furniture. The country practice of arranging the furniture, in a prim and starched manner, along the walls, is, I believe, rather peculiar to America, for both in France and England a negligent affluence of ottomans, sofas, divans, screens and tables of all sorts, appears to be the prevailing taste. I was lately in a drawing-room, here, in which I counted no less than fourteen sofas, *causeuses, chaises longues,* and ottomans, scattered about the room, in orderly confusion. The ottoman appears to be almost exclusively English, for it is rarely seen in Paris, whereas a drawing-room is seldom without one in London. I do not remember ever to have met with one in America, at all. In the wood and silks of furniture, I think we rather excel the English, although it is not as usual to find magnificence of this sort, carried out with us, as it is here. Capt. Hall is unquestionably right, when he says our mode of furnishing is naked, compared to that of England, though the little we have is usually as handsome as any thing here.

I have been much struck with the great number and with the excellence of the paintings one sees in the English dwellings, for, in Paris, a good picture is rarely to be found out of the galleries and the palaces. I should think Rome, alone, can surpass London in this particular.

The offices of the London residences are much more extensive than with us, for, besides occupying a substratum of the house itself, they quite often extend into the yard, where they are covered with a large skylight. I am inclined to think the lodging rooms, generally, not as good as ours. The English get along with moderately-sized town-houses, all the better perhaps from their habits, for the young men quit the paternal roof early, it being usual to put them on allowances, and to let them go at large.

I have heard extraordinary things concerning the distance that is maintained between friends in England, and the *ménagement* that is necessary in conducting intercourse even between the members of the same family. One who ought to know from his official position, a foreigner in charge of a diplomatic mission, has assured me a son cannot presume to go unceremoniously and dine with a father, but that invitations are always necessary, and that the forms of society are rigidly observed between the nearest connexions. There is a secondary and an imitative class, (in England it is very numerous) of whom I can believe any absurdity of this nature, for they caricature usages, breeding, forms, and even principles. These are the people who talk about eating cheese, and drinking beer and port, and lay stress on things insignificant in themselves, as if manners, and taste, and elegance were not far more violated in their fussy pretensions, than they would be in emptying one of Barclay's big butts. In other words, this is the silver-fork school, of whom one has heard a good deal in America, the gentry who come among us, in common, having little other claims to a knowledge of the world than that they have thus obtained at second hand, as the traditions of fashion, or perhaps in the pages of a novel.

I do not say that among the crowd of genteel vulgar that throng the capital of a great empire like this, a pretty numerous array of silly pretenders of this description may not be made, but it will not do to receive these people as the head of society, or, indeed, as a very material portion of it. As a rule, I certainly think mere drill passes for more in London than in most other capitals. This arises, in part, from the manner in which the whole nation is drilled, each in his station, from the valet to the master; but, in a social sense, chiefly, I think, because the same arbitrary distinctions do not prevail in England as elsewhere in Europe, nobility being, in most other countries, an indispensable requisite for admission into the great world. Certainly, as between Paris and London, the advantage in this particular is in favour of the former, where good sense, at all times, appears to regulate good breeding; but, notwithstanding, I am far from attributing to the English all the follies of this nature that it is the fashion to impute to them.

Nothing can have been more simple and unaffected than the intercourse between father and son, that I have witnessed here. It would be improper for a son, having a separate establishment, to come at unseasonable hours to the house of any father, who is in the habit of receiving much, for it might occasion an awkward inconvenience; and if one is bound to treat ordinary friends with this respect, still more so is he bound to manifest the same deference to his own parents.

I have been amused in tracing the many points of resemblance that are to be found between our own manners and those of the English. I should say the off-hand and familiar way in which the seniors of a family address the juniors, is one. Dining the other day with Lord S[pencer], who has filled high ministerial appointments, when the ladies had retired, he said to his eldest son, a man older than I am, and a leading member of parliament, "Jack, ring the bell."* I will not say that this is precisely American simplicity, but it is the way your father and mine would have been very apt to speak, under the same circumstances, and I think it is a manner which belongs to all that portion of our people who really come of the Middle States.

Seated at a table like Lord Grey's, with the company I met there, I have been led to look around me, in quest of the points of difference, by which I could have known that I was not at home. Putting the conversation aside, for that necessarily was English as ours would have been American, it would not have been easy to point out any very broad distinctions. The dining-room was very much like one of our own, in a good house. There was a side-board which stood in a recess, with columns near it. The furniture was a little plainer than it might be with us, for an eating-room in Europe is seldom used for any other purpose. The form and arrangements of the table were very like, with a slight difference in the width of the table itself, ours, in the narrow cramped houses it is now so much the fashion to build, usually wanting width. We dined off of plate, a thing so rarely done in America as to form a substantial difference. The foot-men were powdered and in showy liveries, and the butler was in black. The latter might still be seen at home, but three or four footmen in livery, in the same house, I have never witnessed but once. But remove the cloth, and send the servants away, and I think any one might have been deceived. As the party around this table was composed of men of high rank, and still higher personal consideration, it would be unfair to compare them with the wine-discussing, trade-talking, dollar-dollar set that has made an in-road upon society in our commercial towns, not half of whom are educated, or indeed Americans; but I speak of a class vastly supe-

---

*Jack was shortly after made Chancellor of the Exchequer.

rior, which you know, and which, innovated on as it is by the social Vandals of the times, still clings to its habits and retains much of its ancient simplicity and respectability. Between these men, and those I have met at the table of Lord Grey, and at one or two other houses, here, I confess I have been almost at a loss to detect any other points of difference, than those which belong to personal individuality.

In the phrases, the intonation of the voice, the use and pronunciation of the words, it was not easy to detect any points of difference, although I have watched attentively, for a whole evening. The manner of speaking is identically the same as our own, (I speak now of the gentlemen of the Middle States) direct, simple and abbreviated. There is none of the pedantry of "I can not," for "I can't," "I do not," for "I don't," and all those school-boy and boarding-school affectations, by which a parade is made of one's orthography. These are precisely our own good old New York forms of speech, and, knowing the associations and extraction of those who formed the school, I have always suspected it was the best in the country. I do not mean, however, to exclude from it the same classes in all the other Middle States, and that portion of those in the Southern who live much in the towns. Communion with the world is absolutely necessary to prevent prig-ism, for one insensibly inclines to books in a solitude, getting to be critical and fastidious about things that are better decided by usage than by reason.

The simple and quiet manner of addressing each other that prevails here, helps to complete the resemblance. The term "my Lord," is scarcely ever uttered. I do not think that I have heard it used by gentlemen, six times since I have been in London, though the servants and all of the inferior classes never neglect it. I should say the term "my lady," is absolutely proscribed in society. I have heard it but three times, since I have been in Europe, although one scarcely sees less of the titled English in Paris, than in London. These three cases are worth remembering, since they mark three different degrees of manners. It was used, or rather the phrase "your ladyship" was used by Sir [Henry Halford], a physician, who evidently wanted the tone of one accustomed to associate with equals. It was used by Mrs. _____, an American (we are a little apt to be *ultra* in such things) at Paris, and I saw a daughter of "my lady" turn her head to conceal a smile. Thirdly, and lastly, it was used by Sir _____ _____, a dashing young baronet, to Lady _____ _____, in a sort of playful emphasis, as we should dwell on official appellations, in grave and sounding pleasantry.

Of course, there is more or less of fashion in all this; nor should I be surprised, ten years hence, to find it indispensable to breeding, to be punctilious the other way; so much depends on the mode of doing these things, that any custom of this nature can be brought into vogue, or be condemned. Still, there is so much inherent good taste in simplicity, that, I think, no very laboured exhibitions of the sort, can ever long maintain themselves.

One seldom repeats the terms "your Majesty," and "Royal Highness," in ordinary conversations with sovereigns and princes, any more than one is always saying "your Excellency" and "your Honour" in talking with the Governor and Lieutenant-Governor of Massachusetts; the only two functionaries in America, I believe, who have legal styles of address. In France it is usual to say "*sire,*" "*oui sire,*" and "*non sire;*" but, here, I am told, for I never have had any personal communication with an English prince, it is the practice to say, "sir." The English have rather an affectation of saying that "one uses 'sir,' only to the king and to servants." This word is much less used by the English than with us, as it is much less used by people of the world in America, than by those who, either from living retired, or from not having access to society, are not people of the world. It is, however, a good word, and can be thrown in, occasionally, into American conversation with singular grace and point, though, like other good things it may be overdone. The coxcomb who refrains altogether from using it, with us, in deference to the cockney pandects of the Brummel school, shows neither "blood nor bottom."

I can remember when our old staid ladies used to address the servants as "sir;" but then a servant, being a negro, had something respectable and genteel about him, for it was before he had lost both by too much intercourse with the European peasants who are superceding him. One might indeed say "sirrah," to the new set, but "sir" would be apt to stick in his throat. The philosophy of the practice is obvious enough. In the mouth of one who uses this little word understandingly, it marks distance mingled with respect: used to a superior, the respect is for him; used to an inferior, the respect is for one's self.

It has been cleverly and wittily said that, in America, we have a tolerably numerous class, who deem "nothing too high to be aspired to, and nothing too low to be done." In making my comparisons with any thing and every thing on this side of the Atlantic, I keep these pliant persons entirely out of view. They can be justly compared to nothing else in human annals. They are the monstrous offspring of peculiar circumstances, and owe their existence to an unparalleled freedom of exertion, acting on the maxims of a government that is better understood in practice than in theory, and, which, among its thousand advantages, is obnoxious to the charge of giving birth to a species of gentry perfectly *sui generis*. I compare the gentlemen of no country to these philosophers.

On the continent of Europe, it is rather a distinction to be undecorated in society. Stars and ribbands are really so very common, that one gets to be glad to see a fine coat without them. As mere matters of show, they are but indifferent appendages of dress, unless belonging to the highest class of such ornaments, when indeed their characters change; for there is always something respectable in diamonds. Here it is quite the reverse. You probably may not know that birth, of itself, entitles no one to wear a decoration.* A king, as king, wears his crown and royal robes, but he wears no star, or ribband, or collar. A peer has his coronet, and his robes as a peer, but nothing else. The star and ribband are deemed the peculiar badges of orders of chivalry, and they vary according to the institution. The ribband is worn across the breast, like a sword belt, though usually it is placed under the coat. It is broad, and blue appears to be the honourable colour. At least the "blue ribband," and the "*cordon bleu*," are in most request in France and England, belonging to the orders of the Garter and of the Holy Ghost. The *Légion d'Honneur* and the Bath both use red ribbands. There are gorgeous collars and mantles to all the orders,

---

*"Decoration" is the proper word, I believe, for the badges of an order; the French, however, frequently term them *crachats*, or *le crachat du roi*, the king's spittle!

for occasions of ceremony, but in society one seldom sees more than the ribband and the star, and not often the former. The garter at the knee is sometimes used also.

Lord Grey has no decoration; neither has Lord Lansdowne, nor Lord Holland. Lord Lauderdale, the day I dined in his company in Berkeley Square, wore a star, being a knight of the Thistle; Lord Spencer wore that of the Garter. These two are almost the only instances in which I have seen Englishmen in society, appearing with decorations, in London, though I have frequently seen them in Paris. The difference, in this respect, is striking on coming from the continent. The ribband at the button-hole is very rarely, if ever, used here; the star, of course, only when dressed for dinners and evening entertainments, or on state occasions. It was formerly the practice, I believe, to appear in parliament with stars, but it is now very rarely done.

I tell you these things, since, as they do exist, it may be well enough to have some tolerably distinct notions as to the manner. With the exception of the Bath, the orders of this country are commonly conferred on personal favourites, or are the price of political friendships. There appear to be orders that are pretty exclusively confined to men of ancient and illustrious families, while others, again, have the profession of distinguishing merit. In England, the Garter, the Thistle, and St. Patrick's, belong to the former class, and the Bath to the latter. You will, at once, imagine that the last stands highest in the public estimation, and that it is far more honourable to be a knight of the Bath, than to be a knight of the Garter. This would be the case were reason stronger than prejudice, but as it is not, I leave you to infer which has the advantage.

I had a little aside with one of the guests at Lord Grey's, in the course of the evening, on the subject of the characters of the reigning family. It is true my informant was a whig, and the whigs look upon George IV. as a recreant from their principles; but this gentleman I know to be one worthy of credit, and singularly moderate, or I should not repeat his opinions.

Speaking of the king, he described him as a man more than commonly destitute of good faith. A sovereign must be of a singularly upright mind, not to be guilty of more or less duplicity, and of this my acquaintance seemed perfectly aware; but George IV., he thought, lent himself with more than common aptitude to this part of the royal *rôle*. He mentioned an anecdote as illustrative of the treachery of his character.

Some forty years since, the debts of the Prince of Wales became so pressing as to render an application to parliament necessary for relief. By way of obtaining the desired end, it was promised that "like Falstaff" he would "repent, and that suddenly," and take himself a wife, to insure an heir to the throne. There was a report, however, that he was already privately married to Mrs. Fitz-Herbert. Although such a marriage was civilly illegal, by the laws of the kingdom, many well meaning, and all right-thinking people believed it to be binding in a moral and religious point of view, and as parliament was not absolutely destitute of such men, it became necessary to pacify their scruples. With this view Mr. Fox is said to have demanded authority of the Prince to contradict the rumour, if it might be done with truth. This authority he is understood to have received in the fullest terms, and it is certain Mr. Fox pledged himself to that effect, in his place in the house. After all, it is now confidently affirmed, the Prince was actually married to Mrs. Fitz-Herbert, and I was told Mr. Fox never forgave the gross act of duplicity by which he had been made a dupe.

The Duke of York was spoken of, as a well meaning and an honest man, but as one scarcely on a level with the ordinary scale of human intellect. Neither he nor his brother, however, had any proper knowledge of *meum* and *tuum*, a fault that was probably as much owing to the flatterers that surrounded them, and to defective educations, as to natural tendencies.

My informant added, that, George III. and the Duke of York excepted, all the men of the family possessed a faculty of expressing their thoughts, that was quite out of keeping with the value of the thoughts themselves. The Duke of Kent he said formed an exception to the latter part of the rule, being clever; as, though in a less degree, was the Duke of Sussex. Having so good a source of information, I was curious to know how far the vulgar rumours which we had heard of the classical attainments of the present king were to be relied on. To this question my companion answered pithily, "he may be able to write good Latin, but he cannot write intelligible English." I have seen a letter or two, myself, which sufficiently corroborate the latter opinion, for if one were to search for rare specimens of the rigmarole, he might be satisfied with these. George III. did little better.

As the conversation naturally turned on the tendency to adulation and flattery in a court, and their blighting influence on the moral qualities of both parties, my companion related an instance so much in point, that it is worth repeating. A Scotch officer, of no very extraordinary merit, but who had risen to high employments by personal assiduity and the arts of a courtier, was in the presence of George III., at Windsor, in company with one or two others, at a moment when ceremony was banished. That simple-minded and well-meaning monarch was a little apt to admit of tangents in the discourse, and he suddenly exclaimed "D_____, it appears to me that you and I are just of a height—let's measure, let's measure." The general placed his back to that of the king, but instead of submitting to the process of measurement, he kept moving his head in a way to prevent it. Another tangent drew the king off, and he left the room. "Why didn't you stand still, and let him measure, D_____," asked a looker-on. "You kept bobbing your head so, he could do nothing." "Well, I did'n't know whether he wanted to be taller, or shorter."

George III. has got great credit, in America, for his celebrated speech to Mr. Adams, whom he told "that he had been the last man in his kingdom to consent to the independence of America, and he should be the last man to call it in question, now it was admitted." If he ever made such a declaration, it was a truly regal speech, and of a character with those that are often made by sovereigns, who, if wanting in tact themselves, draw on those around them for a supply. It is now generally understood that the answer of Charles X., when he appeared at the gates of Paris in 1814, as Lieutenant-General of the kingdom, where he is made to say, "that nothing is changed, except in the presence of another Frenchman," was invented for him, by a clever subordinate, at the suggestion of M. de Talleyrand.* The dying speech of Desaix, was put into his mouth by the First Consul, in his despatches I believe, for the Duc de [Valmy], who stood at his side when he

---

Je la revois enfin, et rien n'y est changé, si ce n'est qu'il s'y trouve un Français de plus.

fell, assured me that the ball passed through his head, and that he died without uttering a syllable.

"Is not the truth, the truth?"

It would seem not.

Letter X.

To William Jay, Esq., Bedford, N. Y.

I remember that some five and twenty years ago, you and I had a discussion on the supposed comparative merits of parliament and congress, considering both strictly as legislative bodies. I say supposed, for it was pretty much supposition, since you had never been out of your own country, and although I had actually been twice in England, and even in London at that time, it was at an age so young, and under circumstances so little favourable to obtaining the knowledge necessary to such a subject, that I was no better off than yourself, as to facts. It is true we had both read speeches attributed to Lord Chatham and Mr. Burke, and Fox and Pitt, and sundry other orators, and which were written by Dr. Johnson and his successors in the grinding line, but this was a very different thing from having looked, and listened, and judged for oneself. In short, we did, what most young men of our age would probably have done, under the same circumstances; we uttered valueless opinions in an oracular manner, convincing no one but ourselves, and positively edifying nobody.

I thought of this discussion, which was longer even than a speech in congress, occupying no small portion of the Christmas holidays in the country, as I first put foot in the room in which were assembled the Commons of England.

I went down to St. Stephen's about six o'clock, and, passing through divers intricate ways, I finally reached a place where a man stood in a sort of box, like the box-office keeper in a theatre, with the difference that the retailer of places in the gallery of the House of Commons carried on his business in an open and manly manner, there being no necessity for peeping through a hole to get a sight of his face. I am not quite certain that this is not the only thing connected with parliament, that is not more or less mystified.

Having paid my half crown, I was permitted to go at large in a small room with a high ceiling. Out of this room ascended some flights of narrow steps, mounting which, I reached a narrow lobby, that communicated by two doors in front with the gallery of the House, and by two doors at its ends, with little pent-up rooms, which I afterwards found answered as a sort of reporters' guard rooms. There was also a little door in front, between the two principal entrances, by which the reporters alone went in and out of the gallery.

I found the chapel badly lighted, at least so it seemed from above. There might have been fifty or sixty members present, more than half of whom belonged to the ministerial side of the house, and not a few of whom were coming and going pretty assiduously between Bellamy's and their seats. Bellamy's is the name of the legislative coffee-house, and it is in the building.

The speaker sat buried in a high chair, a sort of open pulpit, under a canopy, with an enormous wig covering his head and shoulders. He looked, by the dim light, like a feeble attenuated old man, or old woman, for really it was not easy to say which; but his "*order*, ORDER," was uttered in a potent bass voice, and in a sort of octave manner, that I have attempted to describe in writing. Whether this ominous mode of calling to order was peculiar to the office, or to the man, I cannot tell you, but quite likely the former, for there is an hereditary deference for such a thing here, as well as for a wig.

The members sat with their hats on, but the speaker was uncovered, if a man can be said to be uncovered who is buried in tow. They sit on benches with backs of the ordinary height, and I counted six members with one foot on the backs of the benches before them, and three with both feet. The latter were very interesting attitudes, a good deal resembling those which your country buck is apt to take in an American bar-room, and which I have seen in a church. I do not mention these trifles to draw any great moral, or political consequences from them, but simply because similar things have been commented on in connection with congress, and ascribed to democracy. I am of opinion political systems have little to do with these *tours de forces*, but that there is rather a tendency in the Anglo-Saxon race to put the heels higher than the head.

Behind the speaker's chair, two members were stretched at full length, asleep. I presume the benches they occupied were softer

than common, for two or three others seemed anxiously watching
the blissful moment of their waking, with an evident intention to
succeed them. One did arise, and a successor was in his place in
less than a minute. That I may dispose of this part of the subject,
once for all, I will add that, during the evening, three young
men came into the side gallery within fifteen feet of me, and
stretched themselves on the benches, where they were not visible
to those in the body of the house. Two were disposed to sleep,
rationally, but one of them kept pulling their coats and legs in a
way to render it no easy matter, when all three retired together
laughing, as if it were a bad job. I should think neither of the
three was five and twenty.

I have now given you an exact account of the antics of the
House of Commons on my first visit, and as I made a note of them
on the spot, or rather in the lobby, to which we were driven once,
in the course of the evening; and shall merely add that, so far
as my experience goes, and it extends to a great many subsequent visits, they rather characterize its meetings. I leave you
to say whether they render the legislature of England any worse
or any better, though, for my own part, I think it a matter of
perfect moonshine. The only times when I have seen this body in
more regulated attitudes, have been occasions when the house
was so crowded as to compel the members to keep their legs to
themselves.

As respects the cries, so much spoken of, some of them are droll
enough. Of the "Hear, hear, hear," I shall say nothing, unless it be
to tell you that they are so modulated as to express different
emotions. There is a member or two, just now, that are rather
expert in crowing like a cock, and I have known an attempt to
bleat like a lamb, but I think it was a failure. I was quite unpre-
pared for one species of interruption, which is a new invention,
and seems likely to carry all before it, for a time. Something that
was said excited a most pronounced dissatisfaction among the
whigs, and they set up a noise that was laughably like the qua-a-
cking of a flock of ducks. For some time I did not know what to
make of it—then I thought the cry was "Bar, bar, bar," and fancied
that they wished a delinquent to be put at their bar; but I believe,
after all, it was no more than the introduction of the common

French interjection "bah!" which signifies dissent. The word is so sonorous, that twenty or thirty men can make a very pretty uproar, by a diligent use of it.

You will ask what the speaker says to these interruptions? He says "*order,* ORDER,"—and there the matter ends. I shall say nothing against these practices, for I do not believe they essentially affect the interests of the country, and, as Fuseli used to tell his wife, when she got in a pet—"*Schwear,* my dear—do; *schwear* a little, it will do you good," it may be a relief to a man to break out occasionally in these vocal expressions of feeling, especially to those who cannot, very conveniently to themselves, say any thing else.

No business of importance was done the night I paid my first visit, although some discussion took place on one or two financial points. Lord Althorp spoke for a few minutes, and in a manner so hesitating and painful, that I was surprised at the respectful attention of the House. But I was told he has its ear, from the circumstance of its having faith in his intentions, and from a conviction that, although he has hard work to get at it, he has really a fund of useful and precise information. He is one of the most laboured and perplexed speakers I have ever heard attempt to address a deliberative body. Mr. Peel said a few words in reply, sufficient to give me an idea of his manner, though I have since frequently heard him on more important occasions.

The voice of Mr. Peel is pleasant and well modulated; he speaks with facility, though in a slightly formal manner, and with a measured accentuation that sometimes betrays him into false prosody, a fault that is very common with all but the gifted few, in elocution. He called "opinion," for instance, this evening, "*o*-pinion," and "occasion" "*o*-casion." If there were a word between persuasive and coaxing, I should select it as the one that best describes the manner of Mr. Peel. The latter would do him great injustice, as it wants his dignity, and argument, and force; and the former would, I think, do injustice to truth, as there is too evident an effort to insinuate himself into the good opinion of the listener, to render it quite applicable. One rather resists than yields to a persuasion so very obvious. It strikes me his manner savours more of *New* than of *Old* England, and I consider it a tribute to his reasoning powers and knowledge, that he is listened to with so much respect, for whatever may be the political and religious mystifications of the English, (and it would not be easy to surpass either), there is a homely honesty in the public mind, that greatly indisposes it to receive *visible* management with favour.

The voice of Mr. Peel is not unlike that of Mr. Wirt, though not as melodious, while his elocution is less perfect, and he has not the same sincerity. Still I know no American speaker to whom he can so well be compared. There is something about him between our eastern and southern modes of speaking. Some of his soft sounds, those of the *u* for instance, were exaggerated, like those of one who had studied Walker instead of obtaining his pronunciation in the usual way, while others, again, came out naturally, and were rather startling to a nice ear.

Sir Francis Burdett spoke, for a few minutes, in the course of the evening. By the way, the English do not pronounce this name Bur*dett*, but *Bur*dit. He is tall and thin, more than ultra in height as in opinions, with a singularly long neck. In personal appearance, though rather handsome than otherwise, he is almost as much out of the common way as John Randolph of Roanoke. He had much less fluency and parliamentary neatness than I should have expected in one of so much practice, though he was quite self-possessed. I do not know whether you ever heard our old friend, Mr. James Morris of Morrisania, speak in public, but if you have, you will at once get an idea of the manner of Sir Francis Burdett. They have the same gentlemanlike deliberation—the same quiet, measured utterance—the same good drawing-room, or dinner-table tone, and a similarity in voice and enunciation that to me was quite startling.

Sir Francis Burdett, whose name once filled all mouths in England, no longer attracts much political attention. He probably struck his first notes on too high a key, not to fall into an octave below, before the air was finished. Your true and lasting melody steals slowly on the ear, commencing with more modulated strains, and rising gradually with the feelings that the sounds awaken. Luther, who has left a steadily increasing impression on the world, would probably have shrunk with horror, at first, from the degree of reformation to which he finally arrived by slower and more certain means. It may also be questioned if Sir Francis Burdett had a mind sufficiently original, or a reason logical enough, either to conceive or to maintain the reform that England needs, and, sooner or later, will have, or take revolution in its stead.

Mr. Hume had something to say, too, during that portion of the debate which referred to some of the minor expenses of the government. He was respectfully heard, and had a business-like and matter-of-fact manner, that was adapted to catch the attention of those who wished for practical details. He seemed earnest and honest, and has as little of the demagogue in externals, as any man in the house; far less than Mr. Peel, who sat on the treasury bench. He has not the smallest pretension to eloquence, but speaks like a man who is indifferent to every thing but his facts, with which he seems to have made himself sufficiently acquainted by plodding investigation. A course like this may certainly be over-done, but in such a government it may also be eminently useful. There is a Scottish industry and perseverance about this member that are respectable, while they are not without amusement to the observer of personal and national traits.

When the principal business of the night was disposed of, there came up a question that was admirably suited to draw out the true and prevailing character of the British parliament. It was a law relating to the servants of the country, and one which, of course, affected the interests and comforts of all who kept them. The legislature of this country controls the mightiest interests, it is true, but it is under the direction of a very few minds, the *oi polloi* of the two houses merely echoing the sentiments of their leaders, in all such matters; but, when a question arises touching the pantry, or the chase, or the preserves, a chord is struck that vibrates through the legislative multitude, coming home to the knowledge and practice of every man who has a seat. Accordingly, this question called up a set of orators who are usually content to be silent.

I am far from undervaluing the importance of a sound and vigorous legislation on the subject of servants, for they stand in a very peculiar relation to their masters, and it would be well for all parties if we had rules of the sort among ourselves. But there was something ludicrous in seeing this important body gravely occupied in discussing this minute feature in domestic economy, and that, too, with an earnestness and zeal that had slumbered while the debate concerning taxation lasted. One or two country members stammered through speeches of great nicety and erudition, and one man was carried away by such an ecstacy of admiration at the improvements of the country, that he boldly affirmed one might now travel through England and find silver forks and napkins in every inn! By the way, if this be true, I have missed my road, for I saw nothing of the sort between Dover and London. Another speaker was clearly a little "how come you so," but this is by no means unusual in parliament, the papers having made five or six allusions to such scenes since I arrived here. I have twice witnessed these exhibitions. I believe they have been also seen in congress, in the night sessions;. the Anglo-Saxon race having a propensity to lower the head as well as to raise the heels.

It would be unfair to cite this sitting as a specimen of what the House of Commons is, in its better moments, though I feel persuaded that the latter instances are the exceptions, while something very like what I have here told you, makes the rule. I do not believe that the average speaking of parliament is any better than that of the state legislature of New York; though I beg you to understand that I am not about to abuse my opportunities to renew the old discussion to your manifest disadvantage. In making comparisons of this nature, it is usual to overlook several important and qualifying circumstances. The American legislative bodies are strictly the representatives of the nation, or of certain geographical sections of the nation. In tone, intelligence, deportment and education, they are but a little above the average of their countrymen; if a small class, that comprehends the very debased and vicious, be excluded, possibly not at all. Parliament represents exclusively not only the rich, in the main, but the landed interest, and is composed, almost entirely, of men taken from the higher classes. Some of the consequences which one would naturally expect from such causes are certainly discoverable. The English of parliament, though far from faultless, is, on the whole, materially better than that of congress. It could hardly be otherwise, with the respective elements of the bodies we are comparing, and when we recollect, moreover, the manner in which population is compressed in England, and how much it is diffused in America. It is the friction of constant intercourse which gives its polish to society, and nothing could save us from downright rusticity but the activity of a circulation that is out of all the ordinary proportions of social communion. It may be too much to say that this active and altogether peculiar blending of persons is *polishing* America, but it is *chiselling* the whole surface of society down to a smoothness that destroys marked inequalities.

The House of Commons contains more than six hundred and forty members,* whereas the House of Representatives contains but about two hundred and twenty. Now a simple proposition in the rule of three, will demonstrate that the former ought to possess nearly three times as many good speakers as the latter, in order to be relatively on a level with it. I greatly question if it has as many, numerically speaking, alone. I believe that one hundred men can be found in congress, who would, on an emergency, make much better extemporaneous speeches, than one hundred of the best speakers in the House of Commons. As between the House of Lords and the Senate, when the relative numbers are considered, there is no comparison.

There is, however, another side to this question, that must not be overlooked. A large proportion of the English Commons are laymen, whereas a majority of Congress, perhaps, belong to a profession in which the art of debating, or something very near it, is cultivated as the means of subsistence. They lay great stress here on these distinctions, as an anecdote that I will relate may give you to understand.

The tories have recently made a great acquisition to their ranks, by the entrance of a Mr. Sadler into parliament. He has just delivered a speech that has made some noise, and which, if not literally so, is deemed to be maiden, in reference to its importance. Walking up St. James's street the day after Mr. Sadler spoke, I met Lord _____, a whig member of the House of Commons. He asked me if I had been in the house the previous night, and then alluded to the effort of Mr. Sadler. "The tories are making a great noise about him," said Lord _____, "but we have found out that he is a *lawyer!* Every one thought, at first, he was a *country gentleman*, but, lo and behold! he turns out to be a lawyer!" It was not so easy, at first, to understand the connexion between the merits or demerits of Mr. Sadler's speech and his profession, but a little further conversation gave me the clue. In a social organization as factitious as this, things get to be estimated by their relations to

*1828.

the different phases of society. Success is *quo ad hoc*. If a duke were to exhibit a picture, though no great thing of itself, thousands would rush to see it, as a good thing for a duke. This spirit is particularly observable in literature; a book written by a lord selling almost as a matter of course, for his inferiors love to live, even in the equivocal familiarity of thinking, in communion with a nobleman. Byron owes no small portion of his popularity to his rank, for the better portions of his works are by no means suited to the common English tastes.

While one smiles at these distinctions, it must not be forgotten that they come fairly into the account in comparing the oratory of parliament and congress. If we urge on one side that the same conventional deportment and purity of pronunciation are not to be expected in an American as in an English legislature, because one represents an entire community and the other an *élite*, we cannot refuse the plea that their system excludes a set of men trained to public speaking, while ours freely admits them. In brief, the question properly divides itself between the fact and its reasons. The fact, I believe, to be as already stated, and I think that some of the strongest qualifying circumstances on both sides, have here been enumerated.

You will be curious to know what may be the effect of the cheering and coughing system; or, perhaps it were better now to term it the *bah-ing* system. There can be no doubt that such practices open the door to abuses of a more serious character than those which arise from the liberty of talking by the day. One puts it in the power of a majority to stifle reason and suppress facts, while the other merely exhausts patience and consumes time. Now time is of much less importance to congress than to parliament, since the powers of the former extend only to certain great interests, while the latter, as I have just shown you, legislates even about the servants of the country.

It would be a great saving of time, and a great furtherance of justice, if there were established a tribunal at Washington, to sit constantly, whose sole business it should be to decide on private claims against the government. An appeal might lie to Congress, on the part of a public advocate appointed to protect the public interests, or it might even be expedient to sanction all the decisions by enactments, but, in nineteen cases in twenty, I think, the two houses would take the reports of the tribunal as conclusive. The auditors, it is true, form some such judicial officers now, but the tribunal I mean would take cognizance of all the claims that at present go before Congress, and might be contested, if improper, by a law officer. We shall have such a court, in time, but not till we think less as Englishmen and more as Americans.

We are too apt to consider parliament and congress as bodies of similar powers, and, consequently, as recognising the same general legislative maxims. This error has led to some of the most serious evils to which our experience has given birth, and which, by insensible means, unless corrected in time, will sooner or later lead to a perversion of the governing principles of our own government.

Whatever may have been the ancient dogmas of the British constitution, parliament is now absolute. It is true that the executive, in theory, forms an integral part of parliament, but by gradual and constant encroachments on the authority of the crown, the ministers have become the creatures of parliament whenever the latter sees fit to assert its authority, although a majority of the latter is apt to be the creatures of ministers, in another and a more limited sense. The members are bought, it will be remembered, however, because they possess the power, and he who traffics away his authority, in this mode, does not part with it entirely, but is merely turning it to his personal account. The only power in England that can resist parliament, is the body of the nation. As this is an extra-legal force, forming no part of the system, it is to be found everywhere, and is only more available in England than in Turkey, because the nation is more enlightened. It is in truth the only elementary check which exists on the action of the omnipotence of parliament, all the others extending no further than they can go by intrigue and management. This practical feature in her government, gives England some sort of claim to be considered a republic. Congress is composed of *attornies in fact*, for not only are its powers expressly limited, but such is the nature of the trusts, that any attempt to exceed them is a direct assault on the omnipotence of the constituency. With us the executive is as much representative as the legislature, the trustee of the power being a direct emanation of the popular will. To attempt to control him, then, in the exercise of his constitutional authority, is for an attorney named for one specific trust to attempt to discharge the duties committed to another, named for quite a different, and for an equally specific trust.

These are the general features of difference, which of themselves are sufficient to give birth to very different legislative maxims, and which *would* give birth to them, were not traditions, more efficacious, in such matters, than principles. But there are many minor points that frequently agitate us, and which are commonly settled on English principles, that are closely connected with a due consideration of the discrepancies between the two polities. I will illustrate my meaning, by an example.

The right of petition is justly esteemed an important English right, whereas with us, it may be made the instrument of doing infinite harm, while I question if a single case of its exclusive and particular usefulness, could be cited.

In England, the right of petition is the only regular mode by which the body of the nation can at all enter into the councils of the nation. Apart from the fact that the constituencies are arbitrarily wielded as mere political machinery, a vast majority of the English have not even this indirect, and inefficient control over the choice of their legislators. One body is hereditary, and the other is chosen by a striking minority, even in theory; and, in fact, by the influence of the aristocracy. Under such a system the right of petition is doubly useful, for while it serves as a lever for the mass, it also serves as a beacon to their rulers. A moderate and timely application of this force may prevent an exercise of it that would overturn the state.

The right to petition Congress existed entirely as a traditionary right, until the constitution was amended. Certainly any man, or any set of men could petition, as much as they pleased, but the question now in consideration is whether there exists any governing and important principle that would render it incumbent on Congress to receive and consider their requests, had not Mr. Jefferson introduced his amendment. As the people are directly, fully and always recently, represented in Congress, there exists no plea on the score of the necessity of adopting this mode of being heard, as in England. Under such a system there is no danger of laws being passed, as in England, to prevent county meetings being called without the sanction of an officer of the government;

and the people, if they wish it, have always the expedient of
assembling when, where and how they please, to make their sentiments known. Congress has no power to pass any such a law at
all. Parliament may curb the press, but Congress is absolutely
impotent on this point. It was impotent, before the amendment
existed, for all these provisions were supererogatory. The tendency of a government like ours, is to the doctrines of pledges and
instruction, (neither of which is tenable as a whole, though true in
part) and it would seem that they who claim a right to *instruct* can
have little need to *petition*. But the objects of a petition can be
better obtained by another mode of proceeding. If the people
assemble in primary meetings, and put the subject of the petition
into the form of a printed memorial, and cause their names to be
published, such a document would be more likely to effect its
object, because it would be more authentic than the old method.
It would be in the way of being read, so as to be understood, a fate
which befals few petitions, and names could not be surreptitiously
annexed without exposure, as is constantly practised with petitions.

All this will probably appear very much like heterodoxy, and
yet I think it all quite true. The subject might easily be extended
to many other practices. You may feel disposed to ask, why Mr.
Jefferson, a lover of independence, so far overlooked these distinctions as to obtain an insertion of a clause in the constitution, by way of amendment, securing the right of petition to the
people. No man is omniscient; and Mr. Jefferson, having been
educated under the monarchy, deferred more to its maxims, than
would have been the case, had he lived later. But General Lafayette has explained to me the reason why several of the supererogatory clauses were introduced, in 1801. Mr. Jefferson was
in Europe when the constitution was formed. This instrument
was a subject of great interest to the liberals of this part of the
world, who know little of the substratum of freedom which exists
with us, in the state governments. It was an awkward thing to
explain that Congress possessed no powers that were not expressly
ceded, when he was asked where were our guarantees for liberty
of conscience, and of the press, and for this right of petition,
which, in Europe, where the people cannot assemble without permission half the time, and are not directly represented, is justly

deemed a right of the last importance. Under the feeling created by the constant inquiries that he heard on these points, Mr. Jefferson got the amendments, mentioned, introduced. At least, such is the history of the transaction that I have received from General Lafayette.

In ninety-nine cases in a hundred, petitions lead to no greater injury, with us, than to a waste of time. Indeed, they are getting to be rather unusual, the public feeling them to be unnecesary. It resorts to a higher power, being the master. But petitions may work peculiar evil, under a system like ours. If recognised as a right, it is a mode of entering Congress with vexed questions, over which Congress may have but a doubtful, or no proper control, and disturb, uselessly, the harmony of its councils. A single member may do this, also, it is true, but with less influence, and consequently with less injury. Petitions are a sort of semi-official consultation, and, besides letting the wishes of the whole, or of a part of the people be known, which can be, at least, as well effected by other means, they insidiously work their way into the debates, and enlist the passions, prematurely, on subjects that may require great forbearance to be disposed of wisely and with safety. It should always be remembered, among other things, that instead of dealing with citizens, our government is often called on to deal with states. There is so strong a bias in men of reading to take warning from history, under the just persuasion, that human nature continues inherently the same, throughout all time, that they too frequently neglect to ascertain whether the facts are identical, in preaching their favourite doctrine, that "like causes produce like effects."

Of course I now speak of petitions for political and general objects, and not of those introduced to obtain private favours. The word itself is unsuited to our form of government, and even in private cases, would be worthily displaced, by substituting "Memorial."

Letter XI.

To James E. De Kay, Esq.

I was passing through Pall Mall, shortly after the town became so crowded, when I saw a mermaid combing her hair before a small mirror, as the crest on a chariot that stood at a door, and I at once thought I recognised the arms of Sir Walter Scott. On examining nearer, I found the bloody hand, which left no doubt that the literary baronet was in town.

Among the persons whom a mistaken opinion that I was the son of [Thomas Cooper], had brought to my door, was Sir G[eorge] P[hilips], a member of parliament, and a strong whig. This gentleman had the good nature not to drop me, when he found his error, but he proffered many civilities, which were commenced by an invitation to dinner.

I do not remember to have seen a house with exactly the same *entourage*, as that of Sir G[eorge] P[hilips]'s. I had the street and number of course, but when I got near the place, I found nothing but shops, or dwellings of an appearance that did not indicate the residence of an affluent baronet. At the precise number, however, I found such a door as one might have expected to meet; and nothing but a door. It had pilasters, fan lights, a neat entrance, and a massive knocker, with two powdered and liveried footmen in waiting. Of course I gave the magical raps, the "open sesame" of London, and was forthwith admitted. "Pray, sir, does Sir G[eorge] P[hilips], live here?" The answer was satisfactory, though *how* he lived was to me still a matter of wonder. An inner door was opened, and a long and wide passage lay before me. At the end of this, we found the apartments of the family, which appeared to be ample, and suited to the condition of my host. As it was half-past seven, I had no opportunity of ascertaining how the light was obtained, or what sort of objects one looked out upon by day-light, though in a subsequent morning visit, I thought, in this particular, London was a little outdone even in obscurity.

We had at dinner, on this occasion, Sir James Mackintosh, Mr. Spring-Rice, Mr. Rogers, Mr. Dumont, a Swiss, known for his remarks on Mirabeau, and other works, and two or three ladies, besides a few gentlemen, connections of the family. I have little to tell you of the entertainment, except that Sir James Mackintosh conversed a great deal, and as usual, exceedingly well. The English do not strike me as being good talkers; even when they have more in them than the French, they appear to have less at command. Still, I think it possible to find, not a pleasanter perhaps, but a more masculine circle in this capital than in that of France. If it were possible to keep our sets distinct, we would not be very far behind them either, for, as a people, we are better talkers than the English, and our practical habits give us generally truer notions of more things than they are apt to possess; but, keeping sets distinct, in a town like New York, for instance, is much like stopping the flock, when a single sheep has escaped.

Sir James Mackintosh, to-day, was severe on some of the provisions of the common law, and frankly admitted that the English system cherished many gross absurdities merely on account of their antiquity. He alluded to the law of the half-blood, which he pronounced to be an atrocity. I ventured to say, that I thought there was one thing connected with the subject that was worse than the law itself, which was Sir William Blackstone's reason for it. At this he laughed, and made several pithy and sound remarks on the aptitude of men to take any absurdity on the credit of great names, and the disposition to find good reasons for practices, however irrational or unjust, that had got to form a part of our habits. I wished heartily that some of our "reading classes" had been present, that they might have heard the manner in which one who has been "brought up at the feet of Gamaliel," venerates their idols. Were I to seek those who entertain false and exaggerated notions of the merits of the "Three Estates," I should not look for them here, among men of reflection and education, but among the book-worms of America, or in that portion of our people, among whom the traditions of their emigrant fathers are still rife; and I would thus seek them, on the principle, that one who wished to see a fashion caricatured, would not look for an example in the streets of a great capital, but in those of a remote provincial town.

The fact is, the *seemliness* of England, its studied and calculated decencies, often deceive near observers, and it is no wonder that ardent admirers, at a distance, should be misled by so specious an outside. I remember just before leaving home to have had a discussion with an intimate friend, on the subject of close corporations. My friend, is as honest a fellow as breathes, and what is more one who loves his native land; not its cats and dogs, because they are *his* cats and dogs, or, in other words, he is not a Broad-way-patriot, but is a man who has a natural sentiment in favour of the land of his fathers, takes an honest pride in its history, looks forward to the future with hope, and has a manly appreciation of the leading and distinctive features of its institutions. But, with all these, and many other excellencies, he has rather a bookish predilection in favour of things that have been prettily and coquetishly set forth in English literature. Among other crotchets of this nature, he had taken it into his head that, while it might be well enough to form a broad base for society in the main, close corporations were very good things, as wheels within a wheel. I remember that he particularly instanced the New York Hospital, in proof of the justice of his notions.

I believe the New York Hospital is almost the only institution we have, that possesses this privilege. Now it is a distinction to belong to any thing exclusive, and this circumstance, alone, has induced a class of men to accept the trust, who would not dream of it, were similar things common. This is one cause why the privilege is not abused. Another reason is, that the community gets a tone, either for good or for evil, by its prevalent habits, and the effects which flow from open corporations, and which must influence a solitary close corporation that happens to exist in their neighbourhood, would be superseded by the effects of close corporations were there more of the latter than of the former. As Rome was not built in a day, neither is one isolated fact to establish a theory.

I mention these things because the abuses of the English close-corporation-system was the subject of conversation, to-day, and I found the sentiment very generally against them. Some reform is declared to be indispensable, in order to get rid of the corruption that has grown up under the practice.

I was the first to quit the table, after the hint was given, and, on entering the drawing-room, I found Sir Walter Scott seated on one side of an ottoman, and his daughter on the other. They were alone, as if they had just got through with the civilities of an entrance, and finding myself so near the great writer, I went up to him and asked him how he did. He received me so coldly, and with a manner so different from that with which we had parted, that I drew back, of course, both surprised and hurt. I next tried the daughter, but she was not a whit more gracious. There remained nothing for me to do, but to turn round and enter into conversation with an agreeable countrywoman, who happened to be present, and who by her simplicity and frankness made me amends for the caustic manner of her neighbour.

In a few minutes, I saw Sir Walter in the centre of a group composed of Sir James Mackintosh, Mr. Rogers, Mr. Dumont and Mr. Spring-Rice. The expression of his countenance suddenly changed, and he held out his hand to me, in the same cordial way, in which he had stood on the landing of the hotel in the rue St. Maur. He had not recollected me, at first; and the extreme coldness of his manner probably proceeded from being overworked in society.

I had been much hurt, at the first reception, as you may well suppose, and as you will better understand, when I explain the cause. Indeed, I own, even after his assurance that he did not at all recall my features when I spoke to him, I felt tempted to remind him of the answer of Turenne, when he was struck by one of his valets who had mistaken his back for that of another servant—"and if I had been Pierre, you need not have struck so hard."

When in Paris, it appeared to me that Sir Walter Scott, in his peculiar circumstances, certainly *ought*, and possibly might reap some considerable emolument from his works, in America. The sheets were sold, I had understood, to the American publisher, but as an illiberal and unhandsome practice prevailed of reprinting on the American edition, the moment it appeared, and of selling it at a reduced price, it was not in the power of the publisher to pay any thing approaching what he otherwise would. Although the sum paid me for the sheets of a work in England, was of no great amount, in itself, yet compared with the value of the two articles, it seemed so much out of all proportion greater than what I had reason to believe Scott received from America, that I felt a sort of shame the fact should be so. I suggested therefore a plan by which I thought the state of things might be altered, and Sir Walter made to receive some small portion of that pecuniary reward for the pleasure he bestowed, of which he was so much in want, and which he so well merited. My plan was not to his liking, although I still think it the best, and he substituted one of his own. Under his suggestion, then, I had made an effort to effect our object, but it totally failed. My zeal had outrun discretion, and I was rightly punished, perhaps, for over-estimating my influence. I communicated this disappointment by letter, and I confess it had first struck me that some displeasure at the failure (though why I did not see, for the expedient adopted was purely his own) had mingled with his coolness. It seems I did him injustice, as his subsequent conduct fully proved.

In touching on this subject, I am induced to recollect the want of policy as respects ourselves, and the want of justice as respects others, of our copy-right law. We shall never have a manly, frank literature, if indeed, we have a literature at all, so long as our own people have to contend with the unpaid contributions of the most affluent school of writers the world has ever seen. The usual answer to this reasoning savours disgracefully of the spirit of traffic that is gradually enveloping every thing in the country in its sordid grasp. If a generous sentiment be uttered in favour of the foreigner who contributes to our pleasures, or our means of knowledge, it is thought to be triumphantly answered by showing that we can get for nothing, that for which we are asked to pay. But there is a much more serious objection, than that of a niggardly spirit, to be urged against the present system. The government is one of opinion, and the world does not contain a set of political maxims, or of social views, more dangerous to its permanency, than those which characterize the greater part of the literature of the country from which we import our books. I do not mean that our principles are more nearly approximated to those of Russia, for instance, than to those of England; but it is the very points of resemblance that create the danger, for where there is so much that is alike, we run the risk of confounding principles. I take it that the institutions of England have more to apprehend from the influence of our own, than from the influence of those of all the rest of the world united; and, *vice versa*, that we have, in the same proportion, more to apprehend from those of England. It is usual to say that the deference we pay to English maxims is natural, being the unavoidable consequence of our origin; all of which is quite true, but in continuing a system, by which this deference is constantly fed, we give it an unnatural and factitious duration. It is high time, not only for the respectability, but for the *safety* of the American people, that they should promulgate a set of principles that are more in harmony with their facts. The mawkish praise of *things*, that is now so much in vogue in America, is no more national, than are the eulogiums which the trader lavishes on his wines, equally when he sells and when he drinks them.

These very works of Sir Walter Scott, are replete with one species of danger to the American readers; and the greater the talents of the writer, as a matter of course, the greater is the evil. The bias of his feelings, his prejudices, I might almost say of his nature, is deference to hereditary rank; I do not mean that deep feeling, which, perhaps, inevitably connects the descendant with the glorious deeds of the ancestor, and which every man of sentiment is willing enough to admit, as it is a beautiful feature in the poetry of life, but the deference of mere feudal and conventional laws, which have had their origin in force, and are continued by prejudice and wrong. This idea pervades his writings, not in professions, but in the deep insinuating current of feeling, and in a way, silently and stealthily, to carry with it the sympathies of the reader. Sir Walter Scott may be right, but if he is right our system is radically wrong, and one of the first duties of a political scheme is to protect itself.

It may be fairly enough answered, perhaps, that the influence of a writer of Scott's powers cannot properly be urged in settling principles, as one such pen in a century would be considered a prodigy. His case forms an exception, instead of a rule. We will grant this, and consider him then as one greatly below his real standard, but possessing the same peculiarity of feeling, for Sir Walter Scott is a great writer, not because he feels this deference for accidental rank, but in spite of it. His talents are a gift from nature, while his notions are the result of social position.

Now what would be the situation of a writer who should attempt, before the American public, to compete with even a diminished

Scott, on American principles? He would be almost certain to fail, supposing a perfect equality of talent, from the very circumstance that he would find the minds of his readers already possessed by the hostile notions, and he would be compelled to expel them, in the first place, before he could even commence the contest on equal terms. As if this were not disadvantage enough, under the present conditions of the copy-right law, he would have to contend with a price bottomed on the possession of a literary waif.

There is no just application of the free trade doctrine to this question, for a fair competition does not suppose one of the parties to obtain his articles ready made to his hands. It is impossible that our literature should make head against these odds, and until we do enjoy a manly, independent literature of our own, we shall labour under the imputation which all foreigners urge against us, with more truth than is desirable, that of being but a second hand reflection of English opinions.

There is a morbid feeling in the American public, it is true, which will even uphold an inferior writer, so long as he aids in illustrating the land and water, which is their birthright. This weakness has been publicly charged upon them, here, as resembling the love of property. The latter accusation is probably urged a little too much in an inimical spirit, but the press has fairly laid itself open to the imputation, for while it has betrayed a total and a most culpable indifference to the maintenance of American *principles*, and even of American character, it has manifested a rabid jealousy of the credit of American *things!*

The day after the dinner at Sir G[eorge] P[hilips]'s, Sir Walter Scott did me the favour to call in St. James's Place. His manner removed any doubts on the subject of the American experiment, for nothing could be more simple and natural than his whole deportment. He spoke of his embarrassments in a way that led me to believe he would soon remove them.* On this subject he seemed cheerful and full of hope. "This fellow Napoleon," he said, in his quiet, humorous manner, "has given me a good lift, and I am only

---

*Coupling this conversation with subsequent knowledge, the writer has been induced to think that Sir Walter Scott, at that time, was not aware of the extent of his own liabilities. He mentioned a sum that was greatly short of that reported to be due, soon after his death, and which held an equitable lien on the estate of Abbotsford.

too well treated by my countrymen." I mentioned to him a remark of a French critic,* in speaking of the Life of Napoleon. This person happened to be the only one, at a large dinner, who had read the book, and every body was curious to know what he thought of it. "Oh! it is a miserable thing," he said, "full of low images and grovelling ideas; just like Shakspeare." I thought he was sensitive on the subject, and changed the conversation.

I was on the point of mentioning to him another anecdote connected with this work, and which it will, at least, do to tell you. Shortly after it appeared, one of the French journals, the Globe, or the Débats, I forget which, in two or three consecutive articles, covered it with the eulogiums with which it was usual to receive the novels of the same author. In a few weeks public opinion in France took high ground against the book. The same journal now came out with a new *critique*, which commenced by saying, "that having originally received the Memoirs of Napoleon with the courtesy due to an illustrious name, and the French character, it was time to take an impartial view of it;" and then it set to work, in good earnest, to cut it up, as one would carve a pig!

I had just published a book, and Scott kindly and delicately inquired whether it had been disposed of to advantage, in England. As compared with English books, it had not, certainly, though I thought it had done very well for a foreign book, written in a foreign spirit, and with no particular claims to English favour. He disavowed this feeling for his countrymen, and frankly offered to serve me with the publishers. As I had no cause to complain of the party into whose hands I had already fallen, but, on the contrary, reason to be satisfied, I could only thank him, and state the fact. As I am writing of England and English character, it is no more than fair to say that the peculiarities I have mentioned did much less to impair the popularity of this work, in England, than I did expect, or could have expected. There is a manliness and a feeling of pride, in the better character of the country, that singularly elevates it above this littleness, and, while I make no doubt a great many did feel this objection, I believe a majority did not. I much question, had the case been reversed, if either the French or the

---

*A man who has since filled one of the highest offices under the French government.

American public, would have received a book with the same liberal spirit. I have been so sensible of this, that I have felt a strong desire to manifest it, by taking a subject from the teeming and glorious naval history of this country. What a theme this would be for one sufficiently familiar with the sea! An American might well enough do it, too, by carrying the time back anterior to the separation, when the two histories were one. But some of their own seamen will yet bear away the prize, and although I may envy, I do not begrudge it to them. It is their right, and let them have it.

Among the acquaintances for whom I am indebted to the letters of Mr. Spencer, is Mr. Sotheby the poet. This gentleman, now no longer young, lives in a good style here, being apparently a man of fortune and condition. He is a good specimen of the country, simple, quiet, and, unless his countenance and manners are sad hypocrites, benevolent and honest. Indeed I have seldom seen any one who has left a more favourable impression, as respects the two latter qualities, on a short acquaintance.

Mr. Sotheby invited me to dinner, pretty much as a matter of course, for all social intercourse in England, as in America, and in France, is a good deal dependent on the table. I found him living in a house, that, so far as I could see, was American, as American houses used to be before the taste became corrupted by an uninstructed pretension. I was one of the first; but Mr. Coleridge was already in the drawing-room. He was a picture of green old age; ruddy, solid, and with a head as white as snow. His smile was benevolent, but I had scarcely time to reconnoitre him, before Sir Walter Scott appeared, accompanied by Mr. Lockhart. The latter is a genteel person, of a good carriage, with the air of a man of the world, and with a sort of Scotch-Spanish face. His smile is significant, and not a bad one for a reviewer. The wife of the Bishop of London, and two or three more formed our party.

At table I sat directly opposite to Sir Walter Scott, with Mr. Coleridge on my left. Nothing passed during dinner, worth mentioning, except a remark or two from the latter. He said that he had been employed, when secretary to Sir Alexander Ball, the Governor of Malta, to conduct a correspondence between the commander of our squadron and the government of Tripoli. I presume this must have been while Commodore Morris was in command, that officer being on very familiar terms with Admiral

Ball, as the following anecdote will show. The late Captain Bainbridge had a duel with an English officer at Malta, and under circumstances that enlisted the public feeling on his side, in which the latter was killed. The same day Commodore Morris breakfasted with the Governor. After breakfast, Sir Alexander Ball mentioned the affair to his guest, with proper expressions of regret, adding it would be his duty to demand Mr. Bainbridge. Of course, nothing was to be said to the contrary, and the Commodore took his leave. While pulling off to his ship he casually observed that Mr. Bainbridge would be demanded. The midshipman of the boat reported it to the lieutenant of the deck, who sent notice to Mr. Bainbridge, forthwith. In due time the official demand appeared. The Commodore sent orders to the different ships to deliver the delinquent, and received answers that he was no longer in the squadron. He had, in truth, hurried off to Sicily in a hired felucca. This showed a good feeling on the part of Sir Alexander Ball, who always manifested a seaman's desire that we should flog the barbarians. Mr. Coleridge did not tell this anecdote, but I had it, many years since, from my old friend Commodore Morris, himself.

One of Mr. Coleridge's observations was in bad taste. He professed to like most of our officers, with a very supererogatory exception in the case of Commodore Rodgers. It was easy to see he had adopted an unworthy prejudice against this officer, on account of the affair of the Little Belt. No transaction of the same nature was probably ever more thoroughly investigated than this, or grosser injustice done any man than was done Commodore Rodgers. I confess I have always viewed his conduct as singularly creditable and humane. He was fired into, and he fired back, as a matter of course. Perceiving that his assailant made a feeble resistance, he ordered his own fire to cease, and it was not renewed until he was again assailed. He ceased a second time, from the same motive, and all in a very few minutes. His own ship was scarcely injured, and but a single boy hurt. His assailant was torn to pieces and had his decks covered with killed and wounded. Now, looking to our previous history, to the wanton attack on the Chesapeake, an attack for which the English government itself had felt bound to atone, it was a great proof of moderation, that Commodore Rodgers did not insist on the absolute submission of the Little Belt. He might have done it, and enforced his demand with no risk to his own vessel, for, as to the fanfaronade of the President's having been beaten off, and silenced, and on fire, besides being contradicted by the fullest testimony, on oath, no seaman who knows any thing of the respective forces of the two vessels can for a moment believe it probable.

That question has been pretty effectually settled by the Constitution, a sister ship of the President, which, in open war, has since whipped with ease, and carried into port, two such ships as the Little Belt, at the same time.

Nothing can better illustrate the monstrous consequences of the mental dependence to which the prevalence of English literature is helping to give an unnatural existence in America, than the manner in which Commodore Rodgers was visited by public opinion in his own country, for his conduct on this occasion. Sad, indeed, is the situation of the military man, who, holding his life in his hand at the service of his native land, meets with reproach, calumny, misrepresentation and malignant hostility from those for whom he has fought, and this because he has humbled their constant and most vindictive enemy! Commodore Rodgers has never recovered the ground he lost, in the public favour at home, for his behaviour, on this occasion, marked as it was by a noble and generous forbearance. It is true men no longer reproach him with the particular act, for after the investigation and all that has since occurred, it would even exceed ordinary audacity to do so, but thousands entertain, unknown to themselves, prejudices which are derived from this source, and which will only cease with their breath.

This it is to serve a people, who will consent to form their estimates of their own servants, from the calculated hostility of their enemies! I believe we may boast of being the only nation in the universe, which submits to so unjust and so dangerous a domination. It unhappily forms our highest claim to originality!

Mr. Sotheby has a son a captain in the navy. This gentleman, I believe, felt the gratuitous character of Mr. Coleridge's remarks, for he expressed himself favourably as regards Commodore Rodgers, whom he had recently fallen in with, on service. I contented myself by saying, a little drily, that he was a highly respectable man, and a very excellent officer, which, at least, had the effect to change the conversation.

When the ladies had retired, the conversation turned on Homer, whom, it is understood Mr. Sotheby is now engaged in translating. Some one remarked that Mr. Coleridge did not believe in his unity, or rather that there was any such man. This called him out, and certainly I never witnessed an exhibition as extraordinary as that which followed. It was not a discourse, but a dissertation. Scarcely any one spoke besides Mr. Coleridge, with the exception of a brief occasional remark from Mr. Sotheby, who held the contrary opinion, and I might say no one *could* speak. At moments he was surprisingly eloquent, though a little discursive, and the whole time he appeared to be perfectly the master of his subject and of his language. As near as I could judge, he was rather more than an hour in *possession of the floor*, almost without interruption. His utterance was slow, every sentence being distinctly given, and his pronunciation accurate. There seemed to be a constant struggling between an affluence of words and an affluence of ideas, without either hesitation or repetition. His voice was strong and clear, but not pitched above the usual key of conversation. The only peculiarity about it, was a slightly observable burring or the *r. r. rs.*, but scarcely more than what the language properly requires.

Once or twice, when Mr. Sotheby would attempt to say a word on his side of the question, he was permitted to utter just enough to give a leading idea, but no argument, when the reasoning was taken out of his mouth by the essayist, and continued, pro and con, with the same redundant and eloquent fluency. I was less struck by the logic than by the beauty of the language, and the poetry of the images. Of the theme, in a learned sense, I knew too little to pretend to any verbal or critical knowledge, but he naturally endeavoured to fortify his argument by the application of his principles to familiar things; and here, I think, he often failed. In fact, the exhibition was much more wonderful than convincing.

At first I was so much struck with the affluent diction of the poet, as scarcely to think of any thing else; but when I did look about me, I found every eye fastened on him. Scott sat, immoveable as a statue, with his little grey eyes looking inward and outward, and evidently considering the whole as an exhibition, rather than as an argument; though he occasionally muttered, "eloquent!" "wonderful!" "very extraordinary!" Mr. Lockhart caught my eye once, and he gave a very hearty laugh, without making the slightest noise, as if he enjoyed my astonishment. When we rose, however, he expressed his admiration of the speaker's eloquence.

The dissertations of Mr. Coleridge cannot properly be brought in comparison with the conversation of Sir James Mackintosh. One lectures, and the other converses. There is a vein of unpretending philosophy, and a habit of familiar analysis in the conversation of the latter, that causes you to remember the substance of what he has said, while the former, though synthetick and philosophical as a verbal critic, rather enlists the imagination than any other property of the mind. Mackintosh is willing enough to listen, while Coleridge reminded me of a barrel to which every other man's tongue acted as a spigot; for no sooner did the latter move, than it set his own contents in a flow.

We were still at table, when the constant raps at the door gave notice that the drawing-room was filling above. Mr. Coleridge lectured on, through it all, for half an hour longer, when Mr. Sotheby rose. The house was full of company assembled to see Scott. He walked deliberately into a maze of petticoats, and, as he had told me at Paris, let them play with his mane as much as they pleased. I had an engagement, and went to look for my hat, which, to escape the fangs of the servants, who have an inconvenient practice, here, of taking your hat out of the drawing-room while you are at dinner, I had snugly hid under a sofa.The Bishop of London was seated directly above it, and completely covered it with his petticoat. Mr. Sotheby observing that I was aiming at something there, kindly inquired what I wanted. I told him I was praying for the translation of the Bishop of London, that I might get my hat, and, marvellous as it may seem, he has already been made Archbishop of Canterbury!

Just as I was going away, one or two ladies, whom I had the honour to know, made their appearance, and I remained a moment to speak to them. You will remember that congress is just now debating the subject of the protective system. You cannot, however, know the interest that is felt on this subject here. I had a specimen of it to-night, in the conversation of these ladies, and in that of one or two more with whom the detention brought me in discourse. When the women occupy themselves with such subjects, it is fair to infer that the nation feels their magnitude. Europe generally, or the north of Europe rather, possesses a class of female politicians that is altogether unknown to us. We have party ladies, as well as England, who enter into the feelings of their male friends; who hate, abuse, and blindly admire, with the best of them; but how rare is it to find one who is capable of instructing a child in even the elementary principles of its country's interests, duties, and rights? A part of this indifference is owing to the natural condition of America, which places her above the necessity of the ordinary apprehensions and efforts; but it would be much better were our girls kept longer at their books, before they are turned into the world to run their light-hearted career of trifling.

With one lady I had a short but a sharp discussion on political economy, to-night. She was thoroughly free trade, and this is a doctrine that I hold to be bottomed on a complete fallacy. It would be quite as easy to prove, in my opinion, that liberty can exist without government, as to show that nations can equally profit by trade, without consulting their peculiar circumstances. She asked me if trade did not consist in an exchange of equivalents. I thought not, in fact, but in an exchange of *apparent* equivalents. I did not believe, that the Indian who sold a beaver skin for half a dollar, in the forest, which, after deducting charges, brought four or five dollars of profit in the market, obtained any thing more than an *apparent* equivalent. He was a loser by his ignorance and his social facts, while the trader was, in the same proportion, a gainer. But free trade would permit the Indian to bring his own peltry down, and pocket the difference himself. True, as a *theory;* but life is composed of stubborn *facts*, that laugh at theories of this sort. He cannot come. Could restriction supply a remedy? Certainly; by appointing a clever agent, for instance, at a salary, to dispose of their peltry in common for them, and by excluding the traders from their territory, they might get double or treble the present prices. Their agent might cheat them. So does the trader. The buyers would go elsewhere. They cannot; the Indian has a monopoly of the article. Did I not believe free trade increased commerce, and indirectly diffused its advantages over the whole world? I made no doubt that many restrictions were absurd, and in this fact I saw all the true argument that can be adduced in favour of free trade. Let us imagine a garden filled with fine fruit, on which the owner sets a moderate price. He refuses, however, to open his gates but once a week, and half his fruit is lost in consequence. This is an abuse of restriction. Convinced of his error, he throws his gates open altogether, and bids all enter and help themselves; and to render things equal, he prohibits the use of ladders, or of climbing. A tall man enters and picks as much as he wants; but the short man at his side can reach nothing. But free trade would let him take a ladder. True, if he could carry one; but he can get none, or is too feeble. Now, knowledge, capital, practice, establishments, skill, and even natural aptitude, compose the difference in stature between nations, and the laws must provide the ladders, or the shorter will go altogether without fruit, or get it at the tall man's prices. But competition would regulate this, as other things, and the market would settle down into a fair system of equivalents. It is easy to make this out in theory, but difficult to prove it in practice. We usually expect too much from competition, whose natural tendency, in trade, is to combination. The thousand interests of life derange the action of the most ingenious theory. The world has never yet seen a fair exchange of equivalents in traffic, and I doubt if it ever will. It is said we can't buy more than we sell, and that the balance of trade regulates itself. This will do on paper, but it is not true in fact. We may sell too low and buy too dear. When England takes a pound of our cotton at ten cents, and sells it back again at a dollar, leaving a clear profit of fifty cents, by which her manufacturers roll in their coaches, while the planter is living from hand to mouth, we are pretty clearly doing one or the other. But let natural efforts regulate this, and do not have recourse to laws. When a strong man gets a weak one down, if the liberation of the latter depends on his natural efforts, he will never rise.

Here I bade my fair antagonist good night, as I do you.

Plate V

St. James's Palace

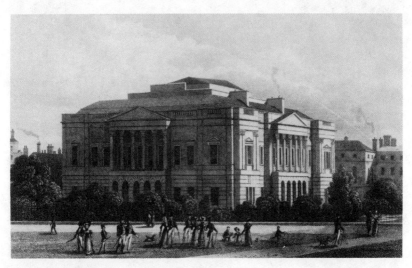

York House, St. James's Park

Plate VI

Holland House

Spencer House, Green Park

Plate VII

Lansdowne House

Somerset House

Plate VIII

Northumberland House, Charing Cross

Statue of Charles I, Charing Cross

Letter XII.

To William Jay, Esq., Bedford, New York.

Although I had been several times at St. Stephen's, I never, until quite lately, got into the House of Lords. A young connexion, who happens to be travelling in Europe, and myself, have, however, just made a visit to the Hospital of Incurables. Several members of this house have offered to procure permission for me, but it has always been in a way that has rendered the civility any thing but a favour. It is a marked fault in English manners, that they extend the factitious system, by which every concession of politeness of this nature has the appearance of being sought, to strangers.*

I may say the same thing of the House of Commons, into which I have had a dozen offers of admission beneath the gallery, though but once in a way that I did not feel it to be a humiliation to accept. The exception was a case of thoroughly gentlemanlike attention, and I record it with the greater satisfaction.

As I am writing with the intention to supply comparisons of national manners, I will relate a recent occurrence that took place at Paris. A party of American travellers arrived at the door of the Chamber of Deputies, and, in the absence of all other means of getting in, they took the bold measure of sending their cards to

---

*The writer had a ludicrous specimen of this feeling, at a later day, in Italy. An English minister's wife gave a great ball, and applications were constantly made for tickets. As the town was small, this ball made a great sensation, and every one was talking of it. It was no great sacrifice for the family of the writer to preserve their self-respect on this occasion, as they lived retired from choice. Hints began to be thrown out, and questions asked if they had yet *procured* tickets. At eight o'clock of the very night of the entertainment, these important tickets arrived *unasked!* Of course, no notice was taken of them. It will be remembered that all this dog-in-the-mangerism had nothing to do with the customs of the country in which the parties were, it being usual for the natives to give their guests more than two hours' notice, when they wished to see them at balls. This social *convoitise* on one side, and coquetry on the other, distinguish the English circles all over Europe.

the president, with a request to be admitted, and immediately had convenient places assigned them. I do not say I would imitate this course, but it is impossible not to admire the courtesy which overlooked the mistake.

There are men who ply about the doors of the two houses of parliament, to show strangers the way into them; for it is almost as much an affair of management and bribery to get into St. Stephen's chapel, after one is elected, as it is to get the legal return. We contracted with a man at the outer door to deliver us safe in the House of Lords, for three shillings sterling, each. The rogue carried us no farther than the first inner door, however, where he turned us over to one a step above him in dignity, coolly demanding a shilling for his pains. Our new guide carried us through a door or two more, when we reached the real vendor of places. We paid the second guide another shilling, and the stipulated price went into the hands of the regular box-office-man.

I am far from complaining of the practice of paying for these admissions, though the price is too high. Members, you will remember, can grant admissions. It is quite impossible for every one to be present, and in a town like London, the half crown may be a very healthful check, both morally and physically. The legislative body that has not the power to clear its hall, would become contemptible. The publicity of congress is only commanded through its journals, the admission of strangers being purely a matter of favour. Here the latter are present, only, by a fiction, as indeed they are sometimes absent; for frequently when ordered to withdraw, they do not budge. The same principles substantially regulate the proceedings of congress and of parliament, though there exists one difference between them, that is founded on a fundamental distinction in the governments. In congress the vote is taken openly, in parliament it is not. It is a great pity that, while we admit of this affinity in forms, we do not always perceive the essential difference that exists in substance.

You know, already, that the hall of the House of Lords is divided into three divisions—that around the throne, that which contains the peers, and that which is set apart for the public. I should think the latter, which is termed below the bar, might hold two or three hundred people, standing. There are no seats, and even the reporters are compelled to write on their knees, or to sit on the floor. Luckily for them, there is little, in general, to report.* There is also a small area around the fire-place which appears to be a no-man's-land, for I heard a commoner ask a peer, lately, whether it was permitted for the members of the other house to occupy it, and the answer was an admission of ignorance, though the peer rather thought it was. The members of the commons, however, usually stand around the throne. Mr. Wortley, a gentleman I had seen in America, was standing on the steps of the throne to-night, while his father, Lord Wharncliffe, made a speech.

We found a thin house, and plenty of space below the bar. The Duke of Wellington was on the ministerial bench, and not far from him was my dinner acquaintance, the Bishop of [Llandaff], in his lawn sleeves. With this exception and that of another bishop, who entered in the course of the evening, besides the chancellor and the other officers of the house, I saw no one that was not in ordinary attire. All but the bishop and the latter wore their hats, and they wore their precious wigs. The chancellor looked like a miller with his head thrust through his wife's petticoat. As for my bishop, he appeared fidgety and out of his place.

Lord Lansdowne and Lord Grey and Lord Holland, were all in their places, but neither said any thing but the first, who spoke for a few minutes. When we entered, I do not think there were twenty peers in their seats, though the number doubled at a later hour. These twenty were mostly clustered around the table, and their meeting strongly resembled that of an ordinary committee. The Marquis of Salisbury, a descendant of Burleigh, was on his feet when we came in, discussing some point connected with the game laws. I doubt if his great ancestor knew half as much of the same subject. The tone was conversational and quiet, and, altogether, I never was in a public body that had so little the air of one. I could not divest myself of the idea of a *conseil de famille*, that had met to consult each other, in a familiar way, about the disposition of some of their possessions, while the members of the house who were listening, resembled the children who were excluded by their years.

Although one so seldom hears the term "my lord" in the world, it was pretty well bandied among the speakers to-night. They

*This arrangement was subsequently changed.

pronounced it "*my lurds*," the English uniformly sounding the possessive pronoun in question more like the Italians than we do, so that is makes "mee lurds." I was a good deal puzzled, when I first arrived here, to account for many abuses of the language, in the middling classes, and which sometimes are met with in the secondary articles of the public prints. "Think of *me* going without a hat," is a sentence of the sort I mean. It is intended to say, "Think of *my* going, &c.;" but, from a confusion between the sound and the spelling, the personal pronoun is used, by illiterate people, instead of the possessive. This species of illiteracy, by the way, extends a good way up English society.

I take it, the polite way of pronouncing this word is by a sort of elision—as m'horse, m'dog, m'gun, and that *my* horse, *my* dog, *my* gun, the usual American mode, and *me* horse, *me* dog, *me* gun, the English counterpart, are equally wrong; the first by an offensive egotism, and the last from offensive ignorance. I think more noble peers, however, said "*me* lurds," than "m'lurds," though the formal tone of public speaking is seldom favourable to simple or accurate pronunciation. It usually plays the deuce with prosody, unless one has a naturally easy elocution. The French, in this respect, have the advantage of us, their language having no emphatic syllables. A Frenchman will often talk an hour without a true argument or a false quantity.

Lord Salisbury appeared to have a knowledge of his subject, which, in itself, was scarcely worthy to occupy the time of the peers of Great Britain. I do not mean that game is altogether beneath one's notice, and still less that the moral enormities to which the English game-laws have given birth, do not require a remedy; but that local authority ought to exist to regulate all such minor interests; first, on account of their relative insignificance, and, secondly, because the reasoning that may apply to one county, may not fitly apply to another.

You may perhaps be ignorant that, by the actual law, game cannot be sold at all in England. My wife was ill lately, and I desired our landlady to send and get her a bird or two, but the good woman held up her hands and declared it was impossible, as there was a fine of fifty pounds for buying or selling game. The law is evaded, however, hares, it is said, passing from hand to hand constantly in London, under the name of *lions!*

I remember once, in travelling on our frontiers, to have received an apology from an inn-keeper, for not having any thing fit to eat, because he had only venison, wild pigeons, and brook trout. I asked him what he wanted better. He did not know, "but the gentleman had quite likely been used to pork!" Absurd as all this seems, I remember, after serving a season on the great lakes, to have *asked* for boiled pork and turnips, as a treat. Our physical enjoyments are mere matters of habit, while the intellectual, alone, are based on a rock. The worst tendency we have at home, is manifested by a rapacity for money, which, when obtained, is to be spent in little besides eating and drinking.

A Lord Carnarvon said a few words, and Lord Wharncliffe made a speech, but it was all in the same conversational tone. The peers do not address the chancellor in speaking, but their own body; hence the constant recurrence of the words "my lurds." The chancellor does not occupy a seat at one end of the area, like a speaker, but he is placed on his woolsack, considerably advanced towards the table.

I should have been at a loss to know the members, but for a plain tradesman-like looking man at my elbow, who appeared to be familiar with the house, and who was there to show the lions to a country friend. I was much amused by this person's observations, which were a strange medley of habitual English deference for rank and natural criticism. "There," said he, "that is Lord L_____, and he looks just like a journeyman carpenter." His friend, however, was too much awe-struck to relish this familiarity.

I was a little disappointed with the *physique* of the peers, who are, by no means, a particularly favourable specimen of the English gentlemen, in this respect. Perhaps I have never seen enough of them together to form a correct opinion. A Lord A_____, whom I met at Paris, told me that his father had taken the trouble to count the pigtails in the House of Lords, at the trial of the late queen, and that he found they considerably exceeded a hundred. I was aware this body was somewhat behind the age in certain essentials, but I did not know, until then, that this peculiarity extended to that precise portion of the head.

The peers of Great Britain, considered as a political body, are usurpers in the worst sense of the word. The authority they wield, and the power by which it is maintained, are the results neither of frank conquest, nor of legally delegated trusts, but of insidious innovations effected under the fraudulent pretences of succouring liberty. They were the principal, and, at that time, the natural agents of the nation, in rescuing it from the tyranny of the Stuarts, and profiting by their position, they have gradually perverted the institutions to their own aggrandisement and benefit. This is substantially the history of all aristocracies, which commence by curbing the power of despots, and end by substituting their own.

There exists a radical fault in the theory of the British government, which supposes three estates, possessed of equal legislative authority. Such a condition of the body politic is a moral impossibility. Two would infallibly combine to depose the other, and then they would quarrel which was to reap the fruits of victory. The very manner in which the popular rights were originally obtained in England, go to prove that nothing of the sort entered into the composition of the government at the commencement. Boroughs were created by royal charters. Even the peers were emanations of the royal will, and, much as might be expected, the creatures of the king's pleasure.

In the progress of events, the servants became too strong for their masters. They set aside one dynasty and established another, under the form of law. Since that time they have been gradually accumulating force, until all the branches of government are absorbed in one; not absolutely in its ordinary action, it is true, but in its fundamental power. Parliament has got to be absolute, and the strictly legislative part of it, by establishing the doctrine of ministerial responsibility, has obtained so much control over the part which is termed the executive, as to hold it completely within its control.

An Englishman is very apt to affirm that the President of the United States has more power than the King of England. This he thinks is establishing the superior liberty of his own country. He is right enough in his fact, but strangely wrong in the inference. The government of the United States has no pretension to a trinity in its elements, though it maintains one in its action; and that of Great Britain pretends to one in its elements, while it has a unity in its action. The president has more real power than the king, because he actually wields the authority attributed to him in the Constitution, and the king has less real authority than the president, because he does not exercise the authority attributed to him by the Constitution, even as the Constitution is now explained, different as that explanation is from what it was a century since.

Were the King of England to name a ministry that did not please his parliament, which in substance is pleasing those who hold the power to make members, that ministry could not stand a week after parliament assembled. If the two houses of parliament were composed of men of different interests, or of different social elements, there would still be something like an apparent balance in the composition of the state; but they are not. The peers hold so much political control in the country, as, virtually, to identify the two bodies, so far as interests are concerned. Without this, there would be no harmony in the government, for where there are separate bodies of equal nominal authority in a state, one must openly control the others, or all must secretly act under the same indirect influence; not the influence of a common concern in the public good, for rulers never attend to that, until they have first consulted their own interests, as far as their powers will conveniently allow. In point of fact then, the peers of England and the commons of England are merely modifications of the same social *castes*.

In looking over the list of the members of the House of Commons, I find one hundred and sixty with those titles which show that they are actually the sons of peers, and when we remember the extent and influence of intermarriages, it would not probably exceed the truth were I to say that more than half the lower house stand, as regards the upper, either in the relation of son, son-in-law, brother, or brother-in-law, nephew, or uncle.* But nobility is by no means the test of this government. It is, strictly, a landed, and not a titled aristocracy. There are seventy-four baronets among the commons, and these are usually men of large

---

*Even in the parliament of 1832, I find no less than seventy-four of the *eldest* sons and *heirs* of peers, sitting as commoners. Among them are Lords Surrey, Tavistock, Worcester, Douro, Graham, Mandeville, and Chandos, all of whom are the eldest sons of Dukes. In the parliament of 1830, were also Lords Seymour, Euston, and Blandford, of the same rank.

landed estates. If we take the whole list, we shall not probably find a hundred names that, socially, belong to any other class than that of the aristocracy, strictly so called, or that are not so nearly allied to them in interests, as virtually to make the House of Commons, identical, as a social caste, with the House of Lords. It is of little moment whether these bodies are hereditary or elective, so long as both represent the same set of interests.

The aristocracy of England is checked less by any of the contrivances of the state, than by the extra-constitutional power of public opinion. This is a fourth estate in England, and a powerful estate every where, that, in an age like this perhaps does more than written compacts to restrain abuses. It has even curbed despotism over more than half of Europe. As the influence of public opinion will always bear the impress of the moral civilization of a people, England is better off, in this particular, than most of her neighbours, and it is probably one great reason, why her aristocracy has not fleeced the nation more than it has, though I dont know that it has any thing to reproach itself with, in the way of neglect, on this score.

The perpetuity of the ascendancy of the English aristocracy is a question much mooted just now, and I have frequently heard in private, sturdy and frank opinions on the subject. There are three prominent facts that, I think, must soon produce essential changes in this feature of the English system. In carrying out the scheme of spreading the power of the peers over the commons, as it has been done by personal wealth, individuals of the body have become offensively powerful to the majority of their own order. Influence is getting into too few hands to be agreeable to those, who, having so much, would wish to share in all. This is one evil; and I think when reform does occur, as occur it must, that there will be a great effort to arrest it, when this one point shall have been rectified.

But there is a far more powerful foe to the existing order of things. The present system is based on property, for, with a king without authority, the power of the Lords, unsupported by that of the Commons, would not be worth a straw in this age; and, though land may not be, the balance of power, as it is connected with money, is rapidly changing hands in England. There has arisen, within the last fifty years, a tremendous money-power, that was formerly unknown to the country. Individuals got rich in the last century, where classes get rich now; and instead of absorbing the new men, as was once done, the aristocracy is in danger of being absorbed by them.

It would not be in nature for a large class of men to become rich without wishing to participate in power. It is a necessity in money to league itself with authority. Were it not for the natural antipathy between trade and democracy, the mercantile and manufacturing classes of England would make common cause with the people and change the government at once; but the affluent dread revolutions; the debt of England is a mortgage on the rich; and, most of all, commerce detests popular rights. It is, in itself, an aristocracy of wealth. When the hour comes, however, it will be found struggling to equalize the advantages of money, I think.

The third danger arises from the fictions of the system. No power on earth can resist the assaults of reason, if constantly exposed to them, since it is the language of natural truth. Liberty of the press is incompatible with exclusion in politics, or at least, with an exclusion that proscribes a majority. Neither throne, nor senate, can withstand the constant attacks of arguments that address themselves equally to the sense of right and to the passions of men. The alternatives are to submit, or to repress.

Now, while the aristocracy has been silently and steadily extending its net over England, it has always been with the professions of a monarchy. It was an offence to speak evil of the king, when it was no offence to speak evil of the aristocrats. The law protected a fiction, while it overlooked a reality. It is too late to change. Feeling an indifference to a power that was little more than nominal, the press has been permitted to deal freely even with the throne, of late, and England would not bear a law which denied her the privilege of censuring the aristocrats. The public mind, on this point, appears to be under the influence of a re-action. The French Revolution so far quickened the jealousies of the English government, that prosecutions for sedition were carried to extremes under Mr. Pitt, and now that the danger is abated, something like a licence on the other side has followed.

The church will do more to uphold the present system than the aristocracy, although there are two sides even to the effect of the influence of the church. It sustains and it enfeebles the government, through dissent. It sustains, by enlisting the prejudices of churchmen on its side, and it enfeebles by throwing large masses necessarily into the opposition.* On the whole, however, it aids greatly in upholding the present order of things. One of the most distinguished statesmen of this country, observed to me pithily, the other day, that we enjoyed a great advantage in having no established church. I understood him to mean that he found the establishment of England a mill-stone around the neck of reform.

One who should judge of the character of the English aristocracy, by inferences drawn solely from the political system, and from the warnings of history, would not come to a fairer decision, than he who should judge of the condition of democracy in America, by the state of the Grecian and Italian republics. There is much, very much, that is redeeming here, though it belongs rather to incidents of the national facts, than to the effects of purely political causes. As one of the chief of the latter, however, may be mentioned the openness to censure and comment, that has arisen from the fraud of considering the government in theory, and in the penal laws, as a monarchy, when it has so few genuine claims to the character. While this circumstance exposes the real rulers to constant assaults, and, as I think, to ultimate defeat, it has, for them, the redeeming advantage (in some measure redeeming, at

---

*Just before the writer left England, the Lords threw out the bill for the repeal of the Test Laws. Shortly after, the matter was brought up anew, and the authorities of orthodox Oxford were assembled to petition *against* the measure. On the day of meeting, however, to the astonishment of every body, speeches were made in *favour* of the repeal by several prominent men. Of course the petition was for repeal, for party is just as well drilled in Europe as it is with us.

A few months later, I had the whole secret explained. A leading dissenter, now a member of parliament, told me that he and his friends gave the government to understand distinctly, that if the Test Laws were not repealed, the dissenters of England would make common cause with the Catholics of Ireland and overturn the establishment.

The following anecdote is also derived from the best authority. About the time nullification was rife in America, a gentleman, also in parliament, went from London to a dinner in the country. He found the Right Rev. Lord Bishop of _____, among the company. "What news do you bring us from town, Mr. _____ ?" asked the consecrated christian. "No news, my Lord." "No news! We were told there was *good* news." "To what do you allude, my Lord?" "Why, we were told there is every reason to expect a speedy dissolution of the American Union."

least) of putting them on their guard, of admonishing them of their danger, and of checking and correcting the natural tendency to abuses. It is, in fact, a means of bringing the moral civilization and knowledge of the age to bear directly on their public and private deportment. Viewed in the first sense, it is usual, here, to say that the families of the peers are as exemplary as those of any other class of subjects. It is absurd to make any essential distinction between the nobility and the gentry, on such a point, for they are identified in all but the mere circumstance that the former are a titled division of the aristocracy. As between *castes*, I do not believe there is any essential moral difference, anywhere. Each has the vices and the virtues of its condition, and if leisure and wealth tempt to indulgences, they also supply the means of those higher mental pleasures which do quite as much as preaching, towards restraining evil. Individuals of rank do certainly abuse their privileges, and others profit by their insignificance. There are cases of profligate vice among the English nobility, beyond a question, but, as a whole, I believe they are externally as decent and moral, as the same number of any class in the kingdom. We misconceive the character of aristocracy quite as much as they misconceive the character of democracy. Both are essentially tempered by the spirit of the age. The practice of marrying for worldly views, causes rather more breaches of the marriage vows among the women, than would otherwise be the case, though they are certainly better than many other European nations in this respect. The English say that the world sees the worst of them, in this particular, a sentiment unknown to the women of the Continent, causing their own to elope, when they have yielded to an illicit attachment. I do not believe in either the fact, or the reason. The disclosures prove that they are discovered half the time, and the elopements that are voluntary, probably proceed from the fact that the law allows divorces, and re-marriages, an advantage, if indeed it be one, that is denied catholics. This is the weak side of the morals of the English nobility, among whom there are probably a larger proportion of divorces, than among the same number of any other protestants. The separations, *a mensa et toro*, are also comparatively numerous.

I have, first and last, been brought more or less in personal contact, with a large number of the nobility of this realm. I have generally found them well mannered and well educated, and sedulous to please. There is a certain species of conventional knowledge, that belongs in a measure to their peculiar social position, that is diffused among them with surprising equality. I can liken it most to the sort of inherent tastes and tact, that distinguish the children of gentlemen from those who are equally well taught in other respects, but have not had the same early advantages of association, and which frequently render them companionable and agreeable when there is little beneath the surface. Judged by a severer standard, they are like other educated men, of course, though their constant intercourse with the highest classes of a nation distinguished for learning, taste, and research, probably imparts to them as a body, an air of knowledge that is, in some degree, above the level of their true intelligence. Of a good many of those with whom I have even conversed, I know too little to speak with sufficient understanding, but among all those with whom I have, I should find it difficult to name one who has left on my mind the impression of vapid ignorance that so often besets us in our own circles. Something is probably owing to their better tone of manners, which, if it does nothing else, by inculcating modesty of deportment, prevents exposure. On the other hand, I could not mention half a dozen who left behind them the impression of men possessing talents above the ordinary level. Perhaps, however, this is in a just proportion, to their numbers. Lord Grey, I have little doubt, has one of the most masculine and vigorous minds among the peers; and I think it will be found, should he ever reach the upper house, that Lord Stanley will possess one of the acutest.

The English appear to me to encourage a fault in their eloquence, that is common to their literature and their manners. The incessant study of the Roman classics has imparted a taste for a severity of style and manner that is better suited to the comprehensive tongue of the ancients, than to our own ampler vocabulary. From this, or from some other cause, they push simplicity to affectation; or, admitting that there is an unconsciousness of the peculiarity, to coldness. This is observable in their ordinary manners, and in their style of parliamentary elocution; the latter, in particular, usually wanting the feeling necessary to awaken sympathy. As respects the Lords, it is rare, I fancy, to hear any thing approaching oratory, the delivery and the language being conversational rather than oratorical. They appear to be afraid of falling into the forensic, as it might detract from a speaker's glory to have it proved upon him he was a lawyer! The English nobleman, however, is usually above the miserable affectations of the drilled coldness of the automaton school. He appears to have imbibed a portion of the amenity of the high society of the continent. In this respect the men are better than the women, as our women are said to be better than the men. I think one would apply the term *gracieuse* to fewer English women than common, though the men of rank merit that of *aimable* oftener than it is adjudged to them. I have often, quite often, met with English women of winning exterior; but their deportment has almost always appeared to be the result of their feelings; inducing one to esteem, as much as to admire them; and, although one of ordinary capacity most respects this trait, where it is wanting he could wish to find its substitute. In reference to the points of a factitious coldness of manner, and a want of feeling in oratory, I should say the peers, as compared to the class next beneath them, are most obnoxious to the latter charge, and the least to the former.

A day or two after my first visit, I went again to the House of Lords to hear Mr. Brougham speak in the case of an appeal. I found but two peers present, the chancellor, and, I believe, Lord Carnarvon. The former sat on the wool-sack buried in flax, as usual, and the latter occupied one of the lateral benches, with his hat on. The appeal was made from a decision of the chancellor, who had ordered that a father should not have the custody of his sons. It was an extraordinary proceeding in appearance, at least, though reflection somewhat lessens its absurdity. In point of fact, owing to a change in the administration, the chancellor from whom the appeal was made, was not the person who now presided, but had not this accidental change intervened, it would have been otherwise. Mr. Brougham spoke several hours, and it would have been irksome to him, indeed, to be compelled to argue, on appeal, a case over again, that had already been presented to the same ears! When one comes to consider the matter, however, he finds that there are many lawyers among the lords, who, if they do not hear the arguments, may read them; and who can rely on their own knowledge in making up their minds, when they come to the vote. The defect was, therefore, one of form rather than one of substance, though it was strangely deficient in appearances, a fault the least likely to occur in this government.

Letter XIII.
To William Jay, Esq., Bedford, N. Y.

Were the people of England, free from the prejudices of their actual situation and absolutely without a political organization, assembled to select a polity for their future government, it is probable that the man who should propose the present system, would at once be set down as a visionary, or a fool. Could things be reversed, however, and the nation collected for the same purpose, under the influence of the opinions that now prevail, the proposer of the system that would be very likely to be adopted in the former case, would be lucky if he escaped with his ears. It is safer that facts should precede opinions in the progress of political meliorations, than that opinions should precede facts; though it would be better still, could the two march *pari passu*. All essential changes in the control of human things, must be attended by one of two species of contests, the struggles of those who would hasten, or the struggles of those who would retard events. The active portion of the former are usually so small a minority, that it is pretty accurate to affirm they are more useful as pioneers than as pilots, while it is in the nature of things that the latter should gradually lose their power by desertions, until compelled by circumstances to yield.

The considerations connected with these truths teach us that reform is generally a wiser remedy than revolution. Still it must be recollected that the progress of things is not always in the right direction. Artificial and selfish combinations frequently supplant the natural tendency to improvement, and a people, by waiting the course of events, might sometimes be the supine observers of the process of forging their own chains. In all such cases, unless the current can be turned, it must be made to lose its influence by being thrown backward.

In continuing the subject of the last letter, I am of opinion that the present system of England is to undergo radical alterations, by the safest of the two remedies, that of reform; a denial of which will certainly produce convulsions. The hereditary principle, as extended beyond the isolated abstraction of a monarch, is offensive to human pride, not to say natural justice, and I believe the world contains no instance of an enlightened people's long submitting to it, unless it has been relieved by some extraordinary, mitigating, circumstances of national prosperity. The latter has been the fact with England; but, as is usually the case with all exceptions to general rules, it has brought with it a countervailing principle that, sooner or later, will react on the system.

Hitherto, England has had a monopoly of available knowledge. Protected by her insular situation, industry has taken refuge in the island; and, fostered by franchises, it has prospered beyond all former example. The peculiar construction of the empire, in which national character and conquest have been mutually cause and effect, has turned a flood of wealth into that small portion of it, which, being the seat of power, regulates the tone of the whole, as the heart controls the pulsations of the body. This is the favourable side of the question, and on it are to be found the temporal advantages that have induced men to submit to an ascendancy that they might otherwise resist.

The unfavourable is peculiarly connected with the events of the last thirty years. In order to counteract the effects of the French revolution, the aristocracy carried on a war, that has cost the country a sum of money which, still hanging over the nation in the shape of debt, is likely to produce a radical change in the elements of its prosperity. In the competition of industry which is now spreading itself throughout Christendom, it is absolutely necessary to keep down the price of labour in England, to prevent being undersold in foreign markets, and to keep up the prices of food, in order to pay taxes. These two causes united have created an excess of pauperism, that hangs like a dead weight on the nation, and which helps to aid the rivalry of foreign competition. Taking the two together, about one hundred and thirty millions of dollars annually are paid by the nation, and much the greater part as a fine proceeding from the peculiar form of the government; for the sacrifices that were made, were only to be expected from those who were contending especially for their own privileges. As the territories of England were impregnable, no mere monarch could have carried on the system of Mr. Pitt, since the rich would not have submitted to it, and as for the people, or the mass, there would have been no sufficient motive. In order to appreciate these efforts, and their consequences, it will be necessary to consider the vast annual sums expended by Great Britain during the late wars, and then look around for the benefits. One undeniable result is, I take it, that industry is quitting the kingdom, under the influence of precisely the same causes as those by which it was introduced. I do not mean so much that capitalists depart, as they left Flanders, for the scale on which things are now graduated, renders more regular changes necessary, but that the skill emigrates, to avoid the exactions of the state. I may, however, go further, and add that capital also quits the country. It takes longer to subvert the sources of national than of individual prosperity, and we are not to look for results in a day. Still these results, I think, are already apparent. They appear in the moderated tone of this government, in its strong disinclination to war, and, in fact, in an entire change in its foreign policy.

It is quite obvious that the English aristocracy is existing in a state of constant alarm. The desperate expedient of Mr. Pitt, that of undertaking a crusade against popular rights, is already producing its reaction. It is seldom that the human mind can be brought to an unnatural tension on one side, without recoiling to the other extreme, as soon as liberated. Men are constantly vibrating around truth, the passions and temporary interests acting as the weights to keep the pendulum in motion. The result of the present condition of the English aristocracy, is to put them, in a political as well as a social sense, on their good behaviour. Although so great a proportion of the peculiar embarrassments of Great Britain may be traced, with sufficient clearness, to the exclusive features of the government, there probably never has been a period in the history of the nation, when the power of the few has been so undisputed in practice, or its exercise more under the sense of correction.

I have already said that one of the consequences of the forced prosperity that grew out of the system of Mr. Pitt, was to raise up a dangerous social caste, that had no immediate connexion with the government, while it became too powerful to be overlooked. Sir James Mackintosh, in his History of the Revolution of 1688, has said, that the Constitution attributes the power of creating peers to the king, "either to reward public service, or to give dignity to important offices, or to add ability or knowledge to a part of the legislature, or to repair the injuries of time, by the addition of new wealth to an aristocracy which may have decayed." Nothing is wanting to the truth of this exposition but to add the words "or any thing else." Mr. Pitt extended these constitutional motives by including that of neutralising an antagonist wealth, which might become dangerous to the particular wealth already in possession of power. The peerage has been essentially doubled since the accession of George III. In addition to these accessions to the House of Lords, a great number of Irish peers have been created, who are also a species of direct political aristocrats. Social bribes have been liberally dealt out, in addition, by an enormous creation of baronets, of whom there are now near a thousand in the empire.

But this is a mode of maintaining a system, that will soon exhaust itself. Knighthood, except in particular cases, is no longer a distinction for a gentleman, and would be refused by any man of a decided social position, unless under circumstances to which I have elsewhere alluded. The exceptions are in the cases of especial professional merit. A lawyer, an artist, a physician, or a soldier, might be knighted without discredit, but scarcely an ordinary civilian. It would throw a sort of ridicule about a man or a woman of fashion, to be termed "Sir John," or "My Lady," without these alleviating circumstances.

The case is a little, but not much, better, as respects baronets. I should think it would no longer be easy to get a man of family, who is familiar with the world, to accept of a baronetcy, except as a professional reward. As we say in America, "the business is overdone." Even Irish peerages are not in favour.

You will readily understand the approaching necessity for change in the institutions of England, by looking a little more closely at facts. The danger comes equally from the rich and the poor. From the rich, because they are excluded from power by the action of the borough system, and from the poor, because they are reduced to the minimum of physical enjoyments, and are formidable by numbers, as well as by their intelligence.

As regards the rich, though the scale of pretension has gradually been extending itself with the wealth of the nation, the latter has outgrown the possibility of meeting its wants. The price of a seat in parliament amounts almost to a tariff, it is true, the average expense for a term of years being set down as a thousand pounds a-year, but the supply is limited, and is in a few hands. Men may submit to a competition, but, though in the case of representation there must be some fixed numbers, they naturally dislike monopoly, and still more, in such cases, the fruits of monopoly. Were the English government strictly a money-power government, its security would be treble what it is to-day, for it would at once neutralize one of the most formidable of its enemies. But it is not; for though based on money, it is so modified as not to give even money fair play. Were there not natural political antipathies between the rich and the poor, they would unite, and speedily produce a change. It would be a master-stroke of policy to bring in all the wealth of the country again, as a loyal ally of the government, by destroying the borough system entirely, equalising representation by numbers, establishing a reasonably high rate of qualification, and, by preserving the open vote, leave money to its influence. I take it, a money-government, that is fairly in action, in an industrious and intelligent nation, is only equalled in strength by one based on popular rights, in a community accustomed to the exercise of political privileges. It is, however, the government most likely to corrupt and debase society.

When I tell you of the intelligence of the poor in England, you are to understand me, not as saying that it extends very far; but the cultivation of intellect dependent on the exercise of the mechanical arts, the cheapness of printing, and the general spirit of the age, have raised up a set of men in England, among what are called the operatives, who are keen in investigation, frequently eloquent and powerful in argument, and alive, by position, to those natural rights of which they are now deprived. These men act strongly on the minds of their fellows, and are producing an effect it would be folly to despise. Paine was of the class.

The popular accounts of the fortunes of the landed aristocracy of England, may lead you into erroneous notions concerning their relative wealth and power, so far as the two are connected. Conversing lately with one of the best informed men in the kingdom on such a subject, I alluded to the reputed income of Lord Grosvenor, who is said to have £300,000 a-year. My acquaintance laughed at the exaggeraton, telling me that he did not believe there was a man in the country who had half that income, and that he knew but five or six who, he thought, could have as much as £100,000.

These large incomes are also liable to many reductions, even when they do exist. The estate is there, certainly, and the incumbent has a life interest in it; but what between widows' dowers, younger children, mortgages, and liens created by the anticipations incident to entails, and other charges, one, who is a good judge, tells me he questions if the proprietors of England touch much more than half the amount of their rent-rolls, if indeed they receive as much. My friend is intimate with a man of rank here, with whom I have, also, a slight acquaintance, and, speaking of his estate, he added, "Now, vulgar rumour will tell you Lord [Lansdowne] has a hundred thousand a-year; he has, in truth, a rent-roll of sixty thousand, of which he actually receives about forty."

There is so much beauty in probity, and one feels such a respect for those who manifest more devotedness to the affections than to worldly interests, that I cannot refrain from relating a circumstance, or two, connected with the history of this nobleman, that were related by his friend in the same conversation.

Lord [Lansdowne] was born a younger son. The improvidence of his father left a debt of the enormous amount of near a million of dollars. The elder brother and heir refused to recognize this claim, which did not form a lien on the estate. A moderate provision had been made for the younger brother. At this period, my friend was commissioned to speak to the latter, concerning a marriage with the heiress of a large estate; not less, I believe, than sixteen thousand a-year. He heard the proposition, coloured, hesitated, and answered that if he ever married, his choice was made. Shortly after he married his present wife, who was virtually without fortune. A few years later the elder brother died childless, when he succeeded to the titles and the estates. From that moment his expenditure was so regulated, that in a few years he was enabled to pay every sixpence of the debts of the father, since which time he has lived with the liberal hospitality becoming his station.

I do not know that the English nobility are at all deficient in liberality, but the charity-*fanfaronades* of Christmas blankets and hogsheads of beer, and warm cloaks, that so often appear in the journals here, have only excited a smile, while I have never seen Lord [Lansdowne], since I learned these traits, without feeling a reverence for the man. He has his reward, for his wife is just such a woman as would remove all cause of regret for having acted nobly.

An English gentleman has just published a book on the subject of the exaggerations that prevail concerning the incomes of the gentry of the country. He has adopted a very simple and a very accurate mode to prove his case, which, it strikes me, he has done completely. "Vulgar rumour gives Lord A———— thirty thousand a-year," he says, at starting. "Now we all know that the estates of Lord A———— consist of such and such manors, in such a county, and of so many more manors," all of which he names, "in some other county." These manors he shows to contain so many acres of land. The rental in each county is pretty well known, and, taking it at two pounds the acre, he calculates that nine thousand acres give but eighteen thousand a-year, *gross* income. This diminishes the popular rental nearly one-half. In this manner he goes on to show, in a great many real cases, (mine being supposititious), how enormously fame has exaggerated the truth in these matters. In estimating the struggle between the wealth that is in possession of power, and that which is excluded by the present political system of England, you are, therefore, to discard from your mind fully one-half of what is popularly said about the former, as sheer exaggeration.

Still the aristocracy of this country is very powerful. It has enlisted in its favour a strong national feeling, a portion of which is well founded, a part of which is fraudulent, and even wicked, and some of which is dependent on one of the most abject conditions of the mind to which man is liable. By aristocracy I do not now mean merely the peers and their heirs, but that class which is identified by blood, intermarriages, possessions, and authority in the government, for you are never to forget, though the House of Commons does contain a few members who are exceptions, that the controlling majority of that body is, to all intents and purposes, no more than another section of the interests represented by the peers. The two bodies may occasionally disagree, but it is as partners discuss their common concerns, and as the lords frequently disagree among themselves.

The English gentlemen have the merits of courage, manliness, intelligence, and manners.—Their morals are overrated, except as to the vices which are connected with meanness. Perhaps there is less of the latter than is commonly found in countries where the upper classes are more directly under the influence of courts, but even of this there is much, very much, more than it is common to believe in America. As between the English and ourselves, I honestly think we have the advantage of them on this point. They are our superiors in manners and in intelligence; they are our superiors in all that manliness which is dependent on opinion, but certainly I have known things practised, and that pretty openly, in connexion with interest, by men of condition here, which could not well be done by a gentleman with us, without losing *caste*. In the northern states we have very few families whose sons would now hesitate about embarking in commerce, at need, and this, of itself, is a great outlet (as well as inlet) for the vices of a pecuniary nature. The prejudices connected with this one subject are the cause of half the meannesses of Europe. The man who would hesitate about suffering his name to appear in a commercial firm would pass his life in a commission of meannesses, not to say crimes, that should put him to the ban of society. This feeling is daily becoming weaker in England, but it is still strong. Men of family scarcely ever engage *openly* in commerce, though they often do things *covertly*, which, besides possessing the taint of trade, have not the redeeming merit of even its equivocal ethics. To them the army, navy, church and government patronage are almost the only resources. The latter facts have given rise to two of the most odious of the practical abuses of the present system. A few occasionally appear at the bar, but more as criminals than as advocates. The profession is admittted within the pale of society, as it opens the way to the peerage and to parliament, but it requires too much labour and talents to be in favour. A physician in England ranks higher, professionally, than almost any where else, but he is scarcely considered an equal in the higher set. The younger sons of peers enter all the professions but that of medicine, but I never heard of one who chose to be a doctor. A curate may become Archbishop of Canterbury, but a physician can merely hope to reach a baronetcy, a dignity little coveted. Like our "Honourables," and "Colonels," it is not in vogue with the higher classes. I cannot better illustrate the state of feeling here, in relation to these minor titles, than by our own in relation to the appellations named, which are of much account in certain sets, but which it is thought bad taste to bandy among gentlemen. The masculine properties of the English aristocracy (I include the gentry, you will remember) have deservedly given them favour with the nation. They owe something of this to the climate, which is favourable to field sports, and something, I think, to the nature of their empire which has fostered enterprise. Physically they are neither larger, nor stronger, nor more active than ourselves, but I think they attend more to manly exercises. The army has been exclusively their property, for it is necessary, in such a government, to keep it in the hands of those who rule. The purchase of commissions is strictly in unison with the spirit of the system. Then the insulated situation of the kingdom, coupled with its wealth, induce travelling. The influence of the latter can scarcely be overrated, and no nation has so many motives for quitting home. The English go abroad for the sake of economy, for while their actual expenses are less, their incomes are increased from five to twenty per cent., by the usual courses of exchange. Formerly none but men of rank went abroad, and they were distinguished from the rest of the nation by their taste and liberality, but now all the genteel classes (and some below them even) travel. It is true the English character on the Continent has suffered by the change, but the English nation is greatly the gainer.

The English gentlemen are not sparing of their persons in war, or in civil troubles. They would not have abandoned Paris to a mob, in 1792.* These are qualities to captivate the mass, who greatly prize daring and physical excellencies. Although there is a considerable and certainly an increasing hostility to the exclusive classes of England, there is also a deep feeling of respect and even of attachment for them, in a portion of the nation. Perhaps no aristocracy was ever less enervated or thrown off its guard, by the enjoyment of its advantages, than this, a fact that must be attributed, too, to the circumstance that the public, by possessing

---

*In 1830-31, when England was menaced with revolution, the English travellers on the Continent of Europe, hurried back to their own country, to be at their posts.

so many more franchises than usual, have kept them constantly on the alert. In the event of any struggle between the aristocrats and the mass, I should say that much may be expected from the manliness and spirit of the former, enough, perhaps, aided as these qualities would be by their habits of control and combination, to secure the victory, were it not that the very affluence of intelligence in this portion of the nation, would always put at the command of the people sufficient men of minds and authority to direct them. Although a wide reform, wide enough to admit themselves, would be apt to be sustained by the *novi homines,* revolution would not; for the new rich, as a body, are always found on the side opposed to popular rights; and the aristocracy would have most to apprehend from seceders from their own body, as leaders, unless events, as probably would be the case, should raise up some man of native fitness for the station, from the ranks of the people themselves.

That part of the present influence of the aristocracy which is fraudulent and even wicked, is connected with a wide-spread system of studied misrepresentation, and with abuses connected with the church. As I shall probably have occasion to write a short letter on the subject of the latter, I will touch on the former alone, at present. While the aristocracy itself is so well mannered and less apt to betray illiberal sentiments than the classes beneath it, I cannot think it free from the imputation of having conspired to circulate the atrocious misrepresentations which have been so industriously promulgated against ourselves, for instance, during the last half century. They may despise the traitors, but they love the treason. The whole code of prejudices and false political maxims which pervade society here, is the offspring of a system of which they are the head. They have differed from the other nations of Europe, in which power is exclusive, in the circumstance of the franchises of the nation. A franchise is not power of itself, but it is an exemption from the abuses of power. As it was not possible to muzzle the press, it has become necessary to make it the instrument of circulating falsehood. No means of effecting such an end are so certain as that of creating prejudice, which instantly becomes an active and efficient agent in attaining the end. The United States, her system, national character, historical facts, people, habits, manners, and morals, for obvious reasons, have been one principal object for these assaults, but as I may have occasion to speak of the Anglo-American question hereafter, I will now allude only to the internal action of the system.

Thirty-six years ago, you and I were school-fellows and classmates, in the house of a clergyman of the true English school. This man was an epitome of the national prejudices, and, in some respects, of the national character. He was the son of a beneficed clergyman in England; had been regularly graduated at Oxford and admitted to orders; entertained a most profound reverence for the king and the nobility; was not backward in expressing his contempt for all classes of dissenters and all ungentlemanly sects; was particularly severe on the immoralities of the French revolution, and, though eating our bread, was not especially lenient to our own; compelled you and me to begin Virgil with the Eclogues, and Cicero with the knotty phrase that opens the oration in favour of the poet Archias, "because their writers would not have had them placed first in the books if they did not intend people to read them first;" spent his money freely, and sometimes that of other people; was particularly tenacious of the ritual, and of all the decencies of the church, detested a democrat as he did the devil; cracked his jokes daily about Mr. Jefferson and Black Sal, never failing to place his libertinism in strong relief against the approved morals of George III., of several passages in whose history, it is charity to suppose he was ignorant; prayed fervently of Sundays; decried all morals, institutions, churches, manners and laws but those of England, Mondays and Saturdays; and, as it subsequently became known, was living every day in the week, *in vinculo matrimonii*, with another man's wife!

You know this sketch to be true. Now, I do not mean to tell you that all the stronger features of this case are at all national, but I think the prejudices, the pretending condemnation of the moral defects of those who did not think exactly as he did, and the blindness to his own faults, are. In this particular, that church of which our old master was a member, in doing the state good service, has done itself a grave injury. The popular mind has been so acted on, by a parade of religious influences, that millions of Englishmen attach a sense of criminality to the efforts of those who would reform the government. I think you must have observed how seldom one has found an active English reformer left in possession of a fair moral character. The course has usually been to commence by assailing the liberals with sneers, in connection with their origin, their pursuits, and their motives. These attacks have been addressed to the abject feeling which the establishment of an aristocracy has formed in the minds of the mass, and which has created a sort of impression that birth and fortune are necessary to the civic virtues. He who should make it matter of reproach against a public man in France, that he came of the people, would lose more than he would gain by his argument, and yet it is a constant weapon of the English party tactics. Failing of success, by these means, the next assault is against the character.

The English themselves are apt to attribute the latter expedient to a creditable feeling in the nation, which invites, by its moral sense, exposures of this nature. The reasoning may be true in part, or it is true up to the level of the dogmas of the decency-and-seemliness school which the system has created, but it is flagrantly false when viewed on pure Christian principles. Coupled with the grossness of language, the personalities, the vindictiveness and the obvious deformities of hostility and art, with which these attacks are usually made, nothing can be more inherently offensive to the feelings of those, of whom the "chiefest virtue" is charity. But we need no better proof that the whole is the result of a factitious state of things, in which a parade of morals is made to serve an end, than the fact, that, while every man who shows a generous mind is peculiarly obnoxious to be accused of vice, they who are notorious for their misdeeds are not only overlooked, but spoken of in terms of reverence, if they happen to belong to the dominant party. You will understand me; I am not now speaking of the common party abuse, which varies with events, but of a deliberate and systematic method of vituperation, by means of which the idea of liberalism in politics has become associated in the public mind, with irreligion, libertinism, pecuniary dishonesty, and, in short, with a general want of moral principle. As a consequence, men habitually think of Mr. A_____, or Sir George B_____, or Lord C_____, as persons to be condemned for their sins, though the very vices of which they are accused are openly practised by half the favourites and leaders of the other side, with impunity as regards the public. I can quote to you the instance of Washington, who was accused of being an unprincipled adventurer, at the commencement of the revolution, as a case in point; and I dare say your own scrupulous and pious father, passed for a fellow no better than he should be, with a majority of the well-intentioned English of that day.

It seems to me that there is a singular conformity between English opinion and the English institutions. The liberty of the country consists in franchises, which secure a certain amount of personal rights, and not in a broad system, which shall insure the control of the numbers. As individuals, I am inclined to think the English (meaning those who are easy in their circumstances) do more as they please than any other people on earth; while the moment they begin to think and act collectively, I know no nation in which the public mind is so much influenced by factitious and arbitrary rules. Something like the very converse of this exists with us.

I have little to say about the influence which the aristocracy possess through the deference of their inferiors. Strange as it may seem, the subordinate classes take a sort of pride in them. Such a feeling can only have arisen from the depression of the less fortunate, and it is quite plain has gathered no small part of its intensity from any thing but that knowledge which leaves "no man a hero with his *valet-de-chambre*." It exists to a singular degree, in despite of all the bluster about liberty, and I can safely say that I never yet knew an Englishman, I care not of what degree of talents, who did not appreciate the merits of a nobleman, to a certain extent, by his rank, unless he lived in free and constant communion with men of rank himself. I have found the nobles of England, certainly, as I have already told you, but it has often puzzled me to discover the aristocratic mien, the aristocratic ears, aristocratic fingers, aristocratic nails, and aristocratic feet that these people talk and write so much about. I have been often led to think of that *jeu d'esprit* of Hopkinson, where he says

> "The *rebel* vales, the *rebel* dales,
> With *rebel* trees surrounded,
> The distant woods, the hills and floods,
> With *rebel* echoes sounded,"

in reading of these marvels. I need scarcely tell you that an English nobleman is morally much as the highest gentleman of a great and polished empire might be supposed to be, and in physical formation very like other men. His ears may, occasionally, be a little more obvious than common, but he possesses no immunity by which they can be made smaller than those of all around him.

I think this feeling of deference, however, is so interwoven with all the habits of thought and reasoning of the nation, that its *prestige* will long confer an advantage on the nobles of England, unless the torrent of change, by being unnaturally and unwisely dammed, gain so much head as to sweep all before it.

There is no great princely nobility in England, like that which exists on the continent of Europe, and which, royal personages in fact curtailed of their power by the events of this and of past ages, is still deemed worthy of forming royal alliances. In blood, modern alliances, and antiquity, the English nobles, as a class, rank among the lowest of Europe, their importance being owing to the peculiarity of their political connexion with one of the first, if not the very first state of Christendom. I do not know that their private wealth at all surpasses that of the great nobles of the continent, those of France excepted; although there is no inferior nobility here, as there, the younger sons sinking at once into the class of commoners. When the Howards of the fifteenth century were just emerging from obscurity, the Guzmans, the Radziuils, the Arembergs, and hundreds of other houses were sinking from the rank of princes into that of their present condition. The ancestors of Talleyrand were deprived of their possessions as sovereign counts, a century before the first Howard was ennobled. As to the ancient baronies that figure among the titles of the English, they are derived from a class of men who would have been followers, and not the equals, of the Guzmans and Perigords, five centuries since. There appear to me to be two errors prevalent on this subject; that of overrating the relative importance and antiquity of the nobility of England, (except when viewed as a political aristocracy, or since the revolution of 1688) and that of underrating the true condition of the English gentry. All this is not of much importance, though I was lately told of a German princess who spoke of a marriage with the House of Hanover, as a *mésalliance!*

Letter XIV.
To Richard Cooper, Esq., Cooperstown, N. Y.

The last month has been one of severe duty with the knife and fork. Through the hospitality and kindness of Mr. Rogers I have dined no less than three times with him alone.

On the first occasion our party consisted of Lords Lansdowne, Grey, and Gower,* Sir Thomas Lawrence, Mr. Luttrell, and myself. I have little to tell you of this dinner, which was like any other. I thought some of the company stood too much in awe of the great man, though I did not see why, for there is no one here with whom I feel less restraint, myself, than with Lord Grey. Of course one defers naturally to a man of his years and reputation, but beyond this, I found nothing to check conversation.

The painter is a handsome, well-behaved man, though he was not at his ease. In the course of the evening he inquired if I knew Gilbert Stuart. He had a slight acquaintance with him, and wished to know if "he were not a very facetious gentleman." I was of opinion that Stuart invented to amuse his sitters. This, Sir Thomas then observed, explained a report he had heard, according to which, Mr. Stuart had claimed him as one of his pupils; an honour I thought he rather pointedly disavowed. Our artist does not appear to be much known here. It is the fashion to decry Mr. West now, quite as much as it was to overrate him while the island, by the war, was hermetically sealed against continental art. We constantly run into the extreme of over-estimating the celebrity of our own people in this part of the world. So far as my experience goes, Washington and Franklin are the only two Americans who enjoy thoroughly European reputations. I mean by this, that were their names mentioned in a drawing-room, every one would know who they were, their peculiar merits, and the leading points in their histories. Jefferson would, I think, come next; after which,

*The present Duke of Sutherland.

the knowledge of individuals would be confined chiefly to the respective professions. There are men who live by writing for the periodicals, and such is the craving for novelty, that they lay heaven and earth under contribution for subjects. In this way, an article occasionally appears that treats of American things and American names, and, in the simplicity of our hearts, we fancy the world is meditating on our growing greatness, when in fact, the periodicals themselves scarcely attract attention. Indeed, one of the things that has struck me favourably here, is the practice which people have of doing their own thinking. Puffs and advertisements may help a work off, but they do not, as with us, bestow reputation. Nothing is more common than to hear opinions of books and pictures, but I do not remember ever to have heard a remark concerning the notions of the reviewers. Reviews may control the inferior classes, but they have little or no effect on the higher. Intelligence, breeding, tone, taste, and manners, rally in such masses in these huge capitals, that they not only make head against the inroads of vulgarity and ignorance, but they even send forth a halo that sheds a little light out of their own proper sphere; whereas, with us, like treasures exposed to invasion, they are in constant risk from an incursion of the barbarians, who sometimes fairly get them in their clutches.

Mr. Allston is less known than I had supposed, though where known he seems to be appreciated. I should say Mr. Leslie is more in possession of the public, here, than any other American artist, though scarcely known out of England, for a painting has not ubiquity, like a book. Mr. Newton's reputation is limited. We boast too much of these gentlemen; not on account of their merits, for each has great merits in his way; but because I think neither is particularly anxious to meet our prurient attachment. Mr. Leslie is a mild man, and cares little, apparently, for any thing but his tastes and his affections; the latter of which do not turn exclusively to America. He was born in London, and has told me that his first recollections are of England. Mr. Newton has quite pointedly given me to understand that he too was born a British subject, and that he thinks himself an Englishman. If any man is excusable for deserting his country, it is the American artist. His studies require it, even, and there is little to gratify his tastes at home. As respects these two gentlemen, the accidents of birth are in unison with the accidents of their profession, and it really seems to me we should show more self-respect by permitting them to choose their own national characters.

At the second dinner we had ladies; the sister of the poet presiding. We were kept waiting a good while for two or three gentlemen who were in the House of Lords, where it seems an interesting debate occurred on a party question, but we sate down without them. We had at table, Mr. Thomas Grenville; a Lord Ashburnham, who, when asked the question, confessed he had not been in the House, except to take the oaths, in seventeen years; and Lady Aberdeen, the wife of the minister. Lady _____ was also of our party. The absentees left large gaps at the board, and our dinner was *tant soit peu* dull.

In the course of the evening, Mr. Grenville related a very amusing anecdote of Scott. They dined in company with the Princess of Wales, while she was in her equivocal exile at Blackheath. After dinner, the party was grouped around the chair of the Princess, when the latter said abruptly, "They tell me, Mr. Scott, you relate the prettiest Scotch stories in the world; do have the goodness to relate me one." This was making a little of a mountebank of the great bard to be sure, but his deference for royal rank was so great that he merely bowed, and said "yes, madam," and began—"In the reign of king such a one, there lived in the highlands of Scotland, such a Laird," going on with his legend, as if he were reading it from a book. The story was short, neatly told, and produced a good effect. "Dear me! Mr. Scott, what a clever story!" exclaimed the Princess, who, if all they say about lineage and blood be true, must have been a changeling, "pray be so obliging as to tell me another." "Yes, madam!" said Scott, and without a moment's hesitation he went on with another, as a school-boy would go through with his task!

Mr. Grenville asked me if John Jay was still alive. On hearing that he was, he spoke of him in high terms, as a man of abilities and sterling integrity. I should say Mr. Jay has left a better name in England, than any diplomatic man we ever had here. In general, I think the disposition is to "damn us with faint praise;" but the respect of Mr. Grenville seemed sincere and cordial. Dr.

Franklin is not a favourite in London; more than one of the prominent men among the English statesmen speaking of him, in my presence, in any thing but terms of admiration.

It is not a safe rule to take the opinion of England concerning any American in public life, for it is very often "*tant mieux, tant pis*" with them, but there is a sturdy honesty in the better part of this nation that gives a value to their judgments in all matters of personal integrity and fair standing.

After dinner, our peers came in full of their debate, and as merry as boys. Lord Holland was one of them, and he was quite animated with what had passed. It seems my bishop had made a speech, which they pronounced rather illogical.

Sir Walter Scott soon after joined us. Although so complaisant to a princess, he showed he had stuff in him, to night. There was a woman of quality present, who is a little apt to be *exigeante*, and who, I dare say, on a favourable occasion, might ask for three stories. No sooner did the great poet appear in the door, than, although in a remote part of the room, she addressed him in a decided voice, asking him how he did, and expressing *her* delight at seeing him. The old man took it all like Ben-Nevis, walking up coolly to Miss Rogers and paying his respects, (a tribute to good manners that scarcely silenced the other) before he made the least reply. This was done with the steadiness, quiet, and tact of Lafayette, certainly one of the best bred men of the age. Scott seems much more at his ease in London than he did in Paris, where the romance and the *empressement* of the women had the effect to embarrass him a little.

The third of Mr. Rogers's dinners was given expressly to Sir Walter Scott, I believe. We had at table, Sir Walter himself, Mr. Lockhart, Mrs. Lockhart, and Miss Anne Scott; Mr. Chantrey, Lord John Russell, and Mr. Sharp, a gentleman who is called "Conversation Sharp," Sir James Mackintosh, and a Mr. Jekyll, who, I was told, from his intimacy with George the Fourth and his wit, has obtained the name of the "king's jester." Mr. Leslie came in before we left the table, and in the drawing-room we had Mrs. Siddons and several more ladies.

There is something too gladiatorial about such dinners, to render them easy or entertaining. As a homage to Scott it was well enough, but it wanted the *abandon* necessary to true enjoyment.

No one talked freely, even Mr. Sharp, who has obtained so much reputation for ability in that way, making one or two ineffectual rallies to set us in motion. I have met this gentleman frequently, and, though a sensible and an amiable man, I have been a good deal at a loss to imagine how he got his appellation. In comparison with that of Sir James Mackintosh his conversation is gossip. I do not mean by this, however, that Mr. Sharp indulges in trivial subjects, but it strikes me, he has neither reach of mind, information, originality, wit, nor command of language, to give him reputation in a town like London, and yet he is every where called "Conversation Sharp." In short, if I had not been told that such was his *sobriquet,* I should have said he was a sensible, amiable, well-read person, of social habits, and who talked neither particularly well, nor yet so ill as to attract attention, and just about as much as a man of his age ought to talk. He seems rather more disposed than usual, to break the stiff silence that sometimes renders an English party awkward, and may have become distinguished in that way, for the man who will put Englishmen at ease in company, meaning Englishmen of a certain class, merits an illustration. Before this dinner, however, I have never observed so much of this social awe, in the better company, here. A caste or two lower in the scale, it becomes characteristic of the national manners, always excluding, of course, those who are so low as to be natural. I think the *people* of England are more hearty, cordial, and free in their modes of intercourse, than the people of America, though certainly less *parochial;* the application of which term I shall leave you to discover for yourself.

Mr. Jekyll has a reputation for chaste wit. Today he was not distinguished in this respect, though I observed that the company occasionally smiled at his remarks, as if they associated cleverness with his conversation. In this particular, I question if there is a man in London, above the level of story-tellers and jokers, who is the equal of Mr. W_____.

It strikes me the English are drilled into a formality that throws a cloud over their social intercourse. As a people they are not fluent, and the itching desire to catch the tone of the highest class has probably a bad effect; for a man may be a peer, or a great commoner, without being much gifted with intellect. It is true, that Englishmen of this class are generally respectable, but mere respectability of mind will not suffice for great models, and when a body of merely respectable men impart a tone to others, which originates in their own incapacity, it has the effect to restrain talents. Individuals like Sir James Mackintosh and Mr. Coleridge overcome this by the force of their impulses, and the consciousness of power, but thousands of men, highly, though less gifted than they, are curbed by the established forms. This is but speculation, after all, and quite likely it is valueless.

I have told you Mrs. Siddons and several other ladies joined us in the evening. Mr. Rogers presented me to the former, but her reception was cold and distant. Drawn out, as I had been, especially for this introduction, I could not withdraw abruptly without saying something, and I remarked that our papers, perhaps idly, had been flattering the Americans that she was about to visit the country. She answered that if she were twenty years younger, she might be glad to do so, but her age now put such a thing quite out of the question. Her air was too much on stilts, I thought, and, though I dare say, it is her natural manner, it reminded me unpleasantly of the heroine. Her voice seemed pitched to the stately keys of a tragic queen, and her enunciation was slightly pedantic. I should say for the drawing-room, her tone, as relates to these peculiarities, was decidedly professional and bad. I may tell you many things of this nature that will be opposed to your previous impressions, but the sources of information, whence the portraits of the periodical literature of the day are drawn, are to be distrusted. There is one distinguished English writer in particular, of whom it is the fashion to celebrate, in constant eulogies, the grace and deportment, who, I shall say, is one of the very worst-mannered persons I have ever met in cultivated society. Flattery and malice, sustained, as both are, by the credulity and compliance of mankind, make sad work with the truth.*

---

*In speaking of personal peculiarities, the writer thinks he has had sufficient care not to wound the parties. His knowledge of Mrs. Siddons does not extend farther than an evening's observation of her mere exterior, but she is removed beyond the reach of his opinion, did it apply to things more essential. Of the persons collected around the table of Mr. Rogers, on the day in question, Sir Walter Scott, Miss Scott, Sir James Mackintosh, Mr. Sharp, and Mr. Jekyll, are, also, already dead!

Mr. Lockhart did me the favour to present me to his wife, who is a daughter of Sir Walter Scott. She is eminently what the French call *gracieuse*, and just the woman to have success at Paris, by her sweet simple manners, sustained by the great name of her father. I thought her quick of intellect and reflective of humour. Scott himself was silent and quiet the whole day, though he had a good stately chat with Mrs. Siddons, who *dialogued* with him, in a very Shaksperian manner.

The next day, in the morning, I had a visit from Sir Walter, to apologise for not keeping an engagement he had made to go with Mr. Rogers and myself to Hampton Court, where his son Major Scott is just now quartered. In the conversation in which this engagement was made, I happened to mention something connected with my consulate, when Sir Walter inquired, with a little interest if I were the consul of America at Lyons. I told him I was so in commission and name, though I had never been in the place. "Ah!" observed Mr. Rogers, with a pithy manner he knows how to assume—"it is a *job*." To this I answered, it was a bad job, then, as it returned neither honour nor profit. Sir Walter had listened attentively to this trifling, and he now came to speak further on the subject, as well as to make his apologies.

The late Lady Scott was the daughter of a native of Lyons it seems, her maiden name having been Charpentier, or *Anglicé*, Carpenter. Some person of the family, as I understood Sir Walter, had gone to the East Indies, where he had accumulated a considerable fortune, and it now became important to his children to establish the affinity, in order to do which, the first step was to get extracts from the local registers, of the birth of M. Charpentier. He brought with him a note of what he required, and I promised to send it to the consular agent, immediately, for investigation. In this note he described M. Charpentier as a *maître d'armes*, or fencing master, a sort of occupation that would just suit his own notions of chivalry.

The excuse for postponing the party to Hampton Court, was a summons from the king to dine at Windsor, a command of this sort superseding all other engagements. He kindly begged me to name another day for the excursion, but, between bad health and business, it was not in my power to do so. Your aunt, too, who was completely excluded from society by her mourning, and who was now in London for the first time, had too just a claim on my time, to be set aside for other persons. She wished to go to Windsor and Richmond, and into Hertfordshire, and these considerations compelled me to forego the rare pleasure of making a third in a party composed of Walter Scott and Samuel Rogers.

I have just missed seeing Mr. Wordsworth too, in consequence of ill health. He dined with Mr. Rogers, and I was asked to meet him, but my old enemy the headache and a severe nervous attack, obliged me to send excuses, though I put them off as long as I could, and drank hot tea all the morning to get myself in trim. Mr. Rogers sent to press me to join them in the evening, but I was then in bed. As country air will now be useful, we have determined to go to Windsor at once.

Letter XV.
To Richard Cooper, Esq., Cooperstown, N. Y.

Whatever may be said of the beauty of the country in England, in particular parts, it scarcely merits its reputation as a whole. I have seen no portion of it that is positively ugly, a heath or two excepted, and yet I have seen more that is below mediocrity, than above it. I am told, however, I have not seen its finest portions. There is certainly little to admire, in the way of landscape, immediately in the vicinity of London, so far as I have become acquainted with its environs, and we have now entered and left the town in nearly every direction.

Taking our own village as a centre, and describing a circle, with a radius of fifty miles, I greatly question if all England could supply the same field of natural beauty. Our landscapes have much the effect of English park scenery, too, aided by the isolated and graceful woods that belong to every farm, and the negligent accidents of clearing, of which the celebrated art of landscape gardening is merely an imitation. But this country has a great advantage, both in its higher finish and in its numerous and interesting artificial accessories. It is only when viewed at the distance of a mile or two, that the scenery of our country, for instance, has the park-like character at all; the foreground of the picture commonly wanting the necessary polish. Still I can recall a portion of the road between Cooperstown and Utica, that comes almost up to the level of what would be thought fine rural scenery even in England, surpassing it in outline and foliage, and perhaps falling as much short of it, by the want of country houses and picturesque dwellings, bridges, churches, and other similar objects. I mention these places, because they are familiar to you, and not because the country has no more; for I think it may be taken as a rule, that the frequency and negligent appearance of our woods, bring the American landscapes, seen in the distance, much nearer to the level of the English, than is commonly believed.

There is a limit, which associates with the ordinary English rural scene, the idea of comfort and snugness, that is in marked contrast to the naked, comfortless aspect of the broad, unrelieved fields of France. This feature makes the great distinction between the landscapes of the two countries. The nature of the continent appears to have been cast in a larger mould than that of this island, and when, to this circumstance, you add the fact of the enclosures by means of hedges, on the one side, and their total absence on the other, you may form a tolerable idea of the different characters of the scenery of the two countries.

I am led out of London, and tempted to these remarks, in consequence of our having profited by the fine weather, to make several excursions into the country, after all of which I am half inclined to say that the town itself, possesses in its very bosom, finer rural beauties than are to be met any where in its neighbourhood. I have great pleasure, as the season advances, in studying the varying aspects of the parks, which, at moments, present singularly beautiful glimpses. The *chiaroscuro* of these pictures is not remarkable, it is true; the darks predominating rather too much. This is a bold criticism, considering that nature is the artist; but what I mean is, that the play of light and shade is not as sweet or as soft, as in milder climates. Still it is more poetical than that of a fierce sun, unrelieved by vapour.

The groupings in the parks contribute largely to their beauty. The mixture of cows and of deer grazing, with children at their sports, horsemen dashing across the view, and stately coaches rolling along the even and winding roads, add the charm of a moving panorama, to the beauties of verdure, trees, flowers, paths, and water. I do not, now, allude to the Sunday exhibitions; for they are cockney, and rather mar the scene; but to the more regular life of the week. You can hardly imagine the beauty of two or three scarlet coats, passing athwart the broad beds of verdure. I have seen battalions parading, but the formalities of lines rather injure than help the effect, though half a dozen soldiers, scattered about the grass, are like so many fine touches of light in a good picture.

One of our first excursions was to Richmond Hill. We were disappointed in the view, which owes its reputation more to the vicinity of a great town, I suspect, than to its intrinsic merits. The best of a capital, is pretty certain to get a name by the mere force of tongues, and the English have a failing in common with ourselves, which may be attributed to the same cause—an insulated position. This precious circumstance is quite certain to breed cockneys. The failing is that of thinking their own best, better than every one else's best. Travelling, however, is making great innovations on this patriotic vice, and Richmond, I think, is losing its parish fame.

The terrace of Richmond overlooks an exquisite bit of foreground, however, in which the Thames makes an admirable sweep, but the nearly boundless back-ground is crowded, confused, and totally without relief. When Mr. Mathews, the comedian, was in America, I took him to the belfry of the capitol at Albany, that he might get an accurate notion of the localities. He stood gazing at the view a minute, and then exclaimed: "I dont know why they make so much fuss about Richmond; now, to my notion, this is far better than Richmond Hill." Mr. Mathews did not recollect that they who *do* make the fuss, scarcely ever saw any other hill.

We were told the view was better from an upper window in the inn, than from the terrace; but I cannot think fifteen or twenty feet in elevation, can make any decided difference in this respect. We went into the park, but were not particularly struck by it. There was a large herd of deer, or I ought to say a drove, for they had a calm and *sheepish* appearance. It is an animal that loses its characteristic charm, in losing its sensitive, listening, bounding wildness, and its elasticity.

We passed Kew and Twickenham, varying the road a little in order to do both. The palace at the former place is to come down, being an old German-looking house that, as a palace, is unworthy of the kingdom, and which has not sufficient historical interest to preserve it. The gardens are valuable for their botanical treasures.

Twickenham is an irregular old village, along the banks of the Thames, whose beauties form its charms. We saw the exterior of the house of Pope, which is very much such a dwelling as would belong to a man of moderate means and habits, in America. Strawberry Hill was our object, here, however, but we were denied admission. The road, which is narrow and winding, like a lane, a beauty in itself, runs close to the building, but a high wall protects the grounds. In arrangements of this sort, the English, or rather the Europeans, much excel us. To the great houses there is space, but they understand the means of obtaining privacy and rural quiet, in situations that we should abandon in despair, on account of their publicity. Indeed few men with us would consent to "hide their light under a bushel," by building a plain rear on the road, shutting in their grounds by walls, and reserving their elegance for themselves and their friends. I am not quite sure the public would not treat a man's turning his back on it, in this manner, as an affront, and take its revenge in biting *his* back, in return. Such, notwithstanding, is the situation of Strawberry Hill, little being visible from the road it touches, but a rear that has no particular merit.

We were much disappointed with the house, seen as we saw it, for it appeared to me to be composed of lath and stucco; in part at least. It is a tiny castle, and altogether it struck me as a sort of architectural toy. And yet the English, who understand these matters well, speak of it with respect, though there is no people with whom "a saint in crape, is twice a saint in lawn," more than with these grave islanders, and it may be possible they see the wit of Horace Walpole, where I saw nothing but his folly. Lady _____, who has so good a house of her own, assures me the interior is quite a jewel, and the grounds, to use an Anglicism, delicious; and that she is in the habit of making a pilgrimage to the place twice a year I'll engage she don't walk on peas to do it.

We took another day to go to Windsor, which is twenty miles from town. Here the Thames is scarcely larger than the Susquehannah at Cooperstown, flowing quite near the castle. The town is neat but irregular, and as unlike Versailles as England is unlike France. This is a snug, compact, beef-and-beer sort of a place, in which one might enjoy a sea-coal fire and a warm dinner, while waiting for a stage coach; the other awakens the recollections of Burgundy and made dishes, and of polite life. One may expect a royal *cortège* to come sweeping down the stately avenues of Versailles at any moment, whereas the appearance of style in the streets of Windsor excites a sense of unfitness. One leaves an impression of a monarch who deems a kingdom erected for his use, who forces nature and triumphs over difficulties to attain the magnificent; the other, of the head of a state, profiting by accident to obtain an abode, in which his comforts are blended with a long chain of historical images.

The English say that Windsor is the only real palace in the country, and yet it struck me as scarcely being a palace at all. We were disappointed with its appearance at a distance, and almost as much with its appearance within. Like most old castles, it is an irregular collection of buildings erected on the edge of a declivity, so as to enclose different wards, or courts. I believe, including its terraces, it embraces twelve acres. The Tuileries and Louvre, together, must embrace forty. I should think the buildings of Versailles, without reference to the courts, cover more ground than are included within the walls of Windsor, and with reference to the courts, twice or thrice as much. A comparison between Vincennes and Windsor would be more true, than one between the latter and Versailles, after allowing for the fact that Windsor is still a royal residence. The round tower of Windsor, or its ancient keep, will not sustain a comparison with the *donjon* of Vincennes, while the chapel and royal apartments of the latter, will not compare with those of the former.

Windsor is a picturesque and quaint, rather than a magnificent place. It has a character of progressive power and civilization, which leads the mind to the associations of history, and which imparts to it an interest greater than that of mere grandeur, perhaps, but it has little pretension to be considered, on the score of taste and splendour, the principal residence of one of the greatest monarchs of the age; great, in connexion with the power of the nation, if not in connexion with his own. It would be an admirable accessory to the state of a king; venerable by time, and eloquent by association; but it is defective as a principal. While it has great discrepancies as a structure, there was a poetical imagery about it, that insensibly led me to see a resemblance between it and the history and institutions of the country; for, like them, it was the pretension of a palace reared on a foundation of feudal usages, aristocratical rather than royal in details, and among which the church has managed to thrust itself with great advantage, for the chapel, in magnificence and extent, is, out of all proportion, the finest and most important part of the edifices.

I have given you this comparative summary, because minute accounts of this venerable castle abound, and because these accounts do not leave accurate notions of the respective merits of things, without details that are fatiguing, and which are understood only by the initiated. Still Windsor has parts that merit particular mention, and which are peculiar to itself as a royal residence. The first of these is its situation, which may be classed among the most beautiful known. The view struck me, as far finer than that from Richmond Hill, though not as extensive. It is not the site that would be apt to be selected for a palace; but, as you can easily understand, when you remember that the Conqueror first established a hold at the place, it has rather the features of boldness and abruptness that belong to a fortress. These have been softened by modern improvements, and a good terrace now lines the brow of the hill on three of its faces.

The entrance is on the side of the town, and Windsor, like Strawberry Hill, turns its worst side to the public. The approach is abrupt and somewhat rude, but not without gothic grandeur. When within the gate, one is in an irregular court, of no great beauty, though large, but which contains the chapel, the pride of Windsor. The courts are not on the same level, the natural formation of the hill still existing, one lying a little above another.

We were shown through the state apartments, which greatly disappointed us, being altogether inferior to those of almost every French palace I have entered. There were a few rooms of a good size, but they all had a cold German air; and their ornaments, in general, were clumsy and in bad taste. In nothing is the superiority of the French taste more apparent than in their upholstery, and in their manner of fitting up apartments, and nowhere is this superiority more obvious than in comparing St. Cloud with Windsor. At the latter we had some ponderous magnificence, it is true, which exhibited itself in such vulgarisms as silver andirons and other puerilities; but of graceful and classic taste, there was surprisingly little. Even the hues of things were generally cold and chilling.

The castle is now undergoing very costly and extensive repairs, however, and as George the Fourth is allowed to have taste, if he has nothing else, and he is openly accused of having sent to Paris for furniture, it is probable that this description of Windsor will soon become untrue. We saw a few of the improvements which promise well, and, one room in particular, a hall in which the Knights of the Garter hold their banquets, bids fair to be one of the finest things in its way, in Christendom. It is to be fitted up in a gothic taste, to correspond with the old style of the architecture, and, seemingly in unison with the original design. In its present condition, I could not tell how far it had been changed.

The general impression of the state apartments, as I have just mentioned, was not favourable. They had a stiffness and a poverty of grace, if one can use such a term, that was obvious from the first. There were some fine pictures, and many that were indifferent. Sir Peter Lely flourishes here, and the state bedchamber of the Queen, for a lady as exemplary as Charlotte of Mecklenburgh, contains a droll collection of female worthies, by that Corydon of artists. Among them were Mrs. Middleton, Lady Denham, and the Duchess of Cleveland! The misers of Quintin Matsys are here. But you can get better descriptions of paintings from the regular books, than my limits, or my knowledge can help you to.

The chapel is a noble structure. It is as old as the reign of Edward the Fourth and it has a nave worthy of a cathedral, with a superb window. The roof is of stone, supported by ribs and groins of beautiful proportions. This chapel is called St. George's, and it is appropriated to the religious ceremonies of the Garter. The knights are installed in the choir, which contains the banners, stalls, and arms of the present members of the order, as Henry the Seventh's chapel in Westminster, contains those of the members of the order of the Bath.

The emblems of the Garter, like those of the Golden Fleece, carry the mind back to the days of chivalry, and to scenes of historical interest; but they awakened in me no feelings of respect, like those of the Bath. Personal rank is almost an indispensable requisite to belong to the order, and this, with personal or ministerial interest, generally suffices. The names of the sovereigns of Austria, Spain, Denmark, France, Prussia, and the Netherlands, were over as many stalls. There were also those of the Dukes of Dorset, Newcastle, Montrose, Beaufort, Rutland, Northumberland, and Wellington. With the exception of the last, did you ever hear of these knights?

There are many monuments in this chapel, one of which, to the Princess Charlotte, is remarkable by the design, and I think imposing, though it is not a favourite. West appears here, also, in a new character, having sketched the designs for some of the windows.

Eton College stands under the hill, beneath the castle, and on the margin of the river. It is a venerable and quaint pile, and I confess it interested me quite as much as its more celebrated neighbour. It was not a bad thought in Henry, to establish a seminary like this, for the early education of the youth of his kingdom, as it were, within the shadow of his throne. At Windsor the king is every thing, and boys that imbibe their earliest impressions in such an atmosphere, will be apt to feel a lasting reverence for monarchy. But none of the English schools, I believe, can be reproached with disloyalty, for the English cultivate a reverence for the throne that would seem to be pretty accurately proportioned to their systematic intention to allow no one fairly to fill it. They honour the king, and feed him, very much as the Egyptians treated their Apis. After all, is there no analogy between the various mystifications of different and remote nations?

There are said to be near five hundred oppidans, or boys who pay for their instruction, in the school, and near a hundred on the foundation.

We strolled in the Long Walk, which is an avenue lined by trees a league in length. This is royal in extent, but it is scarcely in keeping with the rest of the establishment. The park, I believe, is very extensive, and I presume beautiful, but we had not time to enter it. After taking a light repast, we returned to London, by a road different from that by which we had come.

We left Windsor much disappointed in many respects, and highly gratified in others. I had figured to myself a castle that should possess the usual finish which belongs to the English structures of this nature, while it was as much larger and nobler as a king is thought to be greater than a peer, and which was seated in the midst of such gardens and parks as I have been accustomed to see appropriated to royalty elsewhere. Instead of this, the edifices occupied by the family were scarcely better than a first-rate Paris hotel, if indeed any better. In the place of grandeur and state, however, we found quaintness and historical interest, and some of the most lovely rural scenery imaginable brought close to the walls, to supply the places of a broad park and formal alleys. Windsor Great Park is detached from the castle, and, as a part of the scene, it belongs as much to any one else as to the king.

In short, Windsor struck me as being a noble feudal residence; in this sense, relatively royal; but scarcely as magnificent and regal, as a palace.

We passed some very pretty houses on our way back to London. They were not generally larger than our own better sort of country residences, but had fewer incongruities, a better disposition of the grounds, and every thing was much better kept. One in particular attracted our attention, by its shrubbery and wood. A small lawn resembled velvet, and a stream from the setting sun bathed half of it in light, leaving the rest in shadow, producing an effect like the glow of a well-toned painting. It was the noblest colouring I had seen in England.

Letter XVI.

To Mrs. Comstock, Comstock, Michigan.

Although Paris has so much the most reputation for skill in the art, the English certainly do know how to dance, whatever rumour on your side of the Atlantic may say to the contrary. I remember the sensation made in New York, by the circumstance of the wife of an officer of some rank in the British service, not knowing how to join in the quadrilles, or cotillions rather, as far back as the year 1815. This lady, who, by the way, was a distant relative of your own, had been cooped up in the island of Great Britain for twenty years, by the war, and, either through sheer patriotism, or because London and Paris then lay so far asunder, her knowledge in the mysteries of Terpsichore did not extend beyond the minuet and the country dance, although, unlike most of those who then came among us from Europe, she was of gentle blood, herself, and her husband was the son of a lord. When this lady made her first appearance at a New York ball, to adopt a form of expression a good deal in vogue here, and which it is quite fair to use in the way of retaliation, she had been just *caught*, so far at least as dancing was concerned.

Times are altered, and although I will not even now take it upon me to affirm that the English women are as graceful, or as sylph-like, in a ball-room, as our own, they contrive, however, by the aid of their sweet faces, to render their quadrilles very attractive. Since the *pêle-mêle* of society has put an end to the public entertainments of our own large towns, we labour under the disadvantage of being obliged to use rooms so small that there is little space for graceful motion; an evil that is fast undermining our renown, in this particular, by introducing a slovenly and careless movement. You must look to it, or the English will come to be your equals in this accomplishment.

I have been led into these profound reflections, in consequence of having made my own appearance at some eight or ten of the balls of London, not, however, as an actor, but in the more sober character of an observer. It is my intention to endeavour to enliven your solitude near the setting sun, by rendering some account of what I have seen. My first appearance, at a premeditated evening party, did not happen to be at a ball, but at one of the receptions of a bachelor, who, in virtue of his great wealth, high rank, spacious house, and, for any thing I can say to the contrary, personal qualities, is, I believe, quite generally admitted to collect the very social *élite* of London. As there have been some very silly tales told, among our friends, in reference to my introduction to this gentleman, or rather to his house, for to *him* I never spoke, you will pardon a few personal details, if I tell you the truth, by way of preface.

You are to know, that, under the English system of exclusion, and owing to the silliness of man, to say nothing of the certain quality in the ladies, heaven and earth are sometimes moved, in order to obtain access to particular houses. As it may be well to understand each other on the subject of terms, let me explain what is meant here by exclusion. English exclusion is a wheel within a wheel; it is a capricious and arbitrary selection independently often of rank, fortune, birth, accomplishments, learning, or any thing else beyond mere fashion. It probably can no more be accounted for, than the dog, who did not eat hay himself, nor could give a substantial reason why he refused to let the ox have it. It is a sheer and natural consequence of the wantonness that is engendered by extreme luxury and a highly factitious state of things. We make a great mistake in America, in this matter, by blending the selection of society that are connected with education, similarity of habits and modes of living, unison of opinions, tastes, and breeding, with the arbitrary exclusion that is founded on nothing better than the whim I have just mentioned. One is natural, the other forced; one is necessary to the well ordering of society, and to the preservation of manners and tastes, the other is an effort to supplant the useful by the capricious; one is indispensable to all that is respectable in the sense connected with station, and is the only means by which grace can be cultivated, or refinement produced, while the other is inherently and irretrievably vulgar. Wherever civilization exists, society will be separated by castes, for it is not desirable to reduce all to the same level of deportment, tastes, and intelligence, nor possible without making a sacrifice of that which is most estimable. All that liberty assures us, is, entire equality of rights, and there would be little of this in a community, in which the cultivated and elegant were compelled to sacrifice their feelings by an unlimited association with the ignorant and coarse. The common sense of mankind, every where, silently admits this, and they who cry out loudest against it, are men who usually are unyielding to those beneath them, and declaimers for social equality only as respects their betters. They do not understand the reasons of their own exclusion, for they cannot comprehend points of breeding they have never been taught, tastes they have never cultivated, language they have never heard, and sentiments they have never felt. Happily these social divisions are inevitable, but the extreme exclusion of the English, is a diseased excrescence; a sort of proud flesh, that has shot up in a moral atmosphere, in which these natural causes have been stimulated into unnatural action, by the uncalled for aid of artificial stimulants and calculated adjuncts.

I cannot tell you *why* the house of the Duke of [Devonshire] is considered the very centre of exclusion, in the sense last named, at London; but I believe such to be the fact. After a few general admissions in favour of colour, texture, and workmanship, one would be puzzled to say why your sex decided on the fashion of the hat at the last exhibition of *Longs Champs*. The Duke of [Devonshire] is neither the oldest, the richest, the handsomest, the youngest, nor yet the most illustrious man in London, by a great many, and still, in a sense connected with extreme *haut ton*, he is, perhaps, the one most in request. He is the most *fashionable*, and that, until the *mode* shall be changed, is all that it is necessary to establish, to make out my case. Mr. _____ mentioned, in conversation, that the master of this enviable establishment, had expressed a desire that he would invite me to be among the guests on his next evening. "He would have sent his card, but I told him you would not stand on the ceremony," added my friend. It is always so much better that one should conform to the usages that custom and delicacy prescribe, and this the more especially when circumstances may render others doubtful of their reception, that I thought he had much better not have told him any such thing. A card would have removed every obstacle, and, as I was on easy terms with the negotiator, I believe I laughingly intimated as much. All that was said on the occasion, was said in three minutes, and amounted to a delivery of the request, the explanation I have mentioned, and my laughing comment. The next day I dined with two Americans, both of whom have long been resident here, and the conversation happening to turn on visits, I inquired whether there was any exemption in the case of a peer, about making the first visit in England, or, in short, whether our own usage, or that of the continent prevailed. I then mentioned the equivocal sort of invitation I had to [Devonshire] house. They both assured me, I had not received the proper attention, and that I was not bound to notice it, any further than had been done, by a simple acknowledgment of the civility of the messenger. One might go, or not, on such an invitation. In Paris it would have been my duty to leave a card, in such a case, and on its being returned, I might have gone with propriety. Under the circumstances, I determined to let things take their course; or if Mr. _____ said any thing more about it, to go on his account; if not, to stay away on my own. When the evening arrived, however, Sir James Mackintosh very kindly sent a note, to say *he* would be my companion, and I had nothing to do but to express my acknowledgments and readiness to accompany him; for while I cared very little about [Devonshire] house, and exclusion, I did care a good deal about receiving such an attention from Sir James Mackintosh.

I have said more concerning this silly affair than it deserves, but, having related the simple facts, it may be well not to throw away the moral. So much deference is paid here to rank, the cravings of the untitled to be noticed by the titled are so strong, and America is deemed so little worthy of taking place with any thing, that I am not surprised the truth even, in this case, should excite comment among the English. But what are we to say and think of our own manly, and "much beloved country," which, instead of supporting one of its citizens in maintaining what was due not only to himself, but to his nation, helps to confirm its present unseemly position, by decrying what would have been no more than an act of gentlemanly propriety and dignity, had it occurred, and which never having occurred at all, lends itself to the circulation of the falsehoods, that the malignant feelings of a set, in which even the name of America is hated, have seen proper to set in motion!

The American who comes to this country, and, forgetful of self-respect, of national pride, of the usages of society even, becomes the toad-eater of the great, is represented as a gentleman, as a man of sentiment, and of delicate feelings! The crumbs of flattery that are thrown out to him, to lead him on, and render him ridiculous, that the people to whom he belongs may be held up to ridicule through him, are reported at home, with high sounding exaggerations in his favour, while he who would simply maintain that an American gentleman is entitled to be treated like any other gentleman, is rendered liable to exaggerations just the other way. After all, unhappily, there is no more in this, than has marked our career from the commencement. The American who gets the good word of England is sure of having that of his own country, and he who is abused by England will be certain of being abused at home. I doubt if the history of the United States shows an instance to the contrary, except in cases connected with the party politics of the day, and much of the time, not even in them. It is not possible for one living at home, fully to comprehend the extent of the malignancy, or the nature of the falsehoods that are industriously circulated here, at the expense of the country and its citizens, and so far from leaning to credulity, when any thing of this nature reaches his own side of the Atlantic, not only does his character for sagacity require him to receive it with caution, but even his *safety*. If the craven and dependent feeling which exists so strongly in what are called the better classes of America, on the subject of Great Britain, existed in the body of the nation, our political union, or political independence, in my opinion, would not be worth ten years' purchase.

I went to the lodgings of Sir James Mackintosh, in Clarges Street, where we boldly entered a *hackney coach*, together, and drove triumphantly up to the very door of [Devonshire] house. I was quite passive in this daring act, however, and I throw the whole responsibility on the shoulders of my learned companion. We found the entrance thronged with footmen, and carriages were constantly arriving.

[Devonshire] house has one of those ill-contrived entrances, by a flight of exterior steps, which can never be used in bad weather, and which ought never to be used by your sex, at all. To obviate this difficulty, there is a more private entrance, through the basement, by which we were admitted. Here we found, in a sort of semi-subterraneous ante-chamber, ladies uncloaking, amid some fifty lackies. The room was in truth, above ground, but it strongly reminded me of the apartment beneath the rotunda of the Capitol; that which is called the *caucus*. A footman took our names, and we were announced by a line of servants spread through the passages and on the stairs. I believe there were four repetitions, all in good audible voices.

As the groom of the chambers, who stands at the door of the first reception-room, does not announce until you arrive, this mode at least has the merit of letting you know what is about to be said of you, and it affords an opportunity of correcting mistakes. On reaching this personage, he preceded us through one room to the door of a second, where he announced us, in the usual manner. There may be a little more style in this method of sending up names, but it is not easy to see its use, (unless you admit the one already named) especially if there be a convenient ante-chamber to uncloak in. Both the ante-chamber, and the stairs of [Devonshire] house, used to-night, were unworthy of the rest of the exhibition. The latter, in particular, were almost as narrow and mean as a New York flight.

Lord N———, one of the men of fashion and taste here, told me, in speaking of your sex in England, that he fancied he could see a difference between the women one meets with in and about Grosvenor Square, and the women who frequent [Devonshire] house. He gave a decided preference to the latter. When you remember that Grosvenor Square is inhabited by some of the highest nobles of England, and that it is one of the distinguished quarters of the town, you will at once perceive how subtle are the lines drawn by a fastidious taste, or, at least, by a fancy, that is overshadowed by fashion.

We found some two or three hundred of the *élite* of the town, collected on this occasion. The master of the house was not present, and we were received by a sister, Lady ———, who excused his absence by telling us he was indisposed. After this ceremony, we were permitted to stroll through the rooms and to look about us. I was introduced to a dozen people, among whom were M. Palmella, the Portuguese ambassador, and Sir James Scarlett. The former was a short, compactly-built, man, like most of his countrymen, while the latter, whom I had figured to myself, on account of the odious wigs of Westminster Hall, as a staid old gentleman, with a greasy face and a red nose, was a handsome, genteel, well-formed, and well-dressed man of fashion. When I mentioned my surprise to _____, he humourously remarked: "Yes, yes; he is good-looking, and all that, but he is an impudent dog in the house; most of the lawyers are impudent dogs in the house." It is impudence, you will understand, for a new man to let it be seen he knows more than your hereditary legislator.

I cannot say that I was as much struck with the peculiar advantages of the ladies over the rest of their sex, as was the case with my Lord N_____. There were many pretty, and a few beautiful, women present, but nothing of a very extraordinary nature. The Princess Lieven, who is a mirror of fashion, was among them. She looked more like an American woman, than most of the others.

I was a little amused with two or three whom I knew, and who evidently watched my manner, with the idea of detecting provincial surprise at the splendour and beauty by which I was environed. The expectation was too obvious to be mistaken. As respects the magnificence, it was certainly a great deal beyond any thing we have, and as certainly as much below a great deal I had seen on the continent. As an American, perhaps, I ought to have been astonished, though certainly not as a traveller.

The house was spacious, without being remarkably so; the furniture and fixtures were comfortable and heavy, rather than tasteful and rich; and the whole entertainment, the mean approach excepted, was as much respectable as magnificent. As for the company, I saw nothing unusual in its appearance. There may have been certain conventional signals and forms that rendered it peculiarly agreeable to those who were in the secret; but, judging it by those general laws that are supposed to regulate the intercourse of the refined and polished, it struck me as being *tant soit peu* below the tone of one or two *salons* I have entered in Paris. Of course, there was no vulgarity, no noise, and a good deal of ease, and much good sense; but there was a slightly apparent self-felicitation and enjoyment, in a good many, that a little too plainly betrayed a consciousness that they were in [Devonshire] house.

I was a little annoyed by the curiosity to see how an American would be struck with the wonders, and may have attributed this feeling to some who did not entertain it; but still I should say, that while there was possibly less acting on the score of personal vanity and from individual motives, than there would have been among the same number of French people of rank, there was a good deal more of it, from the exultation of belonging to a set so particularly exclusive.

There was present a young Duke of _____, with his wife on his arm; a lady old enough to be his mother. She was a dark Spanish-looking woman, well preserved, and with the remains of great beauty. I thought the faces of your sex less English than common, a circumstance which may have been owing, however, to the *coiffures*, which were generally French. The *toilettes* were rich and handsome, of course; but it is a fact, I think, beyond cavil, that the women of London do not dress as well as their fair rivals, on the other side of the channel; and I can only account for it, by the English lady's maid wanting the tact and taste of her French competitor; for, half the time, the peculiarity is observable at Paris, even, where both parties have access to the same *artistes*.

I went away early, and alone, the latter circumstance occasioning a mistake almost as ludicrous as that which accompanied the well-known Philadelphia experiment in announcing. There is a woman of fashion, here, a Countess [Cowper], whose husband's title is the same as his name, which is the same as our own in sound, though not in spelling. The latter having been varied by one of those caprices that have converted St. Maur into Seymour, and, according to Sir William of that ilk, Pepin into Draper. I gave my name to the groom of the chambers, on leaving the rooms, and at my request, he called for Mr. [Cooper]'s servant, for I had ordered little Smith to be in waiting with a cloak, intending to walk home, the distance being trifling. The first servant on the stairs, however, accustomed to the title of my fair namesake, and aware that she was in the rooms, called out, in a loud voice, for "Lady [Cowper]'s people." This cry preceded me, and when I reached the *caucus*, I found two powdered and liveried lackies ready to cover me with shawls and cloaks! I declined their good offices, but begged one of them to call Mr. [Cooper]'s man. The little fellow made his appearance, amid the sneers and laughter of his taller peers, who seemed to regard his powdered poll, and lack of inches, much as the peacocks regarded the finery of the daw.

I went one evening lately, to three balls, a mode of comparing sets, that I have always found useful in getting accurate notions of the ways of the world. As a brief account of what I saw, may not only amuse you, but serve to give you an idea of how these things are managed here, it shall not be withheld.

The first visit was to a rich merchant, who had risen in the world by his own enterprise, and who had finally come to keep what might be called a pretty good house. The style of building was much the same as that which prevailed in New York among genteel people, some thirty years since, with the exception that there was no stoop. The drawing-rooms were up one flight of steps, that in front occupying the whole width of the building. This is a fashion almost as general here, with the exception of the great houses, as the two rooms and folding doors, at home.

The mistress of this house was nervous, fidgety, and uneasy lest every thing should be not quite as elegant as she desired. I had not been in the room five minutes, before she whispered to me her great sorrow that the *Honourable* Mrs. Somebody had not been able to come, on account of some distressing event; this being positively the first time, in my life, I had ever heard of the honourable personage. There is a class here, that make almost as much use of this word, as the editors who come from New England. The company was exactly what you would suppose it to be when the presence or absence of an *honourable* Mrs. Somebody was a matter of moment.

From this house I went to another, in the neighbourhood, for the mercantile people, who aim at fashion, now live altogether at the west end, where I found very much the same sort of dwelling, but very different company. The mistress of this house, was an American, married to an Englishman of a good estate, and of respectable standing. Here I met with honourables and right honourables, enough; no one appearing to care any thing about them. I should absolutely have nothing to say concerning this ball, which was just like any other ball in a respectable house, did I not feel bound to add that I was much struck with the beauty of the young women, the neatness of their attire, and the accuracy and lady-like manner of their dancing. The quadrilles did not equal those of the Russian embassy, at Paris, already mentioned, it is true; for there was neither the numbers, nor the space, and possibly not the instruction necessary to produce an exhibition of this nature, equal to what one sees in Paris; but they were very graceful, and, what may appear to you as heterodox, quite equal in beauty to what one sees in New York or Washington.

I was looking at the dancers, when an English acquaintance observed, that he had lately met with a young American at a ball, and "really he could not see that she did not dance quite as well as the English girls about her." You will judge of the effect this produced on me, when I tell you, it was said, just as I had silently come to the conclusion that the English girls had, at last, learned to dance *nearly*, if not absolutely as well, as our own!

This may serve to give you some notion how accurately nations understand each other's peculiarities. Since my sojourn in Europe, it has been my good luck to witness the triumph of one American, on a scene far superior to any thing that usually offers in London. I shall not name the place, nor even the country, but it was at a ball given by a woman of royal birth. The palace was magnificent; and the company, the first in Europe. There were present fifteen or twenty royal personages, or those who were closely allied to monarchs, and nearly half in the room were of the titular rank, at least, of princes. I remember there was the heir to an English dukedom among others, and he attracted no more attention than any ordinary young man. A young American girl was invited to stand up in the set of honour. Her quiet, simple, feminine, lady-like dancing, coupled with the artless ingenuousness of a sweet countenance, in which mind was struggling with natural timidity and the reserve of good breeding, caused her, even in that assembly, to be instantly an object of universal admiration. As I stood in the crowd, unknown, I overheard the comments, which were general on every side of me. "Who is it?" was the first question; and when some one told her name and country, I heard no exclamation of surprise, that an American should be a lady, or know how to dance. In the course of the evening, it is true, twenty compliments were paid me on the grace and deportment of my young countrywomen in general, for it was inferred, at once, that they had seen a specimen of the nation!

From the house of Mrs. _____, who, herself, is far more creditable to us, than many who figure in the periodicals, showing her adopted countrywomen in what the true virtues of your sex consist, by being a model for a wife and mother, while she has cleverness and spirit, I went to that of a Lord C_____. Although I was now under a patrician roof, I saw no sensible difference in the building. Even the merchant was as well lodged as the peer, and all three of the houses had precisely the same wearisome monotony as our own. After the taste and variety of the dwellings on the continent of Europe, you may imagine how dull and fatiguing it is to enter twenty houses of a morning, and find precisely the same internal arrangement. They appear to me to be constructed like the coffins one sees in our streets, for some particular market, differing in sizes to suit, not the persons, but the purses, of customers, and, being put one in another, sent away for sale.

The company at Lord C_____'s, was much the same as that at Mrs. _____'s. It was generally well bred and well toned, and, in the principal drawing-room, where the quadrilles were in motion, I saw no difference, beyond that which belongs to personal peculiarity. There were the same pretty faces, the same fine, well-rounded forms, and the same regulated and graceful carriage. Depend on it, the English women will, sooner or later, dance as well as yourselves. Good luck to Free Trade!

You will feel some desire to know how balls, like the two last, will compare with balls of our own. In London, the rooms are a little larger; the music is much the same; the females, to a slight degree, are better dressed, as to freshness, though scarcely as well dressed as to taste; the men also, I think, are a little better dressed. The attendance has much more style, and the refreshments are not as good as with us. As to the essential point of deportment, the distinctions are more obvious than one could wish, especially among the men, and among the very youthful of your own sex.

The young play a very different part in Europe from that which is confided to them at home. On the continent of Europe, though girls of condition are now permitted to mingle a little with the world previously to marriage, it is under severe restraint, and with much reserve. The English have greater latitude allowed them, though infinitely less, than is granted with us. They still play a secondary part in society, and are subjected to a good deal of restraint. I should say that tone, reflection, and perhaps necesssity, impart more *retenue* of manner here, than it is common to see with us, though girls of good families, certainly the daughters of good mothers, at home, come pretty nearly up to the level of English deportment. It is the *pêle-mêle* of society, in towns that double their population in fifteen years, that is so destructive of manners with us. In the general scramble, no set remains long enough in a prominent situation to form a model. The growth of the country has this sin to answer for, as well as many others that are imputed to the institutions. In brief, then, a better manner prevailed at these balls than is usually met with at ours. I say usually, for I know exceptions in America, but our present concern is with the rule. There was less noise, nothing of the nursery, and generally that superiority of air, which is a natural consequence of minds more scrupulously trained and cultivated, and of a breeding subjected to laws more unyielding and arbitrary. Do not whisper these opinions, I beseech you, to any of your acquaintances, lest they murder me.

In making these comparisons, however, I do not wish to be misunderstood. I could fill a drawing-room, even in New York, that Babel of manners, with women who should do credit to any country. The difficulty would not be to select, but to exclude.

I have certainly met with a few instances of the exuberant manner among English women, but never among the higher classes. A caste, or two, lower in the social scale, it is not uncommon, and there is a set in which it actually appears to be the *mode*. Taking one example from this specimen of the nation, I will describe her, in order that you may know, not *whom*, but *what*, I mean.

Imagine a pretty woman, who will put herself in the centre of the floor alone, *entertaining* two or three men! She talks loud, laughs much, and has altogether a most startling confidence about her; she looks her companion full in the eye, with a determined innocence that makes him feel like a victim, and causes him to wish for a fan. This is a decided garrison manner, and has little or no success at London. Something like it might be seen in the house to which I first went this evening, but nothing like it, at the two others.

It ought to be said, that the young of both sexes have greatly improved, of late years, in England. The dandies, of whom you read in novels, have positively no existence here, or if they have, it is not among gentlemen. I have seen a great deal of mannerism of

Plate IX

Tower of London, from Town Hill

Tower of London, from the Thames

Plate X

Cheapside, looking down Poultry and Bucklersbury

High Street, Aldgate

Plate XI

Ludgate Hill, from Fleet Street

The Guildhall

Plate XII

Bank of England

East India House

deportment, in the secondary classes, often to a disagreeable and ludicrous degree, but nothing at all like the coxcombry that figures in the descriptions of the works of fiction. The men, as a whole, are simple, masculine in manner and mind, and highly cultivated, so far as elegant instruction goes. They fail in the knowledge that is practical, though with a certain set, even with this, or that which relates to things as they are connected with the machinery of their own power, they are familiar enough. Nearly all have travelled, and most read four or five languages, though few speak any well but their own. The same is true of your sex. I have hardly ever heard the merits of a novel discussed among them, and to the continental sentimentality they seem to be utter strangers; but it is apparent at a glance, that they understand better things, and have had their minds highly disciplined. Remember, unless in specific cases, I allude always to rules, and not to exceptions.

The English women are a little apt to strike an American as, in a slight degree, less feminine than his own countrywomen. There is something in the greater robustness of their *physique* to give rise to such a feeling, and I think they are, to a trifling extent, more pronounced in air. While they are much more punctiliously polite, they are scarcely as gracious. There is certainly less nature about them, though there is more frankness of exterior. All their conduct is rigidly regulated, and while they give you their hands in the manner of friendship, you do not feel as much at home, as with the American, who does not even rise to receive you, and who protects the extremities of her fingers, as if they were not the prettiest in the world. While the English woman would command the most respect, the American would win most on your feelings, in a general intercourse. I believe both to be among the best wives and mothers, that the world contains. The English aid nature, in all things, while the Americans too often mar it. No women do so much injustice to themselves, as the latter; their singularly feminine exterior requiring softness and mildness of voice and deportment, a tone that their unformed habits have suffered to be supplanted by the rattle of hoydens and the giggling of the nursery. I have seen many a young American, who has reminded me of a nightingale roaring. It is a pity that they do not seek models among the better society of their own country, instead of the inferior sets of Europe.

Letter XVII.

To Richard Cooper, Esq., Cooperstown, N.Y.

Mr. _____ has carried his kindness so far, as to go with me on the Thames. It had been our plan to row to Greenwich but the weather not proving favourable, we determined to go as far as London bridge, and return on foot through the city. We took boat, accordingly, at Westminster stairs, and went down with the tide.

The Thames is both a pretty and an ugly stream. When full, it is a river of respectable depth and of some width, but, at low water, above London bridge, it is little more than a rivulet flowing amid banks of slimy mud. The wherries in use are well adapted to their work, in this part of the river, but lower down they are not sufficiently protected against the waves. Accidents very frequently happen, though probably they are not out of proportion to the number of boats that are constantly plying in every direction. The principal danger is of getting athwart the cables of barges and ships, when the strength of the current is very apt to cause a wherry to fill.

As we went down with the tide, a pair of sculls answered our purpose, for one can have oars or sculls, at pleasure. The banks of the Thames, above Westminster bridge, are quite pretty, and above Chelsea, where the river flows through fields, they may be said to be even more; the villas on the shores, the windings of the current, and the meadows, raising them almost to positive beauty. But below Westminster bridge, little remains to be admired, until you reach the sea. Though on a larger scale, the navigable part of the river has a strong resemblance to the Raritan below Brunswick, being crooked, muddy, and bounded by wet meadows. The latter has a small advantage in scenery, however; the hills lying nearer to the stream. The passage of the Kilns, also, has frequently reminded me of the Thames below London.

Within the town, itself, warehouses blackened by coal-smoke, manufactories, timber-yards, building and graving docks, and watermen's stairs, principally line the shores. There are no magnificent quays, as at Paris, the shipping taking in and discharging by means of lighters, except in the wet docks, of which, however, there are now nearly sufficient to accommodate all the shipping of the port that is engaged in foreign trade. The Thames presents a very different picture today, from what it did when I first entered it, in the year 1806. At that time the river was literally so crowded as to make it a matter of great difficulty to get a ship through the tiers. There were hundreds of galliots alone, engaged in the trade from Holland, and this in a time of vindictive warfare! It was the only place I knew, which gave one a vivid impression of what is meant by a forest of masts. Most of the docks existed, too, at that time, and they were crowded with vessels. I asked the waterman to-day, an old man who remembered the river many years, what he thought might be the visible difference between the number of vessels in the port, during the year 1806 and that of 1828, and he told me fully half. My own eye would confirm this opinion. The trade has gone to the out-ports; particularly to Liverpool. With the commerce of the river much of its life and peculiarities, it seems to me, have departed. The *costumes* have disappeared: the watermen have a less jolly manner, and even Jack wears the bell-mouthed trowsers no longer. These mutations are constantly going on in the world, but the Thames left a vivid impression on my young fancy, twenty-two years ago, and returning to it, after so long an absence, they struck me with force, and in some degree painfully.

Although the Thames is not the Seine, nor the Arno, nor the Tiber, it has a picturesque and imposing beauty of its own, especially between the bridges. There is a gloomy grandeur in the affluence of the dark objects, in the massive piles that cut the stream, in the movement, and in the sombre edifices that line the shores. Here and there a building remarkable in history, or of architectural pretension, is seen, and usually the dome of St. Paul's is floating in the haze of the back-ground. As for the bridges themselves, they are not unsuited to the general sombre character of the view, though I think them in bad taste as to forms. There is an English massiveness about them that is imposing, but they strike me as being out of proportion heavy for the stream they span, and unnecessarily solid. The arches, with the exception of those of Southwark, are not sufficiently elliptical for lightness and beauty. It would have been a poetical and worthy thought to have made the bridge at Westminster gothic. Southwark bridge is of iron, and the open work impairs the effect of its proportions, which are much the finest of any, but could the sides be closed, it would be a succession of bold and noble arches. Between Westminster-hall and the Custom-house, there are now five of these heavy piles, viz. Westminster, Waterloo, Blackfriars, Southwark, and London. Preparations are making to rebuild the latter, and as London has improved so much in nothing, of late years, as in its public architecture, it is fair to suppose that the new work will be more worthy of the capital of a great empire than its predecessor; though, I dare say, it will not be as much extolled, since nations, like individuals, as their minds expand become less vain of their knowledge than they were wont to be of their ignorance. The London bridge of my nursery tales was but an indifferent specimen of national taste, though lauded to the skies.

We passed the Temple gardens, and one or two more belonging to private dwellings, before we got to Blackfriars, after which no signs of vegetation were visible. The Temple buildings are quaint and interesting, and the gardens, as usual in this country, spots of emerald, beautifully arranged.

We landed at London bridge, and my companion had the good nature to point out to me the supposed site of the Boar's Head, in East Cheap.* It must have been what the cockneys call a *rum* place, for an heir-apparent to carouse in, and yet, Shakspeare, who wrote in the century after that in which Henry reigned, would scarcely have presumed to take so much liberty with royalty, in an age like his, without being sustained by pretty well authenticated traditions, in favour of what he was doing.

Mr. _____ threaded the narrow streets of this part of the town, like one who knew them well, kindly pointing out to me every object of interest that we passed. I smiled as we went along the well-remembered thoroughfares, for it was not possible to avoid comparing the cultivated, celebrated, and refined man who gave

---

*The recent improvements in this part of the town, have caused the house to be pulled down, and it is probable the new avenue, which leads from the new London bridge to the Royal Exchange, and which, in 1833, promised to make this one of the finest parts of the town, will have obliterated every sign of its site.

himself this trouble, with an individual who had first introduced me, twenty-two years earlier, into the very same streets.

You must be sufficiently acquainted with family events to know that I was once in the navy. At that time, it was considered creditable as well as advantageous to the young naval aspirant, to show his mettle by going a voyage or two in a merchant vessel, as a common mariner, before he was placed on the quarter-deck of a man-of-war. This was my course, and I had twice visited London, in the capacity of a young tar, before I was eighteen, besides making several other voyages. The first time I came to London, it was fresh from college, a lad of about seventeen. I had then been long enough at sea to get a nautical air, and of course was confounded with my shipmates of the fore-castle. The oldest custom-house officer put on board the ship had been a gentleman's domestic, and he was full of the lore of the servants' hall. He soon singled me out, and I was much edified, for a week, with his second-hand anecdotes of great people, and the marvels of the West-end. The first Sunday after our arrival in dock, he proposed giving me ocular proofs of the truth of his accounts, and we sallied forth in company, he as Minerva, and I as Telemachus. We passed over much of the ground now passed over under the better guidance of Mr. _____ and it was amusing to me to note the difference in the tastes and manner of my two cicerones. When we approached the monument, the ex-valet stopped, and with an important manner inquired if I had ever heard of the great fire in London. I had, luckily, for it singularly raised me in his estimation. With due formalities, I was then introduced to the place where it had broken out, and to the monument. "That is what we call the monument," said Mr. _____, in his quiet way, glancing his eye at it, as he turned away to show me the new Boar's Head. "This is the house of my Lord Mayor, and that is the coach of one of the sheriffs," said Mr. Swinburne, for so was the custom-house officer named. "Wren has been much praised and much censured for this edifice," observed Mr. _____, as we passed beneath the massive walls. I was led by the ex-valet down a narrow street into a quaint, old, gothic, edifice, where, in a large hall, I was confronted with carved monstrosities in wood, which I was told with much chuckling were Gog and Magog. "That is a quaint and rather remarkable building," said the poet, as we passed the head of the same street; "it is Guildhall; you may know that it gets its name, from being used by the guilds, or corporated companies of the city." "This is Bow-church, and those are the bells that Whittington heard, as he was quitting Lunnun," observed the oracular Mr. Swinburne—"*You* were born far enough from this place, to escape the imputation of cockneyism," remarked the poet, as we trudged along. "There, that is St. Paul's!" cried Mr. Swinburne, with an awful emphasis, as if he expected me to fall down and worship it. "It was a great work to be executed by a single architect," the poet simply said, "and it has many noble points about it; I think it has, at least, the merit of simplicity." He was right enough, as to externals, but it wants unity of design, within.

In this way, then, I went along, with my present companion, ir-resistibly tempted to compare his quiet, unpretending manner, with the brimful importance, and strutting ignorance of the guardian of the revenue. One of the contrasts was so droll that I have not yet forgotten it, though it is unconnected with any of the historical monuments. Mr. Swinburne bristled close up to me, when we had got nearer to the court end, and putting his hand to his mouth, as we passed a quiet old gentleman, he whispered ominously, "An earl!"—"Do you see that person on the opposite side of the street," said the poet, within fifty yards of the same spot—"it is Lord _____, known as the husband of the handsomest woman in Eng-land, and for nothing else." I remember to have greatly scandal-ized Mr. Swinburne, by one of my antics. "Did you ever hear of such a man as John Horne Tooke," he inquired. "Certainly; what of him?" "Why that is he who has just passed—the fellow who looks like a half and half parson." I turned in my tracks, incontin-ently, and gave chase, for, at that early age I was not insensible to the pleasure of looking at celebrated men, and I had been taught to regard Horne Tooke as a writer who had got the better of Junius. Favored by the jacket and trousers I passed several times round "the chace," and I believe at length attracted his attention, by my manœuvres. He was an austere looking man, but I fancied he was not displeased at such evident admiration. As for Mr. Swin-burne, he applied some very caustic epithets to my folly, but I succeeded in mollifying him by double doses of admiration for his cockney wonders.

Some of the scenes that I had witnessed, in my first visits to London, returned to my mind so forcibly to-day, that it appeared as if I had gone back to boyhood and the days of fun. We had in the ship a gigantic fellow from Kennebunk, of the name of Stephen Stimpson. He had been impressed into the British navy, and when he joined us, had just been discharged from a frigate called the Boadicea, or the Boadishy, as he termed her, and (quite as a matter of course) he hated England in his heart. This man was particularly desirous of going to the West-end with me, at a later day, having heard Mr. Swinburne descant on the wonders to be seen there. As we were walking up St. James'-street in company, whither I had a great deal of trouble to get him, for he was for philosophizing and speculating on all he saw, and not a little for fighting, he came suddenly to a halt. An elderly lady was walking through the crowd followed by a footman, in a mourning livery. The man carried a cane and wore a cocked hat. Stephen watched this pair some time, and then gravely wished to know why "that *minister* kept so close in the wake of the old woman a-head of him?" I explained to him who they were, but he scouted the idea. It was a regular "minister," as witness the cocked hat, the black coat and breeches, and moreover the cane, and he was not to be bamboozled by any nonsense about servants. I had to let him follow the lady to her own residence, where, as I had foretold, the "minister" took off his hat, opened the door for his mistress, and followed her into the house. It was many months before Stephen ceased to speak of this. After all, the same *promenade* would excite almost as much astonishment in Broadway, at this very moment.

At that time there was a stand of sedan-chairs, in St. James'-street, near the spot where Crockford's club-house has since been erected. I had some difficulty in getting him over this "shoal," for after laughing in the chairmen's faces, he was for having a ride, on the spot.

The ranger of the Green-park, usually a person of rank, has a very pretty residence and garden, that open on Piccadilly. As we passed its gate, on our way to Hyde Park corner, a black footman was standing at it, his master probably expecting company. The negro was dressed in a rich *white* livery pretty well garnished with silver lace, red plush breeches, white silk stockings, a cocked hat, and his head was powdered as white as snow. You may imagine the effect such an apparition would be likely to produce on my Kennebunk companion. As there are no houses, but this of the ranger, on the park side of Piccadilly, and comparatively few people walk there, we had the black porter, for a little time, all to ourselves. It was with a good deal of persuasion that I prevented Stephen from laying hands on the poor fellow, in order to turn him round and examine him. As it was, he walked round him himself, dealing out his comments with particular freedom. All this time, the negro maintained an air of ludicrous dignity, holding himself as erect as a marine giving a salute, and looking steadily across the street. Among other things, Stephen suggested that the fellow might be one of Mr. Jefferson's "niggers," who had decamped with a pair of his master's nether garments! He was so tickled with this conceit, that I succeeded in dragging him away while he was in the humour. When we returned, an hour or two later, the black had disappeared.

Stephen had a desire to enter the Green-park, but I hesitated, for I had once been forbidden admission to Kensington Gardens, on account of wearing a roundabout. While we were debating the point, a worthy citizen came up, and said—"Go in, my lads; this is a free country, and you have as much right there as the King." On this intimation we proceeded. "What queer notions these people have of liberty," observed Stephen, drily. "They think it a great matter to be able to walk in a field, and there they let a nigger stare them in the face, with a cocked hat, red breeches, silk stockings, laced coat, and powdered wool!" I made my own reflections, too, for the first perception I had of the broad distinction that exists between political *franchises* and political *liberty*, dates from that moment. Young as I then was, I knew enough about royal *appanages*, and the uses of royal parks, to understand that the public entered them as a favour, and not as a right; but had it been otherwise, it would have left ground for reflection on the essential difference in principle, that exists between a state of things in which the community receive certain privileges as concessions, and that in which power itself is merely a temporary trust, delegated directly and expressly by the body of the people.

But I am permitting the scenes of boyhood, to divert me from the present moment.

Mr. _____ showed me the Blue-coat School, the new General

Post Office, and divers other places of interest, among which was Newgate. The architecture of the latter struck me as being unusually appropriate, and some of its emblems as poetically just, whatever may be the legal reputation of the place on other points. Pursuing our way down Ludgate-hill, my companion turned short into the door of a considerable shop. It was Rundell & Bridge, the first jewellers and goldsmiths of the world! England has probably more plate, than all the rest of Europe united; at least, judging by the eye alone, I think it would so appear to a stranger, although her wealth in the precious stones appears to be even less than that of some of the smaller countries. One certainly sees fewer jewels in society, although I am told the display of diamonds at Court, is sometimes very great. There are no public collections to compare with those of the continent, and the severe, one might almost say classical, purity of taste, which prevails in the dress of the men here, must have an effect to lessen the demand for jewels.

I was on the same sofa, at a ball in Paris, with Prince [Borghese], one of the richest men of the continent. His arm lay on the back of the seat, in a way to bring the hand quite near me. Every finger was covered with jewels of price, some of them literally having two or three, like the fingers of a woman. A piece of soap would have done more to embellish the hand, than all this finery. Directly before me stood the Duke of _____, one of the richest nobles of England. I took an occasion to look at him, as he drew a glove. He had not even the signet-ring, which it is now so very common to wear, but the hand was as white as snow.

The shop of Rundell & Bridge was large, but it made a wholesale and affluent appearance, rather than the brilliant show one meets with in Paris. As Mr. _____ was known we were received with great attention and civility. One of the heads of the establishment took us up stairs, into a more private apartment, where we were shown many magnificent things, and among others a good deal of the royal plate which had been sent here to be cleaned. It struck me, as a whole, that the same objection exists to the taste of England, as respects her plate, that exists in relation to almost all her works of art—its clumsiness. An English tureen is larger than a French tureen; an English chair, an English plate, an English carriage, even an English razor, are all larger than common. The workmanship is quite often better, but the forms are neither as classical, nor as graceful. As respects the plate, its massiveness may convey an idea of magnificence, but it is a ponderous and, in so much, a barbarous magnificence compared to that in which the beauty of the proportions, or of the intellectual part, is made of more importance than the mere metal. To the eye of taste a vessel of brass may have more value than one of gold.

You can have no just notion of the affluence of the shops of London, generally, in the article of plate. Gold, silver-gilt, and silver vessels, are literally piled in their vast windows, from the bottoms to the summits, as if space were the only thing desirable. I have seen single windows, in which, it struck me, the simple metallic wealth was greater in amount, than the value of the entire stock of our heaviest silversmiths. I am certain we were shown, to-day, single sets of diamonds that would form a capital for a large dealer in America.

While I tell you the taste of the English plate is not generally good, the cultivation of the fine arts being still too limited to extend much of its influence to the mechanical industry of the country, there are some great exceptions. Flaxman, one of the first geniuses of our times, a man perhaps superior to Benvenuto Cellini, in the intellectual part of his particular branch of art, was compelled, by the want of taste in the public and his own poverty, to make designs for the silversmiths, for which he had been fitted by early and severe study in Italy. Perhaps he was really more successful in his sketches than in his completer works. Had there been a dozen such men in England, the tables of the British nobility would have exhibited taste and beauty, as well as magnificence.

Among the royal plate was a salver just finished, which was beautiful, although the conceit was feudal rather than poetical, and conveyed an idea very different from that created by a sight of the steel-yards, and weights, and other familiar objects of domestic use, disinterred at Pompeii. The material was gold, and the ornaments were the stars and other insignia of the orders of chivalry which the present king is entitled to wear. The star and garter of the first English order was in the centre of the salver, drawn in large figures, while the others were arranged on the border, which was wide enough to receive them, on a diminished, but still on a suitable scale. The work resembled line engraving, and was done with truth and spirit, though, after all, it was nothing but a sort of *tailorism*. The history of the salver itself was rather curious. The eastern kings have a practice of enclosing their personal missives in tubes or cases of gold, resembling the tin and copper cases that are used to hold scrolls. In the course of a century, so many of these golden cases had accumulated, that George IV., who is a much greater prince in such matters, than in others more essential, took a fancy to have them converted into this piece of furniture.

I heard an anecdote the other day of this sovereign, which shows he can at least bear contradiction, and that on a point on which the nation itself is rather sensitive. The Duke of Wellington made one of his guests at dinner, and the conversation is said to have turned on the different armies of Europe! "I think it must be generally conceded," observed the king, "that the British cavalry is the best in Europe; is it not Arthur?" for he is said to have the affectation of calling the great man by his christian name, by way of *illustrating* himself, it is to be supposed. "The French is very good, sir," was the answer of a man who had seen a service very different from that which figures in histories, novels, and gazettes. "I allow that the French cavalry is good, but I say that our own is better." "The French cavalry is very good, sir." "I do not deny it; but is not ours better?" "The French is *very* good, sir." "Well, I suppose I must knock under, since Arthur will have it so." You are to remember practical men say the French cavalry is the best of modern times. Had this anecdote come from a *laquais de place,* I should not have mentioned it.

Coming through Fleet-street, Mr. _____ led me into a court, where he had some business with a printer. Here he told me I was in Bolt-court, celebrated as having been that in which Johnson resided. The place seemed now abandoned to printers. Here I left my companion and returned home.

Letter XVIII.

To William Jay, Esquire.

I was walking to a house where I was engaged to dine, the other evening, when a fellow near me raised one of the most appalling street cries it was ever the misfortune of human ears to endure. The words were "Eve-ning Cou-ri-er—great news—Duke of Wellington—Evening Courier," screeched without intermission, in a tremendous cracked voice, and with lungs that defied exhaustion. Such a cry, bursting suddenly on one, had the effect to make him believe that some portentous event had just broke upon an astounded world. I stopped and was about to follow the fellow, in order to buy a paper, when another cry, in a deep bass voice, that harmonized with the first in awful discord, roared from the opposite side of the street, "Contradiction of Evening Courier—more facts—truth developed—contradiction—Evening Courier." In this manner did these raven-throated venders of lies roam the streets, until distance swallowed their yells—worthy agents of the falsehoods and follies of the hour.

This little occurrence has brought to mind the subject of the daily and periodical press, and that of literature, in general, in England, and the duty of communicating to you some of the facts that have reached me in relation to all these interests, which may have escaped one residing at a distance, and who can only know them as they are presented to the world, which is commonly under false appearances.

I presume it is a general rule, that the taste, intelligence, principles, tone, and civilization of a nation will be reflected in its popular publications, which will include the productions of its periodical press of every variety. The only circumstance that will qualify the operation of this law must be sought in the institutions. If these are popular, the rule is pretty absolute; since the press, by being addressed to an average intellect, will be certain to remain on a level with its constituency. Viewed in this light, and compared with the rest of the world rather than with moral and philosophical truths in the abstract, the American press is highly creditable to the American nation, corrupt, ignorant, and vulgar as so much of it notoriously is. If, however, we look to a higher standard, and consider the press as a means of instruction, we find less to take pride in. The first of these facts is owing less to the merits of the public at home, than to the misfortunes of masses of men in other countries; and the second to a system which has created an average opinion that overshadows all ordinary attempts to resist it. The prevailing characteristic of America is mediocrity.

In England, though there are local political constituencies of the lowest scale of reason and knowledge, they exist as servants rather than as masters. The press has no motive to address them, and of course it aims at higher objects. But, while the strictly political constituencies of England are scarcely of any account in the action of the government, there is a public opinion that may be termed extra-constitutional, that is of great importance, and which it is necessary to manage with tact and delicacy. This common sentiment acts through various channels, of which a single example will serve to illustrate my meaning.

A rich man on 'change may not possess a single political right, beyond his general franchises as a subject. He has no vote, and so far as direct representation is concerned, no power in the state.

This is the situation of thousands in England, for while the government is strictly one of money, seats in parliament being bought as notoriously as commissions in the army, the system is one which does not give money its power through qualifications, but by a competition in large sums. But while this stock-jobber may have no vote, in a government so factitious, so dependent on industry, so much in debt, so willing to borrow, and so sensitive on the subject of pecuniary claims, his *opinion* and good-will become matters of the last moment.

I have selected this instance, because the worst features of the English press are connected with the mystifications, false principles, falsehoods, calumnies national and personal, and flagrant contradictions that are uttered precisely with a view to conciliate the varying and vacillating interests that depend on the fluctuations and hazards of trade, the public funds, and all those floating concerns of life, which, being by their very nature more liable to vicissitudes than homely industry, most completely demonstrate the truth of the profound aphorism which teaches us that "the love of money is the root of all evil." It is not necessary to come to England to seek examples of the effect of such an influence, for our own city presses exhibit it, in a degree that is only qualified by the circumstances of a state of society, which, by being a good deal less complicated, and less liable to derangement, calls for less watchfulness and editorial ferocity.

As a whole, then, I should say the predominant characteristic of the English press, is dependent on the necessity of addressing itself to the support of interests so factitious, so certain, sooner or later, to give way, and, at the same time so all-important to the power and prosperity of the nation, for the time being. The struggles of parties are subservient to these ends, on which not only party but national power depend. If it has been said truly, that the sun, in its daily course around the earth, is accompanied by the roll of the British morning drum, it might with equal justice have been added, and followed by the sophisms to which interests so conflicting are the parent.

In guarding these interests all parties unite. In this respect there is no difference between the Times and the Courier, the Edinburgh and the Quarterly. They may quarrel with each other about the fruits of these national advantages, which they proclaim to be national rights, but they will quarrel with all mankind to secure them to Great Britain. It must be remembered that vituperation and calumny are the natural resource of those who are weak in truth and argument, as stones and clubs are the weapons of children. A shameless, ill-concealed, national cupidity, then, I take to be the predominant quality of the English press. I do not mean that the man of England is a whit more selfish than the man of America, or the man of France, but that he lives in a condition of high pecuniary prosperity, (always a condition of peril) and under circumstances of constant and peculiar jeopardy, that keep the evil passions and evil practices of wealth in incessant excitement.

You know the mechanical appearance of the English press already. There is much talent, mingled with much vulgar ignorance, employed in the news departments; the journals, in this particular, appearing to address themselves to a wider range of tastes and information, than is usual even with us. Many of our journals, even in the towns, are essentially vulgar, in their tone and language, adapting both to the level of a very equivocal scale of tastes and manners, but I do not remember ever to have seen in an American journal of the smallest pretensions to respectability, as low and as intrinsically vulgar paragraphs as frequently are seen here, in journals of the first reputation. The language of the shop, such as "whole figure," "good article," "chalking up," "shelling out," and other Pearl-street terms, frequently find their way into the leading articles of a New York paper, whereas those of London are almost always worded in better taste; but, on the other hand, one daily sees the meanest and lowest cockneyisms, united with infamous grammar, (not faults of hurry and inadvertency, but faults of downright vulgarity) in the minor communications of the English press. Of this quality are the common expressions of "think of me (my) writing a letter," "he was agreeable (he agreed) to go," "I am recommended (advised) to stay," &c. &c.

It is the fashion to extol the talents of the Times. I have now been an attentive reader of this journal for several years, and I must say its reputation strikes me as being singularly unmerited. That it occasionally contains a pretty strong article is true, for its circulation would secure the casual contributions of able men, but, as a whole, I rank it much below several other journals in this country, and very much below some in Paris. It is said this paper reflects the times, and that its name has been given with a view to this character. The simple solution of all this is, I fancy, that the paper is treated as a property, and that it looks to circulation more than to principles, humouring prejudices with a view to popularity. The mere calling of names, and the bold vituperation, for which the Times is notorious, does not require any talent, though nothing is more apt to impose on common understandings. The Morning Chronicle appears to me to possess the most true talent of any journal in London. This appearance, however, may be owing to the fact of its espousing liberal and just principles, for, unlike most of its contemporaries, it has no need of resorting to sophisms and laboured mystifications to maintain a state of things which is false in itself; for it should never be forgotten, in contemplating all the favourite theories of England, that the argument has been adapted to the fact, and not the fact to the argument.* I have seen occasional articles from a journal called the Scotsman, that appear to be written with the simple straightforward power of truth and honesty. There is a lucid common sense about this paper, which gives it a high place in the scale of the journals of the day. No article that I have ever met with in either of these two papers betrays the cloven foot of the pecuniary interests mentioned, though I cannot take upon myself to say that they are entirely free from the imputation. Still they have always appeared to me to be conducted with too much talent, to lend themselves to a practice that one would think must offend the moral sense of every right-thinking and right-feeling man.

Mr. Canning, not long before his death, openly vaunted the moral influence of England, by way of supporting his political schemes. Nothing is more evident than the fact that the journals of this country frequently admit articles that are intended to produce an effect in other states. I think they over-estimate their influence, however, for I do not believe that the opinion of England has any material power, except in America. As a people the English are not liked on the continent of Europe, and I think the disposition is rather to cavil at their truths, than to receive their fallacies. The aristocracy of England has a great influence, by its wealth, power, and style, on the *desires* of all the other European aristocracies, which very naturally wish themselves to be as well off, but the dogmas of this school would hardly do for the daily journals. I do not say that the English press totally overlooks this class and its interests; on the contrary, it does much to sustain both, but it is by indirect means, and not by argument, or by appeals to the passions. It tells of the liberal acts of individuals of the body, recapitulates the amount of rent that has been remitted to the tenantry, and the number of blankets that has been distributed to the poor. The left hand is studiously made to know what

*The Examiner, since 1828, has passed into new hands, and, although little accustomed to see the paper itself, the writer was in the constant habit of reading extracts from it, in Galignani's Messenger. Taking these as specimens of its merit, he is of opinion that for vigour, consistency, truth, and distinctness of thought, and for pungent and manly reasoning, this journal stands at the very head of this species of literature.

the right hand has done in this way, among the great and noble, while the charities of the more humble are usually permitted to pass in silence. Not satisfied with this, the world is regularly enlightened on the subject of the large entertainments given by the great, the names of the guests, and not unfrequently with the dresses of the women. The ravenous appetite of the secondary classes to know something of their superiors, is fed daily in this extraordinary manner, (the practice exists no where else, I believe,) and thousands of dreamy bachelors and prim maidens, pass their days in the high enjoyment of contemplating at a distance, the rare felicities of a state of being to which a nearer approach is denied them, and which a nearer approach would destroy.

I remember when I came to London in 1826, to have laughed at an account of the manner in which Lord A., and Lady B., and Sir Thomas C., had passed their mornings, with the usual gossip of fashionable life that the article contained, when an American who had been some time in England, gravely assured me that there were thousands in the nation, who would not buy the paper were this momentous stuff omitted. There have been books, for a very long time, which contain the pedigrees, titles, creations, and family alliances of the peers, and which furnish mental aliment for hundreds of devout admirers of aristocracy. These books, which are useful enough in a certain way, when it is remembered that the peers control the first empire of modern times, have been extended to the baronets and knights, and latterly to the gentry of the country. The whole forms a curious study, when one is disposed to ferret out the true principle of the government, and the modes by which families have attained power,* but they are read

---

*In the reign of Queen Anne, out of a little more than twenty dukes in the empire, six were descended in the direct male line from the natural sons of King Charles II., viz.: the Dukes of Richmond, Grafton, Cleveland, Northumberland, St. Albans, and Buccleugh. The dukedoms of Northumberland and Cleveland, are extinct, though the titles have been revived in other families; but those of Richmond, St. Albans, Grafton, and Buccleugh, are still enjoyed by the descendants of Charles. George I., did not hesitate to ennoble his mistress, whom he made Duchess of Kendal, and George II., had also his Countess of Yarmouth. These two women were made peeresses, because they were the king's mistresses, but no natural child was ennobled. George III. was still more guarded in his

with avidity, in England, as a means of holding an intercourse with beings, who, as respects the mass, form quite another order of creation.

But if the journals, in this manner, contribute to support the aristocracy by feeding these morbid cravings of the excluded, they do more towards overturning it, just now, by their open and rude attacks. I do not say, that I have ever met with an Englishman, who is not, in some degree, under the influence of the national deference for nobility, for to be frank with you, I can scarcely recal twenty Americans, who are exempt from the same weakness; but there are a good many who, by drawing manfully on their reason and knowledge, are enabled to detect the fallacies of the system, and who do not scruple to expose them in the public journals. These men, of whom I may have made the acquaintance of a dozen, remind me of the lasting influence which the ghost stories of the nursery produce on the human mind. We drink in these tales eagerly in childhood, and, in after life, though reason and reflection teach us their absurdity, few of us go through a church-yard in a dark night, without fancying that its sheeted tenants may rise from their graves. Thus do the boldest of the English, when philosophising the most profoundly on the wrongs and inexpediency of aristocratic rule, look stealthily over their shoulders, as if they saw a lord! You may judge of the profoundness of the impression, here, by its remains in America. Certainly, the mass of the American people, care no more for a lord, than they care for a wood-chuck; perhaps, also the feeling of the real gentry of the country, is getting to be very much what it ought to be, on such a subject, seeing no more than a man of the upper classes of another country, in an English nobleman; but take the class immediately below those who are accustomed to our highest associations, and there is still a good deal of the sentiment of the tailor, in their manner of contemplating an English nobleman.

amours, and although he is said to have had several natural children, they were not publicly recognised. The same is true with George IV., though his manner of life was less guarded. The power of the aristocracy had now become so great, that it repudiated such admissions into their ranks. A struggle, however, occurred in 1831, between the different castes of the state, and the king rose in importance. In order to conciliate him, the whigs immediately gave a peerage to the eldest of his natural children by Mrs. Jordan, and ennobled all the others!

Alas! it is much easier to declare war, and gain victories in the field, and establish a political independence, than to emancipate the mind. Thrice happy is it for America, that her facts are so potent, as to be irresistable; for were our fate left to opinion, I fear we should prove ourselves to be any thing but philosophers.

It will not be doing justice to the English press, if we overlook its disposition to indulge in coarse, national, and personal vituperation. The habit of resorting to low, personal abuse, against all who thwart the views of their government, or who have the manliness to promulgate their opinions of the national characteristics, let it be done as honestly, as temperately, or as justly as it may, is too well known to admit of dispute. It may be a natural weakness in man, to attempt to ridicule his enemies, but the English calumniate them. They calumniated every distinguished man of our revolution; no general can gain a victory over them, and escape their vituperation; and the moral enormities attributed to Napoleon, had their origin in the same national propensity. Some of the English, with whom I have spoken on this subject, while they have admitted this offensive trait in their press, have ascribed it to the morality of the nation, to whose wounded sensibilities, the abuse is addressed! This is very much like imputing uncharitableness to sins, to a Christian conscience. Certainly, I am no vindicator of the personal, or political, ethics of Napoleon. As respects his morals, I presume, they were very much like those of other Frenchmen of his time and opportunities, but if the sensibilities of England, were so exaggerated, on such subjects, why did they go abroad in quest of examples to scourge? I doubt, if there be any thing worse in the private career of Napoleon, than the intrigue with the "Fair Quaker," in that of George III., or any thing approaching that, which every well informed man here tells me, is the present condition of the court of Windsor. Did you ever hear the familiar French song of Malbrook?

> "Malbrook s'en va t'en guerre."
> etc. etc. etc.

Malbrook, you know, was the Duke of Marlborough, and the song is the French mode of revenging the nation, for the manifold floggings it received at his hands. The wisdom of thus killing an enemy in doggerel, whom they could neither slay, nor defeat, may be questioned, but imagine, for a moment, that Wellington, and his fortunes had been French, and then fancy the abuse he would have received. I never yet met with a Frenchman, who had not a most sincere antipathy to the Duke of Wellington; they tell fierce stories about the Bois de Boulogne, and other similar absurdities, the outbreakings of the mortified pride of a military people, but I never yet saw, or heard a personal calumny against him, in France, unless it was connected directly with his public acts. They say, he permitted the terms of the capitulation of Paris, to be violated; but they do not enter into his private life, to villify the man. I have, sometimes, been afraid, this tendency to black-guardism, was "Anglo-Saxon," for it manifests itself in our own journals, more particularly among the editors of New England, who, if they have more of the sturdy common sense, and masculine propensities of the Father-land, than their more southern contemporaries, have also the coarse-mindedness. I have industriously sought the cause of this peculiarity, and at one time, I was disposed to attribute it to a low taste in the mass of the nation, which I again ascribed to the effects of the institutions, just as with us, the strongest term of reproach among the blacks, is for one to call his fellow, a "nigger;" but observation has convinced me, that this national taste is only secondary, as a cause. The press now caters to it, it is true, but it first created it. I believe, its origin is to be found in the vulgarity inherent in the active management of capricious commercial interests, the factitious state of the national power, and the genuine and unaffected outbreakings of a pecuniary cupidity. Look at home, and you will see the presses under the control of those, who have the management of floating interests, tainted by the same vice. "The love of money, is the root of all evil," and the propensity to blackguard those who thwart the rapacity of the grasping, is one of its most innocent enormities.

I think it very evident, that there is much writing in this country, that is especially intended for "our market." The English, who control the reviews and journals, are fully aware of the influence they wield over the public mind in America, and you may be quite certain, that a nation, whose very power is the result of combination and method, does not neglect means so obvious to attain its ends. There is scarcely a doubt, that articles, unfavourable to America, low, blackguard abuse that was addressed to the least worthy of the national propensities of the English, were prepared under the direction of the government, and inserted in the Quarterly Review. Mr. Gifford admitted as much as this, to an American of my acquaintance, who has distinctly informed me of the fact. I presume the same is true, in reference to the daily press. Some fifty paragraphs have met my eye, since I have been here, in which the writers have pretty directly exulted in their power over the American mind. This power is wielded to advance the interests of England, and, as a matter of course, to thwart our own. It probably exceeds any thing of which you have any idea. Whether the English government actually employs writers about our own presses or not, at present, I cannot say, but it has, unquestionably, agents of this sort, on the continent of Europe, and I think it highly probable that it has them in America.

We talk of the predestination of the Turks, but I question if the earth contains a people who so recklessly abandon their dearest, and most important interests, so completely to chance, as ourselves. Both the government and the people, appear to me, to trust implicitly to Providence for their future safety, abandoning even opinion to the control of their most active enemies, and shamelessly deserting those who would serve them, unless they happen to be linked with the monster, party. The chief of a political faction may do almost any thing with impunity, but he who defends his country, unconnected with party, is abandoned to the tender mercies of the common enemy. In this respect, we are like the countryman in a crowd of pick-pockets, full of ourselves, but utterly unconscious of our risks.

The young Englishman who aspires to fortune will select his object, and support it, or attack it, as the case may be, with his pen. He will endeavour to counteract democracy, to sustain the English Free Trade system, to excite prejudice against America, to arouse antipathy to Russia, to prove France ought not to possess Antwerp, or, to uphold some other national interest, and, if a clever man, he is certain to be cherished by that government and rewarded. Some of the most eminent men England has produced, have forced themselves into notice in this manner.

Let us fancy an American to run a similar career. So little is the nation brought before the European world that the chances are, as one hundred to one, he would attract no notice here; but, we will imagine him in possession of the ear of Europe, and able to bring his matter before its bar. If England were opposed in either her prejudices, or interests, he would as a matter of course, be vituperated; for whom did the English press ever spare, under such circumstances? No doubt, a thousand honest and generous pens would be ready to be their countryman's vindicator; no doubt the government would throw its broad mantle around its friend, and manifest to the world its sense of its own dignity and interests? No such thing; the abuse of the English press would produce even more effect in America than in England; its tales, however idle or improbable, would be swallowed with avidity, as tales from the capital circulate in the provinces, and, as for the government, it already has a character here for confiding in those who openly repudiate its principles! Well may it be said, that we have reason to be thankful to God for our blessings, for if God did not take especial care of us, we should be without protection at all.

I have been much struck, here, with the little impression that is made by the reviews. Exceptions certainly exist, but the critical remarks that, written here, produce no visible effect, would give a work its character with us. Every body, that is at all above the vulgar, appears to understand that reviewing "is the great standing mystification of the age."

In making all these comparisons, however, we are too apt to overlook the statistical facts of America. A short digression will explain my meaning. If we speak of the civilization of England in the abstract, it is not easy to employ exaggerated terms, for it challenges high praise; but when we come to compare it to our own, we are to take the whole subject in connection. Were the entire population of the United States compressed into the single state of New York, we should get something like the proportions between surface and people, that exist in England. In reflecting on such a fact, one of the first things that strike the mind, is connected with the immense physical results that are dependant on such a circumstance. The mean of the population of New York for the last thirty years, has been considerably below a million; but had it been fourteen millions during the same period, leaving the difference in wealth out of the question, how little would even England have to boast over us! Losing sight entirely of the primary changes that are dependant on a settlement, and which perhaps seem to be more than they really are, we have actually done as much in the same time as England, in canals, rail-roads, bridges, steam-boats, and all those higher modes of improvement, that mark an advanced state of society. These are the things of which we may justly be proud, and they are allied to the great principle on which the future power and glory of the nation are to be based. They are strictly the offspring of the institutions.

We offer our weak side when we lay claim to the refinements, tastes, and elegancies of an older, or, in our case, it would be better to say, a more *compact* condition of society. The class to which these exclusively belong is every where relatively small. I firmly believe it is larger with us, than among the same number of people, in any other country, though this opinion is liable to a good deal of qualification. We know little or nothing of music, or painting, or statuary, or any of those arts whose fruits must be studied to be felt and understood; but, in more essential things, we have even sometimes the advantage; while in others, again, owing to our colonial habits of thought, we have still less reason to be proud.

To apply these facts to our present subject, you will easily understand the manner in which a nation so situated will feel the influence of opinions of an inferior quality. In all communities men will defer to actual superiority, when it acts steadily and in sufficient force to create a standard. Unluckily manners, tastes, knowledge, and tone are all too much diffused in America to make head against the sturdy advances of an overwhelming mediocrity. As a basis of national greatness, this mediocrity commands our respect, but it is a little premature to set it up as a standard for the imitation of others. It even overshadows, more particularly in the towns, the qualities that might better be its substitute. Its influence on the whole is genial, for so broad a foundation will, sooner or later, receive an appropriate superstructure, but, *ad interim*, it places a great deal too much at the disposal of empirics and pretenders. This is the reason (coupled with the deference that the provinces always show to the capital) why reviews and newspaper strictures produce an effect in America, of which they entirely fail in England. Here the highest intellectual classes give reputation, while in America it is derived from the mediocrity I have mentioned, through the agency, half the time, of as impudent a set of literary quacks as probably a civilized country ever tolerated. There are as flagrant things of the sort perpetrated here, as in America, but their influence is limited to the milliners and shop-men. A national *prejudice* may take any shape, in England, for no one is exempt from the feeling, from the king on his throne to the groom in his stable; but, keeping this influence out of sight, the standard of taste and knowledge is too high, to be easily imposed on.

Some one has said, with more smartness than truth perhaps, so far as one's own contemporaries are concerned at least, "that no author was ever written down except by himself." Many an author however, has been temporarily written *up* by others. I have just had a proof of this truth.

A work has lately appeared here, of rather more pretension than common. This book is deemed a failure in the literary circles of London. Of its merits I know nothing, not having read it, but in the fact, I cannot be mistaken, for I have heard it spoken of, by every literary man of my acquaintance, from Sir Walter Scott down; and but one among them all, has spoken well of it, and he, notoriously a friend of the author, "damned it with faint praise" more than any thing else. The bookseller paid too much for the manuscript, however, to put up with a loss, and a concerted and combined effort has been made to write the book up. In England these puffs, which are elaborate and suited to a grave subject, have had no visible effect, while I see, by the journals at home, that the work in question is deemed established, on this authority!

I am told that the practice of writers reviewing themselves, is much more prevalent here than one would be apt to suspect. One can tolerate such a thing as a joke, but it is ticklish ground, and liable to misconstruction. But man loves mystification. The very being who would bristle up and resent a frank, manly vindication of a writer that should appear under his own name, would permit his judgment to be guided by the same opinions when produced covertly, nor would the modesty of the author, who glorifies himself in this sneaking manner, be half as much called in question, as that of him who, disdaining deceit, met his enemies openly!

There is less of simulated public opinion in the English press than in our own, I presume; owing to the simple fact, that public opinion is neither so overwhelming nor so easily influenced. The constant practice of appealing to the public, in America, has given rise to the vilest frauds of this character, that are of constant occurrence. When it is wished to induce the public to think in a particular way, the first step is to affect that such is already the common sentiment, in the expectation that deference to the general impression will bring about the desired end. I have known frauds of this nature, connected with personal malice, which, if exposed, would draw down the indignation of every honest man in the nation, on those who practised them; some of whom now pass for men of fair characters. It is scarcely necessary to say that such fellows are thieves in principle.

There is another all-important point on which, in the spirit of imitation, we have permitted the English press to mislead us. Nothing can be more apparent, in a healthful and natural state of the public mind, than that a lie told to influence an election, or to mislead on a matter of general policy, ought to be just so much the more reprobated than a lie that affects an individual merely, as the concerns of a nation are more engrossing and important than the concerns of a private citizen. In America, an election ought to be, and in the main it is, an expression of the popular will for great national objects; in England, it is merely a struggle for personal power, between the owners of property. The voter with us, is one of a body which controls the results; in England, he is one of a body controlled by direct personal influence. No greater, ordinary crime, against good morals and the public safety, can be committed, than to mislead the public in matters of facts connected with an election; and yet an "electioneering lie," is almost deemed a venial offense in America, because they are so deemed here, where, as a rule, every thing is settled by direct personal influence and bribery.

Some very false notions exist in America, on the subject of the liberty of the press. We give it by far too much latitude, perhaps not so much in the law itself, as by opinion and in the construction of the law. The leaning is in favour of publication; firstly, because man is inherently selfish, and he cares little what private wrongs are committed in feeding the morbid appetites of the majority; and, secondly, by confounding a remedy with diet. When power is to be overturned, the press becomes a sure engine, and its abuses may be tolerated, in order to secure the inestimable advantages of liberty; but liberty attained, it should not be forgotten, that while arsenic may cure a disease, taken as daily food it is certain death. Every honest man appears to admit that the press, in America, is fast getting to be intolerable. In escaping from the tyranny of foreign aristocrats, we have created in our bosom a tyranny of a character so unsupportable, that a change of some sort is getting to be indispensable to peace. Truth appears to be no longer expected. Nor is this all. An evident dishonesty of sentiment pervades the public itself, which is beginning to regard acts of private delinquency with a dangerous indifference; and acts, too, that are inseparably connected with the character, security, and a right administration of the state; political jockeyship being now regarded very much as jockeyship of another order is notoriously esteemed by those who engage in it. In this respect, England has the advantage of us, for here the arts of politics are exercised with greater *ménagement*, being confined to the few; whereas, in America, acting on the public, they require public demoralization to be tolerated.

In ferocity and brutality, I think the English press, under high excitement, much worse than our own; in general tone and manliness, greatly its superior. In both cases the better part of the community is exposed to the rudest assaults from men who belong to the worst. In England, the public is generally spared the impertinence of personal, editorial controversies, a failing of rusticity, and the press is but little used for the purposes of individual malice; while in America, it is a machine, half the time, which, under the pretence of serving the public, in addition to pecuniary profit, is made to serve the ambition, or to gratify the antipathies, of the editor, who obtains, through its use, an importance and power he could, probably, never obtain in any other manner. This distinction is a consequence of presses being stock-property in England, which is not owned by the editors; while in America, the man who writes is master of the limited establishment. It is his machine of personal advancement.

There is one point connected with this subject, on which we admit a degradation unknown to all other countries. Every community is obliged to submit to the existence of its own impurities, but we imbibe those which are generated in the most factitious and high-wrought, and, consequently, the most corrupt state of society, in christendom. This is another of the evils arising from a want of pride and national character, the people which is thrown into convulsions by the worthless strictures of any foreign traveller, on their elegance and tastes, permitting the very putridity of foreign corruption to fester in and pollute its bosom!

Letter XIX.

To James Stevenson, Esq., Albany, N. Y.

All this time, the business of eating and drinking goes on. There is, indeed, too much of it for me; the late hours, and the small, heated, and crowded rooms of London, compelling me to decline a good deal more than half the civilities that are offered. One thing has struck me, as at least odd. Coming, as I did, into this country, without letters, (those sent by Mr. Spencer, excepted,) I had no right to complain, certainly, had I been permitted to go away entirely without a visit; but I have been noticed by more than I had the smallest right to expect; and yet, among all those who have knocked at my door, I am by no means certain there is a single tory! I except the case of Sir Walter Scott, for we were previously acquainted. As we met first in society, the attention was, perhaps, necessary on his part, though I am far from supposing he would have thought himself bound to cut me because I am an American, although I have some reason for thinking that even he does not view us with very friendly eyes.* I

---

*Proofs of *naïveté* and ignorance of the world, are afforded by most of our travellers, who are the dupes of their own national conceit, and the more exaggerated forms of Europe. As a people, I believe, we are in favour in no part of Europe. I could give much proof on this point, and a good deal will be incidentally introduced into these letters, but a single anecdote must suffice here. There is one man who is much visited and flattered by Americans, now living in England, and divers interesting accounts of his kindness and philanthropy are published by our tourists annually. Within a month, conversing with a countryman just returned from a long visit in Europe, he tells me that an acquaintance of his visited this person, while he remained at an inn, where he dined with a near relation of the great man. In the course of conversation, my acquaintance expressed his apprehension that the visit of ＿＿ would annoy ＿＿. "Not at all," said the other, who believed his companion to be an Englishman, "my ＿＿ rather likes ＿＿, *for an American.*" There are two things that every American should understand. In associating with the English, if he betray the least of the toad-eater, he is despised for the meanness; this is human nature; if he manifest self-respect, and a determination to have all the rights of a gentleman, he is hated for presuming to be an Englishman's equal.

do not know the political opinions of Mr. Sotheby, though he is evidently too mild a man to feel strong antipathies on this account; but, I believe, these two excepted, not only every man who has visited me, or asked me to his house, and nearly every man whom I have met at dinners and breakfasts, has been a whig! Is this accident, or is it really the result of feeling?

I have dined in the last month, among other places, twice at Lansdowne-house, and once with Lady _____, who lives in good style here, and keeps a better sort of table, though a widow. Her house was very much like all the second class houses here, with a dining-room below, and the drawing-rooms on the first floor, being a little larger than a second class American town residence!

At table, we had two or three members of the lower house, a Frenchman, and myself. The conversation turned, after the mistress of the house had retired, on the French revolution, which was discussed, with all the usual allusions to national character, ferocity, levity, and jacobinism, just as coolly as if a Frenchman did not make one of the company. The poor fellow sat on thorns the whole time, keenly alive to the awkwardness of his situation, and looking hard at me, the only one who did not join in the discourse, and the only one who appeared to remember his existence.

This indifference to the feelings of others, is a dark spot on the national manners of England. The only way to put it down, is to become belligerent yourself, by introducing pauperism, radicalism, Ireland, the Indies, or some other sore point. Like all who make butts of others, they do not manifest the proper forbearance, when the tables are turned. Of this, I have had abundance of proof, in my own experience. Sometimes, these remarks are absolutely rude, and personally offensive, as a disregard of one's national character, is a disrespect to his principles, but as personal quarrels on such grounds, are to be avoided, I have uniformly retorted in kind, if there was the smallest opening for such retaliation. Sometimes, the remarks are the result of kind feelings, and a misapprehension of facts, when I have always endeavoured to set the matter right. All foreigners complain of the English, in this respect; though so far as my little experience goes, I think, in general, the very highest classes do not merit the opprobrium they receive on this account, although extraordinary things of the sort are told of even them. Down as low in the social scale, as the third or fourth sets, the commercial classes in particular, the failing amounts almost to intolerance.

We, that is to say, the men, were still at Lady _____'s table, when the raps at the front door, announced evening company. It is necessary to understand the eloquence of a London knocker, to appreciate the melody that followed. Two or three messages were sent to the guest most at home, to summon us to the drawing-room, but the French revolution was in the way. At length, we got rid of the bloody tragedy, and mounting to the first floor, found a room already full of company.

I had the honour of being introduced to Lady _____, who came nearer to a dandy in petticoats in her manner, than any woman I ever met with. I can only liken her apparent affectations of speech, to those one sometimes hears on the stage; a lisping, drawling superciliousness, that may be understood, but cannot be described. She is the only instance I have yet met with, of an English woman of rank, who had not an unpretending, simple manner of utterance, for most of them speak the language, not only well, but with a quiet dignity, that is very agreeable. Indeed, I should say, the women of this country, as a rule, speak with great precision and beauty, though they often appear cold and repulsive.

A countrywoman of ours, at _____, was always talking of this Lady _____. Of course, I supposed they were intimate, the official characters of their husbands bringing them necessarily much together. I alluded, therefore, to Mrs. _____, as one of her acquaintances. " _____" " _____," she repeated, with that exquisite lisp of hers, "I do not think I know them." I wish I could impart to paper, the consummate affectation of her manner, as she said this, for it was quite as admirable in its way, as the coolness with which she denied an acquaintance, that I was certain, in the nature of things, she could not readily have forgotten. I was soon tired of this, and stole away at the first opportunity.

There was at table to-day, Mr. _____ _____, the _____ _____. He is a distinguished commoner, a member of parliament, and a rich landholder. I was surprised to find, this person speaking very much in the worst *drawing-room* manner, of our New England dialect. I do not mean, that he said "dooze" and "ben," and "nawthin," for his pronunciation was not amiss, but he had the mean intonation, and sing-song utterance, that we so well understand in America. I should have pronounced him one of us, in a minute, had I not known who he was. This is the second instance of the kind, I have met with here. *Au reste*, he was a benevolent, sensible, modest man, and, as I thought, without prejudice against America. I love such Englishmen.

I have breakfasted, lately, with Sir James Mackintosh, Mr. Sharp, Mr. ＿＿＿＿ ＿＿＿＿; and two or three others. At the house of the first, I met Mr. Wynn, a prominent whig; and at the latter's, we were the host, Lord S ＿＿＿＿, Sir ＿＿＿＿ ＿＿＿＿, and myself. Mr. Rogers was also present, on most of these occasions. At Mr. Sharp's, were Lord ＿＿＿＿, a young tory for a novelty, and Lord [Kerry], a lad, who is the heir of Lord L[ansdowne].. I had seen the former in Paris.

You will be amused with one of my discoveries. I was offered an egg, with the recommendation, that it was "a country laid egg." I had thought myself, until that moment, deeply versed in the mystery of cooking and eating eggs, whether *à la coque*, or, in *omelettes*. Never before, had I heard, that an egg laid in the country, was better than one laid in a town! I was once told, (it was when a boy,) that the fashion in cooking eggs, like every thing else, was running from one extreme to the other, provincial ignorance having been suddenly enlightened, and from boiling them as hard as bullets, we had exaggerated the new mode by barely warming them through. An egg should be cooked, *à la coque*, just enough to allow the centre of the yolk to run while warm, and to become hard when cold. It should always be eaten from the shell, both because it is better taken in that way, and because it is not gentlemanly to be making messes, and more especially unsightly messes, at table. The wine glass or egg-glass, is an abomination, and altogether a most vulgar substitute for the egg-cup, and one quite unfit to be seen any where but in a steam-boat, or a tavern frequented by *gulpers*. All men accustomed to polite life will agree to this, but how many know the difference between a "town-laid" and a "country-laid" egg? You see by these little incidents how far a new country may be from an advanced state of civilization, notwithstanding it possesses gallowses.

The conversation at Mr. L ＿＿＿＿'s, whom I had known in America, turned on the begging mission of Bishop Chase of Ohio.

One of the gentlemen gave an account of this prelate's church statistics that startled me a little. The population of the state was set down at pretty near a million, and the clergy at less than a dozen! I ventured to say that this must be a mistake, unless clergymen of the Protestant Episcopal church were exclusively meant. There is always a period in the first settlement of a region where there is a deficiency in the spiritual ministrations, but the accounts should not go forth unaccompanied by the explanations, for they tend to mislead. The statements relative to drunkenness, got up for effect by the Temperance Societies at home, are giving us an undeserved reputation for that vice, of which I feel convinced we have, relatively, *among the native population*, as little as any other nation I have visited, and much less than most of them. I feel persuaded there is a party in America that wishes to see these misstatements propagated, in order to bring free institutions into disrepute, a party that embraces a large portion of the trading foreigners, and verily they achieve their object, for democracy and drunkenness are closely associated in the minds of millions of the well-intentioned in this hemisphere. If free principles do prevail, it will be under the providence of God, and through their own energies; for those who spout loudest in their praise at home, and even carry out their doctrines to untenable extremes, take the least heed of any thing that does not immediately affect their own personal interests, and as for the government it actually throws its weight into the hostile scale on this side of the Atlantic, opposing its own friends and rewarding its enemies. This is a singular state of things, but such is the result not only of my own observations, but of those of various intelligent countrymen of ours, who have seen much more of Europe than myself. Were I an office seeker, I would at once resort to the meannesses that obtain for an American the outward favours of the aristocracies of Europe, whatever may be their secret opinions, as the most certain method of being deemed worthy of the confidence of the government at Washington, and of obtaining a reputation in the circles at home.

I have lately had an extraordinary proof of what I now tell you. At one of the dinners at Lansdowne house, Mr. Brougham was present. He came late, and took his seat at the table opposite to the end at which I sat. Of course we had no conversation during dinner. As we were retiring to the drawing-room, Lord Lansdowne did me the favour to present me to this distinguished man. The introduction took place at the dining-room door, and we walked across an ante-chamber together, when the usual compliments and civilities passed. We had no sooner reached the ladies and made our bows, than Mr. Brougham turned to me, and abruptly demanded—"What is the reason so many of your people desert the distinctive principles of your government, when they come to Europe?"

I have been thus particular in relating the circumstances under which this extraordinary question was put, for I think they prove what was uppermost in the mind of Mr. Brougham, and the strong impression that had been left by the circumstance to which he alluded. It is quite evident that this impression must have been unfavourable either to the institutions, or to the candour of the national character.

I hoped the fact was not so. "My experience would say it is," was the answer. "To what class of men do you allude, in particular, Mr. Brougham?" "To your foreign ministers, especially," he said. I thought this very extraordinary, and said as much, and, as something might depend on the character of the individual, I begged him to name one of those who left this impression behind him. He did, mentioning, without reserve, a distinguished minister of the republic, who is now dead. To all this, I could only say, that I supposed a mistaken desire to make themselves agreeable must have been at the bottom of such a course; and here the conversation dropped, by mutual consent.

I do not know whether this conversation will strike you as it struck me, for I confess it would seem that we have some "country laid" ministers, or our ministers have felt confident of having had very "country laid" constituents.

Mr. Brougham was desirous of knowing how we contrive to print books so cheaply, as he had understood we did, labour being so dear. He had been told that Scott's novels were sold for a dollar a copy. The secret of this fact, is to be found in the meanness of execution, the extent and the rapidity of the demand, and most of all, in the circumstance, that the author is paid nothing. A reprint, moreover, is not made from a manuscript, and has no alterations, and few corrections. In addition to all this, the press correction of books, is immeasurably more accurate and laboured in England, than in America. Men of education are employed here, as proof readers, and, perhaps, most of the popular authors of England, have very little knowledge of the grammar of their own language. All these people must be paid, and the money is charged against the work.

A novel, of no great merit, will bring its author four or five hundred pounds in England, especially if it be at all supposed to bring the reader in contact with the feelings and sentiments of the "nobility and gentry." So profound is the deference of those who live in shadow, for those who are beneath the sun's rays, in this country, that the price of a lord's pen, is considerably higher, than that of a commoner's! I dare say, it will be a new idea to you, to measure literary merit by a pedigree, but it is a mode much practised here. A lady of condition, lately offered a novel to a fashionable publisher, and the answer was, "two hundred if anonymous, and five hundred with the name of the author;" the latter, you will understand, having no other value than that of rank, the book being a first effort. An application was made to me, to contribute to an annual, and, by way of inducement, I was shown a list of those who had engaged to write for it, among whom, were six or eight lords. Curious to know, how far these people submitted to vulgar considerations, I put the question, and was given to understand, that they were not only paid as writers, but paid as lords. The moon may not be made of green cheese, but rely on it, could we get near enough to discover its substance, it would turn out essentially different from any thing we imagine.

There was a boy, the heir of a very high title, at one of my late breakfasts. He went away the first, to go to school, I fancy, and the master of the house made the mistake of leaving us, while he went to the ante-chamber, to see the lad off. When he returned, he came up to me, with a momentous manner, and muttered, "three earldoms in the family!" I was compelled to compare this, with the total absence of fuss about boys and girls of rank on the continent of Europe. Just before we left Paris, at a child's ball, a little girl, who was selected to dance with one of the princes, was told by her mother, to say, "monseigneur," in speaking to her partner. After they had got a little warmed with the exercise, the pretty little thing turned round to the boy and said—"why am I to call you *'monseigneur,'* are you a bishop?" *"Je n'en sais rien, moi,"* was the answer. There is young [Kerry], he is the heir of vast estates, of palaces without number, and of a collection of pictures and statuary alone, that would constitute a large fortune. There are five or six principalities in the family, and when he is married, he is to take one of these titles, until he succeeds to the ancient and historical distinctive appellation of his race. But, at present, no one calls him by any thing but his Christian name, although nearly a man!

It appears to me, that the nobles of this country, themselves, make very little parade of their claims, but that the fuss comes principally from those who deem it an honour to be their associates. Nothing more deranges the philosophy of one of the true devotees of rank here, than to find that others do not worship the idol with the same zeal as himself.

Letter XX.
To Richard Cooper, Esquire, Cooperstown.

Perhaps, I ought not to confess the weakness, but we have actually been to see the Tower. Luckily, the "lions" have been sold, so we escaped the most vulgar part of the exhibition.

The Tower proper, is a square building, with four turrets, or rather towers at the angles, and is by no means large, though it is said to be as ancient as the conquest. The Romans are thought to have had a fortress, at, or near, its site. In addition to this building, however, there is a little dingy town around it, principally built of bricks, and surrounded by a ditch and walls. The latter have regular bastions, and the former is wide, deep, and wet, feeling the influence of the tides of the river, for the whole stand immediately on its banks.

This place has been so often described, that I shall say little beyond our general impressions. It struck us as much less imposing than Vincennes, though venerable by time and associations. The Tower itself will not compare with the donjon of Vincennes, its French counterpart, and the adjuncts, are equally below those of the Tower of Paris.

The collection of armour disappointed us greatly, being altogether less interesting, than the fine specimens of the *musée de l'Artillerie*, near the church of St. Thomas d'Aquin; a museum of whose existence nine Frenchmen in ten seem to be profoundly ignorant, while it is one of the most curious things in Europe. Unfortunately, some musty antiquarian has lately robbed the armour of the Tower, of all claims to be considered genuine, or as appertaining to the persons of the great men, on whose effigies it is displayed, and therein he has annihilated most of its interest. "Where ignorance is bliss, 'tis folly to be wise." I wish, with all my heart, the man had not been half so learned, for, like a novel by Scott, or a play by Shakspeare, in this case the fiction was probably more interesting, than the reality. We ought not to quarrel with truth, however, since there is little danger of our getting too much of it.

Of course, we looked at the regalia, but with little interest, for it is not handsome, and I suspect most of the stones are false. The precaution is used, of showing it by the light of a lamp. A crown, notwithstanding, is a famous sight for the English multitude. I would rather take, at random, one of the cases of precious articles, in the Louvre, or at the *Jardin des Plantes* than the imperial crown of Great Britain. What between the Stuarts and some of the later princes your *bona fide* jewels must have been made of steel to withstand their rapacity. Depend on it, had the crown been worth any thing, James II^d, would have looked to it, although he ran away from his kingdom.

There are some curious old implements of war, here, but, by no means, as many or as rare as in the collection at Paris. They showed us the axe with which Anne Boleyn was beheaded, and, sure enough, it was a weapon to make quick work of a "little neck." I was most struck with a sword or two, that I could not hold at arm's length, and which would really seem to demonstrate that, as our minds expand, our bodies shrink. Will the day ever come when matter shall disappear altogether, to give place to the ethereal essence of the spirit? The sight of these swords, and of that of some of the armor, is the first position proved, in demonstrating the existence of giants, and where are they, to day?

I went to dine with _____ _____, on our return. This gentleman had been civil enough to send me two or three invitations, and I now went a little out of my way to manifest a sense of his persevering politeness. I was the first there, but a large party came pouring in immediately after, not a soul of whom had I ever seen before. The old Earl of [Rosslin], the Earl of [Charlemont], the son of the chief of the Irish volunteers, and his wife, Lord [Ebrington], Sir [John Newport], and many others were announced, in quick succession. Finding it awkward to stand in a crowd with no one to speak to, I looked at the pictures of which the house was full. While engaged in this way, a young man came up and spoke to me. It was civil in him, for it appeared to me that he saw I was a stranger, the only stranger in the party, and wished to be polite accordingly. We conversed a few minutes, at a window that was a little removed from the rest of the company.

They have become punctual at London, and I do not think it was fifteen minutes from the time I entered, before dinner was announced. Each of the men took a lady, for there happened to be pretty nearly a tie, and disappeared, leaving my companion and myself standing where we were by the window. He seemed uneasy, and I thought the movement a rare specimen of extreme delicacy of deportment. The only stranger, and he old enough to be the father of some of the young men who had dashed ahead of him, was left standing in the drawing room, as if he were a part of the furniture. I looked hard at my companion, to see if he had the family physiognomy, but he had not, and then I ventured to observe that if we were to dine with the rest of them it might not be amiss to follow.

As we are endeavoring to trace national manners, I will relate an anecdote that occurred just before I left Paris. Madame de _____ invited G _____ to a great dinner, where he was the only stranger, with the exception of an unexpected guest. That person happened to be Count Capo d'Istrias, the President elect of Greece. Just before dinner was announced, G _____ removed to a little distance from the lady of the house, for his invitation had been so worded as to give him reason to think that the entertainment was a compliment to himself, and he could not for an instant dream of preferring claims in competition with M. Capo d'Istrias. Madame de _____ took the arm of the President elect, and walking towards him, she did him the favor to present him to Mad. de Talleyrand, who was of the party, and whom he had the honor of leading to the dinner table. These are trifles, but they are just the trifles that mark the difference between the social tact of London, and that of Paris.

I could not divest myself of the idea that, had I been any thing but an American, this cutting neglect could not have occurred, and when I found that precisely the lowest seat at the table was left for me, I endeavored to recall that passage in Holy Writ, where one is directed to take the lowest place at a feast, as a course good for the soul. Although we have no established religion in America, I will be bold enough to say that no one else that day, bethought him of this text.

My companion, after all, proved to be a connexion of the family, for the seat at the foot of the table, had been left for him. The master of the house sat at the other end, and the mistress in the centre, according to the French mode, so you will perceive I was literally *in extremis*, at this banquet. So much care having been taken of myself, I felt curious to see in what manner the others had been provided for. A swarthy, dark haired common-looking young man sat on the right of the mistress of the house, while old Lord _____, who was a full General in the Army, occupied a more humble situation. This young man was also a soldier, for I heard him talking of a campaign he had made, but, by his years he could not have been more than a colonel, at most, if as high in the army. Of course he must have been of a political or social rank higher than either of the two earls, and this, in England, would give him precedence of his own father! I believe he was the Duke of _____.

A handsome, well-mannered young man sat on my left. Indeed our end of the table was pretty much occupied by the boys, and I began to apprehend a roasting on account of a few gray hairs that time is scattering around my temples. They were well behaved lads, however, I suppose on account of their being in parliament, as I found, by the conversation, was the case with the whole of them. They had all been rowing on the Thames, that morning, and as I had urged the oar myself, in my time, we had at least something to talk about.

The black-haired dignitary gave an account of the death of some officer whom he had seen shot in battle. He had himself found the body after the affair; and, he added, "it had been stripped by the French soldiers." "Why not by our own?" put in my young neighbor, rather pithily. "Because I do not think any of ours had been near it," was the answer, but it sounded like an *arrière pensée*.

It appeared well on the part of my neighbor, to suggest the doubt, and I fell into discourse with him. He had discovered that I was an American by a remark of my right-hand companion, who knew the fact, and he soon began to speak of the difference in language between the English and Americans. He told me he had just come from Paris, and that while strolling in the Palais Royal, he had been struck with the pronunciation of three men who were walking before him. Their dialect was provincial, and he had been at a loss to discover from what part of England they had come, when he ascertained, by their discourse, that they were Americans. I told him we had social *castes* in America, as in England, though they were less strongly marked than common, and that men, of course, betrayed their associations in nothing sooner than in their modes of speech. He admitted the justice of this distinction; but I question if he had ever before thought of America, except as a jumble of a whole people in one *omnium gatherum*. He made a remark that I felt to be just, and one could wish it might be made in the ears of all those who concoct the president's and governors' messages, of the critics, and of the writers of the whole nation. He said he was struck with the manner in which we used the word "our." We did not say "America," but "*our* country," "*our* people," "*our* laws," "*our* this," "*our* that," "*our* t'other." I had been disagreeably impressed, myself, with the same peculiarity, for it is clearly bad, since "*the* country," "*the* laws," "*the* institutions," could mean no other than those of the country in discussion, and would be in better taste. I did not admit this, however, for I had been put at the foot of the table, on account of that country, and one never receives scurvy treatment even for a defect or a misfortune that cannot be helped, that he does not begin to defend it. I told my young critic that it was all for want of a name, the term "United States" being too long, and that the institutions favoured the notion of a right of property in every thing national. He acquiesced in the reasons, which no doubt are the true ones, but he did not appear the more to admire the taste; an opinion that, between ourselves, he entertains in common with some others.

This young man amused me with the entire coolness with which he complimented me on my English being as good as usual. These people are so accustomed to think of us as inferiors, that the bad taste of telling a man in society, "really, now, I do not see but you know how to speak, or to use a fork, or to drink your wine, or to go through the manual of polite life, quite as well as one of us," never appears to strike them. One gets a good many of these oblique compliments, here. My young neighbour was modest, and sensible, but he made this obvious blunder.

My brother statue began to speak of America, and his right hand neighbours listened a little too superciliously for men who had so unceremoniously exalted themselves, and I longed for an opportunity to let them understand whereabouts America lay, and the sort of stuff of which she was made. Chance favoured me, for my neighbour happened to express his apprehensions that the difficulties of Europe might bring about a war, to which America would become a party. "I trembled," he said, "the other day, when the Navarino affair took place, for a war would compel us to impress; and then America *might* think fit to resent it." I told him that impressment, continued a week, out of American vessels, would undeniably produce a war. "Why cannot the two governments amicably settle the matter, by admitting a mutual search in each other's ships?" "Such a privilege would be nominal as respects us, as we could not profit by it; the institutions would forbid impressment." "It is a thousand pities the question cannot be settled." "We hold it to be settled, already, by the law of nations and common sense. The right to impress is not an international but a municipal right, and, of course, can be exercised legally only within the jurisdiction of the nation using it. England has no more claim to follow her seamen into our territory, than to follow her criminals. If we were to send constables to London to arrest thieves, or on board ships on the high seas, we should soon hear of it. Jurisdictions cannot conflict, in this manner, or there is an end of the immunities of national character." "What is then to be done?" "You ask us to concede a favour, and a high favour, that of subjecting the citizen to impositions and trouble for your sole benefit. Now, I think a scheme can be suggested by which the matter may be disposed of." By this time, every ear was pricked up, and attentive, I proceeded—"As for permitting English officers to be the judges of the matter, it is out of the question. We never can concede, and never ought to concede that point. But give us a *quid pro quo* and we may be induced to pass laws that shall purge our shipping, as near as may be, of your seamen." "What could we offer?" "There is the island of Bermuda; you hold it, solely, as a hostile port to be used against us; I think for the peaceable possession of that island, our government would make some sacrifice, and"—here I paused a moment, between a reluctance to hurt my brother statue's *amour propre*, and the recollection of my own attitude on the pedestal, the latter prevailing—"and, by way of inducement to make the arrangement you ought to remember that twenty years hence, England will not be able to hold it."*

The dose worked particularly well. Head went to head, until the idea passed up the table, quite beyond the salt. I heard Lord E_____ exclaim "it is too bad!" I did not think it half as bad, however, as putting a foot on the neck of a stranger, and, moreover, it was true.

The effect of the hint, was quickly apparent, for we were no sooner in the drawing-room than I was approached by half a dozen lords, and I dare say if the dinner were to be gone over again, the bearings and distance from the salt would have been materially altered. I shook the dust off my feet, in quitting that house.

I believe I have not told you an adventure at another house. This was at a dinner given by a merchant; a man of the city, but who does not live in the city, for the *cits* are now fairly rooted in the west end. When dinner was announced the master of the house formally bowed to me, and mentioned my name. This is an invitation, all over the world, to take the *pas*. I advanced accordingly, and offered my arm to the lady; but she very coolly refused it, presenting me to a Mrs. Somebody who sat by her, and took the arm† of some one else. As this person certainly had no title, and was an Englishman, and much younger than myself, I was at a loss to discover his claims. It would have been better had the good man and his wife understood each other, previously, for the effect was to make me appear *tant soit peu* ridiculous.

*It is not yet ten years, since this opinion was given. Where the money that the United States this year distributes among the several states, as returned revenue, (near 8,000,000 sterling,) appropriated to a navy, it would *build* and keep at sea for a twelvemonth, fifty sail of the line. It is "too bad" that a nation, with such means, should be so much under the dominion of a false feeling, as to allow another people to occupy an island like Bermuda, at its threshold, with no other view than to its own annoyance. The internal legislation of this country is practically among the best in the world, while its foreign interests seem to be conducted pretty much on the Mahometan doctrine of fatalism.

†The German Prince speaks of giving the *arm* instead of the *hand,* as an English usage. The writer passed five winters in Paris, and never saw anything but the arm given.

Letter XXI.

To Jacob Sutherland, Esquire.

I have had a singular conversation with a foreigner. This person is a cosmopolite, a _____ by birth, who has lived much in England and America, and our discourse had reference to the opinions and expectations that prevail here concerning our own national character and national destiny. As my companion had no doubts as to the manner in which his communication would be received, he spoke without reserve.

He commenced by saying that a very general impression existed in England that the man of America was not equally gifted, in mind, with the man of Europe. This is merely the old opinion continued to our own times, and I was fully aware of its existence. Captain Hall, when he says that there is *no want of natural ability* in the American people, but that their deficiencies proceed from defective educations, is merely addressing his remark to this prejudice. Almost every English traveller, who has written of the republic, betrays the existence of the same notion, in some way or other. But it is so easy for an American, who is not completely blinded by national vanity, to ascertain these truths, by concealing his origin, while travelling in the stage coaches, that, to me, it is matter of surprise any one who has visited England should be ignorant of them.

Almost every American, whose name reaches this country, in consequence of its being connected with any thing that is thought creditable, is incontinently claimed as an expatriated European. You can have no notion of the extent to which this prejudice is carried. I do assure you, that I have myself heard a respectable man, here, affirm that, in one of the counties of England, he had been a school-fellow of Washington, before the latter emigrated! Mr. Irving figures in biographical notices here, as a native of Devonshire, and even my own humble claims have not been overlooked, as by a sketch of a pretended life, which now lies on my table, my origin is traced to the Isle of Man, and in an elaborated sort of Blue Book, which contains a list of English writers, I find myself enrolled among men, who have far more reason to be ashamed of me, than I have to be ashamed of them. I have been asked quite lately, if Macdonough were not an Irishman, and I believe, my affirmation that poor Allen, who was killed in the Argus, was an American, was absolutely discredited. I met with an assertion, some time since, in one of the journals here, that "Commodore Rodgers was a Scotch baker, of the name of Gray!" The periodical publications of the day, are filled with spurious histories of most of our distinguished men, during the revolution, replete with the usual scurrility and untruths; and even the last war, brought with it, the same touches of amiable veracity.

The national prejudices of England, are freely commented on, by all other people. Prejudice, however, belongs to man, rather than to communities, and I am inclined to think France has almost as many as this country, though they are of a different quality, and are infinitely better cloaked. In making this comparison, I always except the subject of America, for that is a point on which an Englishman usually ceases altogether, to be either just, or discerning.

One of the traits which the English attribute to us, is a greater disposition than common to lie. I have no hesitation in saying, that this nation deems our own, addicted to this vice, altogether out of the ordinary way. On this point, there can be no mistake, for Captain Hall, Mr. De Roos, and several other recent writers, even by exonerating us from the charge, betray its existence; but we have high clerical authority for it, that will settle the matter. I quote Bishop Heber; he is speaking of the American sailors. "They are not so grievously addicted to lying, as they were once said to be. *They have less animosity against the English than formerly, and their character seems to have recovered its natural English tone.*" Dr. Heber might have been puzzled to explain, in what the *natural* English character differs from any other, on principles that would harmonize with the Thirty-nine Articles, of which, I believe, we possess a tolerably accurate copy, in our own church. But, putting orthodoxy out of the question, and not descending to a too rigid construction of words, how was this notion of the American people, and especially of their seamen, obtained? I think, I can explain it.

The English were accustomed to consider themselves the most skilful mariners of the earth. When their American competitors boasted of their own ships, that they could outsail those of England, and that their general qualities were better, verifying all by alleged facts, the latter, as a matter of course, were deemed lies. Were a hundred English ship-masters to assert to-day, that their vessels could outsail ours, the American seamen would have no more charity, but, at once, set them down as dealers in fiction. During the long wars, our shipping was the prey of the belligerents, the English, as the most numerous, doing it the most harm; vexing commerce, by impressing the seamen, and as often carrying off the native, as their own subjects. These acts created a bitter feeling, and the American government, influenced by a miserable penny-saving policy, which cost more in the end, than a prompt resistance, almost abandoned the seamen to themselves; writing long diplomatic notes, instead of arming. I know, by personal observation, that many of our ship-masters of that day, boasted they had misled English squadrons and cruizers, by false information, for it was the only means they had, of avenging themselves.

Conversing with Mr. _____, he informed me that, for some time, an acquaintance of ours, a captain in the British navy, was supposed to have been killed in the attack on Fort Bowyer. On my asking how the information had been obtained, he quite unconsciously answered—"Oh! it was only the report of an American captain." I laughed at him, for this confession, and he frankly admitted an opinion prevailed in England, that the American ship-masters were greater liars than usual.

Our facts are astounding, and, when related, appear marvellous to foreigners. *Au reste*, the Americans, more particularly those of New England, are a gossiping people, and though the gossip may not be a liar, he necessarily circulates much untruth. In this manner, the American lies with his tongue, while the rest of the world lie only in their thoughts. But lying is one of the commonest vices of humanity.

It is fortunate that Providence has reserved us for the justice of another state of being, for, it is certain, there is very little in this. Here is a nation, that, if a civil agent of its own, arrest John Doe, for Richard Roe, punishes him severely, throwing the *onus* of the proof of guilt, on the minister of the law, but which goes out of its own jurisdiction, to demand of foreigners proofs of innocence; failing of which, it lays violent hands on them, exposes them to mutilation and death, in a quarrel in which they have no concern, and then vilifies them, by way of atonement! This is bad enough, certainly, but it is, by no means, the worst feature in the affair. Men, in the condition of gentlemen, have been found among the oppressed, to justify the wrong, for you and I are both old enough, distinctly to remember the time, when England was loudly and openly vindicated by a party, at home, in a course that set all national honour, and national justice at defiance. It is said, that the world presents nothing new; that all its current incidents are merely new phases of old events; but, really, it sometimes seems to me, that the history of man has never before presented so strong an instance of national abasement, as is to be found in the feelings, language, reasoning, and acts of a very large portion of what are called the better classes of the American people, towards Great Britain. Of all burthens, that of the mental dependance created by colonial subserviency, appears to be the most difficult to remove. It weighs upon us yet, like an incubus, and, apart from matters of gain, in which we have all our eyes about us, and apart from party politics, in which men will "follow their leaders, though it be to the devil," there is not an American, in my opinion, at this moment, of sufficient note fairly to attract foreign comment, who does not hold his reputation at home, entirely at the mercy of Great Britain. We do not see this fact ourselves, but strangers do, and deride us for the weakness. We have, indeed, reason to thank God, that the portion of the nation, which constitutes its bone and muscle, although of no account in its floating opinions, is so purely practical, so stubborn in its nationality, so right-thinking, at least, in the matters that come properly and fairly before it, and so little likely to be influenced to its destruction!

Another of the notions that exists in England, is that of the hostility of America to Great Britain. All the recent travellers among us, frankly admit that they see no evidence of such a feeling, but of one quite to the contrary. I have frequently told my friends here, that, in my opinion, and it is an opinion formed from a good deal of observation, *in no other country are the English looked upon with as friendly eyes, as in the United States of America.* I feel as certain of this fact, as I do of any other moral truth at which I believe myself to have arrived by investigation and travelling. I do not think that I have succeeded, however, in convincing a single individual.

A few of the public writers here, affect to maintain that there is no general inimical sentiment, or prejudice in England, against the United States, with the Edinburgh Review at their head. It might as well be denied that the sun appears in the east, and sets in the west. The feeling is as apparent as the day; it mingles with every thought, colours every concession, and even tempers the charities. Every American established in the country asserts it, all travellers believe it, even Captain Hall and other writers confess it, and four out of five, on the spot, when circumstances induce frankness, admit it. Let us look for the reasons of these contradictory feelings, in the two nations.

In the collisions between the two people, in the main, America has won and England has lost. The winner is usually complacent, the loser soured. In America facts have preceded opinion, and so far from there being a tendency to aid the first by appeals to prejudices, the disposition has been to retard them by comparisons favourable to the old system. The very opposite of this state of things exists in England. Power, in America, has nothing to apprehend from English example, while power, in England, has much to apprehend from the example of America. This reason applies with peculiar force to the church in England, which ought to be the first to foster the charities. It is natural for a young people to look back with affection to their ancestry, and to the country from which they sprung, and it is human for those in possession of advantages that once were exclusive, to look forward with distrust to the fortunes of a vigorous competitor that has arisen from their own stock.

These reasons might suffice, but there are others, which, though less evident, have perhaps been more active in producing the unfriendly feeling in England. In this country, it should always be remembered, there is a contradiction between the theory of the government and its facts. By the first the sovereign possesses an authority, that is denied him in practice. No well-informed man really thinks that the King of England, of his own free will, could declare war, for instance, and yet the commentators will tell you he may. In curbing his authority, the aristocracy is compelled to keep in view the nation, and the principal means that have been resorted to for influencing it, have been to act on its prejudices. Nothing has struck me more forcibly, here, than the manner in which the higher classes keep themselves free from the national prejudices, that their organs, the press, studiously excite in the mass. This is said without any reference to America, however, for the aristocracy certainly likes *us* as little as any portion of the community, and without alluding to the mere difference that always exists between knowledge and ignorance, but to notions, which if true, ought to be found more general among the instructed, than among the ignorant.

I perceive that Capt. Hall lays much stress on the loyalty of the English, as a healthful sentiment that is quite unknown in America. He has not attached too much importance to this feeling, in my judgment, though he has scarcely analysed it with sufficient penetration. This loyalty is a pure abstraction in England, on which, by dint of management, the self love of the nation has been concentrated. It is national pride, interest, and national prejudice, to all of which this direction has been given, so far as they are connected with sentiment, for to say that the usual personal attachment has any thing to do with it, in regard to a monarch whom his people have quietly seen stripped, one by one, of the free exercise of all his prerogatives involves an absurdity. No one is more loyal in England, than the Duke who is acquiring boroughs, with a view to return members whose principal duty will be to vote down and curb the royal authority. Such a man, it is true, declaims against disloyalty as a crime; he defends the prerogative both in person and by his nominees; but then he takes good care that it shall be exercised by a minister, whom he has an agency in creating, and with whom he can make his own terms. It would not do to transfer this sentiment from him who has not, to those who actually wield the power of the state, and who are compelled to live so much before the common eye, for there are too many of them; they are unsupported by the prejudice of birth, and familiarity would soon destroy the portion of the feeling that is the most useful.* The force of this fiction, loyalty (it is purely fiction, as it relates to the individual), is inconceivably strong; for I question if the English, after their own fashion, are not the most loyal people in Europe. Their feelings, in this particular, give one good reason to doubt whether men will not defer more to an abstraction, than to a reality.

Another of the prejudices of the English arises from the devotedness of the faith with which they subscribe to the fictions of their own system. In no other country is society so socially drilled. Lord _____ observed to me, "England is a pyramid, in which every man has his place, and of which the king forms the point." The remark has some truth in it, but the peer overlooked the essential fact, that where the summit ought to be the base of his pyramid is. This social drilling, however, like almost everything else, has its advantages and its disadvantages. The better soldier you make of a man the more he becomes disqualified to be any thing else. You have no notion of the extent to which the ethics of station are carried, in this country; being probably quite as much beyond the point of reason and manliness, in one extreme, as the canting of the press, and the brawls of low party politicians are driving it to the other, with us. I have seen a footman's manual, in

---

*I am quite aware that it will be affirmed by some of our *doctrinaires,* the king of England *does* exercise the prerogatives of his office. It would be easy to produce proof enough to the contrary, but take a single case. It is notorious that he wishes a tory ministry, at this very moment, and it is equally notorious that he cannot appoint one, on account of parliament. Now his right to name his ministers is almost the only undisputed prerogative, that is left him in theory even, for a minister is made responsible for all the other executive acts. But hear what a witness, whose loyalty will not be questioned says. "It has affected me very much to hear of *our king's being constrained to part with all his confidential friends, and his own personal servants* in the late general sweep. *Out of a hundred stories,* I will only tell you one, which concerns your old acquaintance Lord Bateman; he went to the king, as usual, over night, to ask if his majesty would please to hunt the next day: yes, my lord! replied the king, but I find, *with great grief,* that I am not to have the satisfaction of your company! This was the first intimation he had had of the loss of his place; and I really think the contest with France and America might have been settled, *though the buck hounds had retained their old master."* See, letter of Hannah More to her sister, London, 1782. The Plantagenets were not treated in this fashion, and yet England was said to be governed, even in their day, by King, Lords, and Commons!

which, besides the explanations of active duties, the whole *morale* of his station, is set before the student, with great precision and solemnity. It is a sort of social catechism. So effectually has the system of drill been pursued, that I firmly believe, a majority of Englishmen, at this moment, attach an idea of immorality, to any serious effort to alter the phases of society. It is deemed social treason, and like other treason, the notion of crime is connected with it. The benefits of this drilling, are great order, with perfect seemliness and method, in conducting the affairs of life; the defects, the substitution of artificial for the natural links of society, form for feeling, and the inward festering of the mind, which, sooner or later, will be certain to break out on the surface, and disfigure, if it do not destroy, the body politic. There is no comparison between the *finish* of an English, and that of a French servant, for instance, as regards the thousand little details of duty. One is as much superior to the other, as an English is superior to a French knife. But, when it comes to feeling, the advantage is all the other way. The English servant will not bear familiarity, scarcely kindness: the Frenchman will hardly dispense with both. To the first you never speak, unless to order; the latter is treated as an humble friend. The revolution in France, has shown instances of devotedness and affection, in consequence, that no revolution in England will ever be likely to see equalled.

One of the effects of the prejudices of the country, is to supersede facts and reasoning, by a set of dogmatical inferences, which the Englishman receives quite as a matter of course, and as beyond discussion. I could give you a hundred examples of what I mean, but a recent instance shall suffice.

In a discussion with the conductor of a periodical work, who is friendly to America, I have had occasion to note the following errors in relation to ourselves. Speaking of the expedition of Captain Parry to the north, he bestows very merited encomiums on the conduct of the crews, which he attributes to their good training, as Englishmen. By way of illustrating the difference between such a system, and one that may, with great justice, pass for its converse, he gave an account of an exploring expedition sent out by the government of the United States, to the Pacific Ocean, in which the men had put their officers on shore, and had gone a sealing! You are to understand, that my acquaintance had been pressing me to contribute to his work, with the object of correcting the erroneous notions, which prevail in England, in regard to America.

"Here," said I, "is an instance of the sweeping deductions that you form. You imagine a fact, and directly in the teeth of testimony, go to work to produce your inferences. The United States never sent an expedition of the sort any where, and, of course, no such occurrence could have taken place. Now, as to the principle, I may speak from some personal knowledge, and I tell you that, according to my experience, the English seamen are much the most turbulent, and the Americans much the most tractable, and the least likely to violate law, of any with whom I have ever had any thing to do. In point of fact, the officers of no American cruizer, ever lost the command of their vessel, for an hour, or, perhaps I might say, a minute, though two or three slight instances of insubordination did occur, under the old laws, and when the terms of service of the men were legally up; but, owing to the spirit of the officers, and the habits of subordination in the crews, in every one of even these instances, the resistance was immediately quelled. What is the other side of the picture? Did not the crews of several English vessels, murder their officers, and run away with the ships, during the last war? There are the cases of the Hermione, and the Bounty, for instance, and this assertion of yours is made in face of the notorious historical fact, that, within the memory of man, the British empire was made to tremble to its centre, by the mutiny of the Nore!"

I believe my acquaintance was struck with this representation, and I expected to see an explanation in his work, but the next number contained a paragraph, which deprecated the admission of matter that conflicted with the *national prejudices!*

So far as mere manner is concerned, the English drilling produces better results, in every day life, than our own *pêle-mêle*. A good portion of the *grossièreté*, at home, is for the want of the condensed class of well-bred people, of which I have so often spoken, and the moral cowardice of men, who have too often ardent longings for the glitter of life, without the manliness to enforce its decencies.* Could the two nations meet half way, in

*One of the most ludicrous instances I know of the manner in which terms are abused, in America, was related to me lately, by Judge ____, of Louisiana. A

this respect, both would be essentially gainers, we in appearances, and in the decencies connected with manner, and the English in the more kindly feelings, and in security. There is undeniably, a cant obtaining the ascendancy at home, that is destructive of all manner, in conducting the ordinary relations of life, and which is not free from danger, as it confounds the substance of things with their shadow. Democracy has no necessary connexion with vulgarity, but it merely means that men shall have equal political rights. There can be no greater fallacy than to say, one man is as good as another, in all things. In the eye of God, men are equal, and happy is the country, in which it is not dangerous to declare, also, that they shall be perfectly equal in all their legal privileges. But beyond this, the principle cannot be carried, and civilization maintained. One man has higher tastes, more learning, better principles, more strength, more beauty, and greater natural abilities, than another. I take it, that human institutions, are intended to prevent him, who is the most powerful, in consequence of the possession of these advantages, from injuring him who is weaker. The relations between master and servant, are not all affected thereby, and he who submits to labour for hire, under the directions of an employer serves, while the other commands. These duties may be conducted with too little, as well as too much deference of manner. The tendency in civilized society, is always toward the latter, when the usual proportions between surface and population are obtained, for it is a consequence of the pressure of society, and there is little fear that we shall not get our share of it, in time; though, *en attendant,* we find occasional instances, in which the individual mistakes insolence for independence. Perhaps, after all, *insolence* is too strong a word. I think, I have met more pure insolence from Englishmen in low situations, than from Americans; it is the natural consequence of reaction; though it is rare, indeed, to meet with the same deference from the last, as from the first. Assemble, in any reasonable space in America, a dozen genteel families, and they will, of their own influence, create an atmosphere of decency, about them, that shall contain

---

constable came into court, leading two knaves, and addressed him, by saying ——"Please your Honour, these are the two *gentlemen,* who stole Col. D___'s horses."

all that is really desirable, in this respect. The inherent sense of right, which is implanted in every man by nature, and which becomes conscience in moral things, may be safely confided in, as the surest means of regulating the deportment of the different castes of society, towards each other.

There is a very general notion prevalent in England, that we seized a moment to declare war against them, when they were pressed upon hardest, by the rest of Europe. A portion of their antipathy is owing to this idea, though the idea itself is altogether owing to their prejudices against America, for there is not a particle of truth in it. I do not remember to have conversed on the subject, with any Englishman, who did not betray this feeling. It is of no consequence, that dates disprove the fact. America declared war, on the 18th of June, 1812, after twenty years of submission to impressment, and illegal captures, and at a moment when the government was put in possession of proof of an effort, on the part of England, to dissolve the Union, as well as of her fixed determination, not to alter her Orders in Council. As respects the latter, history gives all the necessary evidence of the expediency of the war, for it had not been declared three months, when the British government offered to do, what it had just before officially affirmed it would not do. In June 1812, Spain and Portugal were in arms, on the side of England, Russia and Sweden, were secretly preparing to join her, and that great effort which finally broke down the power of France, was just about to commence. But in the face of all these facts, the opinion I have mentioned, certainly exists.

The English have been persuaded that a religious establishment is indispensable to religion. As regards the establishments of Italy, France, Spain, Turkey, and all the rest of the world, they are ready enough to admit that there are capital faults, connected with the several religious systems, but having got the truth themselves, it is expedient to fortify it with legal and exclusive advantages. Of all the profane blasphemies the world has witnessed, that of prostituting the meek doctrines of Christ, by pampering his professed ministers with riches and honours, under the hollow pretence of upholding his faith, is the most insulting to evident truths, and offensive to humility. Such are the fruits of establishments, and of enlisting religion in the support of temporal political systems. Good men *may* prosper, even under these disadvantages, but bad men *will*. It is a device of the devil, if that fallen angel is, at all, permitted to meddle with spiritual things.

As we have no establishment, it is the prevalent opinion, here, that we have no religion. Several intelligent English, have confessed this much to me; an admission that was not at all necessary, for I detected the prejudice, before I had been a month in the country: and one person has actually appealed to me for facts, with a view to repel the arguments of those who uphold the present state of things; since it is assumed, that the actual condition of America, is a proof of the necessity of a religious establishment, in the interests of order and morality. My answer was, "that were the upper classes of the English, to be placed in America, with their present habits and notions, there is not one of them in a hundred, who would not immediately begin to declaim against the religious fanaticisms and exaggeration of the country!" This reply, I believe, to contain the truth. There is an exterior affectation of a deference for spiritual things, here, among people of condition, that does not always, or rather so universally exist with us; for, the government being an aristocracy, and the establishment enlisted in its support, it would be a singular indiscretion, in times like these, for those who reap the peculiar advantages of the existing order of things, to neglect so powerful an ally. Some of these persons, often remind me of that anecdote of the English sailor, who, falling into the hands of the Turks, was urged to become a mussulman — "What, change my religion? No, d — n my eyes, never." The religious *tone* of a community, is best ascertained through its facts. Since I have been in Europe, the following circumstances, among many others of a similar character, have come under my eye.

A duel was fought at Boulogne in France, between the Rev. _____ _____, and Mr. _____; the former was attended by his brother, the Rev. _____ _____. Both the reverend gentlemen were ordained clergymen of the Church of England, and the latter was said to be married to the daughter of a bishop.

A complainant appeared before a London magistrate, in the case of an assault. The defendant justified himself, by saying, "that he was driving a gig, with a female; that the complainant passed him on horseback repeatedly, and insulted his companion, by staring under her hat; whereupon he horsewhipped the offender." "You handed this card to your assailant?" said the magistrate, to the complainant. "I did." "With what intention?" "As is usual among gentlemen, when an outrage like this has been committed." "One corner of the card is torn off—why did you tear it off!" "*Because I am in the church*, sir, and I thought the '*Rev.*' *misplaced on such an occasion.*" The substance of this statement, with the names of the parties, has appeared in the police reports, during my visit here.

"The Rev. Mr. O_____, fought Mr. _____, at Boulogne, quite recently, the reverend gentleman hitting his man."

There is, no doubt, much vice among the clergy every where, for they are frail, like all of us. Probably the vicious men in the Church of England, are not at all more numerous, than those of every established church necessarily must be, with the temptations to enter it for the possession of rich livings. But what I wish to lay before you, is a comparison between England and America on these points. I think, it would be hard to find a layman in all America, who would fight a clergyman; much less a clergyman who would openly fight a duel. If "hypocrisy be the homage which vice pays to virtue," the inference is fair, that a public sentiment in America, keeps a clergyman in closer bounds, than he would be kept in England.

It is denying the effects of the most common natural influences, to pretend that a church, whose avenues lead to vast wealth, and to the highest rank in the state, is as likely to be as pure in its ministers, as one which offers less temporal inducements than any one of all the liberal occupations of life. If it be contended that an establishment is indispensable to religion, it must be confessed that its advantages are to be taken with this essential drawback. It is a notorious fact, that sons are set aside for the church here when children, in order that they may receive particular livings, in the gift of the family, or its friends, or that their fortunes may be pushed in it, by family influence. Nothing of the sort exists with us.

Lord _____, at a dinner in his own house, observed to me, that the best thing we had in America, was our freedom from the weight of a religious establishment. Encouraged by this remark, I told an anecdote of a conversation I had once overheard in America. It was while making a passage in a sloop, on the coast, with two young whalers, just returned from sea, as fellow-passengers. A gentleman on board asked me what had become of young Napoleon, then a boy of ten or twelve years. I answered, there was a report that the Austrians were educating him for the church. My two whalers listened intently to this conversation, in which the tender years of the child had been mentioned, when one of them suddenly exclaimed to the other—"Did you hear that, Ben? Bringing a parson *up by hand!*"—"Ay, ay; making a *cosset*-priest!"

I was much amused by the point and sarcasm of these remarks, and every American will feel why; but, I was more so, I think, by the manner in which my English auditors received the anecdote. I do not think one of them felt its point; but as the Sag-Harbourmen used agricultural figures to illustrate their meaning, I was at once applied to, to know whether such people could be more than half-seamen, and whether America could supply mariners sufficient to become a great naval power!

A lady, here, with whom I am on sufficiently friendly terms to converse freely, was speaking of the son of a noble family, a near connexion of hers, who is in the church. "It is very unpleasant," she said, "to find one whom you esteem, getting to be wrongheaded in such matters. Now _____ was becoming quite serious, and a little fanatical, and I was employed by the family to speak to him!" This _____, is a clergyman whose piety has been highly extolled by one of our bishops, and whose devotion to the Redeemer is thought, at home, to be highly creditable to the English aristocracy. So far as he himself is concerned, all this is well enough; but as to the manner in which "the nobility and gentry," of his connexion, regard his course, you have sufficient proof in what I have just told you.

I shall dismiss this part of the subject as unpleasant to myself. The Church of England, so far as its religious dogmas are concerned, is that in which I was educated, and in which I am training my children; and no one is more sensible of its excellencies, when they are separated from its abuses. I should have been silent, altogether, on its defects, but I feel convinced that a grasping, worldly spirit, has made it an instrument, in the hands of artful or prejudiced men, of defaming a state of society which is probably as exempt from its own peculiar vices, as it ever fell to the lot of men to be.

Another notion deeply rooted in the English mind, is a strange opinion, that all men of *liberal* education and gentlemanly habits, must, of necessity, be hostile to popular rights, and, by the same necessity, advocates of some such liberty as their own, if the advocates of any liberty at all. One of the first things that the clerical critic, on the well known sermon of Bishop Hobart, remarks, is his surprise that a man of "gentlemanly habits" should have taken such a view of matters! There is, unquestionably, a strong disposition in men, who do not look beyond the exterior of things, (and this, perhaps, embraces the majority,) to confound "taste" with "principles." There are many things in which the results of the English system are more agreeable to my tastes, and even my habits, than those of our own, though I believe ours will be eventually softened by the pressure of society; but, it does not strike me that this is a sufficient reason, why an honest man should overlook more essential points. One cannot have the thorough, social drilling of a government of exclusion, and escape its other consequences. All power that is not based on the mass, must repress the energies and moral improvement of that mass for its own security, and the fruits are the vast chasm which exists everywhere, in Europe, between the extremes of society.

I shall say little of the mere vulgar prejudices, which piously believe in the inherent superiority, moral and physical, of Englishmen over all the rest of mankind; for something very like it is to be found in all nations. Still, I think, the prejudices of England, in this respect, are more than usually offensive to other people, as, I believe, are our own. Those of England, however, are to be distinguished from those of America, in one important particular. The common Englishman cannot believe himself superior to his transatlantic kinsman, with a whit more sincerity, than the feeling is returned by the common American. But, while the Englishman of the upper classes thinks lightly of the American, the American of the upper classes over-estimates the Englishman. There are doubtless many exceptions, in both cases, especially among those who have travelled; but such, I think, is the rule. Our own weakness is a natural consequence of a colonial origin, of reading English books, and of the exaggerations of distance and dependency. It is a weakness that is seen and commented on, by every body but those who feel it.

I question if the inbred and overweening notion of personal superiority ascends as high in the social scale, or is as general among people of education, in any other community, as in England. In this respect, we are deficient rather than exaggerated; for while all America (I now speak of the upper classes, you will remember) can be thrown into a fever, by an intimation that our *things* are not as good as those of other nations, there is a secret and general distrust of our equality on the points that alone can give dignity and character to man. A friend of yours has been accused of national vanity, and national conceit, (an odd charge, by the way, for I question if there is a man in the whole republic who prides himself less in the national character, than the person in question,) because he has endeavoured to repel and refute some of the grosser imputations that artifice and prejudice, in this quarter of the world, have been studiously and industriously heaping on us; and the simple circumstance that, in so doing, he has conflicted a little with English supremacy, has been the means of destroying whatever favour he may once have possessed with the American *reading* public, as a writer; for England, at this moment, holds completely at her mercy the reputation and character of every American she may choose to assail, who is not supported by the *bulk* of his own nation. As a matter of course, she writes up all who defer to her power, and writes down all who resist it. The statements of your friend have been publicly derided, because they have affirmed the rights and merits of the *mass*, on which alone we are to ground all our claims to comparative excellence; and I now ask you, if, in any review, comment, or speech, at home, you have ever met with the sweeping assertions of an *abstract, innate* national superiority, that is contained in the following paragraph.

"It would be in vain to inquire whether this superiority, which we do not hesitate to say has been made manifest, with very few exceptions, whenever the British have met foreign troops upon equal terms, arises from a stronger conformation of body, or a more determined turn of mind; but it seems certain that the British soldier, inferior to Frenchmen in general intelligence, and in individual acquaintance with the trade of war, has a decided advantage in the bloody shock of actual conflict, and especially when maintained by the bayonet, body to body. *It is remark-*

able also, that the charm is not peculiar to any one of the three united nations, but it is common to the natives of all, different as they are in habits and education. The guards, supplied by the city of London, may be contrasted with a regiment of Irish recruited among their rich meadows, or a body of Scotch, from their native wildernesses; and while it may be difficult to assign the palm to either over the other two, all are found to exhibit that species of dogged and desperate courage, *which without staying to measure force or calculate chances, rushes on the enemy as the bull-dog upon the bear.*"

Lest you should think I have rummaged one of the productions of the Minerva Press, for some of its inflations, it may be well to explain, that this quiet, deeply seated *naïve* proof of ignorance and prejudice, is quoted from Sir Walter Scott's account of the battle of Maida, in the Life of Napoleon. We are justly enough deemed conceited, but our literature contains nothing to compare with this. I have cited this instance of prejudice, in order to prove how high the weakness of believing in the personal superiority of their own people, ascends in the scale of intellect, for I have no doubt, that Sir Walter Scott religiously believed all he wrote.

The exhibition of many of the prejudices of the English, is not always restrained by propriety, even among those who ought to know better.* Of this, all foreigners complain, and I think, with reason. As respects us, there is a quiet assumption of superiority,

---

*That the reader may understand the nature and extent of the prejudices that are inculcated in England, against this country, I extract a sentence from a *school* book, of a good deal of reputation, *written by a clergyman.* The edition is of 1830. "The women every where possess, in the highest degree, the domestic virtues; they have more sweetness, more goodness, *perhaps as much courage,* and more sensibility and liberality, than the men." Prejudice must have taken deep root, indeed, in England, where the bad taste of a sneer on the courage of America, was not self-evident. One of the best informed men I met in that country, told me, that no event, in his time, had produced so deep a sensation in England, as the unexpected and bloody resistance of the *armed population* to the British troops, at Bunker Hill. One of the principal causes of the errors of all Europe, as respects us, is owing to the fact, that their writers, anxious to attract, deal with exceptions instead of with the rules. The whole article of "America," in the book I have just quoted, betrays this fault. Among other absurdities, it says, "there are scarcely in the country, twenty native Americans, (meaning whites, of course,) in the state of domestic servants." There are, beyond question, tens of thousands, including both sexes, and all ages.

that has the appearance of an established right to comment on the nation, its character, and its institutions. There is a mode of doing this, which removes all objections, among men of the world, but there is, also, a mode which amounts to positive personal disrespect.

Of the latter class, is an occurrence that took place at the table of Lord _____, quite lately. One of the guests very quietly went to work, without preface of any sort, to prove, that the improper deportment of the members of congress, as compared with those of parliament, was owing to a want of refinement in the nation! I met him at once (for I never witnessed in the society of gentlemen, a greater instance of personal indecorum,) by denying his premises. Seriously, I believe, of the two, congress is better mannered than parliament, though there is less mystification; all that has been written to the contrary, being founded rather on what ought to be, according to certain notions, than on what is.

Whenever I meet with this dispostion, it chills all my sympathies. I hope I can be just to such men, but I can never like them. What renders these unfeeling and ignorant comments less inexcusable, is the fact, that any attempt to turn the tables, is instantly met with a silence that cannot be misconstrued. Surprised to find the depth, and universality of prejudice against America, here, as well as the freedom with which remarks are made, I determined to try the experiment of retorting in kind. In most instances, I have found that they who were willing to talk all night, on the defects of America, become mum, the instant there is an allusion to any similar weaknesses in England, or in English character. As there can be no wish to keep up acquaintances, on such terms, I have generally dropped them; always unless I have seen that the prejudice is sincere, and acting on a benevolent nature. I presume the history of the world, cannot offer another instance of prejudice in one nation against another, that is as strong and as general, as that which, at this moment, exists in England against America; the community of language, and the art of printing, having been the means of provoking, rather than of mitigating the failing.

Although prejudice must result in ultimate evil, it may measurably produce intermediate good. The prejudices of England are at the base of the nationality of her people. With us the *people* are national, from affection, and a consciousness of living under a system that protects their rights and interests. But true nationality is very much confined to the mass, though national conceit is pretty generally diffused. No man in America, can have national pride, (the ground-work of all true nationality,) who has not pride in the institutions; and this is a feeling that all the training of the higher classes has taught them to repress. Our social aristocracy, in this respect, are a mere reflection of the commoner English prejudices—prejudices that are received ignorantly, in pure faith, and as the stone admits water by constant dropping. A more impudent piece of literary empiricism has never been palmed on the world, than the pretension that the American reading public requires American themes; it may require American *things*, to a certain extent, though it is quite natural and perhaps excusable that it should prefer foreign, which I believe to be the real fact; but as to distinctive American *sentiments* and American *principles,* the majority of that class of our citizens, hardly know them when they see them. A more wrong-headed and deluded people there is not, on earth, than our own, on all such subjects, and one would be almost content to take some of the English prejudices, if more manliness and discrimination could be had with them. Our faults of this nature, are the results of origin and geographical position; those of England are the results of time, power, artifice, and peculiar political and physical advantage.

All great nations are egotistical, and deluded on the subject of their superiority. The constant influence of an active corps of writers, (who from position become so many popular flatterers,) acting on the facts of a strong community, has a tendency to induce men to transfer the credit that is only due to collective power, to national character and personal qualities. The history of the world proves that the citizens of small states have performed more great and illustrious personal acts, and out of all proportion to numbers, than the citizens of great nations, and the reason is probably to be found in the greater necessities of their condition; but, fewer feeling an interest in extolling their deeds, it is not common for them to reap the glory that falls to the share of even the less deserving servitors of a powerful community.

I shall close this brief summary of national peculiarities, by an allusion to one more. Foreigners accuse the English of being capricious in their ordinary intercourse. They are allowed to be fast friends, but uncertain acquaintances. The man, or woman, who receives you to-day with a frank smile, and a familiar shake of the hand, may meet you to-morrow coldly, and with a chilling or repulsive formality. I have seen something of this, and believe the charge, in a degree, to be merited. They are formalists in manners, and too often mistake the spirit that ought to regulate intercourse. Jonathan stands these caprices better than any one else, for he is so devout a believer that he sees smiles in his idol, when other people see grimaces. Your true American *doctrinaire* studies the book which John Bull has published concerning his own merits, with some such faith as old women look into the almanac in order to know when it will snow.*

---

*While this work is going through the press, Tucker's Jefferson has appeared. In allusion to the principles of a memorial written by himself, Mr. Jefferson's language is quoted to the following effect. "The leap I then proposed was too long, as yet, for the mass of our citizens." Nearly seventy years have since passed by; we have become a nation; numerically and physically a *great* nation; and yet in how many things that affect the supremacy of English opinion and English theories, is "the leap" still "too long" for the "mass of our citizens!" It is these "long leaps," notwithstanding, that make the difference between men.

Plate XIII

Piccadilly, from Coventry Street

Regent Street, from Piccadilly Circus

Plate XIV

Waterloo Place and Part of Regent Street

Regent Street, from the Quadrant

Plate XV

Theatre Royal, Covent Garden

Christ Church and Part of Christ's Hospital

Plate XVI

Old London Bridge

London Docks

Letter XXII.

Henry Floyd-Jones, Esq., Fort Neck.

O ur connexion, Mr. McAdam,* who resides in Hertford-shire, has just taken me with him to his house.

It was something to find myself on an English high-way, seated by the side of the man who had done so much for the kingdom, in this respect. We travelled in an open gig, for my companion had an eye to every displaced stone, or inequality in the surface. The system of roads, here, is as bad as can be; the

*The intelligence of the death of this gentleman has reached America, while this book is printing. John Loudon McAdam was a native of Scotland, of the pro-scribed family of McGregor. He was in the line of descent to a small estate called Waterhead; but being cut off from his natural claims, by the act of attainder, he came early to America, as the adopted son and successor of an uncle, who had married and established himself in New York. Here he received his education, and continued seventeen years, or down to the period of the peace of 1783. Returning to Great Britain, he established himself at Bristol, near which town he commenced his experiments in roads, more as an amateur, than with any serious views of devoting himself to the occupation. Meeting with unlooked for success, he gradually extended his operations, until he finally transformed most of the highways of the island, into the best of the known world. For the last five-and-twenty years, his whole time, and all his studies were directed to this one end.

Mr. McAdam was twice offered knighthood, and once a baronetcy; distinctions that he declined. His second son, however, has recently received the former honour, and is the present Sir James McAdam. As this gentleman is much employed about London, he is usually mistaken for the father.

Mr. McAdam was twice married. His first wife was a daughter of William Nicoll, proprietor of the great manor of Islip, Suffolk county, Long Island, the collateral representative of Col. Nicoll, who took the colony from the Dutch, in 1663, and its first English governor; his second wife was the eldest daughter of John Peter De Lancey, of Mamaroneck, West Chester, New York.

Mr. McAdam was a man of a singularly calm and contemplative mind, mingled with an unusual degree of practical energy and skill. Quiet, modest, intelligent, and upright, few men were more esteemed in private life; and while few men have conferred more actual benefit on Great Britain, scarcely any man has been less rewarded. Conscientious and proud, he was superior to accepting favours that were beneath his claims, or to soliciting those which were his due.

whole country being divided into small "trusts," as they are called, in a way to prevent any one great and continued plan. I should say we went through four or five gates, absolutely within the limits of the town; obstacles, however, that probably still exist, on account of the great growth of London. Although Mr. McAdam had no connexion with the "trusts" about London, we passed all the gates without contribution, in virtue of his name.

We had much conversation on the subject of roads. On my mentioning that I had found some of them much better than others, a few, indeed, being no better than very many of our own, Mr. McAdam told me that there was a want of material in many parts of England, which had compelled them to have recourse to gravel. "Now," said he, "the *metal* of this very road on which we are travelling, came from the East Indies!" The explanation was sufficiently simple; stone had been brought into the India docks, as ballast, and hauled thence, a distance of several miles, to make the bed of the road we were on. Gravel-pits are common in England; and there is one open, at this moment, in Hyde Park, that is a blot on its verdure.

We took the road into Hertfordshire, which is the great northern high-way, as well as being the scene of John Gilpin's race. We passed the "Bell, at Edmonton," where there is now a sign in commemoration of John's speed, and bottom, and wig. By the way, the coachmen have a more classical authority for the flaxens than I had thought.

Waltham cross was an object of still greater interest. Edward I. caused these crosses to be erected on the different spots where the body of his wife reposed, in its funeral-journey from Milford Haven to London. Charing-cross, in the town itself, was the last of them. They are little gothic structures, with niches to receive statues, and are surmounted by crosses, forming quaint and interesting memorials. I believe we passed two of them between London and Hoddesdon, by which it would seem that the body of the queen made short stages. The cross at Charing has entirely disappeared.

At Hoddesdon, we were on the borders of Essex; and the day after our arrival, Mr. McAdam walked with me across the bridge that separates the two counties, to look at Rye-house, the place so celebrated as the spot where the attempt was to have been made on the life of Charles II. The intention was to fire on the king, as he returned from Newmarket, on his way to London. The building is certainly well placed for such an object, as it almost projects into the road, which, just here, is quite narrow, and which it enfilades in such a way, that a volley fired from its windows would have been pretty certain to rake the whole of the royal *cortège*. The house, itself, is a common brick farm building, somewhat quaint, particularly about the chimneys, and by no means large. I suspect a part of it has disappeared. It is now used as a poor-house, and, certainly, if it is to be taken as a specimen of the English poor-houses, in general, it is highly creditable to the nation. Nothing could be neater, and the inmates were few.

The land, around this place, was low and level, and quite devoid of landscape beauty. I was told there is evidence that the Danes, in one of their invasions, once landed near this spot, though the distance to the sea cannot now be less than twenty miles! Mr. Malthus has overlooked the growth of the island, in his comparative estimates of the increase of the population.

Some boys were fishing on the bridge, near Rye-house, wearing a sort of uniform, and my companion told me they were cadets studying for the East India civil service, in an institution near by. The New-river, which furnishes so much water to London, flows by·this spot, also; and, in returning, we walked some distance on its banks. It is not much larger than a race-way, nor was its current very swift. If this artificial stream can even wash the hands and faces of the cockneys, the Croton ought to overflow New York.

Hoddesdon was selected as a residence, by several of the American emigrant families, that were driven from their own country, and lost their estates, by the revolution. Its comparative cheapness and proximity to London, must have been its recommendation, as neither the place itself, nor the surrounding country, struck me as particularly attractive. The confiscations were peculiarly hard on individuals; and in some instances they were unmerited, even in a political point of view; but if it be true, as has lately been asserted, that the British ministry brought about the struggle under the expectation of being able easily to subdue the colonists, and with a view to provide for their friends by confiscations on the other side, retributive justice did its usual office. The real history of political events, would scarcely bear the light, in any country.

If any American wishes to hear both sides of the great contest between the colonies and the mother country, I would recommend a short sojourn in one of the places where these emigrants have left their traditions. He will there find that names which he has been taught to reverence are held in hereditary abhorrence; that his heroes are other people's knaves, and other people's prodigies his rogues. There is, in all this, quite probably, the usual admixture of truth and error, both heightened by the zeal and animosities of partizanship.

I had, however, in our connexion, strong evidence of how much the mind, unless stimulated by particular motives, is prone to rest satisfied with its acquisitions, and to think of things changeable in their nature, under the influence of first impressions. He is a man of liberal acquirements, sound judgment, great integrity of feeling, and of unusually extensive practical knowledge, and yet some of his notions of America, which were obtained half a century since, almost tempted me to doubt the existence of his common sense. An acute observer, a countryman long resident here, told me soon after landing that "the English, clever, instructed, fair-minded and practical as they commonly are, seem to take leave of their ordinary faculties, on all subjects connected with America." Really, I begin to be of the same way of thinking.

Our connexion here, was as far from vapouring on the subject of England, as any man I knew; of great personal modesty and simplicity, he appears to carry these qualities into his estimates of national character. He is one of the few Englishmen, I have met, for instance, who has been willing to allow that Napoleon could have done any thing, had he succeeded in reaching the island. "I do not see how we should have prevented him from going to London," he said, "had he got a hundred thousand men fairly on the land, at Dungeness; and once in London, heaven knows what would have followed." This opinion struck me as a sound one, for the nation is too rich, and the division between *castes*, too marked, to expect a stout resistance, when the ordinary combinations were defeated. I have little doubt, that the difference in systematic preparation and in the number of regular troops apart, that a large body of hostile men, would march further in England, than in the settled parts of America, all the fanfaronades of the Quarterly, to the contrary, notwithstanding. He looks on the influence of the national debt too, gloomily, and is as far from the vapid indifference of national vanity, as any one I know. But, the moment we touch on America, his mind appears to have lost its balance. As a specimen of how long the old colonial maxims have been ccntinued in this country, he has asked me where we are to get wool for our manufactures? I reminded him of the extent of the country. This was well enough, he answered, but "the winters are too long in America to keep sheep." When I told him the census of 1825, shows that the single state of New York, with a population of less than 1,800,000, has three millions and a half of sheep, he could scarcely admit the validity of our documents.

All the ancient English opinions were formed on the political system of the nation, and men endeavoured lustily to persuade themselves that things which this system opposed could not be. The necessity of enlisting opinion in its behalf, has imposed the additional necessity of sometimes enlisting it, in opposition to reason.

There is a small building in Hoddesdon, called Roydon-house, that has exceedingly struck my fancy. It is not large for Europe, not at all larger than a second rate American country house, but beautifully quaint and old fashioned. I have seen a dozen of these houses, and I envy the English their possession, much more than that of their Blenheims and Eatons. I am told there is not a good room in it, but that it is cut up, in the old way, into closets, being half hall and stair case. The barrenness of our country, in all such relics, gives them double value in my eyes, and I always feel, when I see one, as if I would rather live in its poetical and antique discomfort, than in the best fitted dwelling of our own times. I dare say a twelvemonth of actual residence, however, would have the same effect on such a taste as it has on love in a cottage.

I returned to town in a post-chaise, a vehicle that the cockneys do not calumniate, when they call it a "post *shay*." It is a small cramped inconvenient chariot without the box, and, like the *interiors* of the ordinary stage-coaches, does discredit to the well established reputation of England for comfort. Those who use post-horses, in Europe, usually travel in their own carriages, but these things are kept, as *pis allers* for emergencies.

As we drove through the long maze of villages, that are fast getting to be incorporated with London itself, my mind was insensibly led to ruminations on the growth of this huge capital, its influence on the nation and the civilized world, its origin and its destinies.

To give you, in the first place, some idea of the growth of the town, I had often heard a mutual connexion of ours, who was educated in England, allude to the circumstance that the husband of one of his cousins, who held a place in the royal household, had purchased a small property in the vicinity of London, in order to give his children the benefit of country air; his duties and his poverty equally preventing him from buying a larger estate further from town. When here, in 1826, I was invited to dine in the sub-urbs, and undertook to walk to the villa, where I was expected. I lost my way, and looking up at the first corner, for a direction, saw the name of a family nearly connected with those with whom we are connected. The three or four streets that followed had also names of the same sort, some of which were American. Struck by the coincidence, I inquired in the neighbourhood, and found I was on the property of the grandson of the gentleman, who, fifty years before, had purchased it with a view to give his children country air! Thus the *poverty* of the ancestor has put the de-scendant in possession of some fifteen or twenty thousand a year.

I should think that the growth of London is greater, relatively, than that of any other town in Europe, three or four on this island excepted. Many think the place already too large for the king-dom, though the comparison is hardly just, the empire, rather than England, composing the social base of the capital. So long as the two Indies and the other foreign dependencies can be retained, London is more in proportion to the power and wealth of the state, than Paris is in proportion to the power and wealth of France. The day must come, (and it is nearer than is commonly thought) when the British Empire, as it is now constituted, must break up, and then London will, indeed, be found too large for the state. In that day, its suburbs will probably recede quite as fast as they now grow. Mr. McAdam considers the size of London an evil.

The English frequently discuss the usefulness of their colonies, and moot the question of the policy of throwing them off. They who support the latter project, invariably quote the instance of America, as a proof that the present colonies will be more useful to the mother country, when independent, than they are to-day. I have often smiled at their reasoning, which betrays the usual ignorance of things out of their own circle.

In the first place, England has very few real colonies at this moment, among all her possessions. I do not know where to look for a single foreign dependency of hers, that has not been wrested by violence from some original possessor. It is true, that time and activity have given to some of these conquests the feelings and characters of colonies; and Upper Canada, Nova Scotia, Jamaica, New Holland, and possibly the Cape, are, more or less, acquiring the title. I thought Mr. McAdam rather leaned to the opinion, that the country would be better without its colonies than with them. He instanced our own case, and maintained that we are more profitable to England now, than when we were her dependants.

All of the thirteen states of America were truly English colonies. One only was a conquest, (New York) but more than a century of possession had given that one an English character, and the right of conquest meeting with no obstacle in charters, a more thoroughly English character too, by means of a territorial aristocracy, than belonged to almost any other. The force and impression of this strictly colonial origin, are still to be traced among us, in the durability of our prejudices, and in the deference of our opinions and habits to those of the mother-country; prejudices and a deference that half a century of political facts, that are more antagonist to those of England than any other known, so far from overthrowing, has scarcely weakened.

In reviewing this subject, the extent and power of the United States are also to be remembered. Our independence was recognized in 1783. In 1793 commenced the wars of the French revolution. About this time, also, we began the cultivation of cotton. Keeping ourselves neutral, and profiting by the national aptitude, the history of the world does not present another instance of such a rapid relative accumulation of wealth, as was made by America between the years 1792 and 1812. It would have been greater, certainly, had France and England been more just, but, as it was, centuries will go by before we see its parallel. Our naval stores, bread stuffs, cotton, tobacco, ashes, indigo, and rice, all went to the highest markets. Here, then, our colonial origin and habits, stood England in hand. Nineteen in twenty of our wants were supplied from her workshops. Had we still been dependants we could not have been neutral, could not have been common carriers, could not have bought, for want of the ability to sell.

Now, where is England, in her list of colonies, to find a parallel to these facts? If the Canadas were independent, what have they to export, that we could not crush by competition? England may take lumber exclusively from British America, as a colony, but were British America independent, we would not submit to such a regulation. Our southern woods, among the best in the world, would drive all northern woods out of the market. Having little to sell, Canada could not buy, and she would begin, in self-defence, to manufacture. Our manufactures would deluge the West-India islands, our ships would carry their produce, and, in short, all the American possessions would naturally look up to the greatest American state as to their natural head.

In the east, it would be still worse. All the world would come in, as sharers of a commerce that is now controlled for especial objects. England would cease to be the mart of the world, and would find herself left with certain expensive military establishments that there would no longer be a motive for maintaining. Were England to give up her dependencies, I think she would sink to a second-rate power in twenty years. Did we not exist, the change might not be so rapid, for there would be less danger from competition; but we *do* exist; number, already, nearly as many people as England, and in a quarter of a century more shall number as many as all the British isles put together.

Can England retain her dependencies, in any event? The chances are that she cannot. It is the interest of all christendom to overturn her system, for it is opposed to the rights of mankind, to allow a small territory in Europe, to extend its possessions and its commercial exclusion, over the whole earth, by *conquest*. The view of this interest, may be obscured by the momentary interference of more pressing concerns, and the alliance of Great Britain purchase temporary acquiescence, but as the world advances in civilization, this exclusion will become more painful, until all will unite, openly or secretly, to get rid of it. Men are fast getting to be of less importance, in Europe, and general interests are assuming their proper power.

It is probable that England will find herself so situated, long ere the close of this century, as to render it necessary to abandon her colonial system. When this is done, there will no longer be a motive for retaining dependencies, that belong only to herself in their charges. The dominion of the east will probably fall into the hands of the half-castes; that of the West Indies will belong to the blacks, and British America is destined to be a counterpoise to the country along the gulph of Mexico. The first fleet of thirty sail of the line, that we shall send to sea, will settle the question of English supremacy, in our own hemisphere.

Were these great results dependant on the policy of America, I should greatly distrust them, for, no nation has less care of its foreign interests, or looks less into the future, than ourselves. We are nearly destitute of statesmen, though overflowing with politicians. But the facts of the republic are so stupendous as to overshadow every thing within their influence. This is another feature, in which the two countries are as unlike as possible. Here all depends on men; on combinations, management, forethought, care, and policy. With us, the young Hercules, is stripped of his swaddlings, and his limbs and form are suffered to take the proportions and shape of nature. To be less figurative—it is a known fact that our exertions are proportioned to our wants. In nothing is this truth more manifest, than in the difference which exists between the foreign policies of England and America. That of this country has all the vigilance, decision, energy, and system that are necessary to an empire so factitious and of interests so diversified, while our own is marked by the carelessness and neglect, not to say ignorance, with which a vigorous youth, in the pride of his years and strength, enters upon the hazards and dangers of life. One of the best arguments that can be adduced in favor of the present form of the British government, is its admirable adaptation to the means necessary for keeping such an empire together. Democracy is utterly unsuited to the system of metropolitan rule, since its maxims imperiously require equality of rights. The secret consciousness of this fitness, between the institutions and the empire, will probably have a great effect on the minds of all reflecting men in England, when the question comes to serious changes; for the moment the popular feeling gets the ascendancy, the ties that connect the several parts of this vast collection of conflicting interests, will be loosened. The secrecy of motive, and the abandonment of the commoner charities that are necessary for the control of so complicated a machinery, are incompatable with the publicity of a popular sway and the ordinary sympathies of human nature.*

Were London to fall into ruins, there would probably be fewer of its remains left in a century, than are now to be found of Rome. All the stuccoed palaces, and Grecian façades of Regent's-street and Regent's Park, would dissolve under a few changes of the season. The noble bridges, St. Paul's, the Abbey, and a few other edifices would remain for the curious; but, I think, few European capitals would relatively leave so little behind them, of a physical nature, for the admiration of posterity. Not so, however, in matters less material. The direct and familiar moral influence of London is probably less than that of Paris, but in all the higher points of character, I should think it unequalled by that of Rome, itself.

---

*A proof of this truth, is to be found in the law emancipating the slaves of the islands, a step which is the certain forerunner of their loss. It is well known to all near observers, that this measure was dictated to parliament by the sympathies of a public, to which momentary causes had given an influence it never before possessed. Mr. Cobbett, however, openly affirmed it was owing to a wish to convulse America, by re-acting on public opinion here! One is not obliged to believe all that Mr. Cobbett said, but such a surmise, even, proves something.

Letter XXIII.

To R. Cooper, Esq., Cooperstown, N.Y.

Mr. Sotheby has had the good nature to take me with him, to see Mr. Coleridge, at Highgate. We found the bard living in a sort of New England house, that stands on what, in New England, would be called a green. The demon of speculation, however, was at work in the neighbourhood, and the place was *being* disfigured by trenches, timber, and bricks.

Our reception was frank and friendly, the poet coming out to us in his morning undress, without affectation, and in a very prosaic manner. Seeing a beautifully coloured little picture in the room, I rose to take a nearer view of it, when Mr. Coleridge told me it was by his friend Allston. It was a group of horsemen, returning from the chase, the centre of light being a beautiful grey horse. Mr. Allston had found this horse in some picture of Titian's, and copied it for a study; but on Mr. Coleridge's admiring it greatly, he had painted in two or three figures, with another horse or two, so as to tell a story, and presented it to his friend. Of this little work, Mr. Coleridge told the following singular anecdote.

A picture-dealer, of great skill in his calling, was in the habit of visiting the poet. One day this person entered, and his eye fell on the picture for the first time. "As I live!" he exclaimed, "a real Titian!" Mr. Coleridge was then eagerly questioned, as to where he had found the jewel, how long he had owned it, and by what means it came into his possession. Suddenly, the man paused, looked intently at the picture, *turned his back towards it, as if to neutralize the effect of sight*, and raising his hand, so as to feel the surface over his shoulder, he burst out in an ecstacy of astonishment, "It has not been painted twenty years!"

This story was told with great unction and a suitable action, and embellished with what a puritan would deem almost an oath. We then adjourned to the library. Here we sat half an hour, during most of which time, our host entertained us with his flow of language. I was amused with the contrast between the two poets, for Mr. Sotheby was as meek, quiet, subdued, simple, and regulated, as the other was redundant, imaginative, and overflowing. I thought the first occasionally checked the natural ebullitions of the latter, like a friend who rebuked his failings. One instance was a little odd, and pointed.

The conversation had wandered to phrenology, and Mr. Coleridge gave an account of the wonders that a professor had found in his own head, with a minuteness that caused his friend to fidget. To divert him from the subject, I told an anecdote that occurred just before I left America.

Meeting a votary of the science, one day, at a bookseller's, he began to expatiate on its beauties. From theory he proceeded to practice, by making an analysis of my bumps. Tired of the manipulation, I turned him over to the head of the bookseller, who was standing by, professing to be a better judge of another man's qualities, than of my own. Now this bookseller was a singularly devout man, and the phrenologist instinctively sought the bump of veneration, as the other bowed his head for him to feel it. The moment the fingers of the phrenologist touched the head, however, I saw that something was wrong, and I had the curiosity to put my own hand to the scull. In the spot where there should have been a bump, according to theory, there was positively a hollow. I looked at the phrenologist, and the phrenologist looked at me. At this moment, the bookseller was called away by a customer, and I said to my acquaintance, "well, what do you say to that?" "Say?— That I have no faith in that fellow's religion!"

Both the gentlemen laughed at this story, but Mr. Sotheby gave it a point, that I had not anticipated, by intimating to Mr. Coleridge, pretty plainly, that when one discussed the subject of phrenology, he should not introduce his own bumps, as the subject of the experiments. Notwithstanding two or three little rebukes of this nature, the poets got on very well together; and finding that they had some rhymes to arrange between them, I left them to discuss the matter by themselves.

This was a poetical morning, for, on leaving Mr. Coleridge, we drove to the house of Miss Joanna Baillie, at Hampstead, a village that lies on the same range of low heights. Luckily, we found this clever, and respectable, and simple-minded woman in, and were admitted. I never knew a person of real genius who had any of the affectations of the smaller fry, on the subject of their feelings and sentiments. If Coleridge was scholastic and redundant, it was because he could not help himself; to use a homely figure, it was a sort of boiling over of the pot on account of the intense heat beneath.

It has often been my luckless fortune to meet with ladies who have achieved a common-place novel, or so, or who have written a Julia, or a Matilda, for a magazine, and who have ever after deemed it befitting their solemn vocation to assume lofty and didactic manners; but Miss Baillie had none of this. She is a little, quiet, feminine woman, who you would think might shrink from grappling with the horrors of a tragedy, and whom it would be possible to mistake for the maiden sister of the curate, bent only on her homely duties. Notwithstanding this simplicity, however, there was a deeply-seated earnestness about her, that bespoke the good-faith and honesty of the higher impulses within.

After all, is it not these impulses that make what the world calls genius? All men are sensible of truths, when they are fairly presented to them, and is the difference between the select few, and the many, any more than a quickening of the powers, by some physical incentive, which, in setting the whole in motion, throws into stronger light than common, the inventive, the beautiful, and the sublime?

Let this be as it may, Miss Joanna Baillie had to me, the air and appearance of a quiet enthusiast. She went with us to look at the village, and, as she walked ahead, to do the honours of the place, in her plain dark hat and cloak, I am certain, no one, at a glance, would have thought her little person contained the elements of a tragedy.

Something was said of a sketch of Napoleon, by Dr. Channing; a work I had not seen. Miss Baillie allowed that it was clever, but objected to some one of its positions, that, though it was right enough for an American, it was not so right for an Englishman. As I had never read the sketch, in question, I cannot tell you the precise point to which she alluded, and I mention it, as another proof of a tone of reasoning that is sufficiently common here, by which there is an *abstract*, and a *quo ad hoc* right, in all things that touch political systems. This peculiarity has frequently struck me, and I think it so marked, as to merit notice. I take it to be the inevitable consequence of all systems, in which the reasoning is adapted to the facts, and not the facts to the reasoning.

As we returned to town, we passed a group in which there was a ring for a boxing match. Not a prize fight, but a set-to, in anger. Mr. Sotheby expressed a very natural disgust, at this *human,* tendency, (not *inhuman,* remember,) and, then, with an exquisite *naïveté,* sympathized with me on the state of things, in this respect, in America, with some sufficiently obvious allusions to gouging! Although, I have not passed ten months in England, in the course of four visits, I believe I have witnessed more fighting in it, between men, than I ever saw in America. But of what use is it to tell this, here? We are democrats, and bound by all the pandects of monarchical and aristocratical opinion, to be truculent and quarrelsome; as, having no establishment, we are bound to be irreligious; and, so far from gaining credit, I should be set down, as one too sensitive to see the faults of his own country.

Conversing with a very clever woman, the other day, on the subject of field sports, she gave a sudden shudder, and exclaimed— "but, then your rattlesnakes!" I laughed, and told her, that I had never seen a rattlesnake, out of a cage, and that, particular places excepted, in a country nearly as large as Europe, they were unknown in America. She shook her head incredulously, closing the conversation, by observing, "that a *country*, which contained rattlesnakes, could scarcely be agreeable to walk in."—What are a thousand leagues to such an opinion?

Such notions is the American condemned to meet with, here, not only daily, but hourly, and without ceasing, if he should mingle with the people. The prejudices of the English, against us, against the land in which we live, against the entire nation, morally, physically, and politically, circulate in their mental systems, like the blood in their veins, until they become as inseparable from the thoughts and feelings, as the fluid of life is indispensable to vitality. I say it, not in anger, but in sorrow, when I tell you, that I do not believe the annals of the world can present another such instance of a people, so blindly, ignorantly, and culpably misjudging a friendly nation, as the manner in which England, at this moment, in nearly all things, misjudges us. And yet, with this fact staring us in the face, known to every man who visits the country, a few *serviles* excepted, told to us by all foreigners, and as obvious as the sun at noon day, there is not, probably, an American, with the exception of political men who are sustained by party, that has a name of sufficient reputation to reach these shores, who does not hold his reputation at home, not only at the mercy of this country, but at the mercy of any miscreant in it, who may choose to insert three or four paragraphs, to his credit or discredit, in any of the periodicals of the day! Really, one is tempted to exclaim with that countryman, who heard a salute from a seventy-four, "now, do I know, we are a great people!"

My admiration of the growth and immensity of London, increases every time I have occasion to pass its frontiers. I was struck with a remark made to me, here, by Lord H_____, who said—"the want of a capital is one of the greatest difficulties, with which you have to contend in America." Of course, he meant by a capital, not a seat of government, but a large town, in which the intelligence and influence of the country, periodically assembled, and whence both might radiate, like warmth from the sun, throughout the nation.

It is not easy for any but close observers, to estimate the influence of such places as London and Paris. They contribute, essentially, to national identity, and national tone, and national policy: in short, to nationality—a merit in which we are almost entirely wanting. I do not mean national sensitiveness, which some fancy is patriotism, though merely provincial jealousy, but that comprehensive unity of feeling and understanding, that renders a people alive to its true dignity and interests, and prompt to sustain them, as well as independent in their opinions. We are even worse off, than most other nations would be without a capital, for we have an anomalous principle of *dispersion* in the state capitals. In nothing is the American government more wanting, than in tone in all its foreign relations. What American, out of his own country, feels any dependance on its protection? No one, who has any knowledge of its real action. Such an accumulation of wrongs may be made, as to touch the community, and then it is ready enough to fight; but the *individual*, who should urge his own injuries on the nation, as a case that called for interference, would be crushed by the antagonist interests of commerce, which is now the only collected and concentrated interest of the nation. An Englishman, or a Frenchman, goes into distant countries, with a consciousness that he leaves behind him, a concentrated and powerful sentiment of nationality, that will throw its protection around him, even to the remotest verge of civilization, but the case is altogether different with the American. If a man of reflection and knowledge, he knows that there is no concentrated feeling, at home, to sustain him; that the moment any case arises to set his claims to justice in opposition to the trading interests, he becomes obnoxious to the plastic ethics of commerce, and that there is no condensed community to sustain the government, in doing what is clearly its duty, and what may even be its inclination. Public opinion, half the time, is formed in America, by downright, impudent simulations; for little more is necessary than to assert, that Boston and Philadelphia think so and so, to get New York to join the cry. Such things are not so easily practised in a capital, where the intelligence of a nation is concentrated, which is the focus of facts, and, where men become habituated to the arts of the intriguing and selfish. I believe Lord H_____ is right, and that the want of a capital, on a scale commensurate with that of the nation, is, indeed, one of the greatest difficulties, with which we have to contend. We shall never become truly a nation, until we get one. These notions will, probably, seem odd, and certainly new to you, as indeed they are new to me; but it is not a good mode of getting correct ideas of even oneself, to remain always at one's own fireside.

Letter XXIV.

J. E. De Kay, Esquire, New York.

Mr. Rogers came to me the other evening, on one of his friendly visitations, and I went out with him, not well knowing what was to be the result of it. We trot along the streets, together, he a little on the lead, for he is a capital and an earnest walker, and I in the rear, getting over the pavement at the rate of four miles the hour.

London has certain private ways, called passages I believe, by which one can avoid the carriages and much of the streets, besides greatly shortening the distances. We took to a line of these passages, and came out in Leicester Square. Crossing this, we pursued our way as far as the theatres, and entered that of Covent Garden. As I had nothing to do, but to follow my leader, who had certain signals, by means of which he appeared to go just where he pleased, I soon found myself in a private box, quite near the stage, and nearly on a level with the pit. There was a sedate elderly man in possession, already, but he proved to be an acquaintance of my companion, who whispered a few words, and then presented me to him, as to the vice chancellor, Sir John Leach.

The play was intended to represent some of the sports and practices of ancient London, but the chief merit was the scenery. As it is fair to presume that the best authorities had been consulted, I had a great deal of pleasure in looking at the quaint pictures that were successively presented to us, by some of which, it was evident that our progenitors built very much in the rude style that is still to be seen in the towns of Picardy and Normandy, and that, whatever London may be now, she has not always been a wonder of the world.

The house was much larger than any of our own, it was better lighted, and had a neater and fresher look, in despite of London and coal dust. The audience was, quite evidently, composed of people of a class much beneath the highest, still it had a well-dressed and a respectable air, and, although its taste was sometimes to be questioned, it was well mannered. In short, it was very

much like what our own better theatres used to exhibit, before the
inroad of the Goths. The playing was scarcely to be distinguished
from what one usually sees in America, though it was perhaps a
little more decided in its English tone. Mr. Charles Kemble was
among the actors. The circumstances that the lower tier was reserved for people in evening dress, and that, the men sat with
their hats off, gave the spectacle an appearance of respectability
and *comfort* (to use an Anglicism) that is now seldom seen in any
of our own places of public resort.

It is an immense advantage to possess a National Theatre. Our
moralists have made a capital blunder in setting their faces against
the stage; since, while demonstrating their own inability to put it
down, they have thrown it almost entirely into the hands of those
who look only to pecuniary advantages. It should be patronized
and regulated by the state, as the best means of giving it a true
direction, and of checking, if not of totally repressing its abuses.
The common argument, that theatres are places of resort for the
vicious, and particularly for women of light manners, is built on
narrow views and great ignorance of the world. In many countries, the *churches* are used for the purposes of intrigue, and yet it
would hardly be thought a sufficient argument for abandoning
them entirely.

The English government retains a supervision of the stage, a
thing that is well enough if well managed; but, in all countries in
which the institutions are not founded on the mass, the tendency
of censorships is to protect the systems, and, in order to do this
with the least odium, they get to be loose on points that are more
essential to a pure morality. Vice is frequently thrown out as a
sop, to keep the mass quiet under the restraints of despotism.

We are still too young and too provincial for a national theatre.
Nothing can be safer than to write or to talk in *praise* of America,
and all it contains, more especially of its *things*, but few men have
yet nerve enough to tell an unpalatable truth. We have a one
sided liberty of speech and of the press, that renders every one
right valorous in eulogies, but even the pulpit shrinks from its
sacred duties, on many of the most besetting, the most palpable
and the most common of our vices. It is bold enough, as to vague
generalities, and sometimes as to personalities, but who ever sees
the caustic applied to the public? The stage, a little later, may be
made the most efficient corrective of American manners, but, in

the true spirit of village resentment and of provincial sensibilities, a dramatist could hardly expose a failing, now, that the whole audience would not be ready to cry out, "do you mean me, sir?"

We are much laughed at, here, just now, for the manner in which the press is resenting the late book of Captain Hall. No nation is very philosophical under abuse, and certainly the English are surprisingly thin-skinned for a people as proud, and possessing so many just claims to greatness. The fact is, both nations are singularly conceited on the subject of national character, giving themselves credit for a good many exclusive qualities to which they have no exclusive pretensions, and by dint of self glorification, in which the presses of the two countries have been particularly active, they have got, at last, to look upon every man who denies their exaggerated demands, as a sort of robber. Perhaps no other people praise themselves so openly, offensively and industriously as those of England and America, and I have no doubt the newspapers are a principal cause that this failing is so coarsely exhibited, for, as to its mere existence, I fancy there is no great difference in the amount of vanity, as between nations, or as between individuals.

I have been much surprised, however, at observing that, while all America appears to be up in arms against Captain Hall, on account of his hits at our manners, no one seems disposed to take up the gauntlet in defence of the institutions! I know no writer who is more vulnerable in his facts, or in his reasoning on politics, than this gentleman, and yet, while so much ink is shed in behalf of a gentility and civilization that it would become us rather to improve and refine, than to defend, the glorious political facts of the country, are treated as if unworthy of attention. Can all this proceed from the circumstance that we are conscious the latter can take care of themselves, while we secretly distrust the claims of the former? No violence would be done to human nature if this should actually be the case.

The greatest objection I have to the book of Mr. Hall, is that it *insinuates* more than it proves, or even asserts. This is the worst species of detraction, for it admits of neither refutation nor denial. But I cannot express to you the disgust I have felt, as a looker on at a distance, at reading in the journals the mean spirited anticipations of what Mr. Hall was to do for us, in the way of raising the

character of the nation, and the low personal abuse that has succeeded, the moment it is found that these anticipations are not
realized. To be frank with you, one appears to be as discreditable
to the tone, feelings, tastes, and facts of the nation as the other.

It would be next to impossible for an Englishman, on a short
acquaintance, to like the state of society that exists in America. I
never knew one that did, nor do I believe that it is agreeable to
any European, let him come from what part of Europe he will. It
is necessary that habit should smooth down many asperities, before this can be the case; nor do I think that many Americans like
England, if they go beyond the outside, until time has done a
similar office in its favour. I am not disposed to quarrel with any
Englishman, who says frankly, your society is not to my liking; it
wants order, tone, finish, simplicity, and manliness; having substituted in their stead, pretension, noise, a childish and rustic
irritability, and a confusion in classes. These defects are so obvious
to a man of the world, that one cannot but distrust the declara-
tions that are sometimes made to the contrary. Notwithstanding
this admission, I have little doubt that most of the books of travels
that have been published in England, and in which America has
been held up to ridicule, have been addressed to the prejudices of
the nation; written in that particular vein, because it has been
believed it would be more likely to please than any other. Very
few of them discover honesty of intention, a trait that is usually
detected even in the midst of blunders, but it happens that this
work of Captain Hall does possess this redeeming quality.*

The pronunciation of the stage is the same, here, as it is with us.
That of the world is not essentially different from the best pro-

---

*Captain Hall says, that the houses of America struck him as being only half
furnished. On the other hand, the Duke Bernhard, of Saxe Weimar, who landed in
Boston, coming from England, says that he thought the houses appeared better
furnished than those he had just left in Great Britain. On this testimony, the
Quarterly joins issue, insinuating that no one can hesitate to believe that a *captain
in his majesty's navy* is a better judge in these matters than a mere *German* Duke!
The exquisite twaddle of such reasoning exposes itself, and yet, in his main fact,
Captain Hall is unquestionably right. So far as we go, our furniture is generally
handsomer than that of England, and Duke Bernhard has possibly formed his
opinion from particular houses, but nothing is truer than that the American
houses appear naked to one coming from either France or England.

nunciation of the Middle States, though, in many respects, much better than that of what is now called their *society*. Certainly, as a nation, we speak better than the English, but it is absurd to set up the general language of the educated classes of America, as being as pure as the language of the same classes here. I do not make this remark in reference to those words whose pronunciation varies, but in reference to those concerning whose provincialism there can be no dispute. The women of this country have a distinct, quiet, and regulated utterance, that is almost unknown in their own sex in America. Their voices are more like *contr'altos* than those of our women, who have a very peculiar shrillness, and they manage them much better. Indeed, we are almost in a state of nature on all these points. The manners of the country are decidedly worse now, in every thing, than they were thirty years since; a fact, that must be attributed to the *pêle-mêle* produced by a rapid growth and extraordinary prosperity.

While on the subject of representations, I will mention one that has been a little out of the usual course, even for England. We have had a birthday lately, and as George IV. seldom appears in public, the festivities on this occasion have been more than usually brilliant. One of the usages, here, is to bring out young females, by presenting them at court, and, so particular are the true adherents to etiquette, that I am told many young ladies, who have passed the proper age, have been waiting two or three years for this ceremony, in order to make their appearance in the world. At all events, every one has seemed disposed to make the most of the opportunity that has just offered, and we have had a greater show of magnificence, and a much greater throng of courtiers, than it is usual to see, even in this country, in which the king is probably as much flattered as fettered.

As our residence is so near the palace, I had every facility for seeing what was going on without putting myself to inconvenience. One of the first movements was the march of the horse-guards from their barracks to the palace. These troops have a wide-spread reputation for size and magnificence. They are large men, certainly, but must be next to useless in a campaign. Indeed, they are kept for state, though they may be of service in quelling riots, in a town like London; their appearance being well adapted to terrifying an unarmed mob. In size, they are considerably beyond the French *gardes du corps*, but the latter are very numerous, while there cannot be more than a few hundred of the former. Nor are these all English, for, walking behind two of them, the other day, I overheard them speaking like foreigners. They are probably picked up, like the tall men of Frederic, wherever they can be found. It is not impossible that there may be a stray Yankee among them, as there are several in the French army.

The march of these imposing troops was preceded by a fine band on horseback, and the music was the signal for the crowd to collect. There were two ways of entering the palace, one private, and the other public. The princes, foreign ministers, accompanied by those they were about to present, the great officers of the kingdom and court, and certain of the privileged, uséd the former, while the more common herd of courtiers went by the latter. The first were set down in a court near what is called the *stable-yard,* and the latter at the foot of St. James' street.

There is a simple good sense, not to call it good taste, that distinguishes the English from their more ambitious kinsmen, our worthy selves, in all matters connected with names. This of "stable-yard" is one in point; for with us it would be the "stadium," or the "gymnasium," if, indeed, it escaped being called the "Campus Martius." The tendency is to exaggeration, in men, to whom learning, modes of living, and, indeed, most other things, are new, and the mass being better educated than common with us, without, however, being sufficiently educated to create a taste for simplicity, and, at the same time, having an usual influence, we are kept a little more on stilts in such matters than one could wish. This defect pervades the ordinary language of the country too, and, sooner or later, will totally corrupt it, if the proportion, of the unformed to the formed, goes on increasing at the rate it has done for the last ten years.*

*Quite lately, the writer got into a rail-road car at Bordenton, at a place where the company have since erected a large warehouse or shed; some one, observing the signs of a building around the car, inquired what they meant. The writer, who sat by a window, was about to say, "They have laid the foundations of a large house here," when a fellow-traveller, who occupied the other window, anticipated him, by saying that, "Judging by external symptoms, they have commenced the construction of an edifice of considerable magnitude, calculated, most likely, to facilitate the objects of the rail-road company." One would not wish to lose the cause of this disposition to the grandiose, but it is to be regretted that sublimity is getting to be so common.

I stood in the "stable yard," vulgar as the name will sound to "ears polite," witnessing the arrival of princes, ambassadors, and dukes, and much struck with the magnificence of their carriages. Certainly, I had seen nothing equalling it, in Paris, though the every-day style of the King of France, materially surpasses that of the King of England. After all, I thought the gorgeous vehicles, with their coronets rising above their tops, the gildings, and the lace, much less pleasing than the simple perfection of the common carriages of the country, in which every thing is beautiful, because nothing is overdone. M. de Polignac, and Prince Esterhazy, were both present, the one as the French, the other as the Austrian ambassador. The Duke of Gloucester, the cousin and brother-in-law of the king, came in state, as it is termed, having three footmen, in elaborate liveries and wearing a sort of jockey caps, instead of hats, clinging behind his carriage. He was himself, a fine looking man, with a good prominent profile, and a full contented face, dressed in the uniform of a field marshal.

But I soon tired of the mere raree show. Accompanied by a friend, I went round to the line of carriages in St. James's street, which, by this time, could not set down the company nearly as fast, as the vehicles arrived at the other end. There were, in fact, two lines, one in St. James's street, and the other in Pall Mall, and overhearing some one speak of the great length of the former, we determined to walk to the other extremity of it, as the shortest method of satisfying our curiosity; to receive the passing, instead of the standing salute.

I should think, that this one line of carriages extended quite two miles. In the whole distance, there was not a hackney coach, for London is as unlike Paris, as posssible, in this respect. The carriages, for a great part of the distance, were drawn up quite close to the side-walks, in order to leave the centre of the streets free for the privileged to come and go, and, perhaps, also, to permit a freer circulation of the crowd. In consequence of the wheels being nearly in the gutters, and the English carriages being hung quite low, our heads were almost on a level with those of the occupants of the different equipages. In this manner, then, we walked slowly along the line, examining the courtiers at our leisure, by broad day-light, and much nearer than we could have got to most of them, in the palace. The crowd took it all in very good part, appearing to regard it as an exhibition to which they were admitted gratis. Some of the people, who, by the way, were well dressed, and well behaved as a whole, stood looking in at the carriage windows, with quite as much coolness as if they were the proprietors, chatting with their own wives and daughters. Now and then, a footman would remonstrate against the impertinence, but, in the main, the women seemed resigned to their fate. Similar liberties with us, would be natural excesses of democracy! For the reasons already mentioned, there was a larger proportion than common, of young women to be presented, and it may be questioned if the world could have offered a parallel to the beauty and bloom, that were thus arrayed before our eyes. I have elsewhere said that the English females have the advantage of ours in high dress, and this was altogether a ceremony in which the advantage was of their side. I do not think, that we could have shown as much beauty, in precisely the same style, although, when one remembers the difference between a scattered and a condensed population, it becomes him to speak with caution, on a point so delicate.

The ancient court dress, particularly that of the women, has undergone some changes, of late, I believe. I am told the hoop is done away with, though it was not easy to ascertain the fact, to-day, as I only saw the ladies seated. The *coiffures* were good, and the *toilettes*, as a matter of course, magnificent. Diamonds sparkled among eyes scarcely less brilliant than themselves. In France, diamonds are seldom used, except at court, though it is probable, that they are oftener exhibited here, the court being so secluded. On this occasion, however, they were seen in great quantities, enthroned on some of the fairest brows of Christendom.

The men, with the usual exceptions of those who wore their regular professional attire, were all in the well known claret-coloured coat, steel buttons, bags, swords, and embroidered vests. As many of those who came alone, preferred walking to and from their carriages, to waiting an hour for their approach, we had a good many of these gentry in the streets, where they gave the crowd a little of the air of a carnival masquerade. There is great simplicity in the dress of the men of England, however; even on great occasions like this, much of the more tawdry taste being reserved expressly for the footmen.

But, apart from the lovely faces of the young and fair of England, the out door glory of the day, was borne away by the coachmen. Every one of them had a new wig, and many of them capped the flaxens with as rare specimens of castors, as ever came out of a shop. It would be scarcely accurate to call these hats cocked, for they were altogether too *coquet* and knowing, for a term so familiar. Figure to yourself, the dignity of a portly man of fifty, with a sky blue coat, laced on all its seams, red plush breeches, white silk stockings, shoebuckles as large as a muffin, a smug wig, a shovel nosed hat, edged with broad gold lace, and a short snub nose of his own, as red as a cherry, and you will get some idea of these dignitaries.

When we had returned from examining the long line of carriages, I met one of the princesses, in a sedan chair, on her way from the palace to her own residence. She was attended by six or eight footmen, in the jockey caps, and scarlet liveries. Her face was pallid and wrinkled, and as she was no longer young, her appearance had that unearthly and unseemly look, that always marks the incongruity between age and the toilet. Some of the most *uncomfortable,* (you see how English I am getting,) some of the most *uncomfortable* objects I have seen in Europe, have been women in the "sear and yellow leaf," tricked out for courts and balls, and bedizened with paint and jewels. This is a folly, at least, which we have as yet escaped, for if we do abandon society to those who had better be practising their *gammes,* or kicking foot-ball on a college green, we do not attempt to still the thoughts of the grave, by these glaring and appalling vanities.

The scene closed with a procession of mail coaches, which, however neat and seemly the set-outs, had too much the air of a cockney show, to detain us from our dinner.

If the English are simple and tasteful in so much of their magnificence, and, apart from its occasional ponderousness, these are its prevailing characteristics, they are more than usually studied and artificial, in extolling it, when all is over. The papers delight in the histories of great dinners, and fashionable balls; and I have been solemnly assured, there are people, that get into society, who are actually guilty of the meanness of paying for the insertion of their names in the list of the company that is regularly published. As to a drawing-room at court, it is a little fortune to the news-

finders. A guinea introduces the name, five guineas insures im-
mortality to the dress, and ten brings in the carriage. This, you
will see, is making great men, and great women, on a principle
still unknown with us, where we manufacture them in such quantities, and swear they are the best in the market.

Letter XXV.
To James Stevenson, Esq., Albany, N. Y.

The question is often asked, in what do the poor of England suffer more than the poor of any other country? I am not sufficiently versed in the details connected with the subject, to speak with authority, but I can give you the impressions received, as a looker on.

In comparing the misery of England with that of the continent of Europe, one must remember the great difference of climate. A man suffers less at Naples, without a coat or a fire, and with three *grani* for his daily pittance, than is undergone in England, beneath woollen, with ten *grani* to furnish the "ways and means." These facts make a great moral difference in favour of England, when we come to consider the merits of systems, though the physical consequences may be against her.

The poor of this country appear to me to be overworked. They have little or no time for relaxation, and instead of exhibiting that frank manly cheerfulness, and heartiness of feeling, that have been so much extolled, they appear sullen, discontented, and distrustful. There is far less confidence and sympathy between classes, than I had expected to see, for, although a good understanding may exist between the great landholder, and the affluent yeoman who pays him rent and farms the soil, the social chain appears to be broken between those below the latter and their superiors. I do not mean that the rich are obdurate to the sufferings of the poor, but that the artificial condition of the country has choked the ordinary channels of sympathy, and that the latter, when known at all, are known only as the *poor*. They are the objects of duties, rather than fellow-creatures living constantly within the influence of all the charities, including those of communion and rights, as well as those which are exhibited in donations.

There is one large class of beings, in England, whose condition I should think less enviable than that of Asiatic slaves. I allude to the female servants of all work, in the families of those who keep lodging-houses, tradesmen, and other small housekeepers. These poor creatures have an air of dogged sullen misery that I have never seen equalled, in any other class of human beings, not even excepting the beggars in the streets. In our lodgings at Southampton there was one of these girls, and her hand was never idle, her foot seemed to know no rest, while her manner was that of wearied humility. We were then fresh from home, and the unmitigated toil of her existence struck us all most painfully. When we spoke to her kindly, she seemed startled, and looked distrustful and frightened. A less inviting subject for sympathy could scarcely be imagined, for she was large, coarse, robust, and even masculine, but even these iron qualities were taxed beyond endurance.

I should not draw a picture like this, on the authority of a single instance. I have seen too much to corroborate the first impressions, and make no doubt that the case of the woman at Southampton was the rule, and that instances of better treatment make the exceptions. In one of my bachelor visits here, I had lodgings in which there was a still more painful example. The mistress of this house was married and had children, and being a lazy slattern, with three sets of lodgings in the house, her tyranny exceeded all I had ever before witnessed. You are to understand that the solitary servant, in these houses, is usually cook, house-maid, and waiter. When the lodger keeps no servant, she answers his bell, as well as the street door knocker, and goes on all his errands that do not extend beyond a proper distance. The girl was handsome, had much delicacy of form and expression, and an eye that nature had intended to be brilliant and spirited. She could not be more than twenty-two or three, but misery had already driven her to the bottle. I saw her only at the street door, and on two or three occasions when she answered my own bell, in the absence of my man. At the street door, she stood with her eyes on the carpet, and when I made my acknowledgments for the trouble she had taken, she curtsied hurriedly, and muttered the usual "Thankee, sir." When she came into my room it was on a sort of drilled trot, as if she had been taught a particular movement to denote assiduity and diligence, and she never presumed to raise her eyes to mine, but stood the whole time looking meekly down. For every order I was duly thanked! One would think that all this was hard to be borne, but, a day or two before I left the house, I found her weeping in the street. She had disobliged her lazy exacting mistress, by staying out ten minutes too long on an errand, and had lost her place. I took the occasion to give her a few shillings as her due for past services, but so complete was her misery in being turned away without a character, that even the sight of money failed to produce the usual effects. I make little doubt she took refuge in gin, the bane of thousands and tens of thousands of her sex, in this huge theatre of misery and vice.

The order, method, and punctuality of the servants of England are all admirable. These qualities probably contribute quite as much to their own comfort as to that of their masters and mistresses. It is seldom that well bred persons, anywhere, are unkind to their menials, though they are sometimes exacting through ignorance of the pain they are giving. The tyranny comes from those who always appear to feel a desire to revenge their own previous hardships, on the unfortunate creatures whom chance puts in their power. I do not know that the English of condition are unkind to their domestics; the inference would fairly be that they are not; but there is something, either in the system that has unfortunately been adopted, or in the character of the people, which has introduced a distance between the parties that must be injurious to the character of those who serve.

On the continent of Europe the art of managing domestics appears to be understood much better than it is here. A body servant is considered as a sort of humble friend, being treated with confidence but without familiarity, nor can I say I have often witnessed any want of proper respect on the part of the domestics. The old Princesse de [Galitzin], who was a model of grace and propriety in her deportment, never came to see my wife, without saying something kind or flattering to her *femme de chambre*, who usually admitted her and saw her out. A French servant expects to be spoken to, when you meet on the stairs, in the court, or in the garden, and would be hurt without a "*bonjour*" at meeting, or an "*adieu*" at parting. A French Duke would be very apt to take off his hat, if he had occasion to go into the porter's lodge, or into the servants' hall; but I think very little of this courtesy would be practised here. It is our misfortune to try to imitate the English in this, as in other things, and I make little question, one of the principal reasons why our servants are so bad, is owing to their not being put on the proper footing of confidential dependants.

The comparison between the condition of the common English house-servant, and that of the American slave, is altogether in favour of the latter, if the hardship of compelled servitude be kept out of view. The negro, bond or free, is treated much more kindly and with greater friendship, than most of the English domestics; the difference in colour, with the notions that have grown up under them, removing all distrust of danger from familiarity. This is not said with a view to turn the tables on our kinsmen for their numberless taunts and continued injustice; for, with such an object, I think something more original and severe might easily be got up; but simply because I believe it to be true. Perhaps the servants of no country have more enviable places than the American slaves, so far as mere treatment and the amount of labour are concerned.

One prominent feature of poverty, in England, is dependant on causes which ought not to be ascribed to the system. If a man can be content to live on a few grapes, and a pound of coarse bread, and to go without a coat, or a fire, in a region like that of Naples, it does not necessarily follow, that another ought to be able to do the same things in a country in which there are no grapes, in which a fire is necessary, and a coat indispensable. The high civilization of England, unquestionably contributes also to the misery of the very poor, by augmenting their wants, though it adds greatly to the comforts of those who are able to sustain themselves. As between the Americans and the English, it is not saying much, under the peculiar circumstances of their respective countries, that the poor of the former are immeasurably better off than the poor of the latter; but, apart from certain advantages of climate in favour of the south of Europe, I am not at all certain that the poor of England, as a body, do not fare quite as well as the poor of any other part of Christendom. I know little more of the matter, however, than meets the eye of an ordinary traveller; but, taking that as a guide, I think I should prefer being a pauper in England, to being a beggar in France. I now speak of physical sufferings altogether, for on all points that relate to the feelings, admitting that the miserable still retain any sentiment on such points, I think England the least desirable country, for a poor man, that I know.

The notion that so generally prevails in America, on the subject of the independence and manliness of the English, certainly does not apply to the body of the poor, nor do I think the tradesmen, in general, have as much of these qualities, as those of France. The possession of their franchises, at a time when such privileges were rare, may have given some claims to a peculiar character of this nature, but while the pressure of society has been gradually weighing heavier and heavier on the nation, creating the dependence of competition and poverty, in lieu of that of political power, the other countries of Europe have lessened their legal oppression, until, I think, the comparison has got to be in their favour. I should say there is quite as little manly independence, in the intercourse between classes, here, as in any country I have visited.

It is a common result of temporal advantages and civilization, and, perhaps, to be accounted for on obvious principles, that they should fail to bestow the happiness at which we profess to aim. I do not think that either the English or the Americans are a happy people. The possession of a certain physical civilization soon becomes necessary to our wants, but we rather miss them when they are lost, than enjoy them when possessed. In this particular, Providence has singularly equalized the lot of men, for being mere creatures of habit, advantages of this kind neutralize themselves. The sort of happiness that is dependent solely on material things, after the first wants are supplied, is purely relative, and the relation is to our knowledge, rather than to any standard that exists in nature. He who has appeased his hunger with bread, and slaked his thirst with water, is just as well off, so far as his appetites are concerned, as he who has eaten a *ragoût*, and drunk Johannisberger. This is said, however, solely in reference to hunger and thirst, for I make little doubt character a good deal depends on diet, and that the art with which materials are put together, is of more consequence than the viands themselves.

Human happiness would seem to be dependent on three primary causes—the intellect, the affections, and that which is physical. A certain portion of all, with their accompanying misery, is unquestionably the general lot, though so unequally distributed. But, making the proper allowances for a common nature, we are to distinguish between the consequences of particular conditions of society. The greatest obstacle to all our enjoyments is worldly care, and as we increase what is deemed our civilisation, we augment the cares by which they are to be acquired or retained. There is, certainly, a medium in this matter, as in every thing else, but as few are disposed to respect it, it may be set down as unattainable in practice. I believe more people are unhappy because they cannot possess certain indulgences, or because, when possessed, they have been bought too dear, than because they never knew them at all.

It has long struck me that the term "happy country," is singularly misapplied, as regards America; and, I believe, also as regards this country. It is true, it has a conventional meaning, in which sense it may be well enough; but, comparing the people of France, or Italy, with those of England, or the United States, all external symptoms must be treacherous, or the former have greatly the. advantage. By placing incentives before us to make exertions, the El Dorado of our wishes is never obtained, and we pass our lives in vain struggles to reach a goal that recedes as we advance. This, you will be apt to say, is the old truism of the moralist, and proves as much against one nation, as against another. I think the latter position untrue. Competition may be pushed so far as to neutralize all its fruits, by inciting to envy and strife. In America, for instance, all the local affections are sacrificed to the spirit of gain. The man who should defend the roof of his fathers, against an inroad of speculators, would infallibly make enemies, and meet with persecution. Thus is he precluded from one source of happiness that is connected with the affections; for, though the law might protect him, opinion, which is stronger than law, would sooner or later drive him from his fireside. I know very well this is merely a consequence of a society in the course of establishing itself, but it shows how ·ulnerable is our happiness.

But, putting all theory out of the question, neither the English nor the Americans have the air and manners of a happy people, like the French and the Italians. The first have a sullen, thoughtful look, as if distrustful of the future, which gives one the idea that their enjoyments are deferred to a more favourable opportunity; while the two last seem to live as time goes on. Something of this is probably owing to temperament, but temperament itself has, in part, a moral origin. As to the Americans, there are very many reasons for their want of happiness. The settlement of an immense country snaps the family ties, though the constant migration has the effect to produce an amalgamated whole. The tendency of things generally, with us, is to destroy all individuality of character and feeling, and to concentrate every thing in the common identity. One would be set down for an aristocrat, who should presume to enjoy himself independently of his neighbours. It is true, that so far as gain is concerned, there is an exception, the absence of restriction giving free exercise to personal efforts; but when money is obtained by individual enterprise, it must be used, in a greater degree than common, in conformity with the feeling of the nation. One disposed to cavil at the institutions, might almost fancy the public had a jealousy of a man's possessing kinsmen that were not thrown into the general stock. But this weakness of the family tie, in America, is to be ascribed to other causes, among which the constant migrations, as I have just observed, have a conspicuous place. Let the reason be what it will, the effect is to cut us off from a large portion of the happiness that is dependent on the affections.

Then the whole Anglo-Saxon race is deficient in the enjoyments that are so much dependent on the tastes. While there is even a vein of higher poetical feeling than common among a few exceptions, as if nature delighted in extremes, the mass have little relish for poetry, scarcely any good music, and appear to be absolutely wanting in those sentiments which throw so much grace around the rustic amusements of other countries. One might account for these peculiarities in the Americans, by their fanatical origin, and peculiar physical condition, but they are almost as true as respects England itself, as they are with us. The Germans, and other northern nations, the nearest to us in extraction, have a wild poetry in their most vulgar superstitions that is not found here. They cultivate music, and have a deep feeling for it, as an art. This single fact is coupled with one of the highest enjoyments with which we are gifted. The music of America is beneath contempt. We are probably worse off in this particular, than any other civilized people, though certainly improving. The English, though greatly our superiors, are much behind all the other European nations, with which I am acquainted. The music of the people has a cast of vulgarity about it, like our own, that of itself denotes a want of feeling for the art. Even the French, by no means a people of poetical tastes, are greatly their superiors in music. One seldom hears a vulgar air even among the *bas peuple*. I make little doubt, that, in time, we shall surpass the English in this art.

All these peculiarities diminish the enjoyments of the English; but, it strikes me, that the principal reason why these people and the Americans are less happy than usual, is to be found in the fact that, by admitting civilization, men admit cares, whose moral evils are not compensated for, until one reaches a degree of cultivation far above the level of mediocrity. There is, unquestionably, much physical suffering, all over Europe, that is virtually unknown with us, but the remarks just made are meant to apply to those who are removed from the first wants of life. Both England and America strike me as being countries of facts rather than of feelings. It is almost purely so, but the English have one great advantage over us, in being a country of ideas, if not of sentiments and affections. The difference is owing to our youth.

Passons au déluge:—Speaking of the music of England, you are not to understand that there is no good music here. The gold of the country attracts the first artists of Europe, as a matter of course; but even the cultivated English have, quite obviously, not much more feeling for the art than we have ourselves. As a greater portion travel, their tastes are a little more cultivated than those of our people, but nothing strikes one sooner, than the obvious difference in feeling between an English audience, at the opera, and one on the continent of Europe.

Still, the street music of London is positively the best in the world. The improvement in the last few years, even, is quite apparent. Respectable artists, such as would gladly be received in our orchestras, walk the streets, and play the music of Rossini, Mozart, Beethoven, Meyerbeer, Weber, &c. &c. beneath your windows. London is not as well arranged for this species of enjoyment as the towns of the continent, for there are no courts in which the performers can get away from the clamour of the streets;

but, about eight, the carriages cease, every body being at dinner, and most of the more private places are quite silent. Since the weather has become mild, I have frequently paused in my evening walks, to listen to airs that have come from the harp, violin, and flageolet, and have almost fancied myself in Venice, or Naples, though surrounded by the dingy bricks of London. A party of French have found us out, and they come regularly, twice a week, and play old French airs beneath the windows; favours that are seldom conferred on private houses, the public hotels being their usual stopping places. The secret of this unusual feature in the town, is in the fact, that where an Italian, or a Frenchman, though filled with enthusiasm, would bestow a few sous, the Englishman, with immoveable muscles, throws out half a crown. Walking to a dinner, the other evening, I heard a grand piano, on which some one was playing an overture of Rossini's, accompanied by a flageolet, and, going a little out of my way to ascertain the cause, I found the artist in the street, seated before the open windows of a hotel. He trundled the machine about on a sort of wheelbarrow, and his execution was quite equal to what one usually hears in society.

I cannot describe to you the influence these sweet sounds, especially when they revive the recollections of other and more genial lands, have over the feelings. These are the moments in which men may be said truly to live, and half an hour of such delight is worth a year passed in listening to the prices of lots, and to the variation of the markets. Music is certainly a good *article!*

Letter XXVI.

To Jacob Sutherland, Esq., Geneva.

Amid the affected disdain, that is so often assumed by the press and orators of England, when there is occasion to allude to America, a lively jealousy of the growing power of the republic is easily discovered. But, one at a distance, like yourself, may not be aware of the extent to which this feeling is allied with apprehension of Russia. The wise policy of Alexander created affinities of an alarming nature between the government of Russia and that of America, and, mingled with a reluctance to give us fair words and honest treatment, that goes nigh to choke them, the statesmen, here, are beginning to feel the necessity of counteracting some of the bad consequences of their own former blunders.

Heaven bless the Quarterly Review, say I! Although I am far from boasting of the mental independence of the republic, for few men can be more strongly impressed with the dangerous character of the practice that so generally prevails at home, of reasoning and feeling on all questions of polity like Englishmen, instead of Americans, I do believe the Quarterly Review has done more towards alienating the feelings of America from Great Britain, than the two wars, the commercial rivalries, the orders in council, impressment, the Henry plot, and all the other points of national dissension, united. This may sound extravagant, but I am not the only person of this way of thinking; and it is certain, the facts being too notorious to admit of dispute, that several of our prominent men, who were formerly most subject to the Anglo-mania, have been converted to a more healthful state of feeling, in consequence of their having been, accidentally, personal sharers in the abuse that has been so lavishly heaped on the nation. I have laughed, heartily, at the writhings of a certain instructor, under whom you and I, when boys, were condemned to hear all things English lauded to the skies, but who, having been roughly handled, as a writer, in this very Quarterly, has since come out manfully in vindication, as it is called, of the country, or, in other words of its *things,* and, in reality, of himself.

This is a species of independence of which there will never be a lack. Let us be grateful, however, for this much, and thank our stars and the Quarterly, accordingly. When I rejoice in the alienation of the feelings of America from England, it is not that I could wish to see our own nation on worse terms with this, than with any other, but, under the full conviction that we must pass through some such process of alienation, before we shall ever get to consider the English in the only mode that is either safe or honourable for one independent people to regard another. The constant infusion of new prejudices and partialities, by the agency of emigrants, and the manner in which we are obliged to depend on England for our literature, has rendered the change singularly slow, nor does it strike me that what is actually going on, is taking the right direction. We no longer believe that an English apple is better than an American apple, it is true; or even an English hog, or a horse; but, we do not the less believe in English political principles, although nothing can be more apparent than the fact that these principles have been established as a consequence of a factitious, and, in some measure, a fortuitous condition of society, to which our own system is, perhaps, more antagonist than that of any other Christian state.

Keeping the question of our moral dependence out of view, and returning to this country, I think the jealousy of Russia is about to produce a change of policy as respects America. It is quite impossible for one never out of America, to appreciate the nature and extent of the interest that all the higher classes, here, feel in their foreign policy. In America, we are almost in a state of nature, as regards every thing of the sort, the world furnishing no example perhaps of a people so much neglecting all the great interests that are not placed immediately before their eyes.* Did the people of

---

*One may form some notion of the condition of the foreign policy of the country, by a fact that has come to the knowledge of the writer, under circumstances that leave no doubt, in his mind, of its authenticity. An American was at Washington applying for some diplomatic appointment, at the moment Congress had the subject of the French reprisals, as recommended by the President, before them. Of so much greater importance did this *diplomatic agent* deem foreign than native support, that he is said to have written letters to Paris assuring his friends there,

the United States understand their true situation, the intentions, expectations, and wishes of this part of the world, they would at once exhibit a naval force, that should demonstrate the hazards of incurring their just resentment.

Some of our early diplomatists in Europe, when men of talents and character were alone employed in such situations, speak of the reasons they had for distrusting the intentions of England, on the subject of our independence, but I have lately been astonished at hearing it suggested, here, that this government has not yet absolutely abandoned the project of attempting recolonization. It is probable that this opinion is now exaggerated, but that such a scheme did exist, until within the last fifteen or twenty years, I make no doubt. There is a remarkable expression in an article of the Edinburgh Review, that appeared shortly after the peace of 1815. I quote from memory, but the words were nearly these, and as to the idea it is accurate, the subject of the article being America—*"We presume that the project of re-colonization is at length abandoned!"* Such a remark would not have been made causelessly. But I have, myself, been present when this subject was discussed, in Paris, by men who are in the secrets of states, and I well remember the surprise I felt at hearing the possibility of re-colonization suggested. On that occasion, when I gave the failure in 1776, as a proof of the impracticability of such a project at this late day, I was significantly reminded of the hundred millions that England had subjugated in India.

One thing is certain; we estimate our own security, very differently from what it is estimated here. It is the expectation of Europe generally, and of England especially, that we shall separate; and to this end, it is probable that the efforts of those who plot our overthrow will be directed. Little, I might almost say nothing, is known in America, of the means that are employed by the privileged classes of Europe to maintain their ascendancy. We have heard a great deal of the machinations of infidelity, and of the

---

that neither the nation nor congress would sustain the president in his proposition! One or more of these letters came into American hands, and were returned to Washington. In two instances, while in Europe, the writer found Englishmen employed in the legations at low salaries; and, of course, the secrets of the government were put at the disposal of foreign mercenaries.

infamous schemes of demagogues to overturn the existing order
of things, in these governments, but scarcely a whisper has been
breathed against the plots and inexcusable agencies that are universally attributed to the friends of despotism and aristocracy, by
the friends of liberty. Little accustomed to think for ourselves,
and with a corrupt and interested press, we have lent greedy ears
to *ex-parte* testimony, and, ready enough to oppose the principles
of the Age of Reason and of the Illuminati, we have overlooked
the essential circumstance that they are merely the reaction of
extreme abuses, and that the root of the evil lies deeper than the
disgusting excesses which have been so zealously paraded before
our eyes. I can know no more of the past than what I hear; but the
fairest minded men of France have assured me of their deep
conviction, that the machinations of their enemies were principally instrumental in bringing about the horrors of their own
revolution. No one pretends that it is unnatural for those who
have been ruthlessly depressed, to break out in acts of violence
when suddenly released, but they believe that agents were employed to excite these passions to fury, and that, finding it impossible to stay the torrent of revolution by resisitance, the privileged here, directed their schemes to bringing it into disrepute,
by inciting the people to acts that would be certain to offend
humanity. One anecdote related to me by General Lafayette, in
person, I consider so remarkable that it shall be repeated, substituting, however, initials of names that do not apply to those that
were actually mentioned, as some of the parties are still living. I
select this anecdote from a hundred, because I so well know the
integrity of the party from whom it is derived, that I feel confident there is no exaggeration or colouring in the account, and
because it is, fortunately, in my power to prove that I had it from
General Lafayette, almost in the words in which it is given to you.

We were conversing on the subject of the probable agency of the
monarchs and aristocrats of Europe, in bringing about the excesses of the revolution. "Count N——— was in England during
the peace of Amiens," said our venerable friend, "and he dined
with Lord G———, one of Mr. Pitt's cabinet. They were standing
together at a window of the drawing-room, when Lord G———
pointed to a window of a house at a little distance, and said,
'that is the window of the room in which F——— lodged, when

in England.' 'F _____,' exclaimed Count N_____, 'what can you know, my Lord, of such a man as F_____!' The English minister smiled significantly, and replied, 'why, *we sent him to France.*'"

By substituting for "Count N_____" the name of a Frenchman who has been a minister under nearly every government in France for the last forty years, and whose private and public character is one of the best of that country; for that of Lord G_____, a well known English statesmen; and that of F_____, one of the greatest monsters to which the Reign of Terror gave birth, you will have the story almost in the words in which it was related to me by General Lafayette, who told me he had it from Count N_____, himself.

Had this anecdote appeared in one of the newspaper comments of the day, I should think less of it, but coming as it did, from a distinguished Frenchman, and he of better reputation than most of the politicians of the period, to a man like Lafayette, who is so perfectly free from the vice of attributing base motives to even his enemies, and· this in a free and friendly conversation, with no apparent reason to misrepresent, I confess it has struck me as worthy of more than ordinary consideration.

When we remember how natural it is to employ the most obvious agencies in effecting our objects, one is not to be surprised that the scheme of pushing the popular feelings into extremes, should suggest itself, on such an occasion; and, as for any restraint imposed by principles, men are so apt to shift a divided responsibility from their own shoulders to those of their associates, so ready to look for justification in the end, and always so much disposed, in politics, to consider "*une faute*" more heinous than "*un crime,*" that I have no difficulty in believing the story, on the score of any moral scruples in the parties. The avowal might cause surprise, but it was two old soldiers talking over the different *ruses* of their late campaigns, and surprising things of the sort leak out in this way.

Mr. Huskisson was a student of medicine in Paris, at the commencement of the French revolution. The French openly accuse him of having worn the *bonnet rouge*, and of having belonged to the most exaggerated of the Jacobins. They add that he was suddenly lost sight of, and when next seen was in the employment of the British government. All this may be true, however, and still no more than a natural consequence of youth and inexperience. Had Mr. Huskisson been less equivocal in his commercial ethics, and more consistent with his own avowed principles, the circumstance would not have much weight with me, for nothing is more natural than for a young mind to be carried away by sentiments that appear to be generous; but I hold it to be a pretty safe rule that the man who is jesuitical on any one fact, is to be distrusted on all others. That Mr. Huskisson is self-contradicted and insincere in his Free Trade doctrines, is as obvious as any moral truth I know.

But, admitting that both these tales are idle, it would be folly for an American to shut his eyes to the confidence with which even the women, here, speak of the dismemberment of the Union. This is the point to which our enemies will be certain to direct their machinations; and if we wish "to calculate its value" to ourselves, we have only to regard the importance that is attached to it, by our enemies. You will judge of my surprise, when a young girl, under twenty years, told me very coolly, in answer to some pleasantry that had passed between us, on the subject of national power, "Oh, but your Union will soon be dissolved!"

Mr. Cobbett, who, though any thing but authority in matters of fact, is a shrewd thinker, and is accustomed to appreciate the means and agencies of states, has just declared in his journal, that, unless we abandon the protective policy, England ought to manifest her real power, and "blow their boasted Union to the winds." Here we have a specimen of the ethics as well as of the means employed, in such matters, by politicians. Unless we abandon a legitimate policy of our own, the social firebrand is to be lighted in our bosom! This savours strongly of the principles contained in the anecdote of General Lafayette. It will be said, however, that Mr. Cobbett is authority for nothing. But other journals have said, in substance, the same thing, and, I think, such is the tone of most political men, here. I have said that we overrate our security. A people, as much in the habit of looking to another nation for opinions, as our own, cannot be otherwise than dependant, to a certain degree, on the mercy of those who give them their impulses. No one can deny that we receive from England a vast deal that is excellent and useful, and it will be the cue of those who wish to influence us to our own injury, to mix their poison so artfully with this wholesome nutriment, that the two shall be swallowed together. Coupled with the most inflated boastings about American literature, in the journals, we may constantly see statements that such and such a work is republished in England, or has gone to a second edition in this country, as the highest eulogium that can be given. Much the greater proportion of our writers still manifest a dependance on English opinion, a dread of its censure, and a desire to secure its favour, in a way that cannot easily be mistaken. God forbid! that any one should indulge in the low calumnies that mark equally ignorance and vulgarity; but it is painful to see the truckling manner in which flattery and homage are interwoven in so many of our works, with a manifest design to secure the favour of a people, who do not care to conceal their contempt. In my own case, how often have I had occasion to see the influence of this spirit, by having it tauntingly thrown into my teeth that such and such abuse has appeared in some English journal—perhaps such and such a puff, by way of flattery! There is not an American writer, at this moment, who does not lie at the mercy of the English critics, should they consider him of sufficient importance to notice; and there are symptoms that this country begins to think seriously, if indeed it has not long thought, of influencing the reputation of our political men. That such are their own opinions of their own power is sufficiently manifest, for they openly boast of it in the newspapers. Obvious attempts are made to influence opinion even in France, a country that is singularly deaf to foreign impressions; and if they can excite a comment in France, they can convulse America.

In regarding this subject, the feelings and dispositions of the English nation are to be kept out of sight; for the human impulses of bodies of men are of no account in the control of interests like these: they who move the wires are behind the scenes, and the mass here, like the mass at home, is wrought on in a way that is perceptible only to the vigilant and the observing. But it is a humiliating fact, accompanying these circumstances, that the English see their influence, and deride us for it, even while they exercise it.

Some peculiarities of a physical nature serve to aid foreigners in perpetuating their power over the American mind. The population is so diffused, that, unless in cases which excite local interest, there is no opinion sufficiently strong to cope with that which is formed in the towns, and these towns, particularly those of the most influence, are quite as much foreign as American. A large portion of even the presses, in the seaports, are directly controlled by men who were born British subjects, and it is a peculiarity about these people, scarcely ever to forget their origin. There is an infatuation in America, on this subject, that one who stands aloof, can hardly credit. Still, when we come to look into all the causes, it can scarcely create surprise that the writers of the nation, look as much to foreign as to native approbation, that the diplomatists court their enemies, instead of their friends, and that public opinion is constantly influenced by interests and rights adverse to our own.

God knows, what is to be the final result. We may grow out of this weakness, as children get the better of the rickets; or we may succumb to the disease, as children often die. There is little use, however, in treating it with an overstrained delicacy, for it is the school of sentimentalists that has aggravated the disease to its present dangerous extent, and nothing will be so apt to cure it, besides time, as a little caustic, properly applied. I very well know, it is said, that the war of 1812, liberated the American mind from its ancient thraldom, and for a time it did; so did the war of the revolution; but no sooner did things, in both instances, revert back to their ancient channels, than the habits of thought appear to have kept them company. We have gained a little, permanently, beyond a question. No one thinks now, that a British frigate has only to say, "boh!" to an American frigate, to cause her to strike her flag; but this very point of manhood in the field, will prove the tendency to drop back into the old train of thinking, for, in despite of all the experience of 1776, thousands and tens of thousands of native citizens, believed we could not resist the English, when war was declared in 1812, either ashore or afloat! I do not mean, that they believed the power of America could not resist the power of England, but that the man of America could not fight the man of England; for to this had the uninterrupted practice of reading the English accounts of themselves, brought the state of public opinion. As no nation has shown a better spirit in the field, when actually called on to serve, does not this fact prove how completely courage is a matter of convention, and how necessary it is to guard all the habits of thought?

There is a feature of English jealousy, that strikes me as particularly odd. Every one reasons here, as if our government is always to be distrusted on account of its tendency to be driven into wars, by the truculent spirit of the democracy! I should say this notion haunts the English imagination, on the subject of America, though it would be difficult to give a good reason for it. The war of 1812, probably took our enemy by surprise, but it could not have been because the people of America rushed into it with precipitation, but because they had forborne so long as to remove every apprehension of their appealing to force at all. There is a professed distrust of General Jackson on this account. They think, or affect to think, that being a soldier, he will profit by the elements of democracy, and bring on a war of conquest, with a view to his own glory and tastes. Some do not hesitate to say, that he will then aim at a crown, like Napoleon!*

*When General Jackson was running alone, in opposition to Mr. Adams, the English, under the impressions alluded to, above, and probably on account of ancient grudges, betrayed a strong disinclination to his success. Still, Mr. Adams was disliked, for he was believed to be unfriendly to England, and favourable to the system of protecting duties. Suddenly, the press of London, altered its tone in reference to the former, and from lavishing the usual scurrility, it began to speak of him in terms of respect. It is said that the English agents in America, notified their government that they were quarrelling with their bread and butter, and that the change of policy took place in consequence. These little occurrences should teach every American, how to appreciate praise, or censure, that comes from sources so venal. Mr. Adams probably understood the true foreign policy of the government, better than any political man who has been in power since the days of Jefferson. The protective system, the congress of Panama, though defeated in its objects by hostile influence, and the protest of the administration of Mr. Monroe, which is understood to have originated with Mr. Adams, are three of the most elevated, far sighted, and statesman-like measures, America ever undertook. The former, though run down by English influence, will quite likely be called for by the very states that now most oppose it, within the next five-and-twenty years. Nothing is more probable, than that the Constitution will be amended, solely with a view to this end, and that the cotton-growing states will first move in the matter. But for the redeeming act of the president, in recommending reprisals against France, the writer, a near looker on for most of the time, should say, that the character of the nation abroad, suffered much less during the administration of Mr. Adams, than during that of his successor, though the diplomatic tone was not what it ought to have been, under either administration. We boast a great deal of the dexterity with which the nation has got out of a difficulty, while we entirely overlook the capital fault by which it got into it. So far from the truculent spirit of democracy, inducing the government to rush into wars, the craven and temporising spirit of trade, the only concentrated interest of much available power in ordinary cases, has prevented it from maintaining the true interests of the country, in a dozen distinct instances, within the last twenty years.

Letter XXVII.

To Richard Cooper, Esquire, Cooperstown, New York.

It would be an occupation of interest, to note the changes, moral and physical, that time, climate, and different institutions, have produced between the people of England, and those of America.

Physically, I do not think the change as great as is usually imagined. Dress makes a sensible difference in appearance, and I find that the Americans, who have been under the hands of the English tailors, are not easily distinguished from the English themselves. The principal points of distinction strike me to be these. We are taller, and less fleshy; more disposed to stoop; have more prominent features, and faces less full; are less ruddy, and more tanned; have smaller hands and feet, anti-democratical as it may be; and are more slouching in gait. The exceptions, of course, are numerous, but I think these distinctions may be deemed national. The American, who has become Europeanized by dress, however, is so very different looking an animal, from what he is at home, that too much stress is not to be laid on them. Then the great extent of the United States is creating certain physical differences in our own population, that render all such comparisons liable to many qualifications.

As to stature, and physical force, I see no reason to think the animal has deteriorated in America. As between England and the old Atlantic states, the difference is not striking, after one allows for the disparity in numbers, and the density of the population here, the eye always seeking exceptions; but, I incline to believe that the southwest will turn the scale to our side. I believe it to be a fact, that the aborigines of that portion of the Union, were larger than those of our own section of the country.

There are obvious physical differences among the English themselves. One county is said to have an undue proportion of red heads, another to have men taller than common, this again men that are shorter, and all to show traces of their remote origins. It is probable, that some of these peculiarities have descended to ourselves, though they have become blended by the unusual admixture of the population.

Morally, we live under the influence of systems so completely the converse of each other, that it is matter of surprise, so many points of resemblance still remain. The immediate tendency of the English system is, to create an extreme deference in all the subordinate classes for their superiors, while that of the American is to run into the opposite feeling. The effects of both these tendencies, are certainly observable, though relatively, that of our own much less, I think, than that of England. It gives good models a rather better chance here, than they have with us.

In England, the disaffected to the government, are among precisely those who most sustain government in America; and the disaffected in America, (if so strong a word can properly be used, as applied to natives,) are of a class wl.ose interests it is to sustain government in England.* These facts give very different aspects to the general features of society. Walking in Regent street, lately, I witnessed an attempt of the police, to compel some hackney coachmen to quit their boxes, and go with them before the magistrate. A crowd of a thousand people collected immediately, and its feeling was decidedly against the ministers of the law; so much so, indeed, as to render it doubtful, whether the coachmen, whose conduct had been flagrantly criminal, would not be rescued. Now, in America, I think, the feeling of such a crowd, would have been just the other way. It would have taken an interest in supporting the authorities of the country, instead of an interest in opposing them. This was not the case of a mob, you will remember, in

---

*When the writer went to Europe, it was so unusual to hear any thing against the system of America, that disaffection may be said to have become extinct. On his return, however, after an absence of less than eight years, he was astonished to hear monarchical sentiments openly declared, and he believes that it will be generally admitted by all candid observers, that their avowal is now more open and more frequent, than they have been at any time, within the present century. This is not the place to discuss the reasons, but this explanation is due from the writer, on his own account, as, without it, a change that has actually taken place among others, may be ascribed to himself. No one need be ashamed of having honestly altered his opinions, for good cause, and after mature examination; but since the publication of these letters has commenced, the writer has been openly accused of changes that, in point of fact, have occurred among other people. Another occasion may offer to examine this point.

which passion puts down reason, but an ordinary occurrence of the exercise of the power of the police. Instances of this nature, might be multiplied, to show that the mass of the two people, act under the influence of feelings diametrically opposed to each other.

On the other hand, Englishmen of the higher classes are, with very few exceptions, and these exceptions are usually instances of mere party opposition, attached to their system, sensitive on the subject of its merits or defects, and ever ready to defend it when assailed. The American of the same class is accustomed to sneer at democracy, to cavil at its fruits, and to colour and exaggerate its faults. Though this latter disposition may be, to a degree, accounted for by the facts, that all merit is comparative, and most of our people have not had the opportunities to compare; and that it is natural to resist most that which most annoys, although the substitution of any other for the actual system would produce even greater discontent; still, I think, the general tendency of aristocratical institutions on the one hand, and of democratical on the other, is to produce this broad difference in feeling, as between classes.

Both the Americans and the English are charged with being offensively boastful and arrog. nt, as nations, and too much disposed to compare themselves advantageously with their neighbours. I have visited no country in which a similar disposition does not exist, and as communities are merely aggregations of men, I fancy that the disposition of a people to take this view of their own merits, is no more than carrying out the well known principle of individual vanity. The English and ourselves, however, well may, and probably do differ from other nations, in one circumstance connected with such a failing. The mass in both nations, are better instructed, and are of more account than the mass in other countries, and their sentiments form more of a public opinion than elsewhere. When the bulk of a people are in a condition to make themselves heard, one is not to expect much refinement or delicacy, in the sentiments they utter. The English do not strike me as being a vainer nation than the French, although, in the way of ordinary intercourse, I believe that both they and we are more boastful.

The English are to be particularly distinguished from the Americans, in the circumstance of their being proud people. This is a

useful and even an ennobling quality, when it is sustained by
facts, though apt to render a· people both uncomfortable and
unpleasant, when the glory on which they pique themselves is
passed away. We are almost entirely wanting in national pride,
though abundantly supplied with an irritable vanity, that might
rise to pride, had we greater confidence in our facts. Most intelligent Englishmen are ready enough to admit the obvious faults of
their climate, and even of their social condition, but it is an
uncommon American that will concede any thing material, on
such points, unless it can be made to bear on democracy. We have
the sensitiveness of provincials, increased by the consciousness of
having our spurs to earn, on all matters of glory and renown, and
our jealousy extends even to the reputations of the cats and dogs.
It is but an indifferent compliment to human nature to add, that
the man who will join, complacently, and I may say ignorantly, in
the abuse of foreigners against the institutions of the country, and
even against its people, always reserving a saving clause in favour
of his own particular class, will take fire if an innuendo is hazarded
against its beef, or a suggestion made that the four thousand feet
of the Round Peak, are not equal to the thirteen thousand of the
Jung Frau. The English are tolerably free from this weakness, and
travelling is daily increasing this species of liberality, at least. I
presume that the insular situation of England, and our own distance from Europe, are equally the causes of these traits, though
there may be said to be a "property qualification" in the very
nature of man, that disposes him to view his own things with
complacency, and those of his neighbours with distrust. Bishop
Heber, in one of his letters to Lord Grenville, in speaking of the
highest peaks of the Himalayas, throws into a parenthesis, "which
I feel some exultation in saying, is completely within the limits of
the British empire," a sort of sentiment, of which, I dare say,
neither St. Chrysostom nor Polycarp was entirely free.

On the subject of sensibility to comments on their national
habits and national characters, neither France nor England is by
any means as philosophical or indifferent as one might suppose.
As a rule, I believe all men are more easily enraged when their
real faults are censured, than when their virtues are called in
question; and, if the defect happen to be unavoidable, or one for
which they are not fairly responsible, the resentment is two-fold
that which would attend a comment on a vice. The only differ-

ence I can discover between the English and ourselves, in this particular, is easily to be traced to our greater provincialism, youth, and the consciousness that we are obliged to anticipate some of our renown. I should say that the English are *thin-skinned*, and the Americans *raw*. Both resent fair, frank, and manly comments with the same bad taste, resorting to calumny, blackguardism, and abuse, when wit and pleasantry would prove both more effective and wiser, and, perhaps, reformation, wisest of all. I can only account for this peculiarity, by supposing that the institutions and political facts of the two countries have rendered vulgar-minded men of more account, than is usually the case, and that their influence has created a species of public opinion which is less under the correction of taste, principles, and manners, than is the case in nations where the mass is more depressed. Of the fact, itself, there can be no question.

In order to appreciate the effect of refinement on this nation, it will be necessary to recur to some of its statistical facts. England, including Wales, contains rather less than fifty-eight thousand square miles of territory; the state of New York, about forty-three thousand. On the former surface, there is a population of something like fifteen millions; on the latter, a population of less than two. One gives a proportion of about two hundred and sixty to the square mile, and the other a proportion of less than fifty. These premises, alone, would show us the immense advantage that any given portion of surface in England, must possess over the same extent of surface in America, in all those arts and improvements, that depend on physical force. If there were ten men of education, and refinement, and fortune, in a county of New York, of one thousand square miles in extent, there ought to be more than fifty men of the same character and means, in an English county of equal territory. This is supposing that the real premises offer nothing more against us, than the disproportion between numbers and surface; whereas, in fact, time, wealth, and an older civilization, more than quadruple the odds. Even these do not make up the sum of the adverse elements. Though England has but fifteen millions of souls, the empire she controls has nearly ten times that population, and a very undue proportion of the results of so great a physical force, centre in this small spot.

The consideration of these truths suggests several useful heads of reflection. In the first place, they show us, if not the absolute impossibility, the great improbability, that the civilization, refinement, knowledge, wealth, and tastes of even the best portions of America, can equal those of this country, and suggest the expediency of looking to other points for our sources of pride. I have said, that the two countries act under the influence of moral agencies that are almost the converse of each other. The condensation of improvement and cultivation is so great here, that even the base of society is affected by it, even to deportment; whereas, with us, these properties are so dispersed, as to render it difficult for those who are lucky enough to possess them, to keep what they have got, in face of the overshadowing influence of a lower school, instead of being able to impart them to society. Our standard, in nearly all things, as it is popular, is necessarily one of mediocrity; a highly respectable, and, circumstances considered, a singularly creditable one, but still a mediocrity; whereas, the condition of these people has enabled them to raise a standard, which, however much it may be and is wanting in the better elements of a pure taste, has immensely the advantage of our own, in most of the obvious blandishments of life. More than half of the peculiarities of America, peculiarities for which it is usual to seek a cause in the institutions, simply because they are so peculiar themselves, are to be traced to facts like these; or, in other words, to the disproportion between surface and numbers, the want of any other than commercial towns, and our distance from the rest of the world.

Every condition of society has its own advantages, and its own disadvantages. To claim perfection for any one, in particular, would be to deny the nature of man. Their comparative merits are to be decided, only, by the comparative gross results, and it is in this sense, that I contend for the superiority of our own. The utilitarian school, as it has been popularly construed, is not to my taste, either, for I believe there is great utility in the grace and elegance of life, and no one would feel more disposed to resist a system, in which these essential properties are proscribed. That we are wanting in both, I am ready to allow; but I think the reason is to be found in facts entirely independent of the institutions, and that the time will come, when the civilization of America will look down that of any other section of the world, if the country can pass that state of probation, during which it is and will be exposed to the assaults of secret combinations to destroy it; and during which, moreover, it is, in an especial degree, liable to be affected by inherited opinions, and opinions that have been obtained under a system that has so many of the forms, while it has so few of the principles of our own, as easily to be confounded with it, by the ignorant and the unreflecting.

We over-estimate the effects of intelligence, as between ourselves and the English. The mass of information, here, probably exceeds that of America, though it is less equally distributed. In *general* knowledge of a practical nature, too, I think no people can compete with our own. But there is a species of information, that is both useful and refining, in which there are few European nations that do not surpass us. I allude, in particular, to most things that serve to embellish life. In addition to this superiority, the Europeans of the better classes very obviously possess over us an important advantage, in their intimate associations with each other, by which means they insensibly imbibe a great deal of current knowledge, of which the similar classes in America are nearly ignorant; or, which, if known at all, is only known through the medium of books. In the exhibition of this knowledge, which embraces all that belongs to what is commonly termed a knowledge of the world, the difference between the European and the American is the difference to be seen between the man who has passed all his days in good society, and the man who has got his knowledge of it from novels and plays.

In a correct estimate of their government, and in an acquaintance with its general action, the English are much our superiors, though we know most of details. This arises from the circumstances that the rights of an Englishman are little more than franchises, which require no very profound examination to be understood, while those of the American depend on principles that demand study, and which are constantly exposed to the antagonist influence of opinions that have been formed under another system. It is true the English monarchy, as a monarchy and as it now exists, is a pure mystification, but the supremacy of parliament being admitted, there can arise no great difficulty on the score of interpretation. The American system, moreover, is complicated and double, and the only true Whig and Tory parties that can exist must have their origin in this circumstance. To these reasons may be added the general fact, that the educated Englishman reasons on his institutions like an Englishman only, while his American counterpart oftener reasons on the institutions of the republic like an Englishman too, than like an American. A single fact will show you what I mean, although a hundred might be quoted. In England the government is composed, in theory, of three bases and one summit; in America, it is composed of one base and three summits. In one, there is supposed to be a balance in the powers of the state; and as this is impossible in practice, it has resulted in a consolidated authority in its action; in the other, there is but one power, that of the entire people, and the balance is in the action of their agents. A very little reflection will show that the maxims of two such systems ought to be as different as the systems themselves.

The English are to be distinguished from the Americans, by greater independence of personal habits. Not only the institutions, but the physical condition of our own country has a tendency to reduce us all to the same level of usages. The steamboats, the over-grown taverns, the speculative character of the enterprises, and the consequent disposition to do all things in common, aid the tendency of the system in bringing about such a result. In England a man dines by himself, in a room filled with other hermits; he eats at his leisure; drinks his wine in silence; reads the paper by the hour, and, in all things, encourages his individuality and insists on his particular humours. The American is compelled to submit to a common rule; he eats when others eat; sleeps when others sleep; and he is lucky, indeed, if he can read a paper in a tavern without having a stranger looking over each shoulder.* The Englishman would stare at a proposal that should invade his habits under the pretence of a common wish, while the American would be very apt to yield tacitly, though this common wish should be no more than an impudent assertion of some one who had contrived to affect his own purposes, under the popular plea. The Englishman is so much attached to his independence that he instinctively resists every effort to invade it, and nothing would be more likely to arouse him than to say the mass thinks

*Exaggerated as this may appear, the writer has actually been driven away, by strangers leaning over him, in this manner, no less than eleven times, at the Astor House, within the last twelvemonths.

differently from himself; whereas the American ever seems ready to resign his own opinion to that which is made to seem to be the opinion of the public. I say *seems* to be, for so manifest is the power of public opinion, that one of the commonest expedients of all American managers, is to create an impression that the public thinks in a particular way, in order to bring the common mind in subjection. One often renders himself ridiculous by a foolish obstinacy, and the other is as often contemptible by a weak compliance. A portion of what may be called the *community* of character and habits in America, is doubtless owing to the rustic nature of its society, for one more easily maintains his independence in a capital than in a village, but I think the chief reasons are to be found in the practice of referring every thing to the common mind.

It is usual to ascribe the solitary and unsocial habits of English life, to the natural dispositions of the people, but I think unjustly. The climate is made to bear the blame of no small portion of this peculiarity. Climate, probably, has an influence on us all, for we know that we are more elastic, and more ready to be pleased in a clear bracing air, than in one that is close and *sciroccoish*, but, on the whole I am led to think, the English owe their habits to their institutions, more than to any natural causes.

I know no subject, no feeling, nothing, on which an Englishman, as a rule, so completely loses sight of all the better points of his character, on which he is so uniformly bigoted and unjust, so ready to listen to misrepresentation and caricature, and so unwilling to receive truth, on which, in short, he is so little like himself in general, as on those connected with America.

As the result of this hasty and imperfect comparison, I am led to believe, that a national character somewhere between the two, would be preferable to either, as it is actually found. This may be saying no more than that man does not exist in a conditon of perfection; but were the inequalities named, pared off from both people, an ingenious critic might still find faults of sufficient magnitude, to preserve the identity with the human race, and qualities of sufficient elevation, to entitle both to be considered among the greatest and best nations of modern, if not of any other, times.

In most things that pertain to taste, the English have greatly the advantage of us, though *taste* is certainly not the strong side of

English character. On this point, alone, one might write a book, but a very few remarks must now satisfy you. In nothing, however, is this superiority more apparent, than in their simplicity, and, particularly, in their simplicity of language. They call a spade, a spade. I very well know, that neither men nor women, in America, who are properly educated, and who are accustomed to its really better tone, differ much, if any, from the English in this particular, but, in this case, as in most others, in which *national* peculiarities are sought, the better tone of America is overshadowed by its mediocrity.* Although I deem the government of this country the very quintessence of hocus pocus, having scarcely a single practice that does not violate its theory, I believe that there is more honesty of public sentiment in England, than in America. The defect at home, I ascribe, in common with the

---

*Mrs. Butler, in her shrewd work on America, has given many good hits at this love for the grandiose. Whenever this lady has gone out of her particular sphere, or that of her sex, her remarks are such as might have been anticipated from a young English woman, visiting America with all her political prejudices about her, and almost as a matter of course, necessarily ignorant of the true machinery and action of governments. Even in this writer, the expectation, not to say the *longing*, for a dissolution of the Union, that has been so often mentioned in these pages, is sufficiently apparent; she, also, has fallen into the very common error of ascribing things to the institutions, such for instance as the *nonchalance* of the trades people, and the noisy, screeching, hoydenish romps of the sexes, which it suits the caprices of certain people to term society, when they ought to be referred, one to the personal independence of a country prosperous beyond example, and the other to the unsettled condition of towns, that double their population every twenty years, and their wealth in ten.

Mrs. Butler has made many other mistakes, beyond a question, for she has written under erroneous impressions at starting. Of this class are all the misconceptions connected with those usages that are thought to be tending daily towards aristocracy. Any one who knows the country well, knows that in all the ordinary appliances of this nature, America has been gradually receding from such forms, for the last forty years. Thus footmen, liveries, hatchments, coats of arms, &c. &c., are all much less common now, than at the commencement of the century. Mrs. Butler has mistaken the twilight, for the dawn; the shadows of the past for those of coming events. This is a common misapprehension of the English, and it arises from a disposition to see things in their own way.

The treatment that this lady has received, cannot be too loudly condemned. She has been derided, caricatured, almost, if not positively, slandered, because she has presumed to speak the truth about us! Mrs. Trollope has met with similar denunciations, though with a greater show of reason, for Mrs. Trollope has calumniated her own sex in America. Besides, one sees, in the book of Mrs.

majority of our national failings, to the greater activity, and greater *unresisted* force of ignorance and cupidity, there, than here. High qualities are nowhere collected in a sufficient phalanx to present a front to the enemy, in America.

The besetting, the degrading vice of America, is the moral cowardice by which men are led to truckle to what is called public opinion; though this opinion is as inconstant as the winds, though, in all cases, that enlist the feelings of factions there are *two*, and sometimes twenty, each differing from all the others, and though, nine times in ten, these opinions are mere engines set in motion by the most corrupt and the least respectable portion of the community, for unworthy purposes. The English are a more respectable and constant nation than the Americans, as relates to this peculiarity; probably, because the condensed masses of intelligence and character enable the superior portion of the community to produce a greater impression on the inferior, by their collective force. In standing prejudices, they strike me as being worse than ourselves; but in passing impressions greatly our superiors.

For the last I have endeavoured to account, and I think the first may be ascribed to a system that is sustained by errors that it is not the interest of the more enlightened to remove, but which, instead of weakening in the ignorant, they rather encourage in themselves.

Trollope, a malignant feeling, and calculations of profit; while the work of Mrs. Butler is as honest as it is fearless. The latter has designated persons too plainly, perhaps, as coupled with unpleasant remarks; but all these faults may be overlooked, as the whims of a very young female.

In one thing Mrs. Butler is singularly mistaken. She says that neither England, nor France, manifests any sensibility on the subject of the comments of travellers! The French do not, ordinarily, understand the comments of the English, or the English those of the French. Neither nation reads nor knows any thing about the comments of the Americans at all. Nothing is easier than to manifest indifference to things of which we are totally ignorant. As respects the English, however, one has only to name Pillet, d'Haussez, and Puckler-Muskau, in order to show how much abuse and calumny they can heap on those whose opinions displease them. The stories circulated in English society, concerning the latter, by way of retaliation for his book, were quite on a level with the Trollopeana of America. Both are a disgrace to civilization.

Letter XXVIII.

To Captain B. Cooper, U. S. Navy.

Having a long-standing engagement to be in Amsterdam, early in June, we have been compelled to quit London, before the termination of the season. I could have wished to remain longer, but the force of things has moved heavier bodies.

Quitting England is, by no means, as easy a matter for a foreigner, as quitting almost any other European state. I was obliged to go first to the alien office, which is near Westminster Hall, and then proceed to the custom-house, a distance of several miles, in order to get the required permission. If all these forms are necessary, (and I shall not take it on myself to say they are not) it would save trouble could every thing be done in the same office, or, at least, in the same building.

My labours in obtaining the permit to embark, and in taking a passage, have taught me a secret in relation to the advantage we possess over the English in sailing ships. The excess of men causes all occupations to be crowded, and as each *employé* must have a livelihood out of his employment, he becomes a charge on the business. If an Englishman could live on a bit of garlic and a few chesnuts, this would not be of so much moment; but he is a beef-eating and a beer-drinking animal, and likes to be neat in his attire, and the trade is compelled to pay a pretty good price for his support. Thus when I went on board the steamboat to take the necessary passage, I was compelled to return to the shore, and walk, at least, half a mile to an office to effect my purpose. The person to whom I was referred, received me civilly, but after making his bow, he put his hands in his pockets, and ordered two or three clerks to receive my money, enter my name, and do the other necessary things. In America the captain would do all this himself, and would find no time to put his hands in his breeches pockets.

You can form no notion, of the intrigues and frauds that are practised, in these old countries, in the struggles for a subsistence.

Few people of any condition have much direct communication with their tradesmen, and the buying, as a matter of course, falls into the hands of servants. A certain per centum is given the buyer, which the seller adds to the price. This is another reason why the servant is a personage of more importance in Europe than with us, for his master's custom usually depends on *his* patronage. A case of this sort has occurred under my own immediate observation. The proprietor of one of the most celebrated vineyards of France, certain that a vast deal of spurious wine was sold under the name of his vintages, determined to make an effort to bring the pure liquor into proper notice, a difficult achievement, by the way, as the palate once set to even a vicious taste, is as little likely to relish perfection, as any thing else. My acquaintance determined to get his wine introduced to the table of the king, at once, as a certain means of making it known. I dare say, now, you will think he had nothing to do, but to request some purveyor to consent to let the liquor be put before his majesty, and to await the issue. So far from taking this simple course, however, he was advised to make interest with a lady of rank, in order to induce her to persuade a connexion of her own, who was one of the most distinguished men of the age, and had great favour with the king, to present the latter with a case of the wine, and this, too, in a way that might insure its reaching the royal mouth. I cannot say whether the experiment failed or succeeded, but I believe it failed, and most probably through the intrigues of those interested.

In America we have not yet reached this pass, although a glorious beginning has commenced in the commercial towns, which, in their way, are probably as corrupt as any in the world. I have seen abundant proof of a disposition in the trading part of our community, abroad, to combine and conspire to attain their ends, without regard to truth, principles, or justice, and I presume we are to go the way of all flesh in this, as in other respects.

I have not mentioned the subject, because I believe England more obnoxious to this charge of management than other European countries, for probably there is less of it here than elsewhere; certainly much less than in France; but it naturally suggested itself when I came to speak of the number of subordinates that are employed in all matters of business.

Our little preparations were soon made, and, on the appointed
day, we went on board the vessel, which was lying off the custom-
house. As we all stood on deck, just as the boat was about to
proceed, the master came round to ask the foreigners for their
permits to quit the country. "You have no need of one," he observed to me, in passing. "I have one, notwithstanding." The man
stared, and asked an explanation with his eyes. I told him I was a
foreigner; an American. "I have been in America," he said, "but
we hardly look on your countrymen as foreigners." There was
more of the feeling which prevails in America towards England
in these words and in this man's manner, than I had ever before
witnessed in England. He proved to be a mild decent man, and
well disposed to introduce some of our improvements into his
boat.

We had a party of cocknies on board, who went as far as Gravesend for the fun of the thing. Great hilarity prevailed under the
excitement of the usual condiments of bread, cheese and porter,
and we were not sorry to be quit of them.

The weather was fine, and the North Sea as smooth as a dish.
The whole night were we paddling through it, and the next
morning I looked out, in vain, for any signs of land. Our boat was
a solid, good vessel, but slow of foot. The construction necessary
to weathering a heavy sea, may cause these boats to make less way
than our own steamers, though those which go round Point Judith
and through the Sound have also need of some of the same qualities. As between them, I think the American boats usually go
three feet to the English's two.

At length a low spit of sand hove in sight ahead, with here and
there a tree or a church tower, that appeared to rise out of the
water. This was Holland, a country, that, in the language of
seamen, may be said to be awash. As we drew in nearer with the
land, the villages and towers were actually made as one makes the
upper sails of a ship before the hull. When fairly between the
islands, by going up a few rattlins in the rigging, I got a glimpse
of meadows that lay beneath the level of tide, from whose inroads
they were protected by embankments. The whole country reminded me of a ship with its dead lights in.

I saw a wagon rattling along a causeway, and it was a *fac simile* of
the wagons that go under the name of Dutch wagons in New-York,

even to the curvature of the side boards. The only difference I could perceive was in the fact that this had no tongue! The country is so level, that holding back is unnecessary, and a short crooked tiller, that is worked by the foot of the teamster answers the purpose of guiding the vehicle. This was Dutch economy, with a vengeance, for the difference in cost could not exceed a guilder, and the difference in security, time and comfort, must be worth twenty. You will easily understand, that when it becomes necessary to stop one of these crafts, sail must be shortened in season, or the momentum would send the whole on the heels of the horses.

Presently, we got a sight of the steeples of Rotterdam, which were well relieved by trees. The verdure was oppressive, for the landscape resembled one seen through a bit of green glass. The boat was soon along side of the Boom Key, and we were all marched off in a body to have our trunks examined. Mine were merely opened and closed again. The passport was glanced at, and we were dismissed to a hotel. Before we entered the latter I had time to look about me, and to see a hundred things that recalled Albany and New York as they appeared in their palmy Dutch condition.

Here, then, we take our leave of England for a time;—England, a country that I could fain like, but whose prejudices and national antipathies throw a chill over all my affections; a country that unquestionably stands at the head of civilization in a thousand things, but which singularly exemplifies a truth that we all acknowledge, or how much easier it is to possess great and useful, and even noble qualities, than it is to display those that are attractive and winning—a country that all respect, but few love.

Explanatory Notes

2.4 tuft-hunters: those who try to become acquainted with titled or high-ranking persons.

5.2 CAPT. W. BRANFORD SHUBRICK: William Branford Shubrick (1790-1874), to whom *The Pilot* and *The Red Rover* were dedicated, was the novelist's closest friend. They served together as midshipmen under James Lawrence on the *Wasp* in 1809-1810; and, after Cooper's resignation from the Navy in 1810, their friendship deepened into a life-long intimacy. Shubrick had a long, distinguished naval career and rose to the rank of rear-admiral (ret.) in 1862.

Shubrick is named also as the recipient of Letter II (15.2).

6.36-39 celebrated hills . . . Shakspeare: See *King Lear* IV.i.73-74.

9.21 "When shall . . . hill?": *King Lear* IV.vi.1.

9.26-34 "Half way . . . high.": *King Lear* IV.vi.14-22.

10.6-8 Dr. Johnson . . . nautical phrases: Possibly a reference to Samuel Johnson's note on *The Tempest* I.i.1: "In this naval dialogue, perhaps the first example of sailor's language exhibited on the stage, there are, as I have been told by a skilful navigator, some inaccuracies and contradictory orders." See *Johnson on Shakespeare*, ed. Arthur Sherbo (New Haven, 1968), VII, 117. Cooper may not have remembered the passage accurately.

10.16-25 chapter . . . pure spite: Chapter V in *The Pilot* (1824). Cooper's auditor was almost certainly Benjamin Cooper. See note for 305.2.

18.17 Shooter's Hill: Located southeast of London on the Dover road, it was, like Blackheath, a notorious haunt of highwaymen.

20.9-10 "Miss Nancy . . . pocket,": a variation of the first line of the well-known nursery rhyme:

> Lucy Locket lost her pocket,
> Kitty Fisher found it;
> Not a penny was there in it,
> Only ribbon round it.

22.2 RICHARD COOPER: Son of Richard Cooper, the novelist's oldest
brother, young Richard (1808-1862) was a rising Cooperstown attorney. Intelligent, good-natured, and loyal, he was Cooper's
favorite nephew, frequently transacting business for his uncle. He
married Cooper's youngest daughter, Maria Frances, in 1850, after
the death of his first wife, Mary Storrs, in 1846.
    Richard Cooper is also named as the recipient of Letter V (43.2),
XIV (159.2), XV (167.2), XVII (189.2), XX (223.2), XXIII (260.2)
and XXVII (294.2).

23.28-29 the son of . . . ministers in Europe: probably Charles King
(1789-1867), a member of Cooper's Bread and Cheese Club, whose
father, Rufus King (1755-1827), was minister to England in 1825-
1826.

24.33-25.18 awkward mistake . . . explanation: The unexpected visit from
William Godwin seems to have been inspired by a mistaken assumption that the novelist was the son of the actor Thomas Abthorp
Cooper (1776-1849), who had once lived in the Godwin household
as a distant relative of the philosopher's mother. And this error
had apparently been prompted by the circumstance that another
well-known English emigrant Dr. Thomas Cooper (1759-1839),
trained in the law, medicine, and natural sciences, was, like the
novelist's father, styled Judge Cooper (see page 116).

25.30 Alnwick Castle: Fitz-Greene Halleck's part romantic, part satiric
celebration of a visit to Alnwick Castle, in Northumberlandshire,
in October 1822.

25.33-34 "nothing . . . Nazareth.": a variation on John i.46.

31.2 THOMAS JAMES DE LANCEY: The son of Mrs. Cooper's brother,
Thomas James De Lancey, Sr., who died in 1822, and Mary Jane
Ellison, Thomas James De Lancey, Jr. (1822-1859) was a talented,
but apparently unmotivated young man in whom the Coopers
took a special interest.

31.14-15 I have . . . this building: See *Gleanings in Europe: France*, Letter
III.

32.30-32 Lady Warren . . . grand-father: Susannah De Lancey (1707-
1791), sister of Lieutenant-Governor James De Lancey of New
York (1703-1760), the grandfather of Thomas James De Lancey, Sr.

33.18-25 "heads of Washington . . . has done it, no doubt.": Cf. *Letters
and Journals*, II, 390.

33.33-34 Ananias . . . swear to it: Acts v.1-10.

37.30-33 The celebrated tapestry . . . than otherwise: Charles Howard,
Baron Howard of Effingham (1536-1624), commander of the
English forces, ordered ten pieces of tapestry depicting the defeat

of the Spanish Armada in 1588. Their elaborate borders contained portraits of the principal commanders of the fleet. Sold to James I in 1616, the tapestries were hung in the House of Lords, where they perished in the fire of 1834. They survive today only in engravings made by John Pine in 1739, reproduced in *Lord Howard of Effingham and the Spanish Armada* (London, 1919).

37.33-35 "The tapestry . . . get along with": On 18 November 1777, William Pitt, Earl of Chatham, rebuked the Earl of Suffolk, expressing strong disapproval of the British use of Indians in the war with America: "From the tapestry that adorns these walls, the immortal ancestor of this noble lord frowns with indignation at the disgrace of his country." *Celebrated Speeches of Chatham, Burke, and Erskine* (Philadelphia, 1835), p. 42. Suffolk's "immortal ancestor" is Lord Howard, who ordered the tapestries. Thomas Howard, first Earl of Suffolk (1561-1626), also distinguished himself in the battle against the Armada.

38.14 Bellamy's: See 104.11-12.

38.21-22 steeple of Trinity . . . its top: The interior of the dome of St. Paul's is 25 feet higher than was the 200-foot steeple of New York's Trinity Church.

39.32-34 a "geometry stair-case" . . . inexplicable: See Nathaniel H. Carter, *Letters from Europe* (New York, 1829), I, 115.

39.35 automaton chess-player: Constructed by Leonhard Maelzel (1776-1855), the supposed automaton was directed by a concealed human player.

44.26 "Jockey of Norfolk,": John Howard, first Duke of Norfolk (1430?-1485), referred to as "Jockey of Norfolk" in *Richard III*, V.iii.304.

44.34-35 Earl of Surrey . . . peer of England: Henry Charles Howard (1791-1856), Earl of Arundel and Surrey until 1842, when, on his father's death, he became Duke of Norfolk.

46.29 *redingote grise*: the gray mantle, with no distinguishing marks, that Napoleon wore in the field.

50.18 his illustrious ancestor lost his head: Lord William Russell (1639-1683) was tried for treason and beheaded, though he denied taking part in the Rye House Plot to assassinate Charles II and his brother James.

51.17-19 Addison's celebrated answer . . . thousand pounds: See *Boswell's Life of Johnson* (Oxford, 1934), II, 256.

51.37-39 an imperfect copy . . . by Mr. Bryant: almost certainly *The Album* (New York, 1824), an anthology of American verse compiled by a person unknown. It contains the first half of "Alnwick

Castle" and two poems, "Song" and "March," by William Cullen Bryant.

54.2 MRS. J[AY]: Mary Rutherfurd Clarkson (1786-1838), daughter of General Matthew Clarkson and Mary Rutherfurd, married Peter Augustus Jay, son of Governor John Jay, in 1807.

55.18 Sully . . . in 1603: Maximilien de Béthune, Duke of Sully (1560-1641), cannot have visited Holland House (orginally Cope Castle) during his mission to James I in 1603, for it was commissioned in 1604 and completed in 1607.

55.33 the Patroon: Stephen Van Rensselaer (1764-1839).

59.19 the Genessee, in Connecticut: The Genesee river is, of course, in New York.

60.4-28 One of my . . . before the hour: Cf. *Letters and Journals*, I, 355-56.

60.28-29 Sir [Henry Halford]: (1766-1844), president of the College of Physicians (1820-1844), and court physician to four monarchs: George III, George IV, William IV, and Victoria. Cf. *Letters and Journals*, I, 356.

60.30 Dr. [Copleston] . . . Bishop of [Llandaff]: Edward Copleston (1776-1849) was elevated to the bishopric of Llandaff in 1827. Cf. *Letters and Journals*, I, 355-56.

61.14-21 "He asked me . . . flatter him.": Cf. *Letters and Journals*, I, 356.

61.23-25 sermon preached . . . established church: Bishop John Henry Hobart, *The United States of America Compared with some European Countries, Particularly England* (New York, 1825). See also 244.6.

62.28 Brooks's: gaming club in St. James's Street.

64.15-65.6 From [Spencer] house . . . in his party: Cf. *Letters and Journals*, I, 356.

67.11 Captain Hall . . . the same: Basil Hall had remarked "the want of cordiality with which . . . the English look upon them [the Americans]." *Travels in North America* (Edinburgh, 1829), II, 21. Cooper reviewed this book in Colburn's *New Monthly Magazine*, 32 (October 1831), 297-311.

68.2 THOMAS FLOYD-JONES: Brigadier General Thomas Floyd-Jones (1788-1851) was Mrs. Cooper's first cousin and a friend and associate of the novelist as sportsman and agriculturalist. Mrs. Cooper's mother (Elizabeth Floyd) and Thomas Floyd-Jones' father (David R. Floyd, later Floyd-Jones) were brother and sister.

71.7 *Revenons à nos moutons:* proverbial French for "Let's get back on the subject," from *La Farce de Maître Pierre Pathelin* (Rouen, 1486), 1. 1191.

71.17 Mississippi sawyer: a partially submerged, snagged log which rides up and down with the current; hence, a rider who bounces.

74.22-23 Peter Pindar . . . to London: If, as Cooper writes, his footman was "about fifty" in 1828, he could hardly have accompanied the painter John Opie (1761-1807) when he was taken to London in 1781 by Peter Pindar, pseudonym of John Wolcot (1738-1819), the satirist and poet.

77.26 Col. Heathcote: Caleb Heathcote (1665-1721), Mrs. Cooper's great-grandfather, whose daughter Anne married Lieutenant-Governor James De Lancey (1703-1760) of New York.

77.35 Lady Affleck: Mary Clark (d. 1835), daughter of Thomas Clark of New York, married her second husband, Sir Gilbert Affleck, 2nd Bart., in 1796.

77.38 Mrs. White: Eve Van Cortlandt (1736-1836), who married Henry White (1732-1786), a Loyalist merchant.

78.1 John De Lancey: (1741-1820), a cousin of Mrs. Cooper's father.

78.1 Mrs. Izard: Alice De Lancey (1746-1832), a cousin of Mrs. Cooper's father, married Ralph Izard (1742-1804), who was elected to the first United States Senate.

78.1-2 John Watts: (1749-1836), last Royal Recorder of New York City and Member of Congress, 1793-1796. A cousin of Mrs. Cooper's father, Watts married Jane De Lancey (1756-1809).

78.2 Lady Mary Watts: Lady Mary Alexander (1749-1831), daughter of William Alexander, the Earl of Stirling, and Sarah Livingston. She married Robert Watts, a cousin of Mrs. Cooper's father.

79.17-18 Cecilia . . . Mrs. Belfield's entry: In Fanny Burney's *Cecilia: or Memoirs of an Heiress* (1782), the heroine visits Henrietta Belfield in a sedan chair to confer her charities.

80.2 EDWARD FLOYD DE LANCEY: (1821-1905), the oldest son of Bishop William Heathcote De Lancey, Mrs. Cooper's brother.

87.20 Mr. McAdam: Cooper's brother-in-law John Loudon McAdam. See 250.3, and note.

88.32-35 Sir Nathaniel . . . he accepted: Sir N. W. Wraxall, *Posthumous Memoirs of His Own Time* (Philadelphia, 1836), p. 38.

90.6-7 our *chargé*: William Beach Lawrence (1800-1881), *chargé d'affaires* in London.

91.2 JAMES STEVENSON: (1789?-1852), prominent citizen and lawyer of Albany, a close friend of Cooper since boyhood.
Stevenson is also named as recipient of Letters XIX (215.2) and XXV (276.2).

93.17-18 Capt. Hall . . . England: See note for 269.29-30.

94.9 Barclay's big butts: Barclay Perkins (Anchor Brewery, Southwark, London) had porter vats of varying size, the largest with a 3000 barrel capacity.

95.6-8 his eldest son . . . "Jack: John Charles Spencer (1782-1845), Viscount Althorp.

96.26-38 The simple . . . associate with equals: Cf. *Letters and Journals*, I, 358.

100.7 "repent . . . suddenly,": *I Henry IV*, III.iii.5.

101.21-25 George III . . . such a declaration: The quotation is an essentially correct paraphrase of what George III said to John Adams when he received him as minister to England. See Charles Francis Adams, ed., *The Works of John Adams* (Boston, 1850-1856), VIII, 257.

101.33-102.4 The dying speech of Desaix . . . It would seem not: At the moment of his victory at the Battle of Marengo, the dying General Desaix is reported to have said: "Tell the First Consul that my only regret in dying is to have perished before having done enough to live in the recollection of posterity." He was buried at Saint Bernard, near the summit of the Alps; and Napoleon reportedly declared: "The tomb of Desaix shall have the Alps for its pedestal, and the monks of Saint Bernard for its guardians."

101.35 Duc de [Valmy]: Cooper's source was undoubtedly his Parisian acquaintance, François de Kellermann (1770-1835), the Duc de Valmy, who led the charge at Marengo.

103.2 WILLIAM JAY: (1789-1858), son of Governor John Jay and lifelong friend of Cooper from their student days in Albany and at Yale.

   Jay is also designated as recipient of Letters XII (131.2), XIII (145.2), and XVIII (199.2).

103.12-14 speeches attributed . . . grinding line: From 1741 to 1744, using only the scantiest notes surreptitiously made by others, Samuel Johnson "reported" a series of Parliamentary debates for the *Gentleman's Magazine*, creating speeches for members of both parties. These debates were taken as authentic by many readers, and some of the speeches even found their way into the collected works of their supposed authors. Other writers besides Johnson performed such hack work.

107.11 Walker: John Walker's *A Critical Pronouncing Dictionary and Expositor of the English Language . . . To Which Are Prefixed, Principles of English Pronunciation* (London, 1791). Many American editions followed in the early nineteenth century.

110.24-27 entrance of a Mr. Sadler . . . spoke: Michael T. Sadler (1780-1835) entered Parliament in 1829 and delivered his maiden speech on 17 March 1829. Thus, Cooper's reference to Sadler's maiden speech is probably not to be interpreted literally.

116.2 JAMES E. DE KAY: James Ellsworth De Kay (1792-1851), natural-
ist, physician, author, and member of Cooper's Bread and Cheese
Club. De Kay published a book of travels, *Sketches of Turkey by an
American* (1833), but his *chef-d'œuvre* was his five-volume *Zoology
of New York* (1842-1844), part of an official natural history survey of
the State.
De Kay is also designated recipient of Letter XXIV (266.2).

117.2-3 Mr. Dumont . . . Mirabeau: Pierre Étienne Louis Dumont's *Sou-
venirs sur Mirabeau* was not published until 1832.

117.20-24 He alluded . . . reason for it: The English common law precluded inheritance of real estate by relatives of the half-blood.
That is, children and collateral descendants of second or subsequent marriages could not inherit from children of first marriages.
According to Sir William Blackstone, this law was intended to
insure that real estate would always descend lineally from the
"first purchaser," the closest antecedent owner to have acquired
the property by means other than inheritance. In fact, as Cooper
apparently intended to suggest to Mackintosh, Blackstone's explanation was absurd because the law, taking cognizance of the impossibility of proof of descent in all cases, permitted inheritance if the
claimant were next of the whole blood to the person last in possession. See Blackstone, *Commentaries on the Laws of England* (Oxford,
1766), II, 228-30.

117.32 merits of the "Three Estates,": See also 136.10-17ff.

119.15-17 he held . . . St. Maur: Cooper refers to his first meeting with
Sir Walter Scott on the stairs of his Hôtel on 3 November 1826. See
Gleanings in Europe: France, Letter XII.

120.5-7 My plan . . . totally failed: Cooper's plan, that Scott permit his
Life of Napoleon Buonaparte (1827) to be copyrighted in whole or
in part as the assigned property of a U.S. citizen, would not have
conformed to the American statute which restricted American copy-
right to works written by United States citizens. Scott's own plan
was essentially an appeal to the generosity of Carey, Lea, and
Carey and other American publishers. See *Letters and Journals*, I,
170-80, and H. J. C. Grierson, ed., *The Letters of Sir Walter Scott,
1826-1828* (London, 1936), 122-24.

123.20-24 I had just . . . English favour: *The Red Rover*, for which Henry
Colburn, the English publisher, paid Cooper £400.

124.30-31 wife of the Bishop of London: Mary Frances Belli, who in 1805
married William Howley (1766-1848), Bishop of London at the
time of Cooper's visit. See also note for 128.28-31.

124.38-39 while Commodore Morris was in command: Cooper is in
error. Commodore Richard V. Morris was recalled to the United
States in September 1803; Coleridge arrived in Malta in May 1804,
became Sir Alexander Ball's private secretary in July, and served
temporarily as public secretary between January and September
1805. The commanders of the American squadron during his
tenure were Commodores Edward Preble, who had followed Morris, Samuel Barron, who assumed command on 10 September 1804,
and John Rodgers, who succeeded Barron on 22 May 1805.

125.1-16 The late Captain . . . hired felucca: It was not Captain William
Bainbridge, but his brother, Midshipman Joseph Bainbridge, who
fought the duel in February 1803. His second was Lieutenant
Stephen Decatur. Although the Englishman has been identified as
a man named Cochran, the secretary of Sir Alexander Ball, Donald
Sultana has pointed out that Ball had no secretary by that name
nor were any of his three secretaries killed (*Samuel Taylor Coleridge in Malta and Italy* [New York, 1969], pp. 160-61). The Americans may, of course, have been mistaken in the official position
of the Englishman.

125.23-25 Commodore Rodgers . . . Little Belt: the 44-gun U.S. frigate
President, Captain John Rodgers, disabled the 20-gun British
corvette *Little Belt* after she failed to identify herself on 16 May
1811 off Cape Charles.

127.1-128.4 the conversation turned . . . eloquence: For Scott's impressions of the incident, see his journal entry of 22 April 1828. *The
Journal of Sir Walter Scott*, ed. W. E. K. Anderson (Oxford, 1972),
p. 462.

127.1-3 Homer . . . translating: William Sotheby's *Iliad* appeared in
1831, his *Odyssey* in 1834.

128.28-31 I told . . . Canterbury: Bishop Howley was translated to the
See of Canterbury in July 1828.

133.7-8 Mr. Wortley . . . America: Cooper had accompanied John Stuart-
Wortley (1801-1855) and several other Englishmen on part of their
sight-seeing trip to Saratoga, Ticonderoga, and Lakes George and
Champlain during their tour of the United States and Canada in
1824-1825.

135.33-34 trial of the late queen: Queen Caroline of Brunswick, spouse
of George IV, was tried in 1820 for adultery.

140.39-40 Why . . . American Union: Compare *Letters and Journals*, I,
288; II, 23.

142.27 Lord Stanley: Cooper first met Edward George Geoffrey Smith
Stanley (1799-1869) on his trip to North America in 1824-1825 and

accompanied him on part of his tour of New York. See also note for 133.7-8.

147.36-148.3 Sir James . . . may have decayed: Sir James Mackintosh, *History of the Revolution in England in 1688* (London, 1834), p. 200.

150.22-36 Lord [Lansdowne] . . . becoming his station: Cf. *Letters and Journals*, I, 357.

155.5 a clergyman of the true English school: Thomas Ellison (1759-1802).

157.33-36 "The *rebel* vales . . . echoes sounded,": Francis Hopkinson's "British Valour Displayed; or, The Battle of the Kegs" (1778), from which Cooper quotes lines 65-68, satirized the British response to American use of floating mines in the Delaware River.

161.5 sister of the poet: Sarah Rogers (d. 1855).

161.16-17 Princess of Wales . . . at Blackheath: After she moved to Montague House, Blackheath, in 1801, rumors of loose conduct circulated about Princess Caroline, who had been separated from the Prince of Wales, later George IV, since 1796.

166.4-5 a party . . . Rogers: Scott made the excursion to Hampton Court with Rogers and Thomas Moore on 25 May 1828.

169.10-16 Mr. Mathews . . . other hill: Cooper escorted Charles Mathews (1776-1835) on a tour up the Hudson in April 1823.

170.3-4 "hide . . . bushel,": See Matthew v.15.

170.17 "a saint . . . in lawn,": Alexander Pope, *Epistles to Several Persons (Moral Essays)*, "Epistle I. To Sir Richard Temple, Lord Viscount Cobham," 1. 88.

176.2 MRS. COMSTOCK: Sarah Sabina Cooper (1812-1846), daughter of Cooper's brother Isaac and Mary Ann Morris, married Horace Hawkins Comstock in 1833. She was taken by her husband to Comstock, Michigan, where she died young.

177.4 a bachelor: William George Spencer Cavendish (1790-1858), sixth Duke of Devonshire, lord chamberlain of the king's household during two intervals.

183.25-26 according to . . . into Draper: See *Gleanings in Europe: France*, Letter XXIII.

184.29-31 The mistress . . . respectable standing: probably Anne Louisa Bingham (d. 1848), wife of Alexander Baring (1774-1848), first Baron Ashburton, and daughter of Senator William Bingham of Philadelphia.

184.37-38 The quadrilles . . . already mentioned: See *Gleanings in Europe: France*, Letter XVIII.

189.28-31 Raritan below Brunswick . . . passage of the Kilns: The "Kilns" refers to the many brick manufacturing plants located during the nineteenth century on the lower Raritan River near Perth Amboy and South Amboy, New Jersey. Brunswick is, of course, New Brunswick, New Jersey.

194.24 monument: a fluted column, 202 feet tall, designed and erected in 1677 by Sir Christopher Wren to commemorate the Great Fire of 1666.

192.38 Gog and Magog: giant wooden warriors in gaudy costumes standing over 14 feet tall, carved in 1708.

195.39 Blue-coat School: Christ's Hospital, so-called for the uniform of its pupils.

196.18-27 I was on . . . as snow: Compare *Letters and Journals*, I, 210.

201.1-2 "the love . . . evil.": I Timothy vi.10; quoted also at 207.29-30.

203.31-204.1 The left . . . has done: an inversion of the idea in Matthew vi.3.

205.38-39 gave a peerage . . . the others: Dorothea or Dorothy Jordan (1762-1816), a well-known actress, became the mistress of the Duke of Clarence, later William IV, in 1790, and bore him ten children, who went by the name of Fitzclarence. The oldest son, George, was created Duke of Munster; the other sons and daughters were given the rank of children of a marquis.

206.28-29 intrigue with the "Fair Quaker,": Although as a very young man, George III may have been infatuated with Hannah Lightfoot, the "Fair Quaker," the legend that flourished later in his life of a love affair—and even a marriage—between the two seems unfounded.

206.32-36 French song . . . Marlborough: The subject of "La Chanson de Malbrough," the first verse of which Cooper quotes, was John Churchill (1650-1722), first Duke of Marlborough, commander of the British army at the victory of Blenheim (1704).

211.14-26 A work . . . authority: Possibly Edward Bulwer's *Pelham*, published 10 June 1828 by Henry Colburn, who paid £500 for it. Ignored by the great reviews and treated contemptuously or coldly by most others, the book did not sell well for the first two months, but became, shortly thereafter, a great popular and financial success.

211.20 "damned it with faint praise": See Alexander Pope, "An Epistle to Dr. Arbuthnot," 1. 201.

218.40 the begging mission of Bishop Chase: Bishop Philander Chase (1775-1852) went to England in 1823 to raise funds to establish Kenyon College.

223.4-5 the "lions" have been sold: Since a large menagerie was still kept at the Tower of London in 1829 and was not moved to the

Zoological Gardens in Regent's Park until 1834, Cooper may be recalling here his visit of 1833.

223.27-30 Unfortunately . . . its interest: Cooper probably refers to Sir Samuel Rush Meyrick's *A Critical Inquiry into Antient Armour*, 3 vols. (London, 1824).

223.31 "Where ignorance . . . wise.": Thomas Gray, "Ode on a Distant Prospect of Eton College," 11. 99-100.

224.16-18 showed us the axe . . . "little neck.": On the morning of her execution, Anne Boleyn reportedly observed that the headsman was said to be "very good—and I have a little neck," at which she put her hands about it "laughing heartily." See Hester W. Chapman, *Anne Boleyn* (London, 1974), p. 223. Anne was beheaded not with an axe, but with a two-handed sword.

225.33-35 that passage . . . for the soul: Luke xiv.7-11.

229.12-13 I shook . . . quitting that house: a variation of Matthew x.14 (also in Mark, Luke, and Acts).

230.2 JACOB SUTHERLAND: A lawyer and jurist from Blenheim, Schoharie County, New York, Sutherland (1787?-1845) was a friend of the novelist from their student days at Yale. Cooper dedicated *The Pioneers* to him.

Sutherland is also designated as recipient of Letter XXVI (285.2).

230.14-16 Captain Hall . . . educations: Basil Hall attributes the insufficiency of American education to the lures and rewards of active life. See *Travels in North America* (Edinburgh, 1829), II, 170-75.

231.21-26 One of the traits . . . its existence: Basil Hall, *Travels in North America* (Edinburgh, 1829), II, 45; and Frederick F. De Roos, *Personal Narrative of Travels in the United States and Canada in 1826* (London, 1827), p. 54.

231.27-31 I quote . . . *English tone*.": Bishop Reginald Heber, *Narrative of a Journey Through the Upper Provinces of India* (London, 1828), I, xxv. The italics are Cooper's.

234.13-14 Captain Hall . . . confess it: See note for 67.11.

235.15-19 Capt. Hall . . . penetration: See Basil Hall, *Travels in North America* (Edinburgh, 1829), III, 393-94.

236.29-38 "It has affected . . . London, 1782: *Memoirs of the Life and Correspondence of Mrs. Hannah More* (London, 1834), I, 251; (New York, 1835), II, 146. The exclamation points and italics are Cooper's.

237.29-39 the conductor . . . a sealing: Samuel Carter Hall (1800-1889), editor of Colburn's *New Monthly Magazine*, wrote in "Captain

Beechey's Narrative" (*New Monthly Magazine*, XXXI [April, 1831], 373-82): "it has just been announced that the crew of a discovery ship, fitted out by the American Government, has actually mutinied and landed their officers 'bag and baggage,' on the coast of Peru" (pp. 373-74). For Cooper's refutation of this account, see his letter to S. C. Hall, 21 May 1831 (*Letters and Journals*, II, 83-85).

238.22-26 Hermione . . . Nore: The mutinies of the *Bounty*, 28 April 1789, and the *Hermione*, 22 September 1797, involved single ships. The mutiny at the Nore near the mouth of the Thames involved a fleet of more than twenty ships and lasted from 12 May to 15 June 1797.

240.18 Orders in Council: Between 1793 and 1810, the British ministry issued a series of orders curtailing and ultimately forbidding under penalty of seizure all trading of neutral vessels with French controlled ports. United States commerce was severely affected.

242.19-20 "hypocrisy . . . virtue,": François, Duc de la Rochefoucauld, *Maxims*, No. 218.

249.14-17 In allusion to . . . our citizens: The quotation may be found in George Tucker, *The Life of Thomas Jefferson* (Philadelphia, 1837), I, 61. Jefferson refers to a paper he had written—"A Summary View of the Rights of British America" (1774)—in which he presented the grievances of the colonies in a manner that many were not yet willing to accept.

250.2 HENRY FLOYD-JONES: Major General Henry Onderdonk Floyd-Jones (1792-1862), a cousin of Mrs. Cooper and a brother of Thomas Floyd-Jones. See also note 68.2.

250.10-11 the death of . . . John Loudon McAdam: John Loudon McAdam (1756-1836) died on 26 November. His first wife was Gloriana Margaretta Nicoll (1759-1825); his second was Anne Charlotte De Lancey (1786-1852), Mrs. Cooper's sister.

251.21-25 John Gilpin's race . . . I had thought: Cooper's "classical authority" for the use of wigs by coachmen is William Cowper's poem "The Diverting History of John Gilpin." For the "Bell, at Edmonton," see 1.11.

252.25 the Croton: The Croton aqueduct, authorized by the legislature in 1834, was intended to bring water to New York City from the Croton watershed over thirty miles away.

254.23 Blenheims and Eatons: Blenheim Palace, near Oxford, seat of the Duke of Marlborough, was designed in 1705 and completed in 1724; Eaton Hall, near Chester, was rebuilt on an extensive plan by Robert Grosvenor between 1804 and 1812.

254.30 love in a cottage: the phrase apparently derives from George
Colman and David Garrick's *The Clandestine Marriage* (1766),
I, ii: "Love and a cottage! Eh, Fanny! Ah, give me indifference
and a coach and six!"

259.21-23 Mr. Cobbett . . . proves something: See *Cobbett's Political
Register*, LXXXV, 7 (16 August 1834), 402. See also LXXXIV, 1
(5 April 1834), 13-14.

266.21-25 The play . . . presented to us: Cooper may refer to James
Robinson Planché's *The Merchant's Wedding; or, London Frolics in
1638*, performed five times during his stay in London: 25 March,
8 April, 12 April, 17 April, and 21 May 1828.

269.29-30 Captain Hall . . . only half furnished: Cooper's references to
Basil Hall's *Travels in North America* (Edinburgh, 1829) here and
at 93.17-18 are puzzling. Most of Hall's explicit statements concern
well-furnished houses in Canada and the United States (I, 264,
274; III, 178, 316). Cooper may be recalling a reference to the ball
room in the White House ("The suite of apartments thrown open
consisted of two handsomely furnished drawing-rooms, leading to
a well proportioned ball-room, which, however, I was surprised to
find entirely unfurnished and bare," III, 14), or drawing an inference from Hall's stated belief that a society without laws of entail
and primogeniture cannot achieve a permanently wealthy class
who "consider refinements and luxuries as necessaries of life" (II,
27). See also note for 269.33-34. The review mentioned there may
also have influenced Cooper's memory of the book.

269.30-32 Duke Bernhard . . . Great Britain: See *Reise Sr. Hoheit des
Herzogs Bernhard zu Sachsen-Weimar-Eisenach durch Nord-America
in den Jahren 1825 und 1826* (Weimar, 1828), pp. 80-81.

269.33-34 Quarterly joins issue . . . *German* Duke: See the *Quarterly
Review*, 41 (Nov. 1829), 417-447, esp. 421.

270.19 birthday: 23 April 1828, St. George's Day, kept as the anniversary
of the King's birthday.

271.4 tall men of Frederic: The Potsdam guard of Frederick William
I of Prussia, a regiment of giants recruited — and sometimes
kidnapped — from all over Europe, later disbanded by his son,
Frederick II, "the Great."

273.32 bags: silk pouches for the back hair of wigs.

274.22 "sear and yellow leaf,": *Macbeth* V.iii.23.

274.25 *gammes*: musical scales (French).

276.12 *grani*: Neapolitan coins used from the fourteenth to the nineteenth century.

283.23 *Passons au déluge*: Colloquially, "Come to the point," from Racine's *Les Plaideurs*, III.iii.

285.8 The wise policy of Alexander: Alexander I of Russia cultivated United States commerce while still an ally of Napoleon because he wished to lessen British commercial dominance.

285.23 the Henry plot: In 1812 President Madison purchased from John Henry, a former spy for the Canadian governor, papers purporting to disclose a British plot to destroy the American union.

285.31-286.2 certain instructor . . . of himself: Probably Timothy Dwight (1752-1817), President of Yale while Cooper and Sutherland were students. He was attacked in the *Quarterly Review*, 2 (Nov. 1809), 330. Dwight responded vigorously to unfavorable comments on American culture in the *Edinburgh Review* and the *Quarterly Review*. His *Travels in New England and New York*, published posthumously in 1821-1822, was intended, in part, to refute foreign misrepresentations of the United States.

287.13-18 article of the Edinburgh Review . . . abandoned: Cooper probably refers to Article XII in the *Edinburgh Review*, 24 (Nov. 1814), 243-65, with the running title "War with America." See esp. pp. 250, 252.

288.8 Age of Reason . . . Illuminati: Thomas Paine's *The Age of Reason* (1794-1795) and the Illuminati, a secret society founded in Bavaria in 1776, were widely attacked as being rationalistic and anti-religious.

289.34-290.10 Mr. Huskisson . . . truth I know: William Huskison (1770-1830), associated with French liberals in Paris before the Revolution, was present at the fall of the Bastille, and, in 1790, joined a monarchical constitutional club, the Club of 1789. He later broke with the club over French economic policy and became private secretary to the British ambassador to France. Though Huskisson was known for his free trade opinions and policies, Cooper may be referring to an incident in 1828 when, as a member of the government, he was forced by the Duke of Wellington to withdraw a statement that a free trade policy would continue under the Duke, the new Prime Minister.

290.21-25 Mr. Cobbett . . . Union to the winds: See *Cobbett's Political Register*, LXXIX, 4 (26 Jan. 1833), 202. See also LXVI, 7 (16 Aug. 1828), 209-14; LXVIII, 2 (11 July 1829), 56-61; LXXIV, 5 (29 Oct. 1831), 302.

293.24 congress of Panama: called by Simon Bolivar for 1826 to form a defensive union of American republics.

297.20 the Round Peak: probably Round Top Mountain in the Catskills, about nine miles northwest of the town of Catskill, New York.

297.29-31 "which I feel . . . British empire,": Bishop Reginald Heber, *Narrative of a Journey Through the Upper Provinces of India* (London, 1828), II, 407.

303.15n-304.30n Mrs. Butler . . . comments of travellers: Frances Anne Kemble (1809-1893), the English actress, came to America in 1832 and married a southern planter, Pierce Butler, in 1834. The opinions of Mrs. Butler cited by Cooper may be found in her *Journal* (Philadelphia, 1835): on American love of largeness, II, 93; on the dissolution of the Union, I, 188, II, 23-24; on the independence of tradespeople, I, 232-33, II, 11-12; on the noisy romps of the young, especially girls, I, 160-61, 202; on the tendency toward aristocracy, I, 196-97, II, 204; on English and French insensitivity to travellers' criticism, II, 103.

303.41n-304.25n Mrs. Trollope . . . calculations of profit: Frances Milton Trollope (1780-1863) preceded her husband to Cincinnati in 1828 to start a business and recoup their fortunes. Her sharply critical book, *Domestic Manners of the Americans*, was published in 1832.

304.35 Pillet, d'Haussez, and Puckler-Muskau: Europeans who wrote unfavorable reports of England: Réne Martin Pillet, *L'Angleterre vue à Londres* (Paris, 1815); Charles le Mercher de Longpré, Baron d'Haussez, *La Grande-Bretagne en 1833* (Paris, 1833); Hermann Ludwig Heinrich, Fürst von Pückler-Muskau, *Briefe eines Verstorbenen* (Stuttgart, 1831).

305.2 CAPTAIN B. COOPER: Benjamin (d. 1850), a distant relative of the novelist (their grandfathers were cousins), who served with Cooper on the *Wasp* in 1809-1810 and became his life-long friend.

307.24-25 Point Judith . . . Sound: Point Judith, R.I.; Long Island Sound.

308.14 Boom Key: probably Boompjes ("little trees"), principal quay in Rotterdam harbor.

Appendix A
Bentley's Analytical Table of Contents

LETTER I.   Page 5
Embark for Dover. Straits. Town. Cliffs and Port. Contrast
between England and France. Military Works. Shakspeare's
Cliff. View from the Heights. Feelings regarding England.
Alien Office. English Post-coach. Rotten Roads. Tea in
England.

LETTER II.   15
Canterbury. The Cathedral. Road to London. Rating of
Ships. English Roads. Arrival in London. English order.
Yankee Doodle. Lodging-houses.

LETTER III.   22
A London Season. Love of Travelling. Letters of
Introduction. Odious Duplicity. Visiting List. Interview
with Mr. Godwin. Godwin's Opinions. A literary Lady.
Mr. Rogers. American Pronunciation. Mr. Rogers's House.
Dwellings near the Parks. Mr. Rogers's Library. Chantrey
the Sculptor.

LETTER IV.   33
Westminster Abbey. Poets' Corner. Chapel of Henry VII.
Monuments in the Abbey. André's Monument. English Art.
The Parliament Houses. Westminster Hall. St. Stephen's
Chapel. House of Lords. St. Paul's. Statue of Queen Anne.
View from the Dome. English Cicerones. Catholic
Cathedrals. Interior of St. Paul's. St. Peter's and St. Paul's.
Clerical Officials.

LETTER V.   43
English Society. Continental Society. Gentry of England.
English Nobility. Social Ambition. Social Condition of
England. Aristocratical Knocking. Artificial Behaviour.

Tyranny of Custom. Easy Impertinence. Lord John Russell.
Sir James Mackintosh's Opinions of America. Mr. Rogers's
Déjeûners. Breakfasts of St. James's Place.

LETTER VI.   54
Invitations. Mania of Scribbling. Holland House and
Grounds. Dinner. Dutch Herrings. Curious Mistake.
Punctuality. Bishop of London. Saying Grace. Dr. Hobart.
The Ballot. Fashionable Coachman. Tuft Hunting. Coup de
Politesse. Prejudice against the Americans.

LETTER VII.   68
London in the Season. English Coachmen and Carriages.
Abuse of Words. Mr. William Spencer. The Parks. English
Horses. The King's Equipage. Fashionable Marriages.
Equipages. Armorial Bearings. English Footmen. The
Higher Classes. Englishmen and Americans. Stature of
English Women. Duration of Human Life. Complexion of
the English. Lady Affleck. Englishwomen. Sedan Chairs.

LETTER VIII.   80
Squares and Parks. Norfolk House. Houses of the Nobility.
Regent Street. Regent's Park. Climate of London. The
Thames. Climate of England and America. The Spring in
England. Hyde Park. St. James's Park. Exclusiveness.
Privilege of the Entrée. Reception of Americans.

LETTER IX.   91
Dinner at Lord Grey's. Furniture of English Houses. Forms
of Society. The Genteel Vulgar. Domestic Manners.
Decorations of the Nobility. George the Fourth. The late
Duke of York. Courtly Manners. Charles the Tenth.

LETTER X.   103
The English Parliament. Lord Althorp and Mr. Peel. Sir
Francis Burdett. Mr. Hume. Parliamentary Debates. Mr.
Sadler. Power of the Parliament. The Right of Petition.

LETTER XI.   116
Sir Walter Scott. Sir James Mackintosh. Seemliness of
England. Close Corporations. Copyright. English
Literature. Works of Sir Walter Scott. Mr. Sotheby.

Mr. Coleridge. Commodore Rodgers. Conversations of
Mr. Coleridge. English Ladies. Free Trade.

LETTER XII.   131
The House of Lords. Chamber of Deputies. Marquis of
Salisbury. Affected Pronunciation. Parliament of England.
The King and the Parliament. Peers and Commoners. Public
opinion. The Mercantile Class. The Public Press. The
Church. English Aristocracy. Nobility and Gentry. Mr.
Brougham.

LETTER XIII.   145
The People of England. Reform. Condition of England.
Taxes and Commerce. Condition of the Aristocracy. New
Peerage. Institutions of England. A Money-Government.
Wealth of Lord Grosvenor; and of the Nobility and Gentry.
Power of the Aristocracy. Morals of the Upper Classes.
The Professions. Manliness of the Gentry. Prejudices of the
Aristocracy. National Prejudices. Respect paid to Rank.
Princely Nobility.

LETTER XIV.   159
Sir Thomas Lawrence. Mr. Leslie. Mr. Newton. Dinner at
Mr. Rogers's. The Princess of Wales and Sir Walter Scott.
Mr. "Conversation" Sharp. English Society. Mrs. Siddons.
Mrs. Lockhart. Sir Walter and Lady Scott. Mr. Rogers.

LETTER XV.   167
Vicinity of London. English Landscapes. Parks. Richmond
Hill. Twickenham. Strawberry Hill. Windsor Castle. St.
George's Chapel.

LETTER XVI.   176
Dancing. Englishwomen. Balls. Exclusive Society. American
Toad-eaters. A subtle distinction of Character. Sir James
Scarlett. Ludicrous Mistake. Visit to a Merchant.
Honourables and Right Honourables. English Dancing. A
Young American Girl. Visit to a Patrician. English Girls.
Unfeminine Manners. English Ladies and Gentlemen.

LETTER XVII.   189
The Thames. Its Bridges. The Boar's Head. First Visit to
London. My two Cicerones. An American Sailor at the
West-end. Notions of Liberty. Rundell and Bridge.
Jewellery. English Plate. A Royal Salver. Anecdote of
George IV.

LETTER XVIII.   199
Venders of Lies. Periodical Press. Influence of Money. The
English Press. Influence of the Aristocracy. Personal Abuse.
Abuse of America. English Reviews. American Enterprise.
Influence of Mediocrity. Literary Quackery. Literary Fraud.
Electioneering Lies. Abuses of the Press. The Press in
England and America.

LETTER XIX.   215
My Reception in England. Rudeness of the English. A
female Dandy. A Discovery. Eggs. Democracy and Drunkenness. Conversation with Mr. Brougham. Fashionable
Novels. Children of Rank. Homage to Rank.

LETTER XX.   223
Tower of London. Old Implements of War in the Armoury.
English Rudeness and French Politeness. Order of
Precedence. American Pronunciation. National Peculiarity.
Right of Impressment. Effect of a Hint. Anecdote.

LETTER XXI.   230
English Prejudice. Misrepresentations. National
Abasement. Jealousy of America. Unfriendly Feeling.
English Loyalty. Social Drilling. English and French
Servants. English and American Seamen. Subordination.
Gradations in Society. Declaration of War. Established
Religion. Duelling Clergymen. Young Napoleon. Strange
Opinion. Vulgar Prejudices. Absurd Accusation. National
Conceit. Deportment of Congress. Prejudice against
America. Literary Empiricism. National Peculiarities.

LETTER XXII.   250
Mr. M'Adam. English Highways. Rye-house. American
Emigrants. Partisanship. Invasion of England. Roydon-
house. Growth of London. English Colonies. Power of the

United States. Independence of Canada. Colonial System of
England. Foreign Policy. Popular Feeling. Influence
of London.

LETTER XXIII.   260
Mr. Coleridge. Singular Anecdote. Phrenology. Joanna
Baillie. Boxing. Prejudices of the English against America.
Immensity of London. Want of a Capital.

LETTER XXIV.   266
London Passages. National Theatres. The Stage. Captain
Hall. American Society and Pronunciation. Royal Birth-day.
The Horse-Guards. American Grandiloquence. Gorgeous
Spectacle. Line of Carriages. Female Beauty. Coachmen.
A Royal Princess. Newspaper Reports.

LETTER XXV.   276
Poor of England. Servants of all-work. Continental
Domestics. American Slaves. Poverty in England. Human
Happiness. Spirit of Gain. Want of Happiness. Music in
England. Street Music.

LETTER XXVI.   285
Apprehension of Russia. Anglo-mania. Foreign Policy.
Re-colonization. Schemes of Demagogues. Anecdote.
Mr. Huskisson. Mr. Cobbett. English Critics and English
Influence. National Weakness. English Jealousy.
Administration of Mr. Adams.

LETTER XXVII.   294
Physical Differences between the English and Americans.
Moral Differences. Resistance to Law. English and
American Pride. Sensibility to Comments. Statistical Facts.
Peculiarities of America. Its Civilisation. The American
System. English Independence. Unsocial Habits. English
Taste. Mrs. Butler and Mrs. Trollope. English Intelligence.

LETTER XXIII.   305
Alien Office. Taking a Passage. Struggles for a Subsistence.
Our Embarkation. Approach to Holland. Dutch Wagons.
Farewell to England.

TEXTUAL APPARATUS

Textual Commentary

With the exception of one leaf of manuscript, the copy-text of *Gleanings in Europe: England* is the first American edition, a single impression of 2,000 copies,[1] published by Carey, Lea and Blanchard in two volumes in Philadelphia on 2 September 1837.[2] Set from Cooper's manuscript, it is the only printed text to which Cooper gave close attention; and, except for one leaf (recto and verso) of the manuscript, it is the only authorial form. All known evidence indicates that Cooper followed the procedures he established for his three earlier travel books (*Switzerland*, *The Rhine*, and *France*) in supplying Richard Bentley, his English publisher, with printer's copy: that is, he submitted manuscript to Carey for the American edition, corrected Carey's proofs carefully, and then transmitted to England the corrected sheets or revises pulled from Carey's formes. He thus assisted Bentley to obtain the priority of publication requisite to British copy-right and avoided the inconvenience and delay that would have resulted from reading Bentley's proofs.[3] Bentley's edition of *England*, entitled *England. With Sketches of Society in the Metropolis*, appeared in London on 29 May 1837 in three volumes, from an impression of 1,250 copies[4]—more than three months before the Carey, Lea and Blanchard.[5] The only other contemporaneous edition was published under the separate imprints of Baudry's European Library and A. and W. Galignani on 12 August 1837.[6] Printed by J. Smith and deriving from the Bentley, it is twice removed from possible authorial intervention and need not be considered further.

The copy-text for a portion of Chapter XX—224.8 through 227.5 in the Cooper Edition (*Plantes* than the imperial crown of Great Britain . . . nothing sooner than in their modes)—is a single leaf of manuscript.[7] The leaf is part of Carey's printer's copy, for the compositor's signature "Gates" precedes the paragraph beginning "There are some curious old implements . . ." (224.14); a compositor's bracket indicates the page division between the words "just before" (225.18-19); and a hand other than Cooper's has written towards the bottom of the recto: Vol ii/II/121. For these five pages of the Carey printing, the Cooper Edition follows the manuscript as copy-text.

If the comparison between the leaf and its corresponding Carey text is any indication, Cooper seems to have paid close attention to the sheets when he traveled to Philadelphia to read proof.[8] Comparison between the manuscript leaf and the Carey edition shows bold revisions reminiscent of those Cooper made for other works like *The Prairie*. At 224.12-13, for example, after commenting on the rapacity of James II^d, he seems to have added the ironic clause, "although he ran away from his kingdom." At 226.13-14, the manuscript suggests that Cooper did not inquire after the identity of the father of a young man seated on the right of his dinner hostess, but his apparent revision in proof implies the opposite: "I believe he was the Duke of _____." The anecdote describing French manners (225.14-29) undergoes a complex series of changes. The experience, the manuscript reveals, was Cooper's own, for he speaks of his own treatment by Madame de _____ at a party given in his honor. But the Carey edition attributes it to G_____ and assiduously renders all the first-person references in the third person, displaying a series of related authorial revisions in proof. Other less striking differences show Cooper's pursuit of a more precise style: at 225.6, "thought it altogether" becomes "thought the movement"; at 225.28, "social tones" becomes "social tact"; at 225.36-37, "that I was the only one . . . who bethought" becomes "that no one else . . . bethought." In addition, other revisions manifest efforts towards a more colloquial style (at 226.10-11, "high military station" becomes "high in the army") and resolution of ambiguity (at 226.24-25, "His body he had himself found" becomes "He had himself found the body"). In short, the comparison between the manuscript leaf and the corresponding Carey text demonstrates Cooper's characteristic scrupulous attention to the proof while it evidences the usual corruption of punctuation and spelling—and, in two instances, apparent misreadings[9]—imposed by the compositors.

Striking differences between the text and format of the American and British editions of England would insinuate Cooper's intervention in the Bentley edition, a possiblity dispelled by the circumstances of the two publications. While Cooper was completing *England* and preparing to see it through the press, its publication was uncertain. The poor sales of *Switzerland, The Rhine,* and *France* had almost exhausted Carey's and Bentley's qualified interest in the travel series. On the supposition that "[t]his work will excite more interest in your world than the others," Cooper had offered *England* to Bentley for £350 as early as 19 November 1836.[10] Then, in an unlocated letter of 26 December 1836, he sounded out Carey, Lea and Blanchard, who replied on 4 January 1837; "Send on the M.S. at your convenience and we shall try to get on with it [with] as little trouble to you as may be."[11] Pleading a "long continued

XVII. Manuscript leaf of pp. 224.8-225.24 (*recto*)
(*Courtesy Paul Fenimore Cooper, Jr.*)

took the arms of the President-elect, and walking towards me, she did me the honor to present me to Mad. de Talleyrand, who was of the party, and whom I had the honor of leading to the dinner table. There are trifles, but they are just the trifles that mark the difference between the tones of London, and that of Paris. 135

I could not divest myself of the idea that, had I been any thing but an American, this gross neglect could not have occurred, and when I found that precisely the lowest seat at the table was left for me, I endeavoured to recall that passage in holy writ, where one is admonished to take the lowest seat at a feast; although we have no established religion in America, I will be bold enough to say that I was the only one that day, who bethought him of this text.

My companion, after all, proved to be a connexion, for the seat at the foot of the table, has been left for him. The master of the house sat at the head of the table, and the mistress in the centre, according to the French mode. As so much care had been taken of myself, I felt curious in what manner the others had been provided for. A swarthy, dark haired, young man sat on the right of the mistress of the house, while old Lord B—— who was a full General in the army, occupied a more humble situation. This young man was also a soldier, for I heard him talking of a campaign he had made, but by his years he could not have been more than a colonel. Of course he must have been of a position or social rank higher than either of the two earls, and this, in England, would give him precedence of his own father! I did not enquire who he was.

A handsome, well-mannered young man sat on my left. Indeed our end of the table was pretty much occupied by the boys, since I began to apprehend a vanity on account of a few grey hairs that time is beginning to scatter on my temples. They were well behaved lads, however, I suppose on account of their being in parliament, as I found, by the conversation, was the case with the whole of them. They had all been rowing on the Thames, that morning, and as I had urged the oar myself, in my time, we had something to talk about.

The black haired dignitary who gave an account of the death of some officer whom he had seen shot in battle. His body he had himself found after the affair, he added, and, "it had been stripped by the French soldiers." "Why not by our own?" put in my young neighbor, rather pettishly. "Because I do not think any of ours had been near" was the answer, but it sounded like an evidence pre-dice.

It appeared well on the part of my neighbor, to raise the question, and I fell into discourse with him. He had discovered that I was an American by a remark of my right-hand companion who knew whom I was, and he soon began to speak of the difference in language between the English and Americans. He told me he had just come from Paris, and that in walking in the Palais Royal, he had been struck with the pronunciation of three men who were walking before him. Their dialect was provincial, and he had been at a loss to discover from what part of England they had come, when he ascertained by their discourse, they were Americans.

I told him we had several castes in America, as in England, though they were less strongly marked than common; and that men, of course, betrayed their association in nothing, sooner than in their

XVIII. Manuscript leaf of pp. 225.24–227.8 (verso)
(Courtesy Paul Fenimore Cooper, Jr.)

illness," Bentley responded to Cooper's letter of 19 November on 19 February: "[T]he result of the publication of the last two portions of your Works of Travel has not been favorable leaving me in fact without profit. Under these circumstances I trust you will be induced to modify the sum proposed by you for the purchase of the work on England."[12] On 6 March, before he received this implicit acceptance from Bentley, Cooper had written the British publisher in some concern: "The book is nearly printed, and it must go to England, at once, or be lost, as I believe Mr. Carey will publish in May. I therefore send you about half (Vol I. and a few sheets of Vol IId), under the impression that as you have so much of the work already (Switzerland and France, being parts of the same work) it would be unfair to send it to any one else."[13] On 14 April, after receiving Bentley's letter of 19 February, Cooper sent Volume II.[14] In short, the correspondence reveals that Cooper had time to perfect the Carey revises sent to Bentley, and so would have had little incentive to make further revisions.

On 1 May, acknowledging receipt of Cooper's letter of 6 March and the "portion of your Work on England therein alluded to," Bentley disclosed a significant change in his attitude towards *England*. Though he reiterated that "the publication of your two previous Series of Travels has been attended with loss to me," he now agreed with Cooper on the possibility of an increased appeal of *England*, and he proposed to act accordingly: "As the nature of the present work is likely to render it more interesting to the English public than the others[,] I am desirous to consider this book apart from others."[15] The likelihood of greater popular interest and increased sales had persuaded Bentley to turn his edition of *England* into a work substantially more ambitious than the Carey edition.

Though collation indicates that Bentley's text derived, as usual, from Carey's sheets, Bentley treated *England* with far more freedom than he did the previous three travel works. He maintained the improvements of format made for the earlier volumes: a meticulously analytical Table of Contents organized chapter by chapter with appropriate sections repeated as topical summaries at the beginnings of chapters,[16] running heads prepared individually for each page, and handsome 12-point type with heavy leading. The most drastic change, however, was the expansion of Carey's two-volume work to the three-volume format popular with British readers by the inclusion of an appendix containing matter from Cooper's polemic *A Letter to His Countrymen*, published originally in 1834 by John Wiley in New York and John Miller in London. Acting on his own to obtain copy to supplement *England*, Bentley selected — apparently without authorization from Cooper — excerpts from *A Letter to His Countrymen* that dealt specifically with British people, customs, and institutions, freely adapting the Wiley text and encompassing about half of the original work.[17] In the text of *England* itself, at 100.33-101.2, the Bentley edition excised part of a paragraph critical of George III, probably because Bentley advertised himself as "Publisher in Ordinary to His Majesty." It also supplied information to fill blank spaces in the Carey edition: "Lord Holland" and "Holland House," for example, consistently replace "Lord _____" and "_____ house" at appropriate points in Volume I.[18]

Bentley's attempt to generate interest in *England* was unsuccessful. Even though the impression was small, the poor sale required that he reissue the book twice in different formats. The first, with a new title page dated 1837 proclaiming it the "Second Edition," appeared on 30 August.[19] The second, with yet another title page, this time undated and entitled *Travels and Excursions in Various Parts of the World: England*, appeared in 1838 or later as Volumes V, VI and VII of an eleven-volume set of Cooper's travel works.[20]

Though more numerous than in the earlier travel books, the Bentley variants in the text of *England*—3,917 in all—are not notably different in kind. Most of them—3,796—are in punctuation, spelling, capitalization and paragraphing, [21] house-styling changes easily predictable in British reprints of American books. The reasons for the 121 substantive variants are also understandable. More carelessly printed than the Carey *Switerland*, the Carey edition of *England* contains more incorrect or ambiguous readings than the first travel book, and the number of actual or apparent corrections of errors in the Bentley—fifty-five—is about double.[22] In addition, the Bentley introduces nine substantive errors of its own.[23] Two substantive variants ("their own," which becomes "English women" at 141.28, and "It is," which becomes "We are" at 283.20) are transparently adaptations of an American text for British readers. The remaining substantive variants—forty-two in all, none longer than six words—do not exhibit Cooper's characteristic boldness in revision.[24] Rather, they follow Bentley's usual patterns of deletion, addition, substitution and transposition, changes well within the competence of a skilled British copy editor.

The accumulated evidence, then, tends to confirm the hypothesis that, after correcting proof for the Carey edition, Cooper made no alterations in the revises pulled from Carey's corrected formes. The Bentley edition, with its unauthorized appropriation of matter from *A Letter to His Countrymen*, its more than 100 substantive variants, its changes in format, its extensive adaptation of the Carey edition's punctuation, diction, spelling and styling to supposed preferences of British readers, cannot be regarded as a faithful reproduction of the copy-text. Since these variants are in no sense authorial, they are not reported on a separate Rejected Readings list.[25]

Although the Bentley edition corrects numerous errors in the copy-text, other errors are perpetuated in the British and French editions. To fulfill Cooper's intention, illustrated in his careful revisions in proof, and to present a correct and readable text, the Cooper Edition emends all errors in wording and in punctuation—whether corrected by the Bentley or not—wherever they are detected. It also emends punctuation to clarify confusing or ambiguous readings. Where the Bentley reading is the proper correction, the emendation of the Cooper Edition parallels it, but since the Bentley text is nonauthorial, the authority for all emendations in the copy-text (save one) is the Cooper Edition, designated CE in the Emendations list, or, for pages 224-227, the Carey edition, designated A. One emendation derives from a letter Cooper wrote to Bentley on 17 October 1837, over a month after the latest edition of *England* appeared. "England, and indeed all the travels," he commented, trying to draw Bentley's attention to the need for careful proofreading of the sheets of *Homeward Bound*, "contain outrageous blunders—I am made to call a sister of the Duke of Devonshire for instance, a 'sister lady'—I wrote a sister, Lady _____."[26] Accordingly, at 181.34, the editors adopt Cooper's emendation, which appears in none of the early printed texts.

The Cooper Edition continues the work of correcting "outrageous blunders" by emending substantive errors in the copy-text. These emendations are illustrated by the following examples:

Addition of Necessary Missing Words: at 18.2-3, "such navies as those England" is emended to "such navies as those of England";

Substitution of Correct Parts of Speech: at 290.26, "as well of" is emended to "as well as";

Elimination of Doubled Words: at 1.14, "an an effort" is emended to "an effort";

Neologisms: at 252.38, "bare" is emended to "bear," and at 174.14, "their" to "there";

Agreement of Subject and Verb: at 246.20, "exhibition . . . are" is emended to "exhibition . . . is";

Proper Spellings of Persons and Places: at 88.32, "Nicholas Wraxall" is emended to "Nathaniel Wraxall";

Letter Numbers: these are emended throughout Volume II of the Carey;

Dates: at 147.37, "1668" is emended to "1688";

Transposition for Accuracy: at 17.7-8, "the edge of Woolwich, and Gravesend" is emended to "Gravesend, and the edge of Woolwich."

Most of the CE emendations correct errors in accidentals:

Insertion of Missing Punctuation:
Terminal: at 151.8, "country He" is emended to "country. He";
Internal: at 174.6, "were within" is emended to "were, within";
Apostrophes: at 33.17, "St. Pauls" is emended to "St. Paul's";
Correction of Misspellings:
Typographical: at 18.22, "wuch" is emended to "much," and at 189.17, "atwhart" is emended to "athwart";
Others: at 277.15, "corrobate" is emended to "corroborate";
Correction of Forms of Foreign Words and Phrases:
Spelling: at 5.5, "*gensdarmes*" is emended to "*gendarmes,*" and at 141.36, "*thoro*" is emended to "*toro*";
Accent Marks: at 46.22, "mélée" is emended to "mêlée";
Adoption of Conventional Capitalization: at 223.4, "tower [of London]" is emended to "Tower [of London]."

The Cooper Edition also emends erroneous inconsistencies in the spelling of British persons and places: for example, Volume I incorrectly prints "M'Intosh" for "Mackintosh," while Volume II usually misspells the name as "Macintosh." *The Dictionary of National Biography* provides the source for the emendation of the incorrect forms in both volumes, as it is the usual source for correct alternative spellings of such names. *Webster's* (1847) and *OED* are secondary sources for names, but primary sources for all other alternate spellings. When inconsistent spellings—of any kind—are limited in the copy-text to acceptable alternatives, no emendation has occurred. Shakespearean citations in the Explanatory Notes are keyed to *The Riverside Shakespeare*, ed. G. Blakemore Evans (Boston: Houghton Mifflin, 1974).

The Cooper Edition has also clarified a few ambiguous passages. These clarifications, which manifest themselves as emendations of punctuation, are made only when the punctuation of a passage in the copy-text, though not strictly erroneous, is disturbingly idiosyncratic or unusual, creating difficulty for the reader:

Elimination of Fragments: at 55.24, "explanation. Lord" is emended to "explanation; Lord";
Addition of Needed Commas: at 268.3, "me sir" is emended to "me, sir";
Deletion of Confusing Commas: at 35.10, "though, the rude magnificence" is emended to "though the rude magnificence."
Without exception, all corrections are reported on the Emendations list.

The Cooper Edition augments the copy-texts in one important particular. Following the convention of the time, the copy-text often refers to the names of persons and places by a letter followed by a three- or four-em dash, or, less frequently, by a three- or four-em dash without the letter. As the manuscript leaf indicates, this practice existed in his manuscript, and, in a few cases (see 224.31-32), was initiated by Cooper during his revision of proof. When possible, the Cooper Edition supplies these names within square brackets: for example, at 9.1, "W_____" becomes "W[illiam]"; and at 55.8, "Lord _____'s" becomes "Lord [Holland]'s." Like the corrections, all these additions are reported on the Emendations list.

The present edition of *Gleanings in Europe: England* is an unmodernized text, no portion of which has been silently emended. Visual appurtenances of the copy-texts, however, such as general typestyling and the styling of chapter openings, spacing of indentations, and the use of periods after the letter numbers, have not been retained. The present edition reproduces the copy-texts in their entirety except for revisions judged to be made by Cooper in proof, one emendation suggested by Cooper's correspondence, corrections of obvious errors, resolutions of troublesome ambiguities, the insertion of names in square brackets, and ordinary visual appurtenances.

NOTES

1. David Kaser, *The Cost Book of Carey & Lea 1825-1838* (Philadelphia, 1963), p. 221.
2. Robert E. Spiller and Philip C. Blackburn, *A Descriptive Bibliography of the Writings of James Fenimore Cooper* (1934; rpt. New York, 1968), p. 91.
3. See "Textual Commentary," *Gleanings in Europe: Switzerland* (Albany, N.Y., 1981), pp. 326-30, for a description of Cooper's usual practice of sending revises to Bentley, and its implications regarding the nonauthorial status of the Bentley edition of *Switzerland*.
4. Bentley Papers, publications list 1829-1873. *Bibliography of American Literature*, Jacob Blanck, comp. (New Haven, 1957), I, 228, erroneously gives 27 May 1837 as the publication date of the Bentley edition.
5. The depression of 1837 forced Carey to delay publication; see "Historical Introduction," pp. xxviii-xxix.
6. *Bibliographie de la France* (Paris, 1837), 26, 1422-1423.
7. Owned by Paul Fenimore Cooper, this leaf measures 8″ x 13⅛″, consists of lined, light-weight paper without watermark, and contains

Cooper's black-ink holograph filling both recto and verso. The
text shows numerous alterations in Cooper's hand, most significantly the deletion of the heading "To Richard Cooper Esquire"
and a whole sentence immediately following.

8. See JFC to Susan Fenimore Cooper, 5 April 1837; *The Letters and
Journals of James Fenimore Cooper,* ed. James Franklin Beard.
6 vols. (Cambridge, Mass., 1960-1968), III, 259. (Hereafter cited as
Letters and Journals.)

9. At 225.31, Cooper's formation of the initial two letters of "could" suggest
the likelihood that the compositor read it as "would"; at 227.1, Cooper
inserts the relative pronoun "that" so faintly that the compositor
might easily have missed it. In both cases the Cooper Edition retains
the manuscript reading and lists the rejected forms in an abbreviated
Rejected Readings list immediately following the Emendations list.

10. *Letters and Journals,* III, 249.

11. Carey, Lea & Blanchard to JFC; MS: Yale Collection of American
Literature, Beinecke Rare Book and Manuscript Library, Yale
University.

12. Bentley Papers, BM Add Mss 46, 640, 171v.

13. *Letters and Journals,* III, 257.

14. Ibid., p. 261.

15. Ibid., p. 258.

16. The Table of Contents is reproduced for the reader's convenience in
Appendix A, pp. 325-329.

17. Bentley selected the portions of *A Letter to His Countrymen* most
appropriate in tone and subject matter to complement *England* by
excising Cooper's discussions of American subjects. For example,
on p. 4 of the Wiley edition, the names of newspapers engaged in
attacks on Cooper—the *New-York American,* the *New-York Courier &
Enquirer* and the *New-York Commercial Advertiser*—are deleted in
the *England* appendix to prepare for the excision of the whole
controversy, which Cooper addresses on pp. 18-51 of the Wiley
edition. Thus, the discussion of the "Cassio" review of *The Bravo*
and the *Courier & Enquirer* article (quoted by Cooper on pp. 36-39)
disappear; Cooper's relation to the American press does not serve
Bentley's purposes. The anecdote of Hazlitt immediately following, however, is retained. Many other evidences, both large and
small, of Bentley's streamlining the text are obvious throughout
the *England* appendix.

18. "Lord _____" becomes "Lord Holland" at 55.8 ("Lord Holland's"),
55.8, and 59.13; "_____ house" becomes "Holland House" at 55.8,

55.23, 56.1, 57.28, and 59.13; "Lady _____" becomes "Lady Holland" at 55.17 and 58.4; "Earls of _____" becomes "Earls of Holland" at 55.21-22.

19. Bentley Papers, publications list 1829-1873. Two other binding formats use the first issue title page: three volumes in two and three volumes in one.

20. The separate title pages and the state of the letterpress—slightly broken letters, thinned serifs, etc., are virtually identical to the earliest forms—indicate that *Travels and Excursions* is a reissue of the original sheets rather than a new impression. While the first (1837) reappearance was not available for examination by the present editors, it is unlikely that this intervening form is other than a reissue. This is also suggested by Bentley's practice with *Gleanings in Europe: Switzerland*, the second issue of which carries the designation "Second Edition" on its title page. The *Travels and Excursions* also attributes authorship to C. Fenimore Cooper throughout, an error probably originating in the mis-set title page of *Gleanings in Europe: Italy*, the last travel work printed.

21. These variants fall into twelve general categories:

Internal punctuation	2,755 instances
Hyphenation of compound words	
Two words to one hyphenated word (e.g., ground swell→ground-swell)	181 instances
Hyphenated word to two words (e.g., Parliament-Houses→Parliament Houses)	21 instances
Hyphenated word to one word (e.g., India-man→Indiaman)	27 instances
One word to hyphenated word (e.g., ahead→a-head)	5 instances
Words and phrases in roman italicized	3 instances
Spelling	
Correct spellings changed to British preferences (e.g., favorable→favourable)	76 instances
Corrections of incorrect spellings (e.g., forthnight→fortnight)	73 instances
Capitalization	
Uncapitalized to capitalized (e.g., continent→Continent)	227 instances
Capitalized made lower case (e.g., Abbey→abbey)	36 instances
Accent marks in foreign words corrected, added or deleted (e.g., pèle-mèle→pêle-mêle)	26 instances

Two words compressed to one word (e.g., any
  thing→anything)   126 instances
One word expanded to two words (e.g.,
  meanwhile→mean while)   3 instances
Italicized words and phrases made into roman
  (e.g., *people*→people)   10 instances
Variant in terminal sentence punctuation (e.g.,
  air. While→air: while)   98 instances
Addition or deletion of apostrophes (e.g.,
  wont→won't)   16 instances
Change in paragraphing (e.g., pleased. I had
  . →pleased. ¶I had)   113 instances

22. Actual and apparent substantive corrections of errors in the Carey
    edition: 1.14, an an [in the Carey]→an [in the Bentley];
    8.10, Wrights'→Wright's; 15.35, farmer's→farmers'; 17.7-8,
    the edge of Woolwich, and Gravesend→Gravesend, and the
    edge of Woolwich; 18.2, those→those of; 41.13, prebend's→
    prebends'; 48.23, going→go; 68.26, Charles II→Charles I;
    70.28, pasty→ pastry; 80.2, DELANCEY→DE LANCEY;
    87.34, the the→the; 88.32, Nicholas→Nathaniel; 122.14,
    imputations→imputation; 122.19, which is→which are; 133.13,
    the→this; 141.11, differences→difference; 144.1, no→on; 145.1,
    LETTER XIV→LETTER XII; 147.16, on an→in an; 147.37,
    1668→1688; 155.16-17, have had→have; 159.1, LETTER XV→
    LETTER XIV; 161.14, peut→peu; 167.1, LETTER XVI→LETTER
    XV; 174.14, their→there; 176.1, LETTER XVIII→LETTER XVI;
    179.19, I I→I; 179.29, the the→the; 181.11, hast→has; 189.1,
    LETTER XVIII→LETTER XVII; 190.20, waterman→watermen;
    190.7, Southwark, Blackfriars→Blackfriars, Southwark; 196.6-7,
    Rundle & Bridge→Rundell and Bridge's; 196.28, Rundle &
    Bridges→ Rundell and Bridge; 199.1, LETTER XIX→LETTER
    XVIII; 202.1, both both→both; 211.36, and met→met; 212.15,
    that→than that; 215.1, LETTER XX→LETTER XIX; 218.10,
    Winn→Wynn; 223.1, LETTER XXI→LETTER XX; 224.8, Jar-
    dins→Jardin; 234.20, their→there; 236.38, Moore→More; 246.20,
    are→is; 248.14, its→it is; 252.38, bare→bear; 256.22, be→to be;
    263.2, set-too→set-to; 268.13, they they→they; 271.15, St.
    James'→St. James's; 278.37, servant's→servants'; 286.3, their→there;
    298.39, suggest→suggests; 301.25, eats→eat.

23. Substantive errors initiated in the Bentley edition:
    95.37, or [in the Carey]→nor [in the Bentley]; 119.36, for the sheets
    of→ for; 189.35, waterman's→watermens'; 216.4, and→but; 239.7,

has→ha; 241.6, this→thus; 284.14, heard→head; 287.31, in America→inAmerica; 307.31, awash→ a wash.

24. Substantive stylistic changes in the Bentley edition: 1.7, events [in the Carey]→event [in the Bentley]; 3.18, largest →larger; 15.12, &c. &c.→&c.; 15.27, fully→full; 16.23, residences →residence; 20.38, had, quite→had,; 24.20, &c. &c.→&c.; 36.16, &c., &c.→&c.; 41.21, cathedrals at→cathedrals of; 47.39, conduct →behave; 69.30, steamboatish in the motion of→resembling the motion of a steamboat in; 69.32, do→are; 70.20, should call→call; 93.27, quite→very; 99.30, aside→gossip; 113.36, of adopting→for adopting; 125.3, feeling of→feeling on; 135.12, A Lord→Lord; 140.2, churchmen of→churchmen on; 146.3, people's→people; 155.25, of Sundays→on Sundays; 161.9, a Lord→Lord; 162.27, to embarrass→of embarrassing; 173.36, by→for; 176.3, the most→ greater; 183.14, as→so; 191.1-2, to have made→to make; 197.1, quite often→often; 217.35-36,_____ _____→_____; 220.38, correction→ corrections; 222.27, antiquarian→antiquary; 223.2, ESQUIRE →ESQ.; 232.27, admitted→admitted that; 236.22, that the king→the king; 254.28, dwelling→ dwellings; 266.2, ESQUIRE→ESQ.; 283.36, &c. &c.→&c.; 284.15, Rossini's→ Rossini; 296.40, being→being a; 300.22, to be→that is; 304.27, as coupled→ coupled; 308.26, or how→how.

25. Five copies of the Carey edition and one of the Bentley edition were collated in the preparation of the present edition: Carey, Lea and Blanchard (1837): copies 1,2,3, and 4 of James F. Beard; the copy from the American Antiquarian Society ("First Eds"). Bentley (1837): copy 1 of James F. Beard.

26. *Letters and Journals*, III, 298.

Textual Notes

The following comments refer to specific decisions to emend requiring fuller explanation than could be provided in the Textual Commentary.

8.10 The Cooper Edition emends this name to the singular possessive to agree with the mention of the tavern at 12.37ff.

9.21 *The Riverside Shakespeare*, ed. G. Blakemore Evans (Houghton Mifflin, 1973), completes this quotation from *King Lear*, IV.vi.1, with a question mark. The misquotation of "we come" for "I come," however, is not emended.

17.7-8 The Cooper Edition corrects this error in geographical order.

26.25 The addition of "as" in this sentence completes the parallel construction implied by the context.

70.28 The word "pastry" seems to be called for by the context here.

122.14 The context here calls for the singular form "imputation."

125.3 Although both prepositions are possible here, "on" seems more appropriate.

191.7 The Cooper Edition corrects this error in geographical order.

212.15 The addition of "than" in this sentence completes the comparison.

218.36 The quotation marks are emended here so that the expression " 'country-laid' " parallels the immediately preceding " 'town-laid.' "

224.30 Cooper deleted these two names in the manuscript, making the manuscript read "of _____" in both cases. Since the names are recoverable, the Cooper Edition has followed its usual format of inserting them in square brackets in the present text.

224.31-32 Cooper apparently deleted both these names in proof; the Cooper Edition, following its usual format, reinstates them in square brackets.

225.38 The unusual manuscript readings of commas here and the comma-period at 226.2-3 are the result of unadjusted punctuation following a manuscript insertion.

226.2-3 See Textual Note for 225.38.

226.10 The period following this word in the manuscript is the result of unadjusted punctuation following the insertion of the phrase "at most, if of as high military station." in the manuscript.

248.14 Since Cooper does not use contractions in the expository prose
of *England*, this form is emended to "it is."

249.20 The quotation marks are emended here so that the phrase " 'long
leap' " parallels the phrase "is 'the leap' still 'too long' " immediately preceding it.

Emendations

The following list records all changes in substantives and accidentals introduced into the copy-text. The reading of the present edition appears to the left of the square bracket; the authority for that reading, followed by a semicolon, the copy-text reading and the copy-text symbol appear to the right of the bracket. Within an entry, the curved dash ~ represents the same word that appears before the bracket and is used in recording punctuation variants; the caret ʌ signifies a punctuation mark missing in the copy-text. An asterisk before an entry indicates that the entry is discussed in Textual Notes. A dagger † before an entry indicates that the entry is discussed in Explanatory Notes. The Cooper Edition, designated CE, is the authority for all emendations save those first appearing in the Carey, Lea and Blanchard edition when the manuscript is copy-text.

The following texts are referred to:

AMS Author's manuscript (one leaf)

A *Gleanings in Europe: England.* Philadelphia: Carey, Lea and Blanchard, 1837.

1.14	such an]CE; such an an A
5.5	*gendarmes*]CE; *gensdarmes* A
5.8	*commissionnaire*]CE; *commissionaire* A
*8.10	Wright's]CE; Wrights' A
9.1	W[illiam]]CE; W———A *Also emended at* 13.20 *and* 74.27
9.1	Mrs. [Cooper]]CE; Mrs. ———A *Also emended at* 12.21 *and* 15.31
9.18	supererogatory]CE; superogatory A
*†9.21	hill?]CE; ~ A
†10.17	shipmate [Midshipman], now Captain [Cooper])CE; shipmate———, now Captain———A
10.34	husbandry.]CE; ~ ʌ A
12.36	*calèche*]CE; *caléche* A

15.35	farmers']CE; farmer's A
17.6	*l' Anglaise*]CE;*l' Anglaise* A
*17.7-8	Gravesend, and the edge of Woolwich]CE; the edge of Woolwich, and Gravesend A
18.2-3	of England]CE; England A
18.13	earnest]CE; ~, A
18.22	much]CE; wuch A
24.27	Mr. de [Lancey]]CE; Mr. de _____ A
24.31	Spencer's]CE; Spenser's A
26.19	acquaintance]CE; acqnaintance A
*26.25	us as]CE; us A
27.33	Cary]CE; Carey A
27.35	introduced, our]CE; introduced. Our A
28.11	Cary]CE; Carey A
29.17-18	Spencer-house]CE; Spenser-house A
29.22	*chef-d'oeuvre*]CE; *chef d'oeuvre* A
30.5	Chantrey]CE; Chantry A
31.12	your [aunt]]CE; your _____ A
32.34	Louisbourg.]CE; ~ ⋏ A
33.10	Chantrey]CE; Chantry A
33.17	St. Paul's]CE; St. Pauls A
33.19	*bas-relief*]CE; *bas rélief* A
33.30	Bartholomew Fair]CE; Bartholemew's fair A
35.3	Now]CE; ~, A
35.10	though]CE; ~, A
38.38	colonnade]CE; colonade A
39.9	monstrosity]CE; monstrocity A
39.13	Almacks']CE; ~ ⋏ A
39.25	dome]CE; ~, A
40.29	woman in]CE; woman, in A
41.13	canons']CE; ~ ⋏ A
41.13	prebends']CE; prebend's A
41.23	Paul's,]CE; Paul's ⋏ A
42.4	colonnades]CE; colonades A
43.30	*pêle-mêle*]CE; *pèle mèle* A *Also emended at* 238.32 *and* 270.15
46.22	*mêlée*]CE; *mélée* A
†46.29	*redingote grise*]CE; *redingotte gris* A
46.33	fortnight]CE; forthnight A
47.17	Berkeley]CE; Berkley A *Also emended at* 82.16
48.23	and go]CE; and going A

50.1	Mackintosh]CE; M'Intosh A *Also emended at* 50.19, 50.33, 51.5, 51.21, 51.21[*bis*], 51.24, 56.14, 56.37, 59.25, 117.1, 117.5, 117.17, 119.13, 128.6, 128.12, 147.37 *and* 218.8.
50.13	Ridgely]CE; Ridgley A
52.29	*déjeuners*]CE; *déjêuners* A
†54.2	Mrs. J[ay]]CE; Mrs. J⎯⎯ A
54.31	*littérateurs*]CE; *litterateurs* A
54.32-33	*littérateurs*]CE; *litterateurs* A
55.6	sooth),]CE; ~) ∧ A
55.6	mad!"]CE; ~ ! ∧ A
55.8	[Holland]]CE; ⎯⎯ A *Also emended at* 55.8[*bis*], 55.17, 55.21-22, 55.23, 55.24, 56.1, 57.28, 58.4, 59.13, *and* 59.23.
55.24	explanation; Lord]CE; ~ . ~ A
55.25	first [Pitt]]CE; first ⎯⎯ A
56.27	second]CE; seeond A
59.15	*bonhomie*]CE; *bonhommie* A
60.4	[Spencer] house]CE; ⎯⎯ house A *Also emended at* 62.23 *and* 64.15.
60.16	Stuart]CE; Stewart A *Also emended at* 159.17, 159.19, *and* 159.21
†60.28-29	[Henry Halford]]CE; ⎯⎯ ⎯⎯ A
†60.30	[Copleston]]CE; ⎯⎯ A
†60.30	[Llandaff]]CE; ⎯⎯ A
61.6	m'a]CE; m 'a A
61.6	étoient]CE; etoient A
61.10	[Spencer]]CE; ⎯⎯ A
62.8	N[ugent]]CE; N⎯⎯ A *Also emended at* 62.31 *and* 63.9.
62.15	chosen by]CE; chosen hy A
62.24	A[lthorp]]CE; A⎯⎯ A
†62.28	Brooks's]CE; Brookes's A
63.4	landlord, the]CE; landlord. The A
63.9	A[lthorp]]CE; A⎯⎯ A
64.15	Mr. [Rogers]]CE; Mr. ⎯⎯ A
63.9	A[lthorp]CE; A⎯⎯ A
64.15	Mr. [Rogers]]CE; Mr. ⎯⎯ A
64.16	Berkeley]CE; Berkely A
64.17	Lord [Essex]]CE; Lord ⎯⎯ A *Also emended at* 64.26, 64.34, 64.36, 65.3, *and* 65.33.
68.26	Charles I]CE; Charles II A
70.10	what does]CE; whatdoes A
70.19	"Do]CE; ∧ ~ A

70.21	chair, "what]CE; chair," what A
*70.28	pastry]CE; pasty A
71.2	he answered]CE; she answered A
¦76.2	statisticians]CE; staticians A
77.21	C[ooperstow]n]CE; C_____n A
78.3	octogenarians]CE; octagenarians A
†79.21	Belfield's]CE; Benfield's A
†80.2	De Lancey]CE; DELANCEY A
80.29	Northumberland-house]CE; Northumbeland-house A
84.14	McAdamized]CE; M'Adamized A
85.27	background]CE; back ground A
86.9	exhilarating]CE; exhilirating A
87.34	the]CE; the the A
87.35	Allston]CE; Alston A *Also emended at* 160.23, 260.13, *and* 260.15.
88.12	coveted]CE; covetted A
†88.32	Nathaniel]CE; Nicholas A
†88.32	Time]CE; Times A
88.38	'*Comme*]CE; " ~ A
88.38	*voilà*]CE; *voilá* A
88.38	*bâti!*' "]CE; *bâti!* ʌ " A
91.25	*bonhomie*]CE; *bonhommie* A
93.10	*chaises*]CE; *chaiss* A
95.5	S[pencer]]CE; S_____ A
95.35	dollar-dollar]CE; dollar-dollar, A
96.36	Sir [Henry Halford]]CE; Sir _____ _____ A
98.34	*Légion*]CE; *Legion* A
99.6	Berkeley]CE; Berkeley A
99. 12	here; the]CE; here. The A
100.4	since,]CE; ~ ʌ A
100.7	"like Falstaff"]CE; ' ~ ~' A
†101.33	Desaix]CE; Dessaix A
†101.35	de [Valmy]]CE; de _____ A
106.5	*order,*]CE; *order* ʌ A
111.1	*quo ad*]CE; *quoad* A
111.2	thing]CE; things A
114.26	people.]CE; ~ ? A
116.10	[Thomas Cooper]]CE; _____ _____ A
116.10-11	Sir G[eorge] P[hilips]]CE; Sir G_____ P_____ A *Also* emended *at* 116.16, 116.25, *and* 122.27
117.2	Spring-Rice]CE; Spring ʌ Rice A
119.14	Spring-Rice]CE; Spring ʌ Rice A

*122.14	imputation]CE; imputations A
122.24	maintenance]CE; maintainance A
124.11	Spencer]CE; Spenser A
*125.3	on]CE; of A
126.29	it is]CE; is it A
133.12	[Llandaff]]CE; _____ A
133.13	this exception]CE; the exception A
133.19	fidgety]CE; fidgetty A
135.3	pigeons]CE; pidgeons A
137.36	Chandos, all]CE; Chandos. All A
138.16	reason]CE; resaon A
140.2	on]CE; of A
141.11	difference]CE; differences A
141.36	*toro*]CE; *thoro* A
142.39	Lords]CE; Lord's A
144.1	on their]CE; no their A
145.1	Letter XIII]CE; LETTER XIV A
147.16	in an]CE; on an A
†147.37	1688]CE; 1668 A
†150.14	[Lansdowne]]CE; _____ A *Also emended at* 150.22 *and* 151.2
151.8	country.]CE; ~ ∧ A
151.10-11	"Vulgar rumour . . . a-year,"]CE; "Vulgar" rumour . . . a-year, ∧ A
151.13	manors," all . . . names, "in]CE; manors, ∧ all . . . names, ∧ in A
151.19	supposititious]CE; suppositious A
155.17	them placed]CE; placed them A
157.7	secure]CE; secures A
159.1	Letter XIV]CE; LETTER XV A
159.7	Lords Lansdowne]CE; lords Lansdown
161.14	*peu*]CE; *peut* A
162.32	Mackintosh]CE; Macintosh A *Also emended at* 163.6, 164.4, 164.37, 179.18, 179.22-23, *and* 180.29
165.23	*Anglicé*]CE; *Anglice* A
165.31	*maître*]CE; *maitre* A
166.6	Wordsworth]CE; Wadsworth A
167.1	Letter XV]CE; LETTER XVI A
168.16	*chiaroscuro*]CE; *chiaro scuro* A
170.13	stucco]CE; stuccoe A
170.32	*cortège*]CE; *cortege* A
172.13	Strawberry]CE; Stawberry A

174.6	were,]CE; ∼ ∧ A
174.14	there]CE; their A *Also emended at* 234.20 *and* 286.3
176.1	Letter XVI]CE; LETTER XVIII A
176..25	*pêle-mêle*]CE; *pêle* ∧ *mêle* A
178.17	[Devonshire]]CE; _____ A *Also emended at* 178.23, 179.8
	179.21, 180.31, 180.36, 181.18, 181.25, *and* 182.37
179.19	I]CE; I I A
179.29	the truth]CE; the the truth A
181.4-5	Capitol]CE; capitol A
181.11	has]CE; hast A
181.18	ante-chamber]CE; ante-chambcr A
181.34	sister, Lady _____]CE; sister ∧ Lady ∧ A
183.22	Countess [Cowper]]CE; Countess _____ A
183.28	[Cooper]'s]CE; _____'s A
183.32	Lady [Cowper]'s]CE; Lady _____'s A
183.36	[Cooper]'s]CE; _____'s A
184.11	stoop]CE; stoup A
184.15	fidgety]CE; fidgetty A
186.38	*retenue*]CE; *retenu* A
188.15	unless]CE; ∼, A
189.1	Letter XVII]CE; LETTER XVIII A
189.17	athwart]CE; atwhart A
189.35	watermen's]CE; waterman's A
190.20	watermen]CE; waterman A
190.32	St. Paul's]CE; St. Pauls A
191.6	Custom-house]CE; custom-house A
*191.7	Blackfriars, Southwark]CE; Southwark, Blackfriars A
193.27	inquired.]CE; ∼." A
194.17	some time]CE; sometime A
196.6-7	Rundell & Bridge]CE; Rundle & Bridges A
196.18	Prince [Borghese]]CE; Prince _____ A
196.28	Rundell & Bridge]CE; Rundle & Bridges A
197.5	proportions]CE; propertions A
199.1	Letter XVIII]CE; LETTER XIX A
201.29	England]CE; Fngland A
202.2	both]CE; both both A
205.36	repudiated]CE; rcpudiated A
209.6	countryman's]CE; countrymen's A
211.36	deceit,]CE; deceit, and A
*212.15	mind, than that]CE; mind, that A
215.1	Letter XIX]CE; LETTER XX A
215.9	Spencer]CE; Spenser A

215.19	*naïveté*]CE; *naiveté* A
216.17	coolly]CE; cooly A *Also emended at* 229.20 *and* 290.18
217.26	husbands]CE; husband's A
218.10	Wynn]CE; Winn A
218.14	Lord [Kerry]]CE; Lord _____ A
218.14	Lord L[ansdowne]]CE; Lord L _____ A
218.19	*coque*]CE; *coq* A
218.26	*coque*]CE; *coq* A
*218.36	a "country-laid" egg?]CE; "a country-laid egg?" A
219.15	misstatements]CE; mistatements A
219.37	dinners]CE; dinner's A
221.32	earldoms]CE; earldom's A
222.1	young [Kerry]]CE; young _____ A
	Letter XX]CE; LETTER XXI A
223.4	Tower]CE; tower A *Also emended at* 223.7, 223.19, *and* 223.28
223.24	*l'Artillerie*]CE; *l'artillerie* A
224.8	*Jardin*]CE; *Jardins* A *Begin AMS copy-text*
224.10	jewels]A; jewelry AMS
224.12-13	to it, although he ran away from his kingdom]A; to it AMS
†224.16	Anne]CE; Anna AMS
224.21	ethereal]CE; etherial AMS
*224.30	of [Rosslin]]CE; of R _____ AMS; of _____ A
224.30	the Earl] A; the old Earl AMS
*224.30	of [Charlemont]]CE; of C _____ AMS; of _____ A
*224.31-32	Lord [Ebrington]]CE; Lord Ebrington AMS; Lord _____ A
*224.32	Sir [John Newport]]CE; Sir John Newport AMS; Sir _____ _____ A
224.34-35	was full]A; is full AMS
224.38	accordingly]A; to him AMS
225.6	the movement]A; it altogether AMS
225.16	G_____]A; me AMS
225.16	he was]A; I was AMS
225.17	exception of]A; exception of one who came AMS
225.19	G_____]A; I AMS
225.20	his invitation]A; my invitation AMS
225.21	him reason]A; me reason AMS
225.22	himself]A; myself AMS
225.22	he could]A; I could AMS
225.24-25	towards him]A; towards me AMS

225.25	did him]A; did me AMS
225.25	present him]A; present me AMS
225.26	he had]A; I had AMS
225.28	tact]A; tones AMS
225.31	cutting]A; gross AMS
225.32	place]A; seat AMS
225.35	good]A; that was good AMS
225.36	no one else]A; I was the only one AMS
225.37	bethought]A; who bethought AMS
*225.38	convexion]A; ~, AMS
*226.2	mode,]CE; ~,. AMS; ~; A
226.3	So much]A; As so much AMS
226.3	having been]A; had been AMS
226.5	common-looking]A; looking AMS
226.7	Lord _____]A; Lord R_____ AMS
*226.10	colonel,]A; ~. AMS
226.10-11	as high in the army]A; of as high military station AMS
226.13-14	believe he was the Duke of _____.]CE; did not enquire who he was. AMS; believe he was the Duke of _____ ∧ A
226.22-23	at least something]A; something AMS
226.24-25	He had himself found the body]A; His body he had himself found AMS
226.25	and, he added]A; he added and AMS
226.31-32	suggest the doubt]A; raise the question AMS
226.34	the fact]A; who I was AMS
226.36	while strolling]A; in walking AMS
	End AMS copy-text
227.15	laws,]CE; ~. A
227.16	discussion]CE; dicussion A
228.4	trembled,]CE; ~ ∧ A
230.1	Letter XXI]CE; LETTER XXII A
231.34	Thirty-nine Articles]CE; thirty-nine articles A
232.18	misled]CE; mislead A
232.31	gossiping]CE; gossipping A
†236.38	More]CE; Moore A
237.24-25	supersede]CE; supercede A
238.4	"Here," said I, "is]CE; "~, ∧ ~ ~, ∧ ~ A
238.33	*grossièreté*]CE; *grossieretè* A
241.34	Church]CE; church A
242.13	Church]CE; church A
243.19	hers]CE; her's A
244.13	ours]CE; our's A
246.20	is]CE; are A

*248.14	it is]CE; its A
*249.20	It is these "long]CE; "~ ~ ~ ʌ ~ A
250.1	Letter XXII]CE; LETTER XXIII A
252.38	bear]CE; bare A
253.31	Dungeness]CE; Dungenness A
254.26	gives]CE; give A
256.6	hers]CE; her's A
256.22	still to be]CE; still be A
257.2	workshops]CE; workships A
259.24	Cobbett]CE; Cobbet A
260.1	Letter XXIII]CE; LETTER XXIV A
263.2	set-to]CE; set-too A
263.5	*naïveté*]CE; *naiveté* A
266.1	Letter XXIV]CE; LETTER XXV A
266.28	whatever]CE; ~, A
268.3	me,]CE; ~ ʌ A
268.13	particularly]CE; particularily A
268.13	they]CE; they they A
268.32	former?]CE; ~. A
†269.30	Bernhard]CE; Bernard A
269.37	Bernhard]CE; Bernard A
276.1	Letter XXV]CE; LETTER XXVI A
277.15	corroborate]CE; corrobate A
278.29	de [Galitzin]]CE; de _____ A
278.34	*bonjour*]CE; *bon jour* A
278.37	servants']CE; servant's A
280.32	*ragoût*]CE; *râgout* A
281.20	El Dorado]CE; El Derado A
†283.23	*déluge*]CE; *deluge* A
283.39	get away]CE; ~, ~ A
285.1	Letter XXVI]CE; LETTER XXVII A
286.4	us]CE; ~, A
288.38-289.3	said, 'that . . . England.' 'F_____,' exclaimed Count N_____, 'what . . . F_____!' The English . . . replied, 'why . . . *France*.'"]CE; said "that . . . England." "F_____," exclaimed Count N_____, "what . . . F_____!" The English . . . replied "why . . . *France*." A
290.26	well as]CE; well A
294.1	Letter XXVII]CE; LETTER XXVIII A
294.18	looking an]CE; a looking A
297.29	Himalayas]CE; Himilayas A
298.39	suggests]CE; suggest A
301.25	eat]CE; eats A

302.25	bigoted]CE; bigotted A
303.22	apparent;]CE; ~, A
305.1	Letter XXVIII]CE; LETTER XXIX A
306.36-37	elsewhere]CE; elesewhere A
308.28	love.]CE; love./ THE END. A

REJECTED READINGS

225.31	could not]AMS; would not A
227.1	that they were]AMS; they were A

Word-Division

List A records compounds or possible compounds hyphenated at the end of the line in the copy-text and resolved as hyphenated or one word as listed below. If the words occur elsewhere in the copy-text or if Cooper's manuscripts of this period fairly consistently followed one practice respecting the particular compound or possible compound, the resolution was made on that basis. Otherwise first editions of works of this period were used as guides. List B is a guide to transciption of compounds or possible compounds hyphenated at the end of the line in the Cooper Edition: compounds recorded here should be transcribed as given; words divided at the end of the line and not listed should be transcribed as one unhyphenated word.

LIST A

2.16	mole-hills	89.6	horse-guards
8.21	dining-room	91.18	well-proportioned
9.19-20	short-winded	95.34-35	wine-discussing
17.11	marrow-chilling	107.26	dinner-table
20.30	drawing-room	112.26	extra-legal
21.6	town-house	132.2	fire-place
30.4	drawing-room	163.32	story-tellers
32.32	grand-father	167.22	park-like
34.37	church-yard	169.27	German-looking
42.5	one-sixth	180.23	ball-room
48.2	drawing-room	181.2	ante-chamber
49.18	-by-rule	184.24-25	lady-like
55.38	manor-house	186.15	drawing-room
60.27	drawing-room	187.17	drawing-room
72.18	post-chariot	200.30	good-will
80.29	Northumbe[r]land- house	202.8	Pearl-street
83.29	club-houses	207.15	Father-land
88.18	narrow-minded	218.33	steam-boat

246.31	self-evident		271.35	fellow-traveller
249.4	to-morrow		274.25	foot-ball
252.1	Newmarket		276.29	fellow-creatures
252.18	Rye-house		277.1	housekeeper
253.19	Fair-minded		297.39	two-fold
256.24	mother-country		298.6	blackguardism
259.8	Regent's-street		299.11	overshadowing
270.35	wide-spread		306.9	vineyards

LIST B

3.27	heart-burnings		156.15	decency-and-
5.15	seamanship		157.3	well-intentioned
5.32	square-rigged		182.3	well-formed
9.9	two-thirds		182.35	self-felicitation
9.19	short-winded		183.8	Spanish-looking
12.29	gentlemanlike		183.20	well-known
16.17	deep-mouthed		185.24	lady-like
19.4	lodging-houses		186.17	well-rounded
20.14	lodging-houses		192-13	custom-house
28.21	thoroughfare		194-28	St. James'-street
29.17	Spencer-house		203.2	straight-forward
30.1	bookseller		217.8	drawing-room
33.4	much-talked-		243.12	-Harbour-men
38.5	coffee-house		243.20	wrong-headed
41.45	organ-loft		250.21	-and-twenty
70.32	half-bred		252.9	poor-houses
73.7	shovel-nosed		253.19	fair-minded
76.1	common-place		254.35	post-horses
81.19	thirty-three		257.12	self-defense
87.28	stage-coaches		257.22	second-rate
92.1	drawing-room		266.33	well-dressed
92.32	first-floor		270.33	horse-guards
93.12	drawing-room		271.14	*stable-yard*
95.34	wine-discussing		273.31	claret-coloured
101.10	simple-minded		277.23	house-maid
105.34	-a-cking		287.21	re-colonization
118.34	close-corporation		293-29	-and-twenty
137.29	son-in-		307.2	custom-house
155.4	class-mates			

INDEX

Index

This index includes persons, places, things, and topics of concern mentioned or alluded to in Cooper's text, including his own footnotes. Subjects glossed in the Explanatory Notes of this edition are indicated by an asterisk (*) placed before the appropriate page number. The letter n following a numeral indicates a reference to a note in Cooper's text.

Abbotsford, 122n
Aberdeen, Lady, 161
Adam Street, 18-19
Adams, John, *101
Adams, John Quincy, 293
Addison, Joseph, *51, 55-56
Adelphi, 18
Admiralty, 85
Affleck, Lady, *77
Age of Reason, The (Paine), *288
Albany (N.Y.), 55, 169, 308
Alexander I (Rus.), *285
Allen, William H., 231
Allston, Washington, 87n, 160, 260
Almacks' Assembly Rooms, 39
"Alnwick Castle" (Halleck), *25, *51-52
Althorp, Lord, 62-63, 91, 106
America or American, see United
   States
Amsterdam, 36, 305
Ananias, *33
André (monument), 33
Angevine (Westchester), 77
Anglo-Saxon: language, 1; women, 78;
   race, 109, 282; character, 207
Anne, Queen (Eng.), 39, 204n
Anson, Captain George, 32
Antwerp, 208
Apis, 174
Apsley-house, 81
Arabian horses, 71
Archias (poet), 155

Aremberg (family), 158
Argus (ship), 231
Arno, river, 190
Ashburnham, Lord, 161
Astor House, 301n
Austria: sovereign, 173; church, 243;
   ambassador, 272

Baillie, Joanna, 261-62
Bainbridge, Joseph, midshipman, *125
Bainbridge, William, captain, *125
Ball, Sir Alexander, *124-25
Baltimore (Md.), 15
Bank of England, Plate XII, following
   188
Barclay's (brewers), *94
Barlow, Joel, 25
Bartholomew Fair, 33
Bateman, Lord, 236n
Bath, city, 22
Bath, Order of the, 32, 98, 99, 173
Beaufort, Duke of, 173
Becket, Thomas à, 16
Bedford Square, 82
Beethoven, Ludwig Van, 283
Belfield, Mrs. *79
Bell, at Edmonton, see John Gilpin
Bellamy's, *38, 104
Ben-Nevis, 162
Berkeley Square, 47, 64, 82, 99
Berlin, 80
Bermuda, 228-29

Bernhard, Duke of Saxe-Weimar,
*269n
Bible, quoted or cited, *25, *33,
*170, *201, *203-04, 207, *225
Bingham, Anne Louise, *184
Blackfriars Bridge, 191
Blackheath, *18, 161
Black Sal, 155
Blackstone, Sir William
(*Commentaries*), *117
Blandford, Lord, 137n
Blenheim, *254
Bloomsbury Square, 82
Blue-coat School (London), *195
"blue ribband," 98
Boadicea, ship, 194
Boar's Head Tavern, 191-92
Bois de Boulogne (Paris), 70, 80, 207
Boleyn, Anne, *224
Bolt-court, 198
Boom Key, *308
Bordentown (N.J.), 271n
Borghese, Prince, *196
Boston (Mass.), 15, 265, 269n
Boulogne, 241-42
Bounty, ship, *238
Bow-church (Marylebone), 193
Bowyer, Fort, 232
Bridgewater House, 29, 81
Brighton, 22
Bristol (Eng.), 6, 250n
Bristol (Pa.), 15
British America, 257-58
"British Valour Displayed; or, The
Battle of the Kegs" (Hopkinson),
*157
Broadway (N.Y.), 68, 194
Brooks's, club, 62
Brougham, Lord, 143, 219-20
Brummel school, 97
Brunswick, *see* New Brunswick
Brussels, 80
Bryant, William Cullen, 25, *51-52
Buccleugh, Duke of, 204n
Bunker Hill, battle, 246n
Burdett, Sir Francis, 29, 107
Burke, Edmund, 51, 103
Burleigh, 133
Burlington (N.J.), 15
Burlington House, 81

Butler, Mrs. Frances Kemble, *303-04n
Byron, Lord, 111

Caesar (Rom.), 7
Calais, 8, 10, 12
Campbell, Thomas, 24
Canada, 257
Canning, George, 82, 203n
Canterbury, Archbishop of, *128, 152,
see William Howley
Canterbury, cathedral, 16, 41
Canterbury, town, 13-15
Cape of Good Hope, 256
Capitol (Washington, D.C.), 181
Carlton House, 83
Carnarvon, Lord, 135, 143
Caroline, Princess of Wales, 161;
Queen of England, *135
Carter, Nathaniel H., *39
Cary, Henry F., 27-28
Catholic Church, 16, 34; cathedrals,
40-41; worship, 41; m. 140-41
Cavendish Square, 82
Cecilia (Burney), *79
Cellini, Benvenuto, 197
Chamber of Deputies, 131
Channing, Dr. William E., 262
Chandos, Lord, 137n
Chantrey, Sir Francis, 30, 33, 162
Charing Cross, 19, 68, 251
Charles I (Eng.), statue of, 68, Plate
VIII, *following* 130
Charles II (Eng.), 204n, 251
Charles X (Fr.), *101
Charlotte of Mecklenburgh, 173
Charlotte, Princess, 173
Charlemont, Earl of, 224
Charpentier, family, 165
Chase, Bishop Philander, *218
Chatham, town, 17
Chatham, Lord, *37, 103
Chelsea, 189
Cheltenham, 22
Chesapeake, ship, 125
Chester (Pa.), 15
Chestnut Street (Philadelphia), 68
chiaroscuro, 168, 175
Chinese ornaments, 93
Christ, 16, 240; *see also* God, Providence
Christ Church, Plate XIV, *following* 250

Christ's Hospital, Plate XIV, *following* 250
Christendom, 78, 146, 158, 172, 214, 273, 279
Christianity, 156, 206
Christmas, 22, 103, 150
Church of England, 15, 139-40, 241-43
Cicero, 155
Clanricarde, Lord, 81
Clarges Street, 180
Cleveland, Duchess of, 173
Cleveland, Duke of, 204n
Cobbett, William, *259, *290
Cockney or cockneys, 28, 31, 74, 97, 169, 193, 252, 254, 307
Coleridge, Samuel Taylor, *124-28, 164, 260-62
Comstock (Mich.), 176
Comstock, Mrs. Horace H., letter to, *176
Congress (U.S.), 103-04, 110-15, 128, 132, 247, 286n
Congress of Panama, *293n
Connecticut, 59
Constitution, ship, 126
Cooper, Capt. Benjamin, *10; letter to, *305
Cooper, James Fenimore: arrival in England, 6-9; earlier visits, 6, 38-39, 68, 79, 82, 103, 192-95, 204, 255; visits Canterbury, 13-17; takes house in St. James's Place, London, 20-21; introduced by William Spencer, 24; visited by William Godwin, 25-27; courtesies of Samuel Rogers, 27-30; inspects Westminster Abbey, 31-35; Parliament, 36-38; St. Paul's, 38-42; enters English society, 43-66, 215-22; sightseeing in London, 68-79; London parks and squares, 80-90; entertained by prominent Whigs, 91-101; Parliamentary and Congressional proceedings compared, 103-15; renews friendship with Sir Walter Scott at dinner of Sir George Philips, 116-23; meets Coleridge, Scott, and Lockhart at dinner of William Sotheby, 124-28; visits House of Lords, 131-44; reflections on British aristocracy, 145-58; dinners with Samuel Rogers,

159-66; excursion to Richmond and Windsor, 167-75; observations on English society, 176-88; tours about London, 189-98; American and British press as cultural indicators, 199-214; personal discourtesies, 225-29; opinions on national prejudices of British and Americans, 230-49; attacked for repelling and refuting British prejudices and imputations on American character, 245-48; a trip to Hertfordshire, 250-54; prognosis for British colonial system, 255-59; visits Coleridge and Joanna Baillie, 260-62; importance of national cultural capital, 264-65; American and British civilizations compared, 268-304 (*see also entry for United States*), passage from London to Rotterdam, 305-08
Cooper, Susan Augusta (Mrs. JFC), 9, 12, 15, 31, 165
Cooper, Richard, letters to, *22, 43, 159, 167, 189, 223, 260, 294
Cooper, Dr. Thomas, *24, 116
Cooper, Thomas Abthorp, *24
Cooper, Judge William (JFC's father), *24, 26, 95
Cooper, William Yeardley (JFC's nephew), 9, 13, 74
Cooperstown (N.Y.), 77, 159, 167, 170
Copleston, Dr. Edward, *60
copyright law, *119-22
cordon bleu, 98
Corinthian capitals (architecture), 37
Corydon, 173
Cowper, Lady Emily Mary, 183
Cowper, William ("The Diverting History of John Gilpin"), *251
Covent Garden, 74, 266, Plate XV, *following* 250
Crockford's club-house, 194
Croton, aqueduct, *252

Dante, 27, 34
Declaration of Independence, 1
De Kay, Dr. James E., letters to, *116, 266
De Lancey, Edward Floyd, letter to, *80

De Lancey, John, *78
De Lancey, John Peter (JFC's father-in-law), death of, *24, 250n
De Lancey, Thomas James, letter to, *31
Delaware, 11
Denham, Lady, 173
Denmark: sovereign, 173; invasion by, 252
De Roos, Frederick F., 231
Desaix de Veygoux, Louis Charles Antoine, *101-02
Dessin (hotel-keeper), 5, 8
Devonshire, 230
Devonshire, Duke of, *177-78
Devonshire House, 81, 179
Dorset, Duke of, 173
Douro, Lord, 137n
Dover: town, 5, 7-8, 10, 13-14, 109; cliffs, 6-7, 9
Dover, Straits of, 5-6
Downs, anchoring ground, 6
Draper, Sir William, 183
Dresden, 80
Dudley, Lord, 24
duelling, 125, 241-42
Dumont, Pierre, *117, 119
Duncannon, Lord, 91
Dungeness, 6-7, 253
Durham, Lord, 91
"Dutch herring," 58
Dwight, Timothy, *285-86

East Cheap, 191
East Indies, 165, 251, 255
East India Civil Service, 252
East India House, Plate XII, *following* 188
Easter season, 22
Eaton, *254
Ebrington, Lord, 224
Eclogues (Virgil), 155
Edgar (*King Lear*), 9
Edinburgh Review, 201, 234, *287
Edmonton, bell at, *251
Edward I (Eng.), 251
Edward IV (Eng.), 173
Edward VI (Eng.), 37
Egypt: sculpture, 29; gods, 174

El Dorado, 281
Elizabeth, Queen, 55
Ellison, Thomas, *155
England or English, *see also* London *and* United States
amusements
    balls, 176-88, 274
    dancing, 176, 184, 186
    hunting, 15, 22, 133-34, 236
    rowing, 189, 226
    riding, 69-71
    theatre, 29, 266-68
architecture, 11, 34-41, 55, 81, 84, 92, 116, 170, 173, 180-81, 184, 190-91, 193, 196
aristocracy, 3, 26, 80, 136-41, 146-47, 149, 151-54, 203-05, 235, 296, *see also* nobility *and* caste system
army, 66, 198, 226, 245, 253, 270-71
art, 29, 31, 37, 93, 159-60, 173, 196, 260
caste system, 43-44, 46-49, 61, 65, 70-71, 74, 81, 92, 94, 109, 137-39, 147, 152, 158, 163, 177-79, 184, 186-87, 204-05, 216-17, 221-22, 238, 253, 276-77, 296, *see also* aristocracy *and* nobility
church and Church Establishment, 42, 139-40, 240-41
climate, 22, 85-87, 276, 297, 302
coaches and coachmen, 12-13, 18-19, 21, 23, 64-65, 68-70, 72-73, 87-89, 168, 180, 250-51, 254, 272-75, 295
coats-of-arms, 21, 73, 116, 303n
colonies and former colonies, 255-59
Constitution, 112, 137, 147
Court, 196
crown, imperial, 224
custom-houses, 9, 12, 191, 305, 307
decorations and chivalric orders, 32, 98-99, 148, 172, 250
dinners, 49, 52-58, 60-61, 70, 95, 117, 124, 159, 161-63, 179, 199, 215-17, 219, 225, 274, 301
dress, 15, 39, 57, 60, 64, 72-73, 133, 186, 190, 196, 273, 294
empire, 54, 146, 201, 238, 255-58, 297-98
exclusion, system of, 118, 157, 177-79, *see also* caste system

England or English *continued*
government, 3, 136, 301, *see also*
Parliament, House of Commons,
House of Lords
horses, 13, 18, 22, 69, 71-73, 79
houses, 20-21, 27-29, 36, 49, 54-56,
81-82, 85, 92-93, 95, 116, 169-71,
175, 177-78, 180, 182, 184, 186, 216,
254, 260
king (monarchy), 72, 97-98, 136, 170,
174, 235-36, 272, 300
landscape, 7, 10-11, 13, 39-40, 83,
85, 167-68, 189-90
language, 11, 16, 27-28, 60, 62, 69-71,
96-97, 100, 105, 107, 109-10,
133-34, 142, 163-64, 170, 183, 199,
217-18, 226, 247, 267, 269-70
literature, 31, 54, 80, 94, 118, 126,
187-88, 199, 211, 220-21, 223, 231,
244, 262, 268-69, 300
manner and manners, 15, 40, 48-49,
56-57, 60, 71-72, 89-90, 93-96,
104-06, 108-09, 114, 117, 119,
131-32, 135, 142-43, 152, 155,
162-64, 176, 178-79, 181, 186-88,
190, 216-17, 225, 229, 237, 239,
247-49, 262-63, 295, 302
music, 19-20, 283-84
navy, 194, 232
nobility, 21, 43-49, 54, 56, 59, 64, 73,
80-81, 88, 92, 94, 97, 133 37, 141-43,
147-48, 150-52, 155, 157-58, 162-63,
193, 197, 221-22, *see* aristocracy
and caste system
order (systematic disposition), 19, 55
parks and squares, 20, 22, 28-29, 55,
71, 80-84, 86-88, 167-69, 174, 191,
194-95, 260
periodical press, 160, 185, 199-203,
205-13, 237, 285, 287, 289, 291, 293n
plate, 57-58, 95, 196-97
poor, the, 146, 148-49, 216, 252, 276-82
prejudice, 59, 82, 121, 124-25, 152, 154,
157, 162, 211, 235-38, 244-46, 248-49,
309, *see* United States, British
prejudice towards
publishing, 54, 119-21, 123, 211,
220-21, 247, 291
reform, 59, 64, 108, 118, 140, 145,
148, 154-55, 158

religion, 240-43
roads, 13, 18-20, 23, 68, 72, 88, 191-92,
250-51
servants, 19, 47, 57, 72-74, 94-95,
97-98, 108, 116, 128, 180-81, 183,
192, 194-95, 236, 273-74, 276-79,
303n, 306
stature (of people), 6, 15, 74-75, 135,
153, 169, 188, 245, 294
taste, 33, 83, 97, 111, 125, 160, 172-73,
178, 190, 199, 207, 227, 244, 271,
298-99, 302
travellers and travelling, 13, 22-23,
153, 188, 214, 244, 264
vanity, 268, 296
vessels, 5, 10, 17-18, 189-90, 232, 292,
305, 307
weather, 17, 85-87, 168
women, 40, 78-79, 128-29, 141, 143,
162, 176, 181-88, 217, 262, 273-74,
277, 303-04n
Erasmus, 34
Esop, 58
Essex, county, 77, 251
Essex, Lord, 64-65
Esterhazy, Prince, 272
Eton College, 174
Europe, 12, 22, 34-35, 43, 45, 61, 69,
80-81, 84, 86-87, 91, 93, 96-98, 129,
131, 141, 152-53, 158-59, 168-69,
185-86, 196, 198, 203, 208-09, 215n,
219-21, 223, 228, 230, 240, 246, 254,
257, 259, 269, 274, 276, 278, 280,
283, 287n, 295n, 297, 305-06
Euston, Lord, 137n
Evening Courier, 47, 199, 201
Examiner (journal), 203n

"Fair Quaker," *206
Falstaff, Sir John, 100
Fielding, Henry, 18
Fitz-Herbert, Mrs., 100
Flanders, 147
Flaxman, John, 197
Fleet-street, 198
Florence (It.), 36, 81
Floyd-Jones, Henry, letter to, *250
Floyd-Jones, Thomas, letter to, *68
Fox, 51, 100, 103

France or French, compared to England or English: seamanship, 5-6; travelers and travelling, 13, 304n; public safety, 18; neatness of domestic arrangements, 19; decorations and chivalric orders, 32, 98; press, 123-24; manners and taste, 172, 183, 216; prejudices, 231; servants, 237, 278, 306; poorer classes, 279-80; national vanity, 296-97
Franklin, Benjamin, 159, 162
Frederick William I (Pr.), *271
Freeman, Jack, 6
free trade, 59, 122, 129-30, 186, 208, 290
French Revolution, 43-44, 146, 155, 216-17, 256, 288-89
Fuseli, Henry, 106

Galignani's Messenger, 203n
Galileo, 34
Galitzin, Princesse de, 278
Gamaliel, 117
Garter (order of), 32, 98-99, 172-73, 197
General Post Office (London), 195-96
Genessee River, *59
Geneva, 285
genius, defined, 262
George I (Eng.), 204n
George II (Eng.), 204n
George III (Eng.), 81n, 100-*01, 148, 155, 204n, 206
George IV (Eng.), 99, 162, 172, 198, 205, 270
Georgia (state), 50
Germany or German: music, 20; watering places, 22; capitals, 80; nobility, 158, 229n, 269n; architecture, 169, 172; superstitions, 282
Gifford, William, 208
Gilpin, John, *251
Globe, Le (French journal), 123
Gloster (*King Lear*), 9
Gloucester, Duke of, 272
God, 16, 41, 209, 219, 233, 239, 291-92, *see also* Christ, Providence
Godwin, William, *25-26
Gog and Magog, *192
Golden Fleece (order), 173
Gothic architecture, 31-42, 172-73, 192, 251
Gower, Lord, 159

Grafton, Duke of, 204n
Graham, Lord, 137n
Gravesend, 17, 307
Gray, Thomas, quoted, *223
Great Fire of London, monument, *192
Great Lakes (U.S.), 135
Greece or Grecian: architecture, 84, 259; republic, 140; president-elect, 225
Green Park, 28-29, 83, 88, 194-95
Greenwich, 189
Grenville, Lord, 297
Grenville, Thomas, 161
Grey, Lord, 91-92, 95-96, 99, 133, 142, 159
Gros, Baron A. J., 39
Grosvenor, Lord, 149
Grosvenor Square, 82, 181
Guildhall, 193, Plate XI, *following* 188
Guzman, family, 158

half-blood, law of the, *117
Halford, Sir Henry, *60, 96
Hall, Captain Basil, *67, *93, *230-31, *234-35, *268-69
Hall, Samuel Carter, *237
Halleck, Fitz-Greene, 25, 51
Hampstead, 261
Hampton Court, 165
Hanover Square, 72, 82
Hastings, 7
Haussez, Charles le Mercher de Longpré, Baron d', 304n
Heathcote, Colonel Caleb, *77
Heber, Bishop Reginald, *231, *297
Hell Gate (Hurl Gate), 70
Henry V (Eng.), 191
Henry VI (Eng.), 174
Henry VII (Eng.), 173; Chapel of, 32, 34
Henry plot, *285
Hercules, 258
Hermione, ship, *238
Hertfordshire, 166, 250-51
Highgate, 260
Himalayas, 297
History of the Revolution of 1688 (Mackintosh), *147
Hobart, Bishop John Henry, *61-63, 244
Hoddesdon, 251-52, 254

Holland, Earls of, 55
Holland, Lady, 55, 58
Holland, Lord, 55, 59, 91, 99, 133, 162
Holland House, 55-57, 59, Plate VI,
  following 130
Holy Ghost (Order of the), 98
Holy Writ, 225
Homer, *127
Hopkinson, Francis, *157
Horner, Francis (statue by Chantrey), 33
Hospital of Incurables, 131
House of Commons, 62, 103-06, 109-10,
  131, 137-38, 151, 182, 236n
House of Hanover, 158
House of Lords, 36-37, 110, 131-33, 135,
  138, 143, 148, 161, 236n; *see* St.
  Stephen's Chapel
House of Representatives (U.S.), 110
Howard, family, 44, 158
Howley, Mrs., *124
Howley, William, *124, *128
Hume, David, 108
Humphrey, David, 25
Huskisson, William, *289-90
Hyde Park, 83, 87-88, 194, 251

Illuminati, the, *288
impressment, 228, 232, 240
India docks, 251
Indian (American), 129
Indies, 216, *see also* East Indies, West
  Indies
Ireland or Irish: peerage, 88, 148;
  differences with England, 140n, 216;
  the military, 224, 246
Irving, Washington, 230
Isle of Man, 230
Islip (L.I.), 250n
Istrias, Count Capo d', 225
Italy or Italian: architecture, 84;
  pronunciation, 134; republic, 140;
  silversmithing, 197; religion, 240;
  national temperament, 281
Izard, Mrs. Ralph, *78

Jackson, Andrew, 293
Jacobins, 216, 289
Jamaica, 256
James II, (Eng.), 224
Jardin des Plantes, 84, 224
Jay, John, 77-78, 161

Jay, Mrs. Peter Augustus, letter to, *54
Jay, William, letters to, *103, 131, 145,
  199
Jefferson, Thomas, 90, 113-15, 155, 159,
  195, *249n, 293n
Jekyll, Joseph, 162-64n
Jockey Club (N.Y.), 71
"Jockey of Norfolk," *44
Johannisberger, 280
John Bull, 20, 249
John Gilpin, *251
Johnson, Dr. Samuel, *10, *103, 198
Johnson, Sir William, 32
Jonathan (epithet for Americans), 249
Jonson, Ben, 31
Jordan, Mrs., *205n
Journal de Débats (Paris), 123
Jungfrau, mountain, 297
Junius, 193

Kemble, Charles, 267
Kendal, Duchess of, 204n
Kennebunk, 194-95
Kenney, James, 60
Kensington, 56; Gardens, 83, 88, 195
Kent, county, 15, 59, 77
Kent, Duke of, 100
Kerry, Lord, 218, 222
Kew, 169
Kilns, *189
King, Charles, *23

Lafayette, General, 114-15, 162, 288-90
Lansdowne, Lord, 99, 133, *150-51, 159,
  218-19
Lansdowne House, 81, 216, 219, Plate
  VII, *following* 130
Latin, 16, 100
Lauderdale, Lord, 91, 99
Lawrence, Sir Thomas, 159
Lawrence, William Beach, *90
Leach, Sir John, 266
Légion d'Honneur, 32, 98
Leicester Square, 80, 266
Leipsig, 80
Lely, Sir Peter, 173
Leslie, Charles R., 160, 162
Lieven, Princess, 182
Life of Napoleon (Scott), 122-23, 245-46
Lightfoot, Hannah, *206
Lincoln's Inn Fields, 80

Little Belt, ship, *125-26
Liverpool, 6, 190
Llandaff, Bishop of, *60, 133
Lockhart, John G., 124, 127-28, 162, 165
Lockhart, Mrs., 162
London, *see also* England or English:
    impressions of physical features, 5,
    18-20, 23-24, 31, 54, 68-69, 80-89,
    167, 189-97, 199, 259, 264, 266, 272,
    284
    compared or contrasted to,
    Philadelphia, 15
    Paris, 43, 49, 78, 80, 92-94, 96-97,
        176, 179, 202, 225, 259, 264, 272
    New York, 57, 68-69, 79, 92, 176,
        202, 216
    Rome, 259
    illustrations, *see plates following* 68,
        130, 188, 250
London, Bishop of, *see* William
    Howley
London Bridge, 189, 191, Plate XVI,
    following 250
London, Tower of, *223, Plate IX,
    following 188
Long Island (N.Y.), 71, 250n
Long Island Sound, 307
Long Walk, 174
Lord Mayor, 192
Louis XIV (Fr.), 36
Louisbourg (N.S.), 32
Louisiana, 238n
Louvre, 171, 224
Low Countries, 36
Ludgate-hill, 196, Plate XI,
    following 188
Luther, Martin, 107
Luttrell, Henry, 60, 159
Lyons (France), 165

McAdam, John Loudon, *87, *250-51,
    255-56
McAdam, Sir James, 250
Macdonough, Thomas, 231
Mackintosh, Sir James, 50-51, 56, 59,
    117, 119, 128, *147, 162-64, 179-80,
    218
McGregor (family), 250n
Maida, Battle of, 246
Malbrook, 206

Malta, 124-25
Malthus, Thomas, 252
Mamaroneck (N.Y.), 250n
Mandeville, Lord, 137n
Marlborough, Duke of, 70, *206
Marlborough House, 81
Maryland, 11
Massachusetts, 97
Mathews, Charles, *169
Matsys, Quintin, 173
Mediterranean, 6
Medway, river, 17
Mexico, Gulf of, 258
Meyerbeer, Giacomo, 283
Michael Angelo, 39
Michigan, 176
Middle States, 28, 95-96, 270
Middleton, Mrs., 173
Milford Haven, town, 251
Miller, John, bookseller, 51
Milton, John, 31
Minerva, 192
Minerva Press, 246
Mirabeau, Honoré Gabriel, comte de,
    *117
Misers, The, painting, 173
"Miss Nancy Locket lost her pocket,"
    *20
Mississippi sawyer, *71
Mohawk River (N.Y.), 33
Monroe, James, 293n
Montrose, Duke of, 173
More, Hannah, *236n
Morning Chronicle (London paper),
    202
Morris, Commodore Richard
    Valentine, *124-25
Morris, James, of Morrisania, 107
Morrisania (N.Y.), 107
Mozart, W. A., 283
Munich, 80
Musée de l'Artillerie (Paris), 223
music, 283-84
mutiny, 237-38

Nancy Locket, *20
Naples, 50, 86, 276, 279, 284
Napoleon I (Fr.), 6, *46, 101, 206, 243
    253, 262, 293
National Theatre, 267

Navarino, naval battle, 228
Nazareth, 25
Netherlands: sovereign, 173; trade, 190; colonies, 250; landscape, 307; "Dutch" wagons, 307-08; economy, 308
New Brunswick (N.J.), 189
New England: editors, 184, 207; dialect, 217; gossips, 232; houses, 260
New Holland, 256
New Jersey, 11
New-river (London), 252
New York City, 15, 54, 57, 69, 79, 117, 176, 185, 187, 202, 252, 265, 308
New York Hospital, 118
New York, 21-22, 32, 56, 59, 61, 77, 86-87, 96, 103, 131, 145, 159, 167, 181, 184, 189, 209, 215, 250n, 254, 256, 260, 266, 276, 294, 298, 307
New York State Legislature, 109
Newcastle, Duke of, 173
Newgate, 196
Newmarket, 252
Newport, Sir John, 224
Newton, Stuart, 60, 160
Nicoll, Colonel, 250
Nicoll, William, 250
Nore, *238
Norfolk House, 80-81
Normandy, 266
North Sea, 5, 307
Northumberland, Duke of, 82, 173, 204
Northumberland House, 80-81, Plate VIII, *following* 130
Nova Scotia, 256
Nullification, 140

Ohio, 218
Old Palace Yard, London, 71, Plate III, *following* 68
Opie, John, *74
Orders in Council, *240
Oxford, town, 77; University, 140n, 155

Pacific Ocean, 237
Padua, 36
Paine, Thomas, 149, *288
paintings, 29, 39, 93, 173, 224, 260
Palais Royal, 226

Palazzo Gran Duca, 36
Pall Mall, 116, 272
Palmella, Duke of, 181
Panama, 293n
Paradise Lost, 29-30
Paris, 10, 12, 23, 40, 43, 45, 49, 57, 68, 70, 78, 80-81, 84-85, 87, 92-94, 96-97, 99, 101, 119, 128, 131, 153, 162, 165, 172, 174, 176, 179, 182-83, 185, 190, 196, 202, 207, 218, 221, 224-26, 229n, 255, 259, 264, 272, 286n-87, 289
Paris, Tower of, 223
Parliament, 22, 34, 50, 60, 95, 103, 105, 108-12, 114, 116, 132, 136-37, 149, 200, 247, Plate III, *following* 68
Parry, Captain William E., 237
Patroon, *55
Peace of 1783, 250n
Pearl Street (N.Y.), 202
Peel, Sir Robert, 106-08
Pelham (Bulwer), *211
Pepin, 183
Perigord, family, 158
Peter Pindar, *see* John Wolcot
petition, right of, 113-15
Philadelphia, 15, 183, 265
Philips, Sir George, 116, 122
phrenology, 261
Picardy, 266
Piccadilly, 29, 68, 83, 194-95; Plate XIII, *following* 250; church, 72
picturesque, the, 7, 167, 171, 190
Pillet, René Martin, *304n
Pilot, The (Cooper), 10
Pimlico, 56
Pitt, William, the elder, 51, 55, 103
Pitt, William, the younger, 55, 88n, 139, 146-48, 288
Plantagenets, 236
"Pleasures of Memory, The" (Rogers), 27
Poet's Corner, the, 31, 34
Point Judith (R.I.), 307
Polignac, Jules de, Prince, 272
Polycarp, 297
Pompeii, 197
Pope, Alexander, 169-*70, *211
Portland Place, 84
Portman Square, 82
Portugal or Portuguese, 181, 240

Posthumous Memoirs of His Own Time (Wraxall, Sir Nathaniel W.), *88n
Prater (Vienna), 80
President, ship, 126
Protestant churches, 42
Protestant Episcopal Church, 139-40, 219, 240-41
Protestant régime, 41
Providence, 208, 232, *see also* Christ, God
Prussia, sovereign, 173
Puckler-Muskau, Herman Ludwig Heinrich, Prince of (*Briefe eines Verstorbenen*), *304n

Quarterly Review, The, 201, 208, 253, 269, 285-86
Queen's County (N.Y.), 69

Racine, Jean (*Les Plaideurs*), quoted, *283
Radziuil, family, 158
Randolph, John, 107
Raritan River (N.J.), 189
Red Rover, The, *123
Regent's Crescent, 84
Regent's Park, 83-85, 88, 259
Regent Street, 68-69, 83-84, 259, 295; Plates XIII and XIV, *following* 250
Reign of Terror, 289
Revolution of 1688, 158
Richmond, 166
Richmond, Duke of, 204n
Richmond Hill (London), 168-69, 172
Ridgely, Captain Charles G., 50
Rochefoucauld, François, Duc de, (*Maxims*), *242
Rochester (Eng.), 17
Rodgers, Commodore John, *125-26, 231
Rogers, Miss Sarah, *161-62
Rogers, Samuel, 24, 27-30, 49, 51-52, 56, *60, 64, 117, 119, 159, 162, 164-66, 218, 266
Roman architecture, 223
Roman Catholicism, *see* Catholic Church
Roman classics, 142
Rome, 78, 93, 118, 259

Rossini, Gioachino A., 283-84
Rosslin, Earl of, 224
Rotterdam, 308
Round Peak, the (N.Y.), *297
Royal Exchange, 191n
Roydon House (Hoddeston), 254
Rundell and Bridge, jewelers, 196
Russell, Lord John, 49, *50, 62, 91, 162
Russell Square, 82
Russia or Russian, 120, 184, 208, 240, 285-86
Rutland, Duke of, 173
Rye (N.Y.), 55
Rye House, 251-52

Sadler, Michael T., *110
Sag Harbour, 243
St. Albans, Duke of, 29, 80, 204n
St. Chrysostom, 297
St. Cloud, 172
St. George's Chapel (Windsor), 173
St. George's Church (Hanover Square), 72
St. James's Church (Piccadilly), 72
St. James's Palace, 20, 60, 72; Plate V, *following* 130
St. James's Park, 28-29, 83, 89
St. James's Place, 20, 24-25, 27, 53, 59, 122
St. James's Square, 80-82
St. James's Street, 79, 110, 194, 271-72
St. Maur, rue, 119
St. Patrick's, order of, 99
St. Paul, *38-39, 61
St. Paul's cathedral, 33, 38-39, 41-42, 85, 190, 193, 259; Plate I, *following* 68
St. Peter, 61
St. Peter's (Rome), 38, 41-42
St. Stephen's Chapel (Westminster), 36-*37, 103, 131-32
St. Thomas d'Aquin, Church of (Paris), 223
Salisbury, Lord, 133-34
Sapphira, 33
Saxe-Weimar, 269
Scarlett, Sir James, 181
scirocco, 86-87
Scotland or Scottish, 50, 101, 108, 161, 231, 246
Scotsman, The (journal), 203

Scott, Sir Walter, 50, 55, 116, *118-24, 127-28, 161-62, 164-66, 211, 215, 220, 223, 246; family, 119, 162, 164-65
Seine, river, 190
Senate (U.S.), 110
Seymour, Lords, 137n
Shakespeare, quoted or cited, *6, *9, *10, 31, 34, 71, *100, 123, 165, 191, 223, *274
Sharp, Richard, "Conversation," 162-64, 218
Sheerness, naval station, 17
Sheridan, Richard B., 51
Shooter's Hill, *18
Shubrick, William Branford, letters to, *5, 15
Sicily, 125
Siddons, Mrs., 162, 164-65
silver-fork school, 94
Sittingbourne, 17
Smith (JFC's manservant), 183
Soho Square, 80
Somerset House, 85, Plate VII, *following* 130
Sotheby, William, 24, 124, *126-28, 216, 260-61, 263; family, 126
Southampton, 277
Southern states (U.S.), 96
Southwark, 190
Southwark Bridge, 191
Spain or Spanish, 173, 183, 240
Spencer, Lord, 95, 99; son "Jack," *95
Spencer, William, 24, 27, 70, 124, 215
Spencer House, 29, *60, 62, 64, 81, Plate VI, *following* 130
Spring-Rice, Thomas, 117, 119
Stadt House (Amsterdam), 36
Stafford House, 82
Stafford, Marquis of, 82
Stanley, Lord, *142
Stevenson, James, letters to, *91, 215, 276
Stimpson, Stephen, 194-95
Strand (London), 18
Strawberry Hill, 169-70, 172
Stuart, Gilbert, 159
Stuart-Wortley, John, *133
Stuart family, 136, 224
stucco, 83-84, 170, 259

Suffolk County (N.Y.). 250n
Sully, M. de Bethune, duc de, *55
Surrey, Earl of, *44, 137n
Surrey Hills, 85
Susquehannah River (N.Y.), 170
Sussex, Duke of, 100
Sutherland, Duke of, 82, 159
Sutherland, Jacob, letters to, *230, 285
Sutherland House, 82
Sweden, 240
Swinburne, Mr., 192, 194
Switzerland, 22, 117

Talleyrand-Perigord, Charles M. de, 101, 158
Talleyrand, Mad. de, 225
Tavistock, Lord, 137n
Telemachus, 192
Temple Bar, 74
Temple buildings (London), 191
Temperance Societies, 219
Temple gardens, 191
Terpsichore, 176
Test Laws, 140
Thames, river, 6, 17, 85, 169-70, 189-90, 226
Thistle, Knights of the, 99
Thirty-nine Articles, 231
Thornhill, Sir James, 39
"Three Estates," *117, 136
Tiber, river, 190
Tierney, George, 56
Times, The (London), 201-02
Titian, 260
Tooke, John Horne, 193
Tories: British, 110, 215; American, 300
Tower of London, *223
Travels in North America (Hall), 67
Trenton (N.J.), 15
Trinity Church (N.Y.), *38
Tripoli, 124
Trollope, Mrs. Frances, *303-04n
Tucker's *Jefferson*, *249n
tuft-hunters, *2, 65
Tuileries, 171
Turenne (Henri de la Tour d'Auvergne, Vicomte), 119
Turkey, 112, 208, 229n, 240-41
Twickenham, 169
Two Admirals, The (Cooper), *124

United States, *see the general sequence
for specific American persons, places,
and things*
  arts:
    architecture, 11
    painting, 159-61
    literature, 25, 51-52, 120-22
  characteristic attitudes between British
  and Americans:
    ambivalence, 11-12, 20, 25, 27, 38, 51,
      54, 61-65, 67, 126, 131, 135,
      141, 215-16, 219-20, 228-29, 235, 241,
      285
    hostility, American to British, 11-12,
      25-26, 233, 240, 285-86
    hostility, British to American, 33, 54,
      64, 125, 206-10, 213-17, 219, 225, 227,
      240, 268-69, 285-87, 290-92, 302-04
    harmful effects of American cultural
      dependence on England, 1-3, 11,
      118, 126, 149, 180, 209-12, 233-34,
      244, 248-49, 280, 285-86, 291-92, 304,
      307
  selected points of comparison or
    contrast between England and the
    United States:
    miscellaneous affinities, 11, 95-97,
      104-07, 134, 226-27
    speech, pronunciation, and lan-
      guage, 11, 27-28, 69-70, 96-97,
      133-34, 226-27
    dress, 15, 273-74, 294
    maritime proficiency, 17-18, 232
    letters of introduction and invita-
      tion, 23-24, 178-79
    caste attitudes, 43-48, 205, 227
    country houses and town houses,
      55-56, 92-93, 169-70, 184, 186
    table settings, 57-59, 95
    squatters, 59
    livery, 64, 73, 95, 272
    street crowds, 68
    horses and carriages, 69-72,
      272-75
    proprieties and forms of
      etiquette, 71-72, 93-94, 131-32
    stature, of men and women, 75
    climate, 77-78, 86-87
    female faces, 78
    city squares, 83

    institutional effects on attitudes
      and habits, 89, 120-23, 140-41,
      154-58, 200-07, 210, 302
    legislative procedures, 108-15,
      134-40
    protective system, 128-29
    agreement of theory and practice
      in government, 135-42, 300,
      303
    status of professions and
      commerce, 139, 152-53, 306
    constitution of society, 177-78
    press and journalism, 199-202,
      207, 210-13
    diffusion of population, 209, 291
    high culture, 210, 298-99
    general intelligence, 230
    honesty, 231
    social and political indoctrin-
      ation, 236-39
    religion, 240-42
    popular rights, 244-45
    national vanity, 268, 296-98
    servant class, 277-80
    happiness, 280-82
    taste, 280-84, 302-03
    future prospects, 299-304
    individuality, 301-02
Upper Canada, 256
Utica (N.Y.), 167

Valmy, Duc de, *101
Van Cortlandt, Augustus, 77-78
Van Rensselaer, Gen. Stephen, III, *55
Venice, 284
Versailles, 36, 170-71
Vienna, 80
Vincennes, 171, 223
Virgil, 155

Wales, 298
Wales, Prince of, 83, 100
Wales, Princess of, 161
Walker, John, *107
Walpole, Horace, 170
Waltham cross, 251
War of 1812, 292-93
Warren, Lady, *32
Warren, Admiral Sir Peter, 32

Warrensbush (N.Y.), 33
Warwick, Lady, 55
Washington (D.C.), 111, 185, 219,
    286-87n
Washington, George, *33, 156, 159, 230
Waterhead, 250n
Waterloo Bridge, 18, 191
Waterloo Place, 83, Plate XIV, *following*
    250
Watts, John, *78
Watts, Lady Mary, *78
Weber, Karl Maria von, 283
Wellesley, Lord, 81
Wellington, Duke of, 9, 18, 133, 173,
    198-99, 207
West, Benjamin, 159, 173
West-Chester (N.Y.), 77, 250
West-end (London), 192, 194
West Indies, 255, 257-58
Westminster (London), 22, 54, 68, 74, 78
Westminster Abbey, 31-34, 38-*39, 41,
    173, 259, Plate II, *following* 68
Westminster Bridge, 189, 191, Plate IV,
    following 68
Westminster Hall, 34-35, 87, 182, 191,
    305, Plate II, *following* 68
Westminster House, 81
Westminster stairs, 189
Wharncliffe, Lord, 133, 135
Whigs, 91, 99, 110, 116, 205n, 216, 218,
    300
White, Mrs. Henry, *77

White-Hall (London), 85, Plate IV,
    following 68
White House (U.S.), 82
Whittington, Sir Richard, 193
William the Conqueror, 7, 172
William II (Eng.), 35
Wilmington (Del.), 15
Windsor Castle, 72, 101, 165-66, 170-72,
    174-75, 206
Windsor Great Park, 174
Wirt, William, 107
Woolwich, 17
Wolcott, Dr. John, *74
Worcester, Lord, 137
Wordsworth, William, 166
Wortley, John, *see* Stuart-Wortley,
    John
Wraxall, Sir Nathaniel, 81n, *88n
Wren, Sir Christopher, 192, *194
Wright families (tavern-keepers), 12-14,
    18-19
Wright's tavern, 8
Wynn, Charles W. W., 218

"Yankee Doodle," 20
Yankees, 6, 271
Yarmouth, Countess of, 204n
"Year of Sorrow, A" (Spencer), 24
York, Frederick, Duke of, 29, 82, 100
York House, Plate V, *following* 130

Zoological Garden (London), 84